SONGS OF WORSHIP

10 hymns arranged for guitar Starter, Intermediate, Advanced

By Ged Brockie

www.guitarandmusicinstitute.com

ISBN 978-1-7399473-5-4

First published in Scotland in 2022 by GMI - Guitar & Music Institute

Cover - Ignacio Andrés Luna Borrás

Proof read by Douglas Urquhart

PLEASE NOTE THAT THE DOWNLOAD INSTRUCTIONS FOR THE PACK THAT ACCOMPANIES THIS BOOK CAN FOUND ON PAGE 197.

Songs Of Worship

10 hymns arranged for guitar

Starter,

Intermediate,

Advanced

GUITAR
MUSIC INSTITUTE

Ged Brockie

TABLE OF CONTENTS

LEGEND

Understanding The Rhythmic Placement Of The Chords

In this example, D Major starts on beat 1 and is strummed for 3 beats. A7 is played on beat 4.

In this example, G Major starts on beat 1 and is strummed for 2 beats. A7 is played on beat 3.

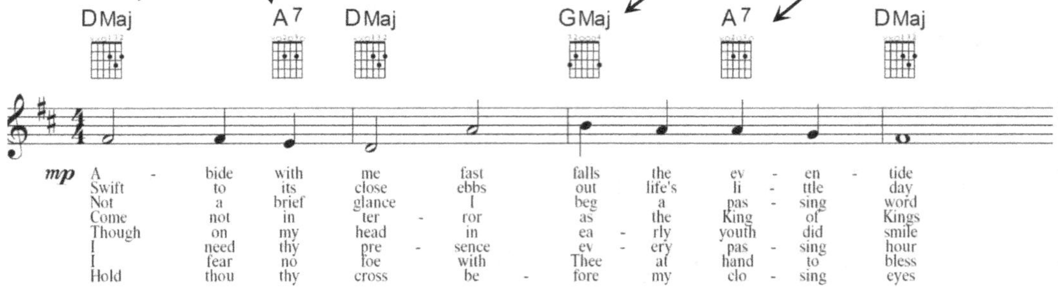

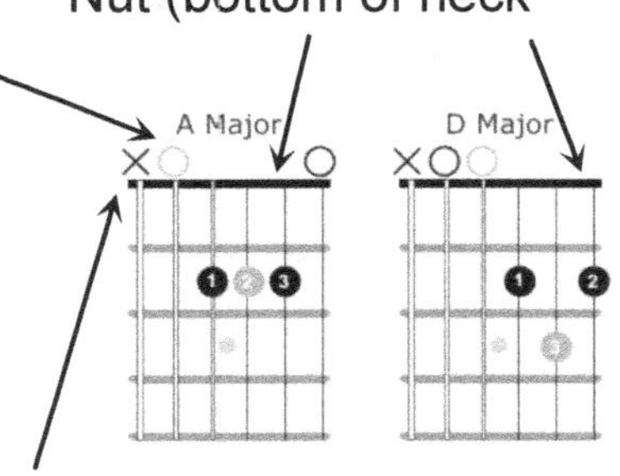

Understanding Chord Boxes Starter

Open string (non fretted)

Nut (bottom of neck

NOTE: Lighter shaded open strings are the root note (note name) of the chord.

This is a barre chord and the fret to barre is shown here.

Note that in a barre chord one finger is placed across all the strings as shown below.

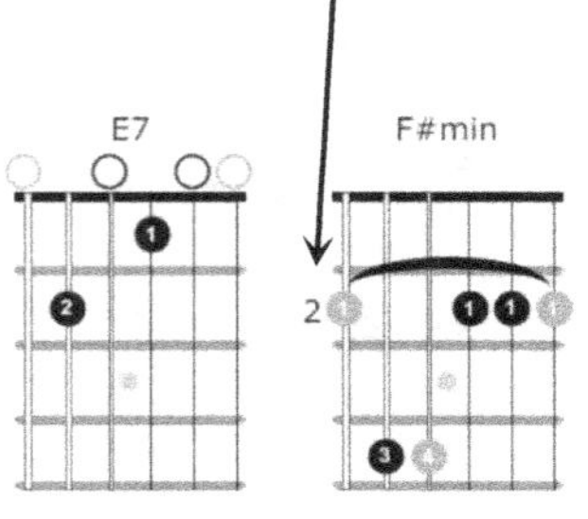

An "X" means do not play the string.

Understanding Chord Boxes Intermediate

Order of notes played - circles of any type first, triangles of any type, cubes on side of any type, then squares of any type.

Triangles are played *after* the circles.

Cubes on side are played *after* triangles.

Round filled in black circles show what finger of left hand is used.

1 - 1st notes

2 - 2nd note

3 - 3rd note

4 - 4th note

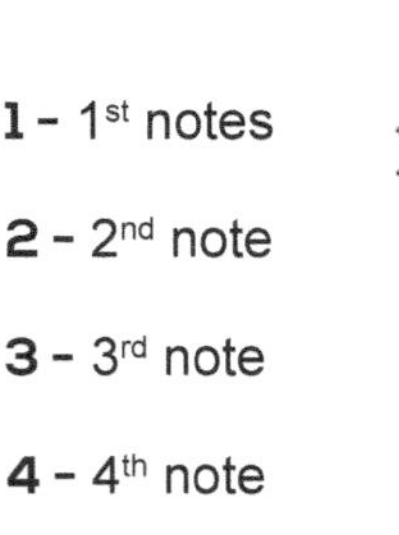

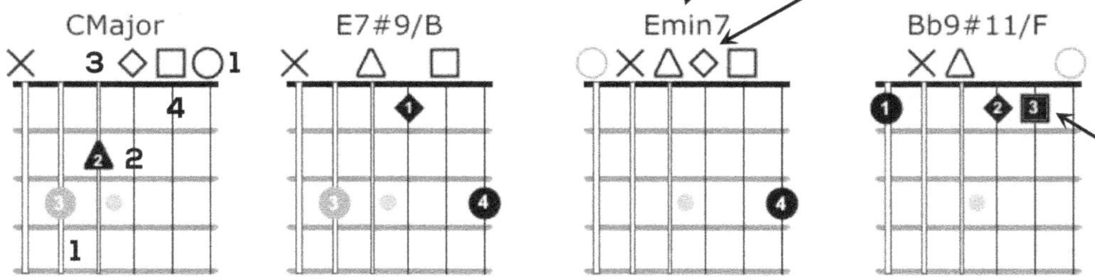

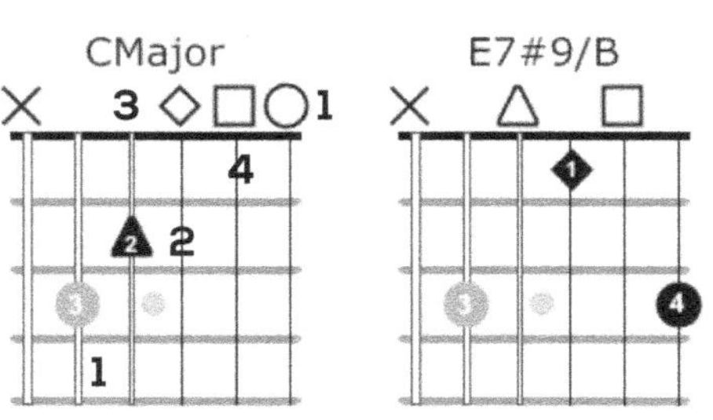

Squares are played *after* cubes on their side.

Understanding Chord Boxes Advanced

Due to the complexity of the chords and lines played in the advanced arrangements, in most cases, the chord boxes will only show the initial chord form. The player is advised to double check with the music notation and TAB, using the chord forms as a general guide.

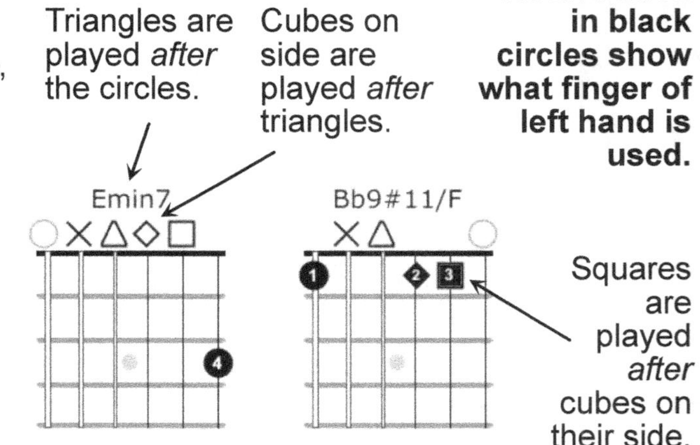

A Word From The Author

This book covers a wide technical range with respect to guitar knowledge and playing ability. It's for guitarists who have not played that long or use the guitar as an accompaniment for vocal or other instrument. It's for the advancing guitar player who is looking to take their playing to a higher level where chords and melody are played together. Finally, this book is for guitarists searching for arrangements that could be used in a performance scenario within church, or played as part of their wider repertoire at a professional level.

The structure of the material will also provide guitar teachers with a range of teaching resources. Play along material, duet playing opportunities, as an example and platform to help students understand how chords function within progression. The arrangements will also aid student comprehension as to how chords are used across the guitar neck with respect to inversion.

The hymns included in this book were chosen for varied reasons. Some were played for personal reasons. Others were chosen because of the lyrical content, the stories of the authors behind the songs, or the quality of the music composed. Finally, hymns were chosen because of their importance to the Christian community around the world and as an acknowledgement of the joy, comfort and solace these words and melodies have played in the lives of countless people in both happy and sad times.

Although only ten hymns are presented, they are offered in many forms. I have included two versions of each "starter" song in two different keys. I'm hopeful that everyone will be able to sing along with at least one version. All chords presented within the starter versions are also displayed in larger chord forms for ease of viewing. I have included a simple music and TAB (tablature) version of the song with chord symbols included for players to either play along with a friend or the downloadable backing track mp3 files.

The intermediate version of the hymns are a jump in technique from the starter, however, the harmonies used are more or less those found in the basic hymn with some exceptions. All chords are provided in large format and video and mp3 recordings are provided to help you understand how the arrangements can be practised and performed.

The advanced version of each hymn is where I've stretched out harmonically. I've often created intros/outros, made use of key changes and other musical techniques. Although challenging, these musical ideas are possible due to the more rigorous technical demands made on the player. I've looked to vary the musical styles, but undoubtedly, jazz harmony has been used extensively throughout the advanced hymn arrangements.

The specific techniques from both a physical and arranging perspective are discussed in the supporting download files. Combining both intermediate and advanced arrangements of a song, where possible, would certainly lengthen the overall piece and would take the listener on a musical journey.

I hope you find these beautiful songs and words and the stories of those that composed them as enthralling as I have. In many ways, creating this book has helped me rediscover and reconsider a lost treasure.

Ged Brockie

Hymn 1
Abide With Me

Resources

Performance of Intermediate version

Audio Talk through of Intermediate version

Performance of Advanced version

Audio Talk through of Advanced version

Use a QR code reader on your cell/mobile phone or tablet to view and listen to the files above. There's a large selection of completely free QR code reader apps available which work on all operating platforms.

To download all resources and other support files, follow the instructions on page 197 of this publication.

Hymn Notes - Abide With Me

The lyrical text for Abide With Me were written by Scotsman Henry Francis Lyte (1793 – 1847), who by all accounts had an upbringing with little input from his father. The one good thing that Henry's father did do, however, was send him to Ireland to receive an education.

Henry then moved to England and eventually rose in the church ranks to become an Anglican clergyman. It is said that he wrote the words to Abide With Me while being aware that his life may well be ending.

William Henry Monk (1823 – 1889) was a church organist and composed the song "Eventide" which is the melody and chordal arrangement that most people will be familiar with. Note that many hymns were sung with alternate melodies and chords. Monk stated that the music for the lyrics of Abide With Me was completed in ten minutes.

Monk was a prolific composer and was eventually elevated to professor of vocal studies at King's College, London.

William Henry Monk   *Henry Francis Lyte*

Lyrics

Verse 1

Abide with me, fast falls the eventide

The darkness deepens Lord, with me abide

When other helpers fail and comforts flee

Help of the helpless, oh, abide with me

Verse 2

Swift to its close ebbs out life's little day

Earth's joys grow dim, its glories pass away

Change and decay in all around I see

O Thou who changest not, abide with me

Verse 3

Not a brief glance I beg, a passing word,

But as Thou dwell'st with Thy disciples, Lord,

Familiar, condescending, patient, free.

Come not to sojourn, but abide with me.

Verse 4

Come not in terror, as the King of kings,

But kind and good, with healing in Thy wings;

Tears for all woes, a heart for every plea.

Come, Friend of sinners, thus abide with me.

Verse 5

Thou on my head in early youth didst smile,

And though rebellious and perverse meanwhile,

Thou hast not left me, oft as I left Thee.

On to the close, O Lord, abide with me.

Verse 6

I need Thy presence every passing hour.

What but Thy grace can foil the tempter's power?

Who, like Thyself, my guide and stay can be?

Through cloud and sunshine, Lord, abide with me.

Verse 7

I fear no foe, with Thee at hand to bless;

Ills have no weight, and tears no bitterness.

Where is death's sting? Where, grave, thy victory?

I triumph still, if Thou abide with me.

Verse 8

Hold Thou Thy cross before my closing eyes;

Shine through the gloom and point me to the skies.

Heaven's morning breaks, and earth's vain shadows flee;

In life, in death, O Lord, abide with me.

ABIDE WITH ME - Starter

ABIDE WITH ME - Starter alternate key

Chords: Abide With Me Starter

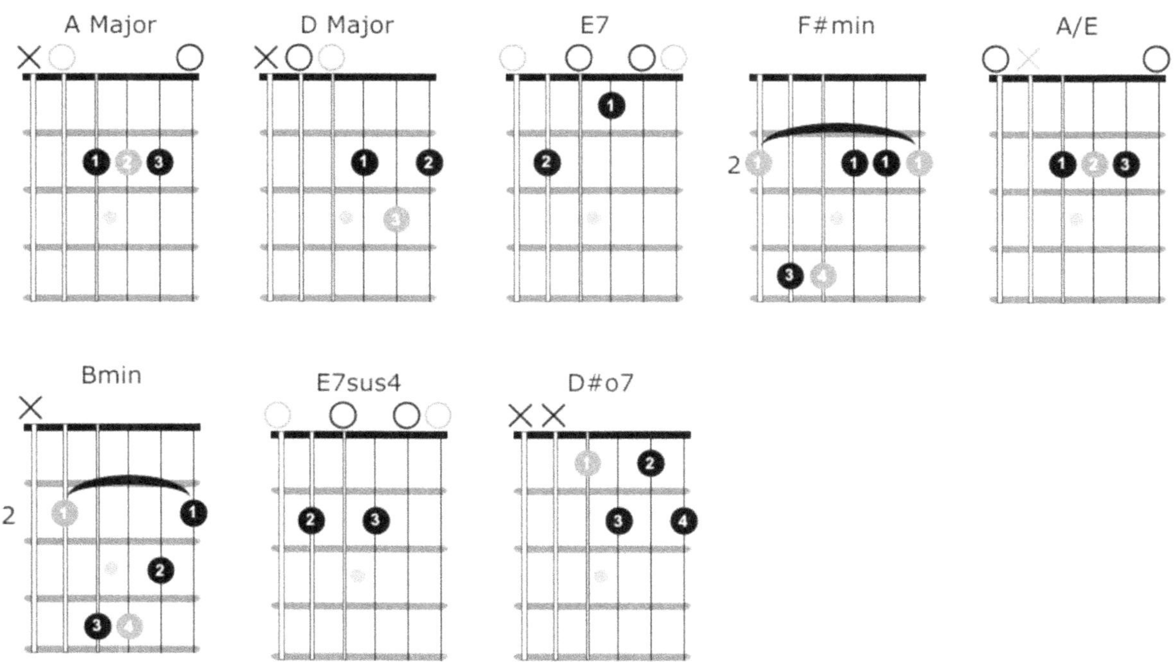

Chords: Abide With Me Starter Alternate Key

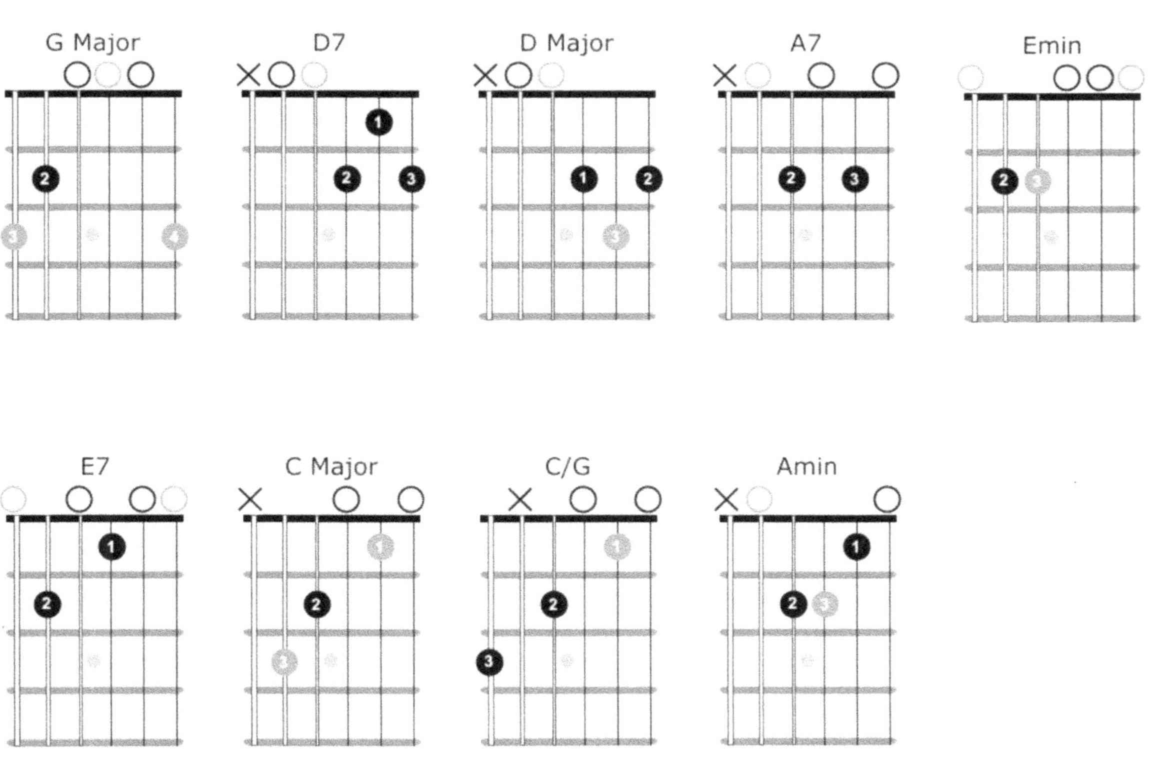

Abide With Me play along

bpm = 80

Abide With Me + Melody
Abide With Me Backing Track

Count of 4 then play

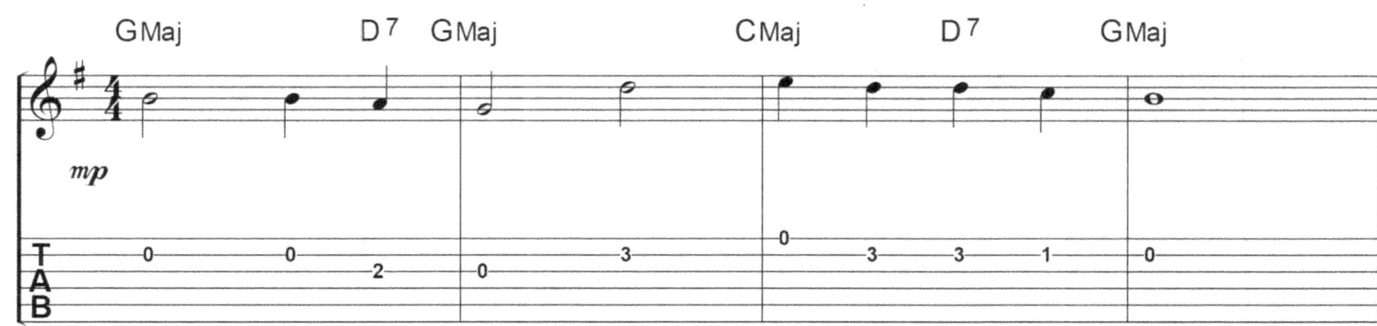

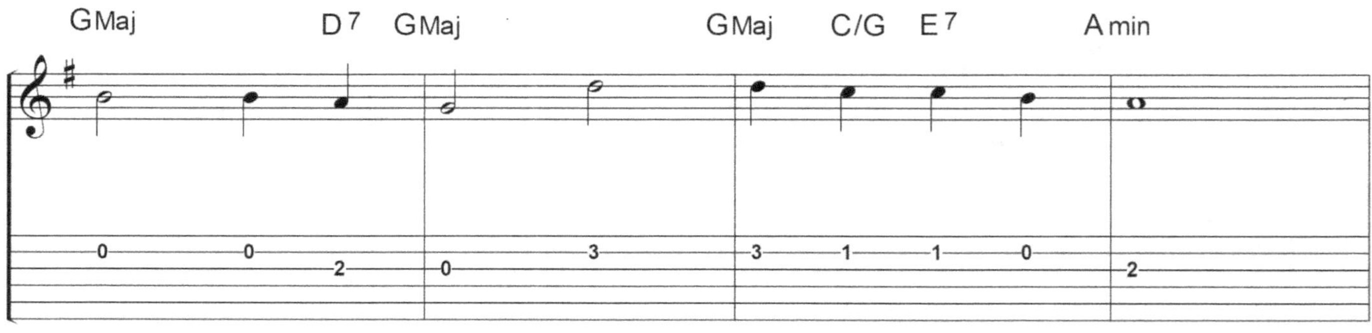

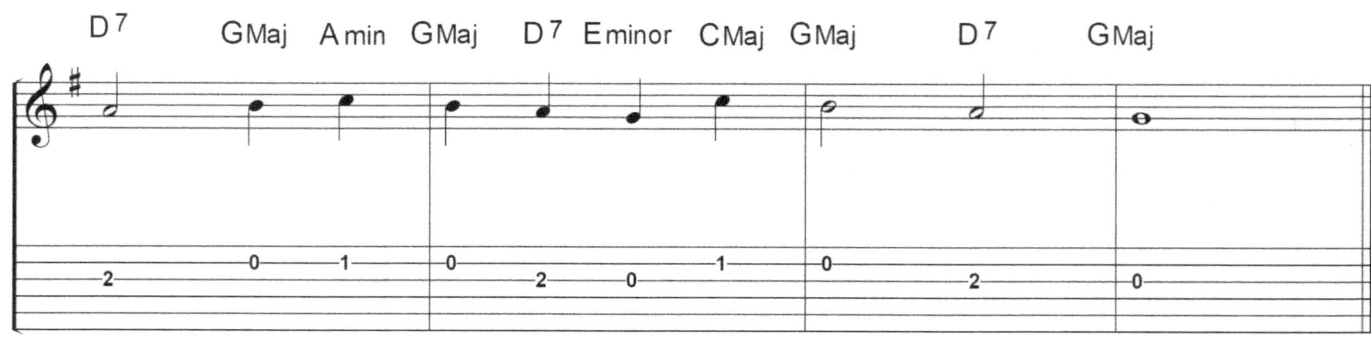

ABIDE WITH ME - Intermediate

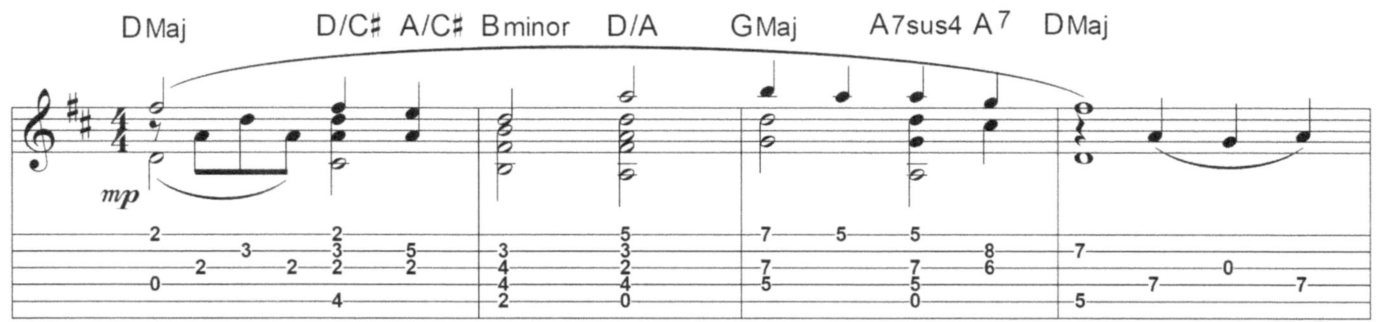

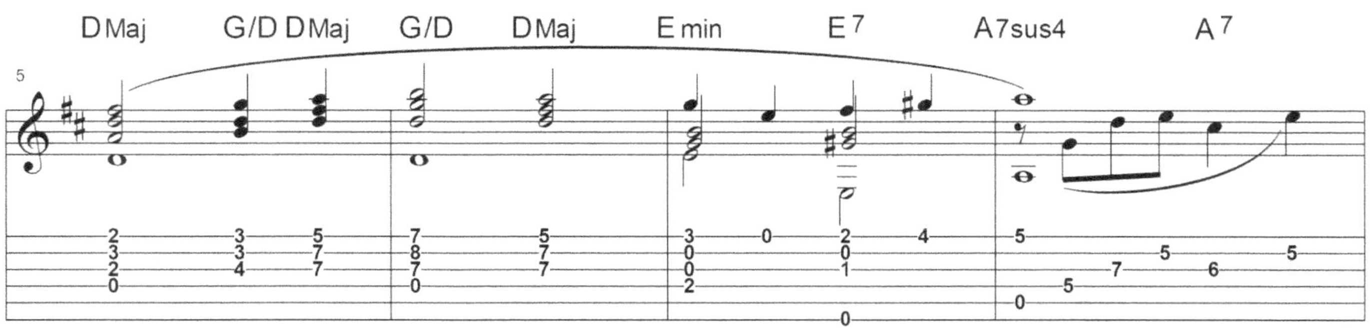

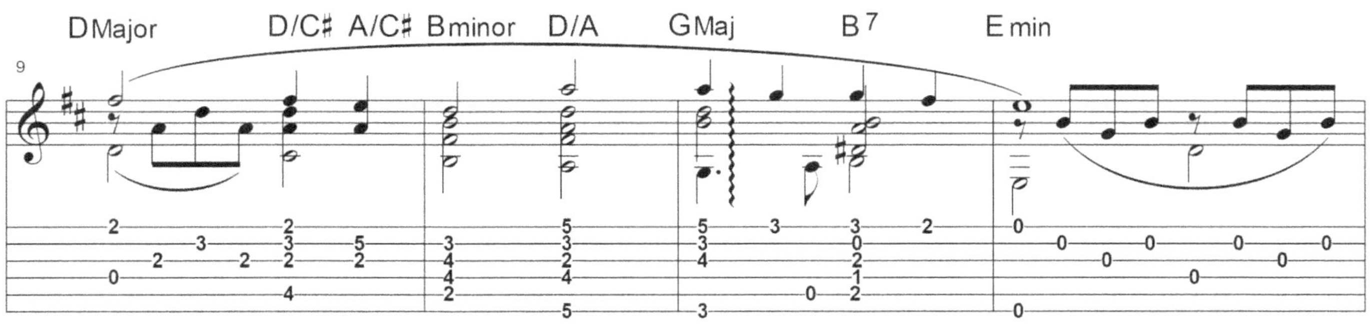

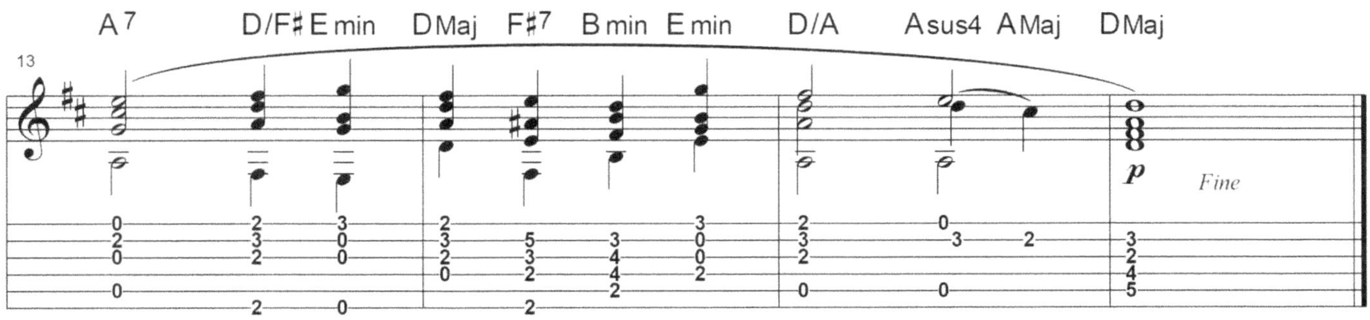

Chords: Abide With Me Intermediate

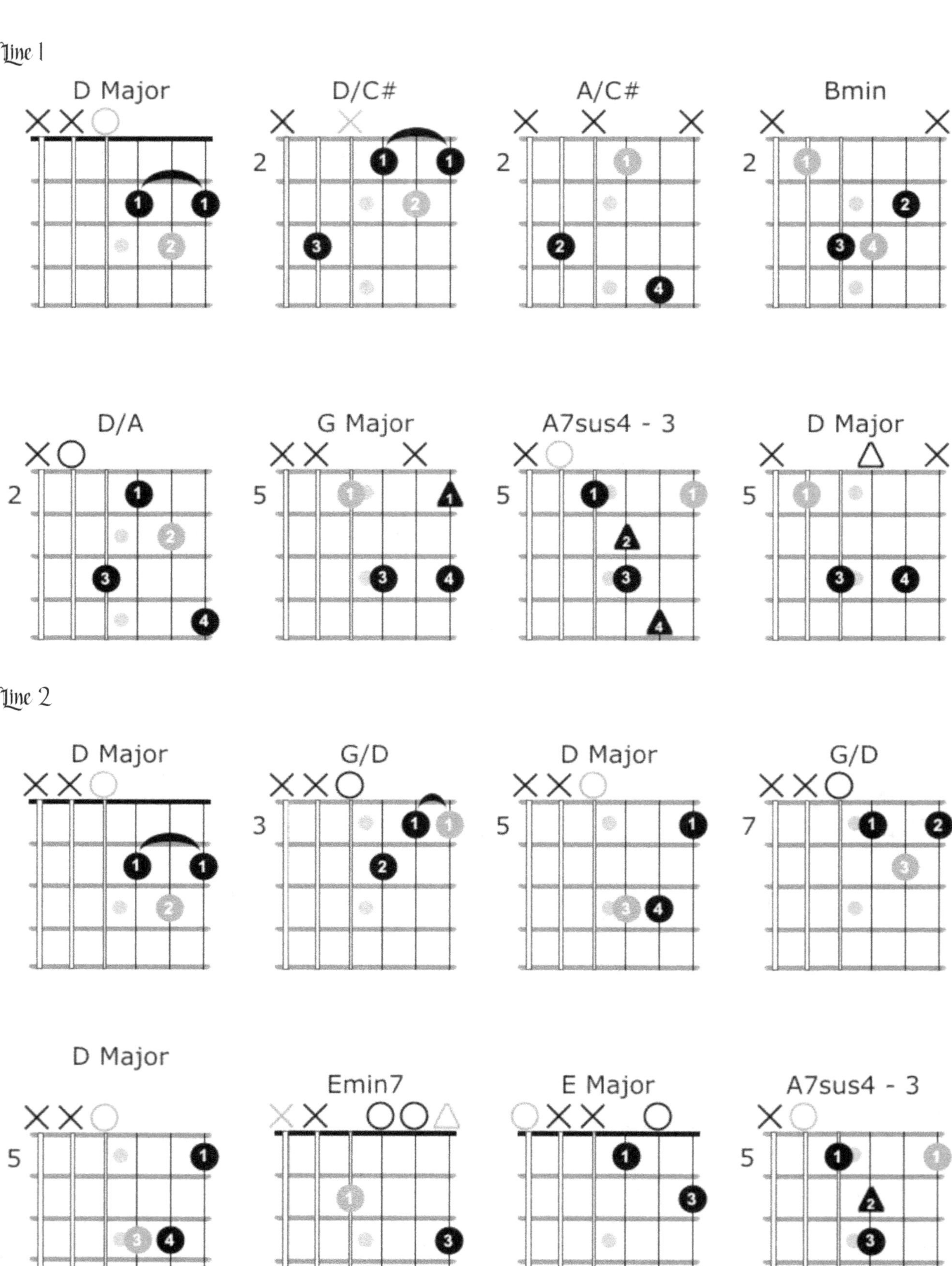

Line 3
D Major
D/C#
A/C#
Bmin
D/A
G Major
B7
Emin
Line 4
A7
D/F#
Emin
D Major
F#7
Bmin
Emin
D/A
Asus4 - 3
D Major

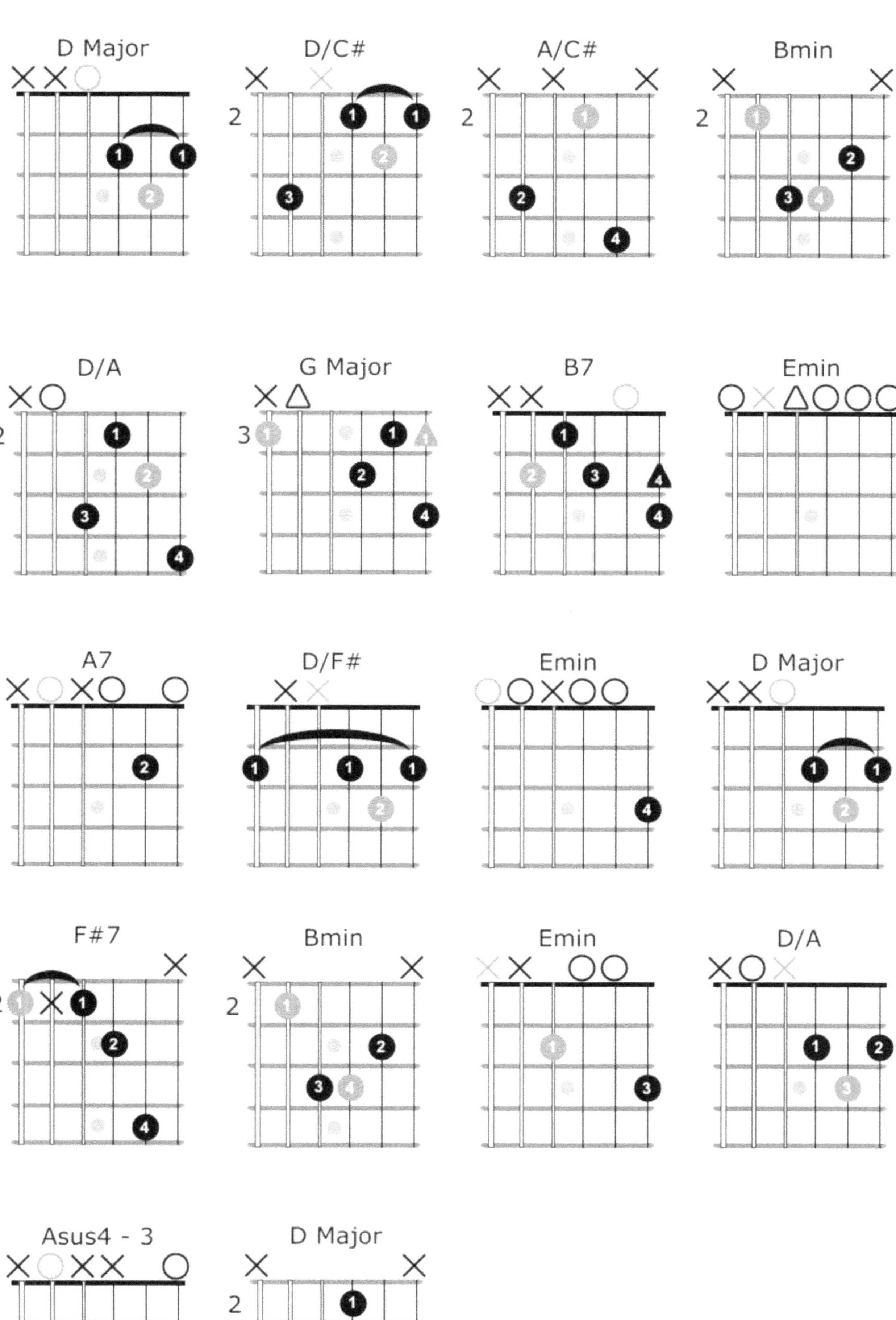

ABIDE WITH ME - Advanced

Arranged by
Ged Brockie

Rubato

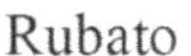

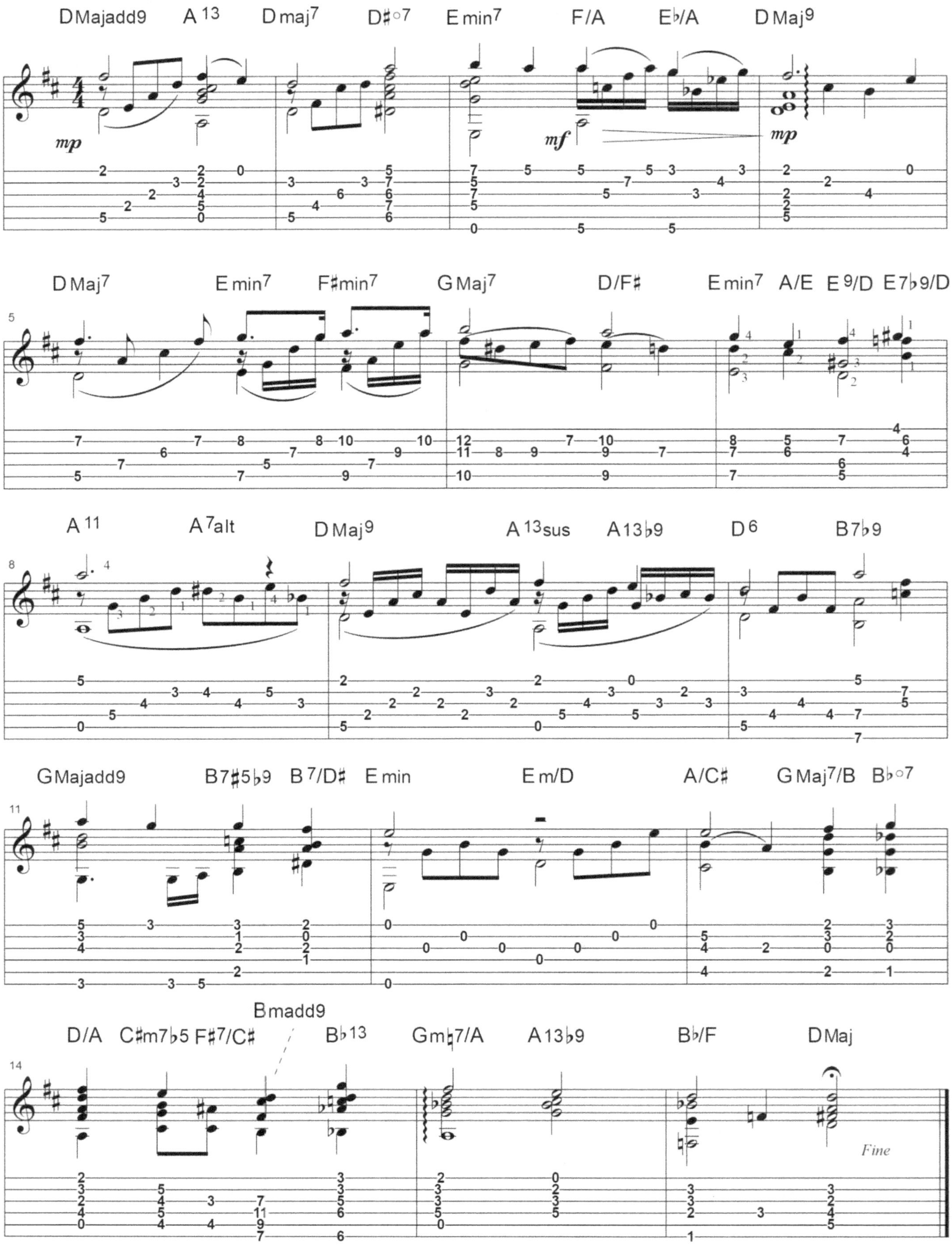

Chords: Abide With Me Advanced

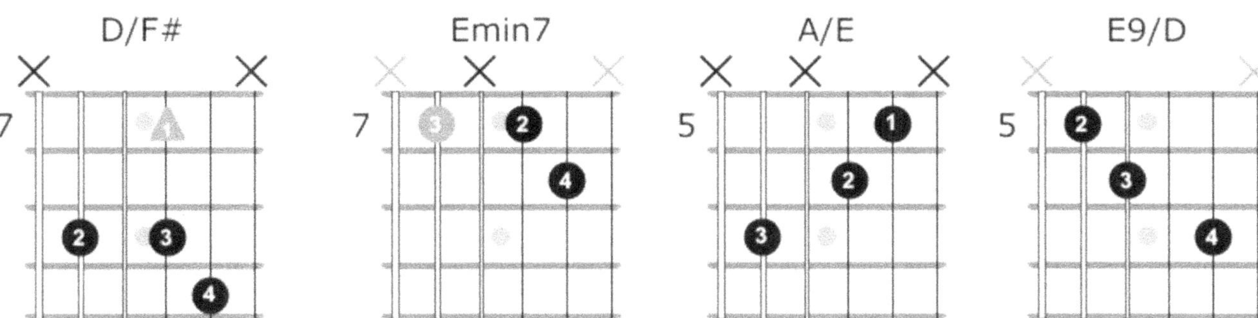

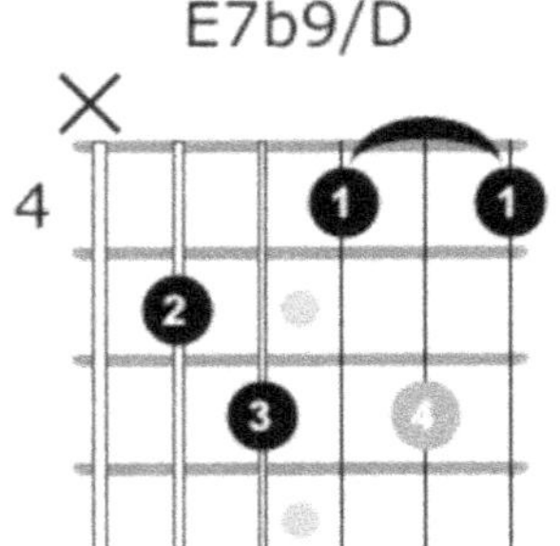

E7b9/D

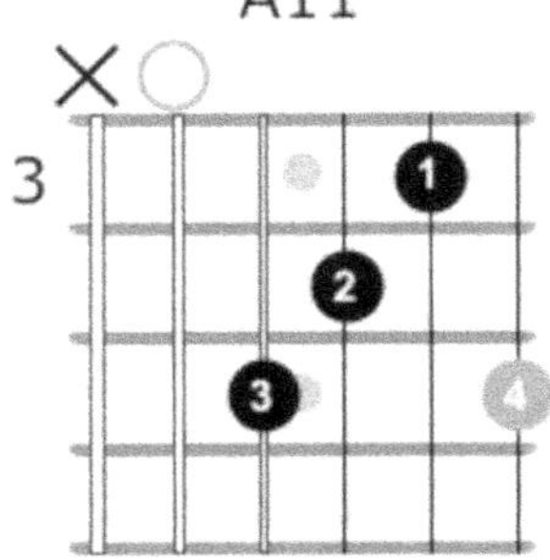

A11

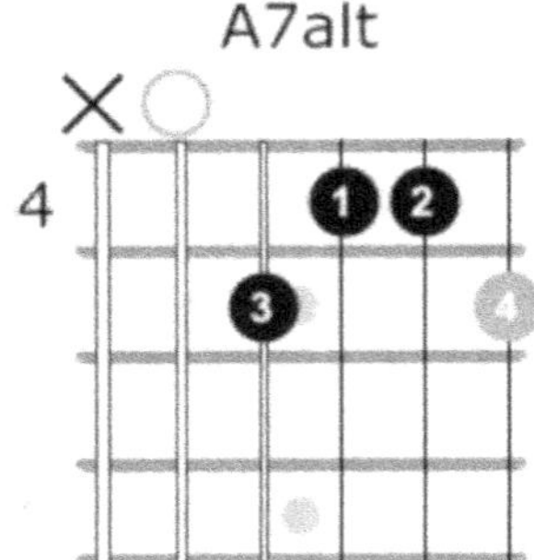

A7alt

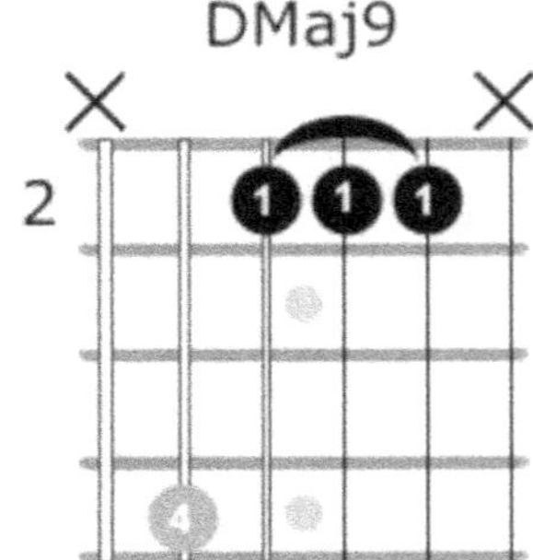

DMaj9

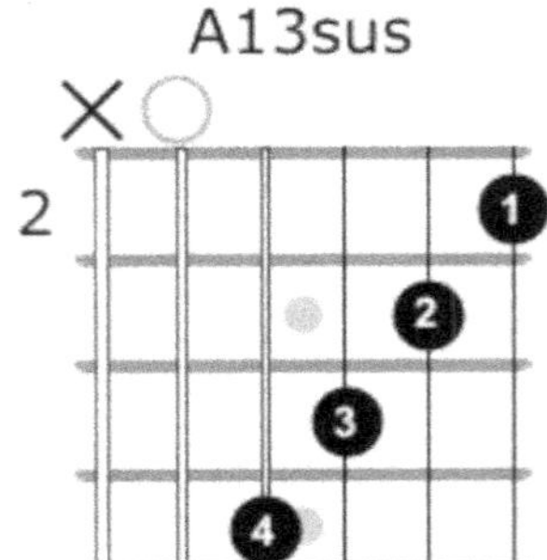

A13sus

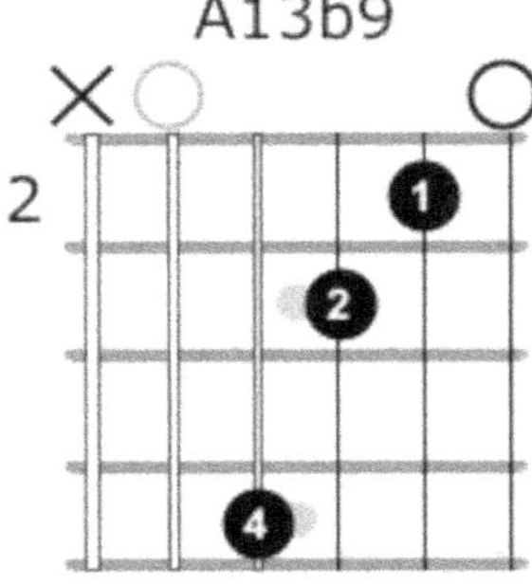

A13b9

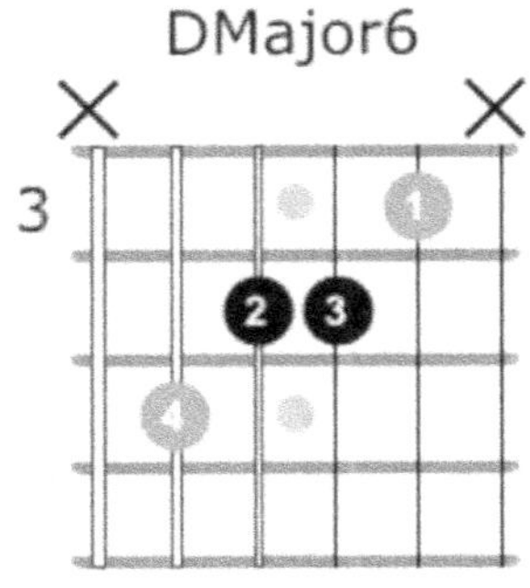

DMajor6

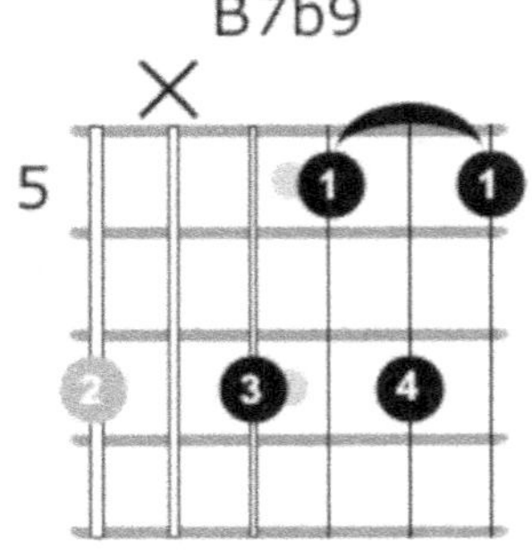

B7b9

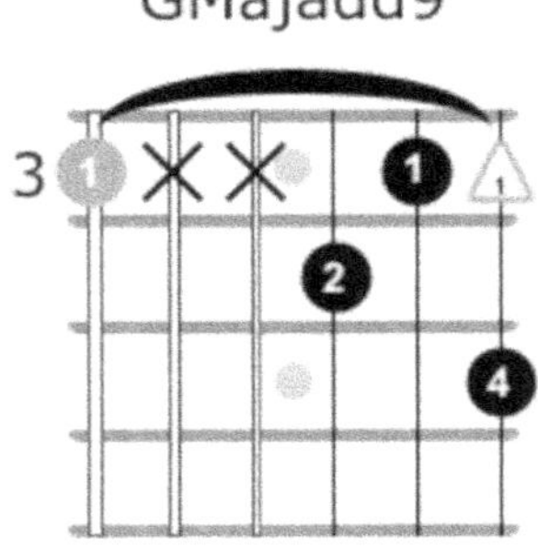

GMajadd9

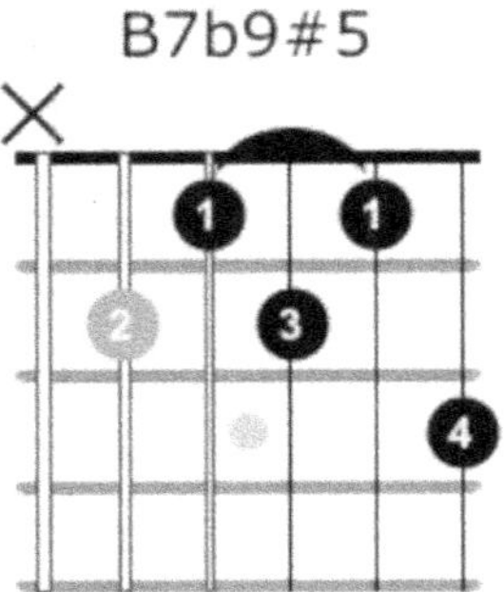

B7b9#5

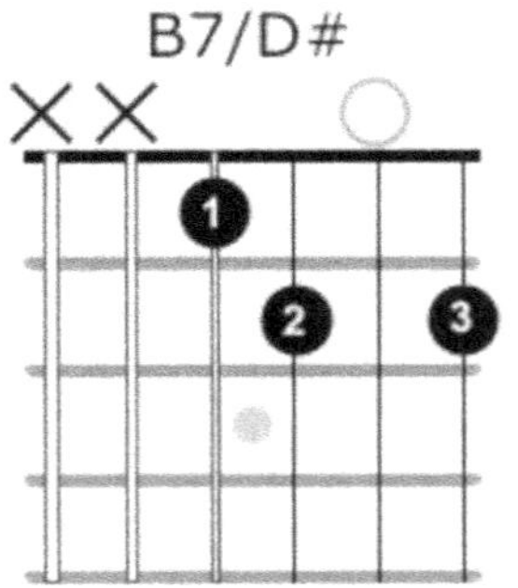

B7/D#

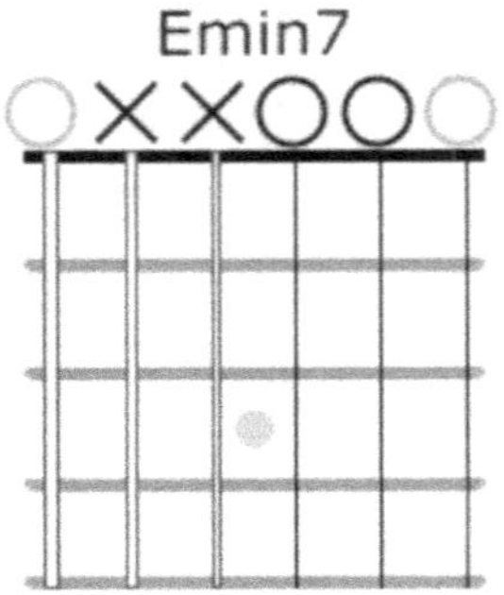

Emin7

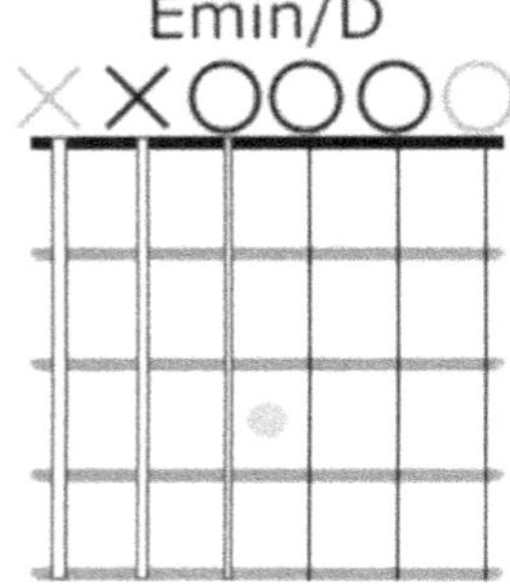

Emin/D

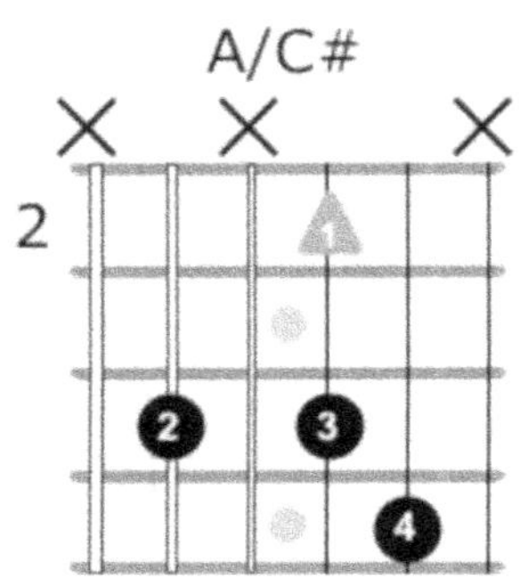

A/C#

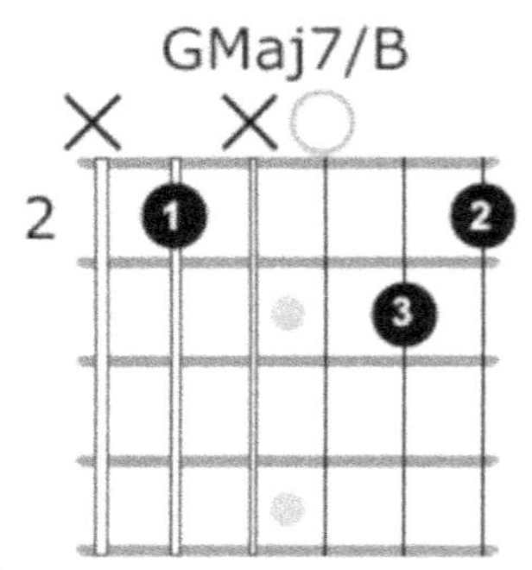

GMaj7/B

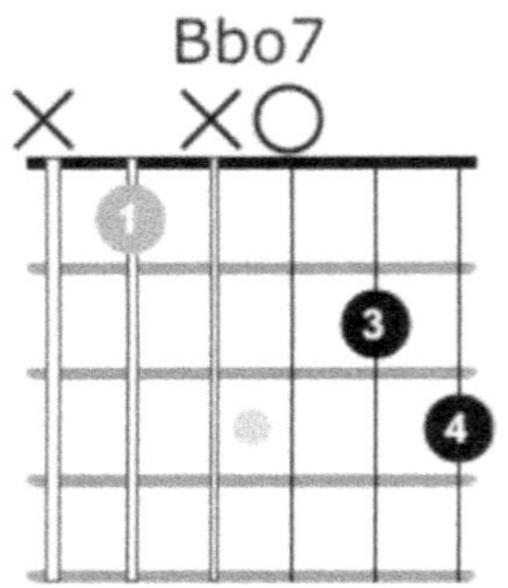

Bbo7

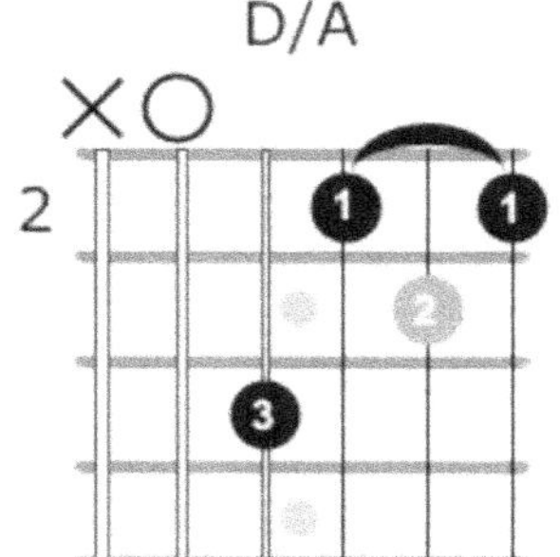

D/A

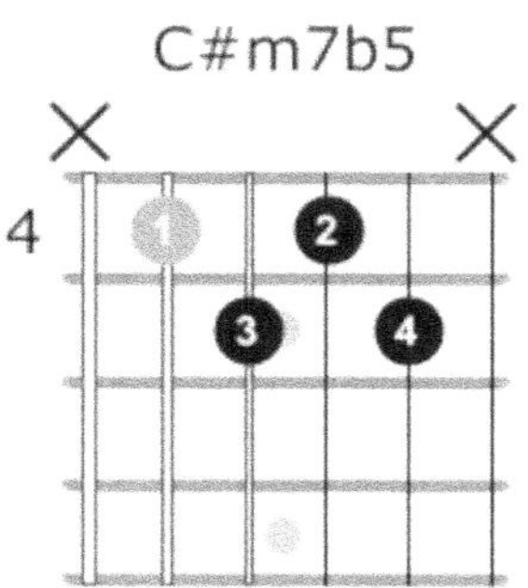

C#m7b5

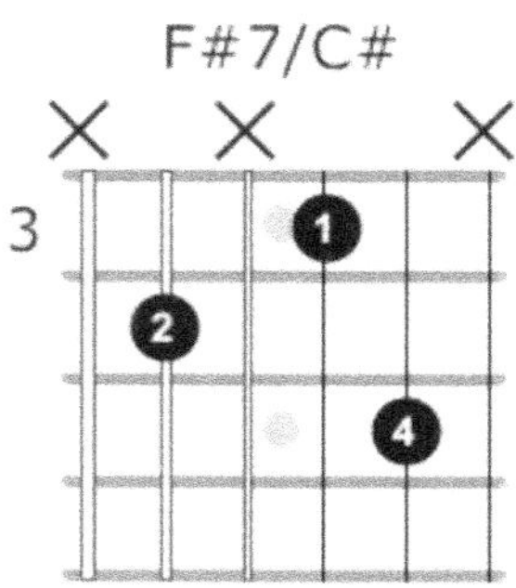

F#7/C#

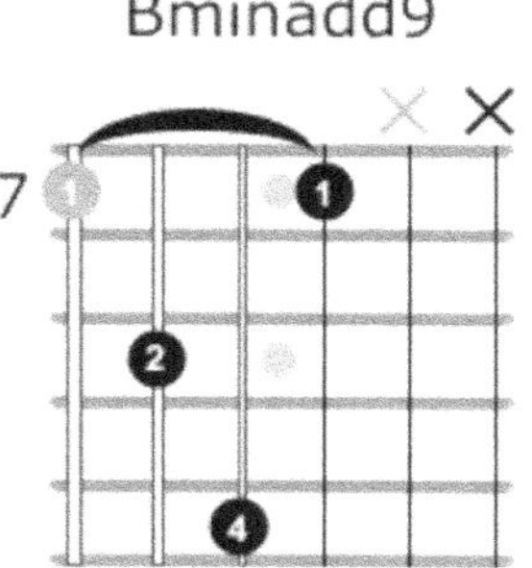

Bminadd9

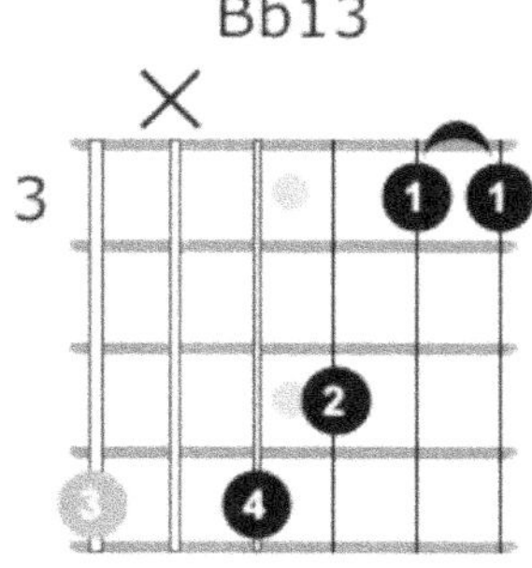

Bb13

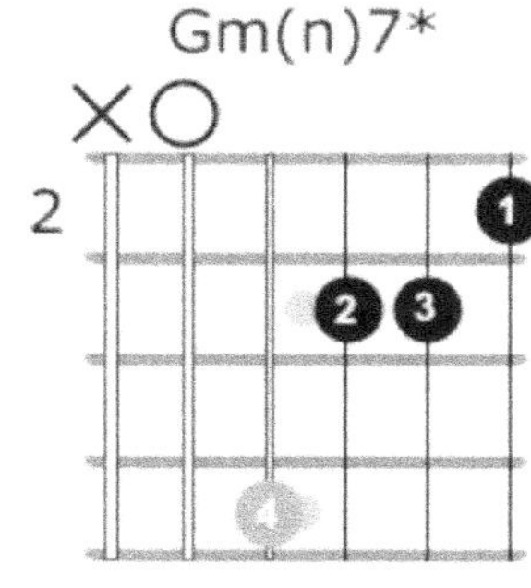

Gm(n)7*

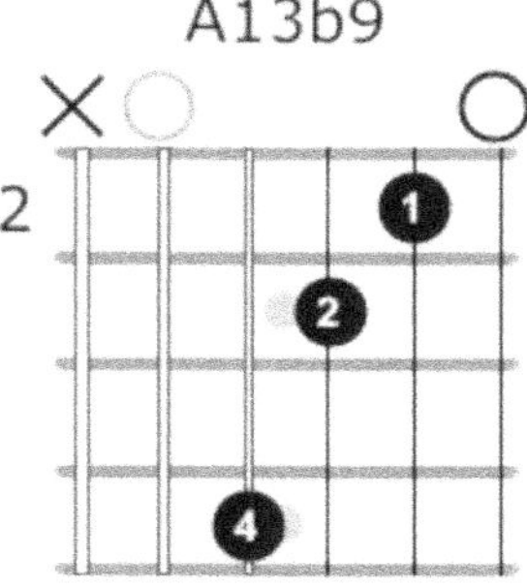

A13b9

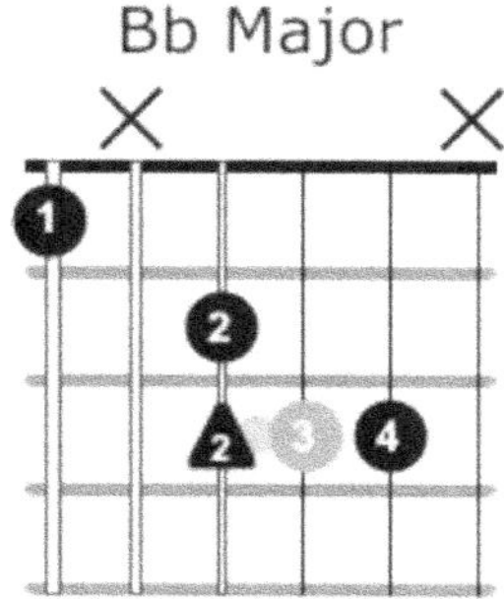

Bb Major

* n = natural

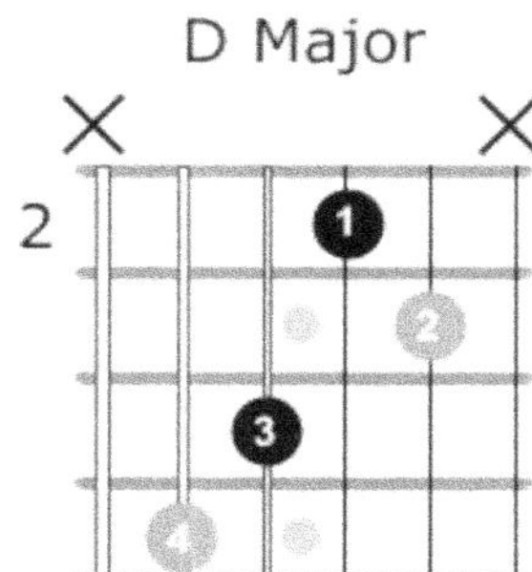

D Major

Hymn 2
Amazing Grace

Resources

Performance of Intermediate version

Audio Talk through of Intermediate version

Performance of Advanced version

Audio Talk through of Advanced version

Use a QR code reader on your cell/mobile phone or tablet to view and listen to the files above. There's a large selection of completely free QR code reader apps available which work on all operating platforms.

To download all resources and other support files, follow the instructions on page 197 of this publication.

Hymn Notes - Amazing Grace

A song that resonates throughout the decades & centuries since it was first penned by English poet John Newton (1725 – 1807) in 1772.

The music that is most closely associated with the words of Amazing Grace were composed by American musician William Walker (1809 – 1875) over fifty years later and was originally set to the tune "New Britain".

Amazing Grace is one of those songs that can affect at an emotional level when played instrumentally. There are many instrumental examples, however, being scored for brass is common. One of the greatly loved songs from the hymnal repertoire.

William Walker   John Newton

Lyrics

Verse 1

Amazing Grace how sweet the sound

That saved a wretch like me

I once was lost, but now am found

Was blind but now I see

Verse 2

'Twas grace that taught my heart to fear

And grace my fears relieved

How precious did that grace appear

The hour I first believed

Verse 3

Through many dangers, toils, and snares

I have already come

'Tis grace has brought me safe thus far

And grace will lead me home

Verse 4

When we've been there ten thousand years

Bright, shining as the sun

We've no less days to sing God's praise

Than when we'd first begun

Reprise

Amazing Grace how sweet the sound

That saved a wretch like me

I once was lost, but now am found

Was blind but now I see

AMAZING GRACE - Starter

AMAZING GRACE - Starter alternate key

Music by William Walker
Lyrics by John Newton

With a steady rhythm

DMaj   D7   GMaj   DMaj

A - maz - in - g grace how sweet the sound that
Was grace tha - t taught how my heart to fear and
Through ma - n - y dan - gers toils and snares we
When we've be - en there ten thou - sand years bright

For verse five repeat verse one.

DMaj   E7   AMaj   A7

saved a - a wretch like m - e I
grace m - y fears re - lie - ved how
have a - lrea - dy co - me 'Twas
shi - ni - ng like the s - un we've

DMaj   D7   GMaj   DMaj

on - ce wa - s lost but now a - m found was
pre - ci - o - us did that now grace a - p - p - ear The
gra - ce ha - s brought us sa - fe thu - s far And
n - o le - ss days to si - ng Go - d's praise Than

E7   A7   DMaj   A7

blind bu - t now I see
hour I - first be - lieved
grace wi - ll lead us home
when we - 'd first be - gun

Chords: Amazing Grace Starter

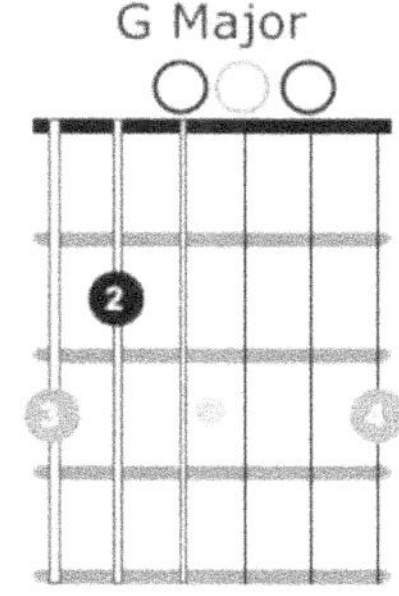

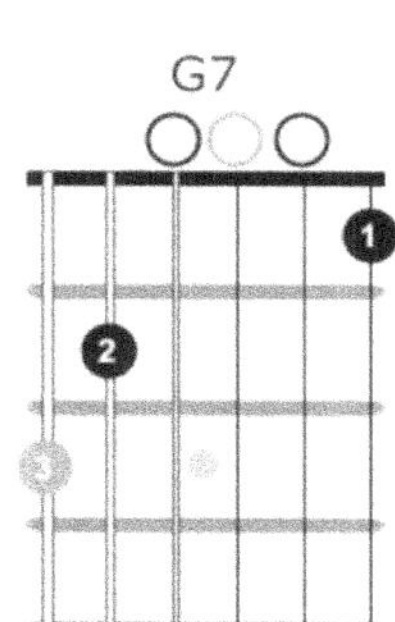

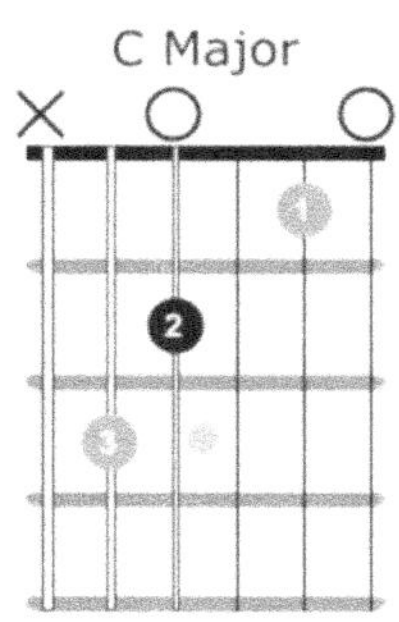

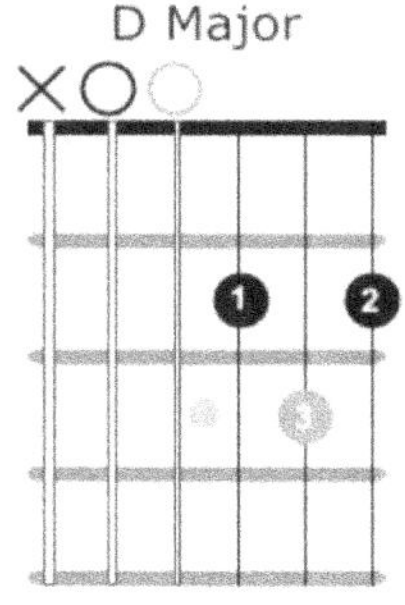

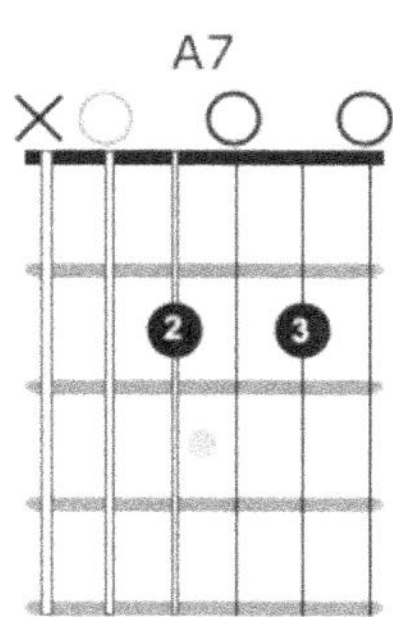

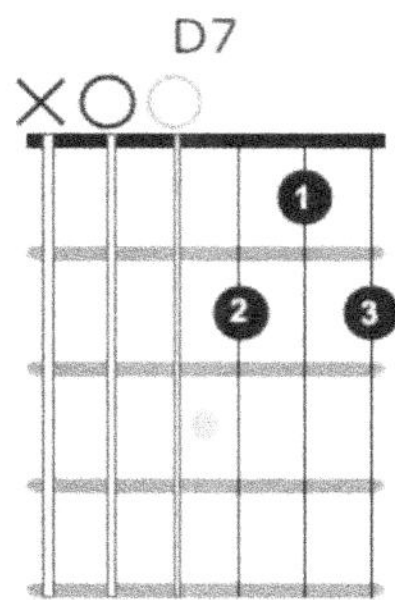

Chords: Amazing Grace Starter Alternate Key

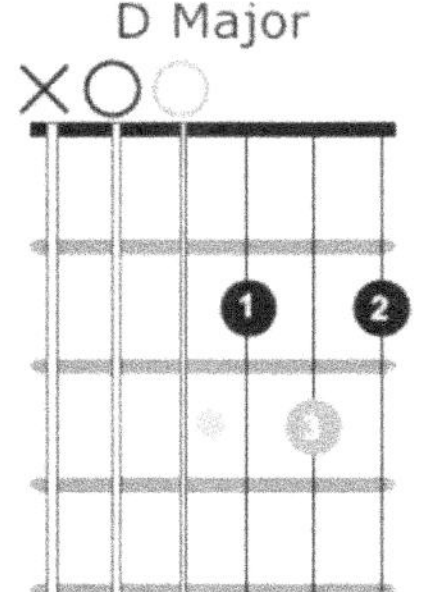

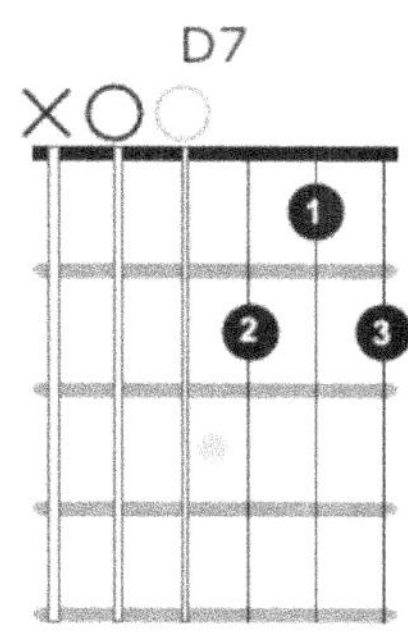

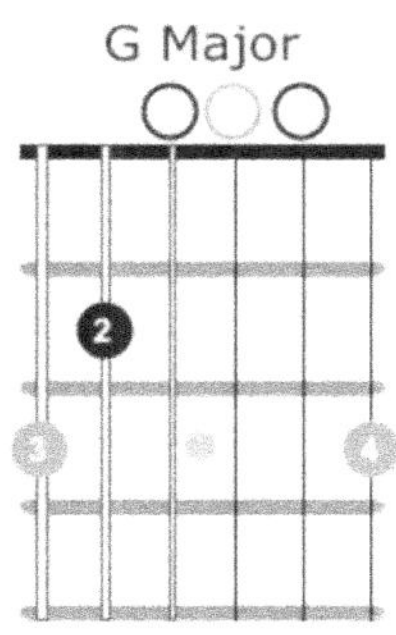

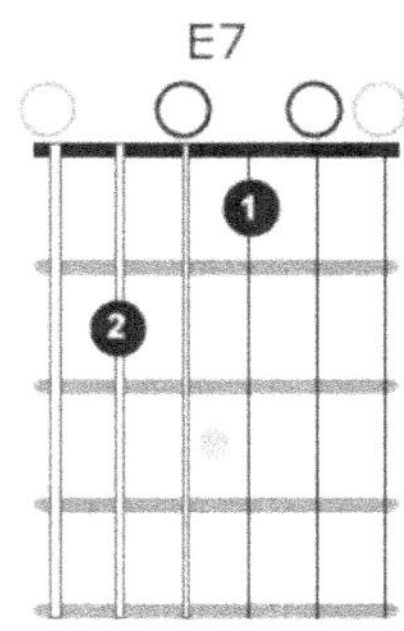

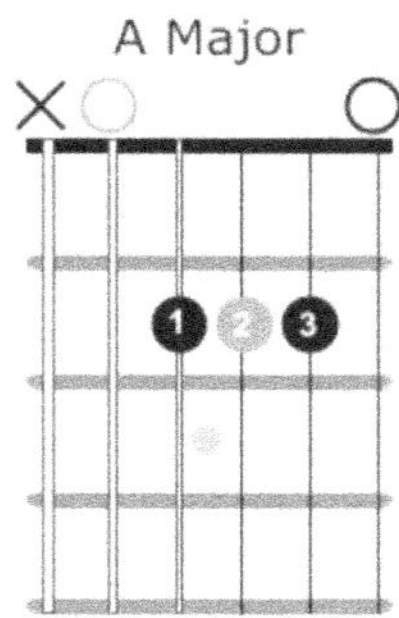

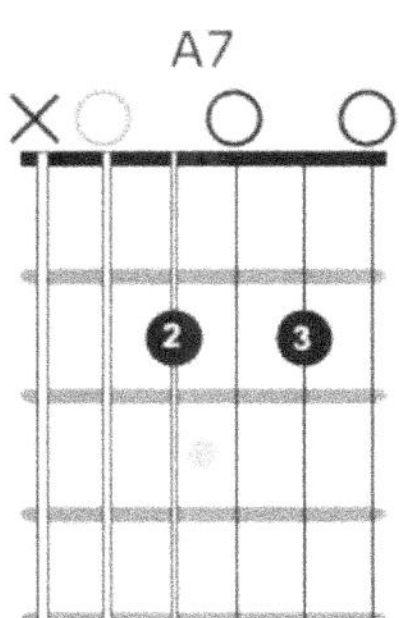

Amazing Grace play along

bpm = 72

Count of 2 then play

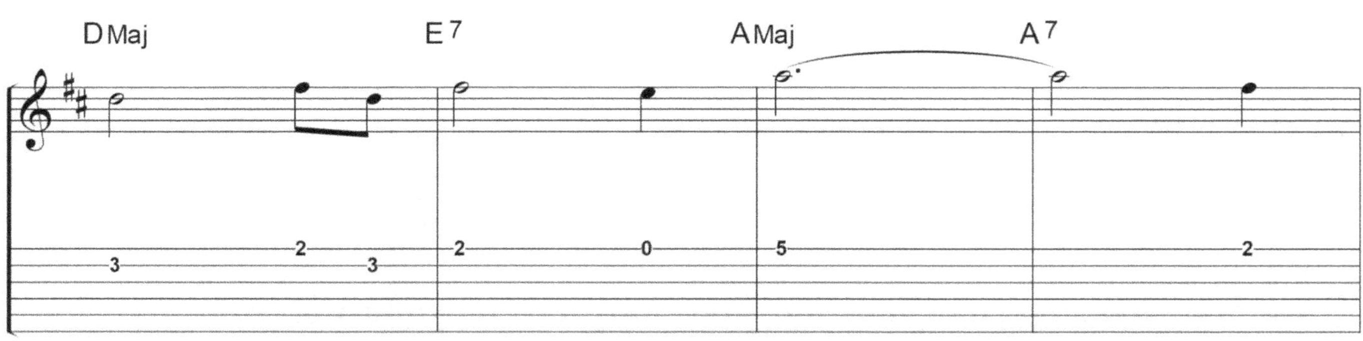

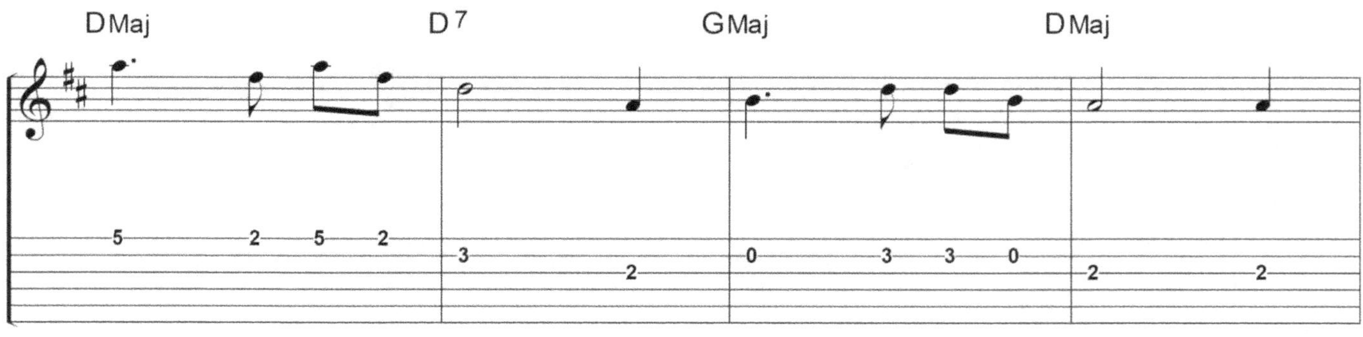

AMAZING GRACE - Intermediate

Not too slow

Arranged by
Ged Brockie

Chords: Amazing Grace Intermediate

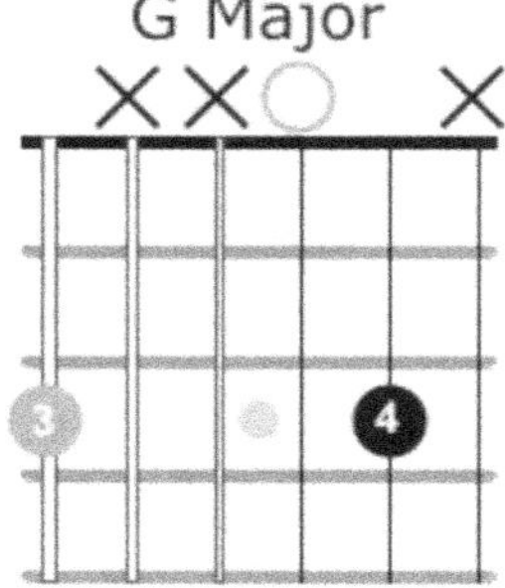

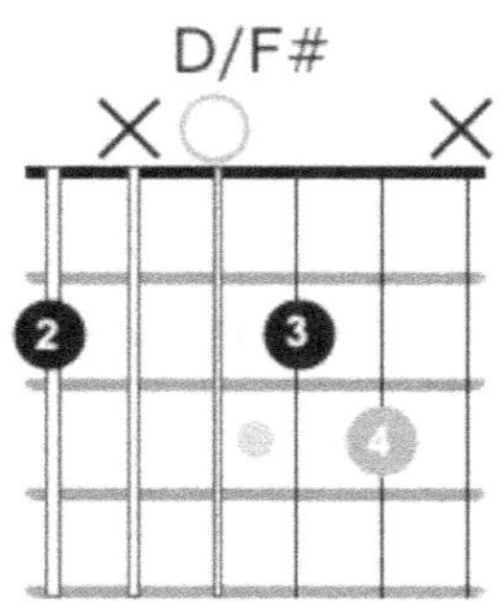

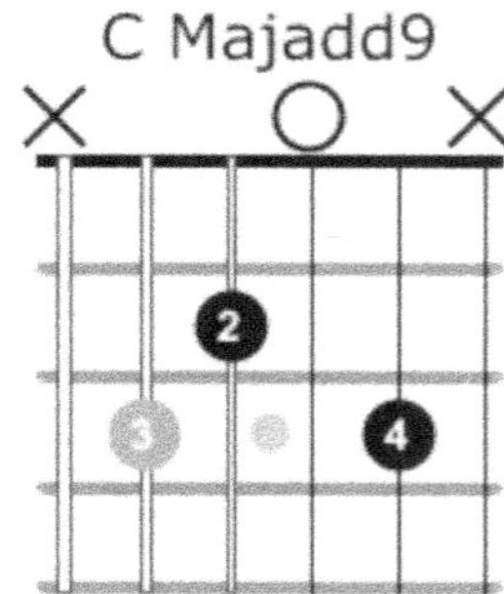

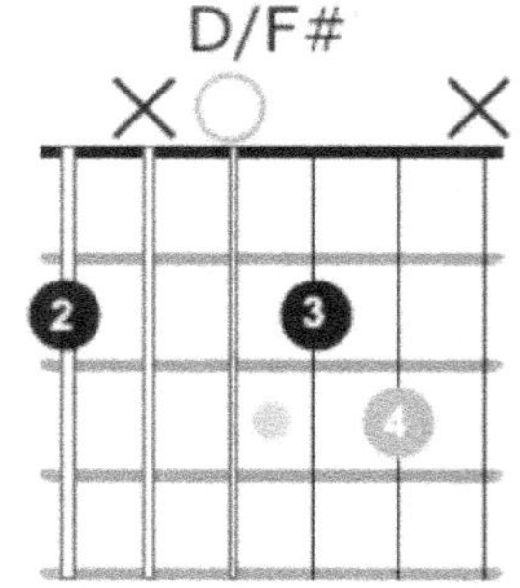

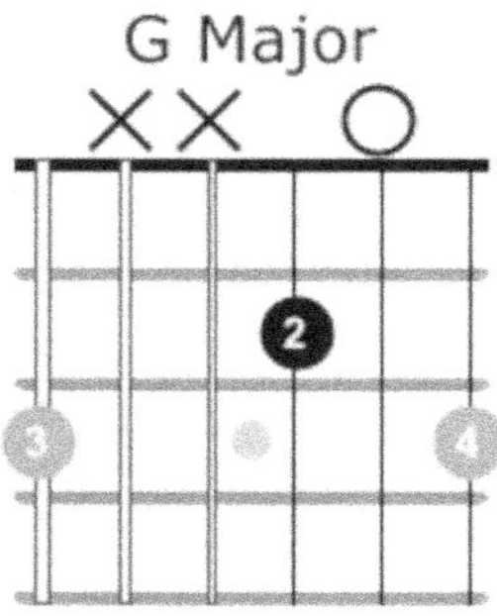

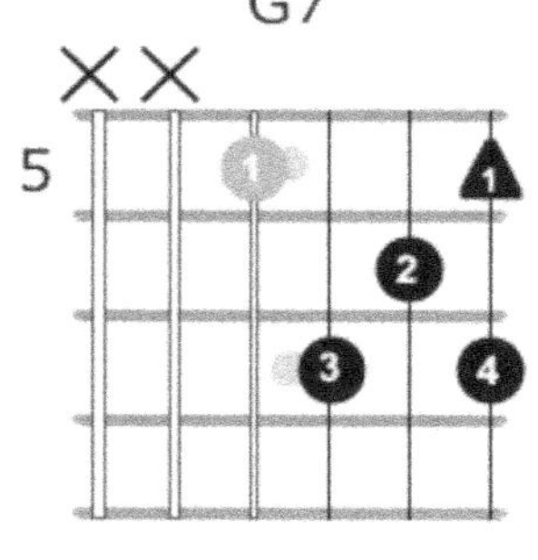

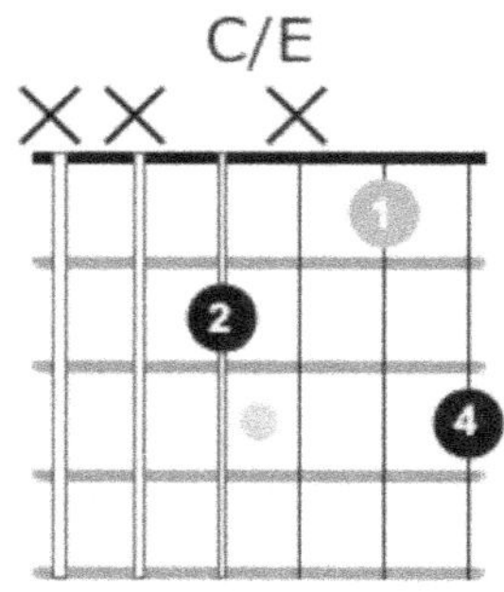

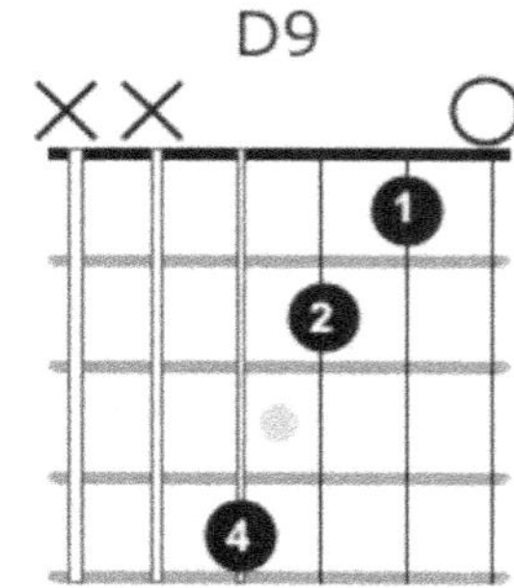

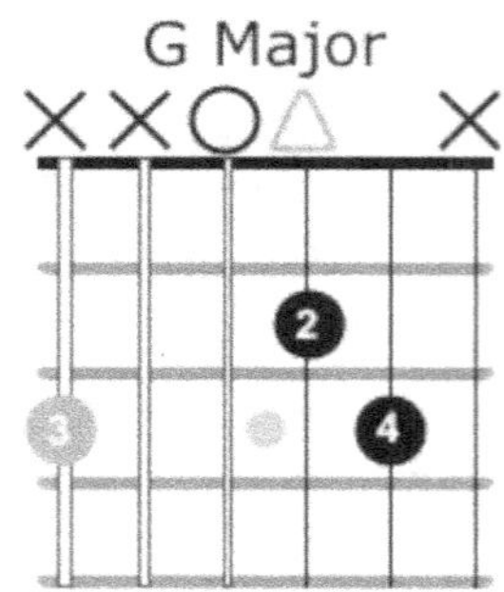

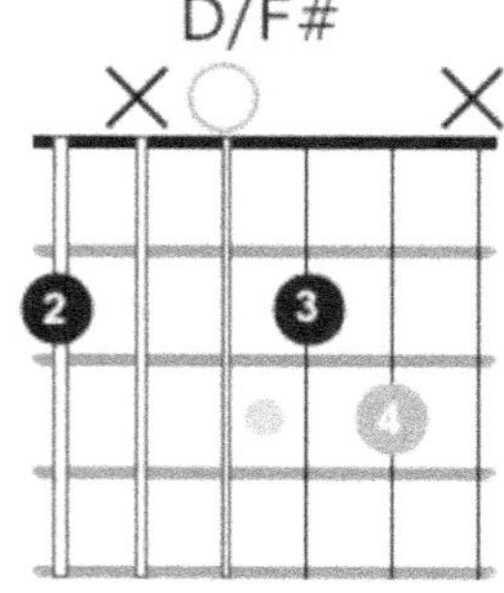

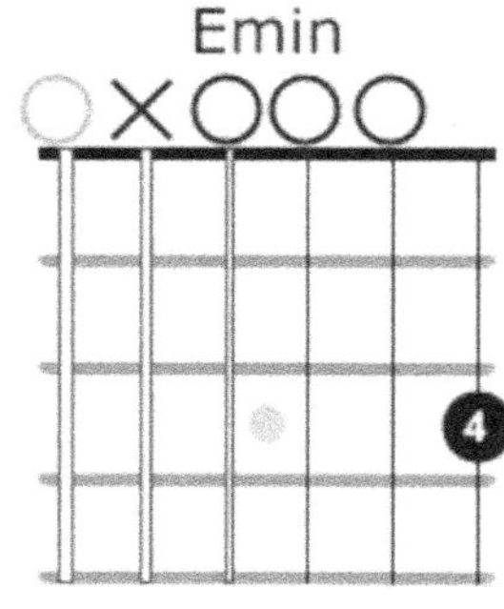

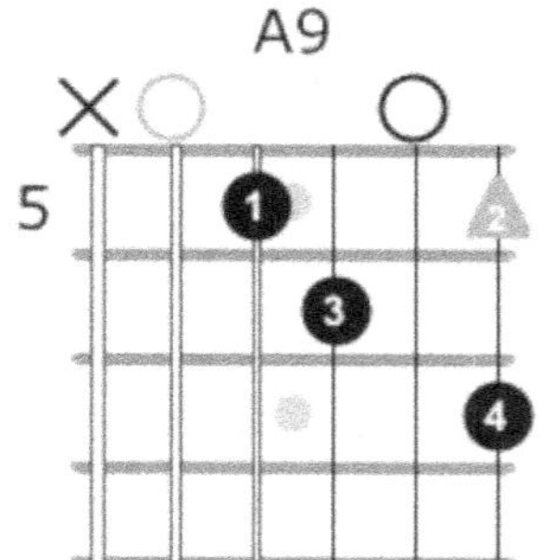

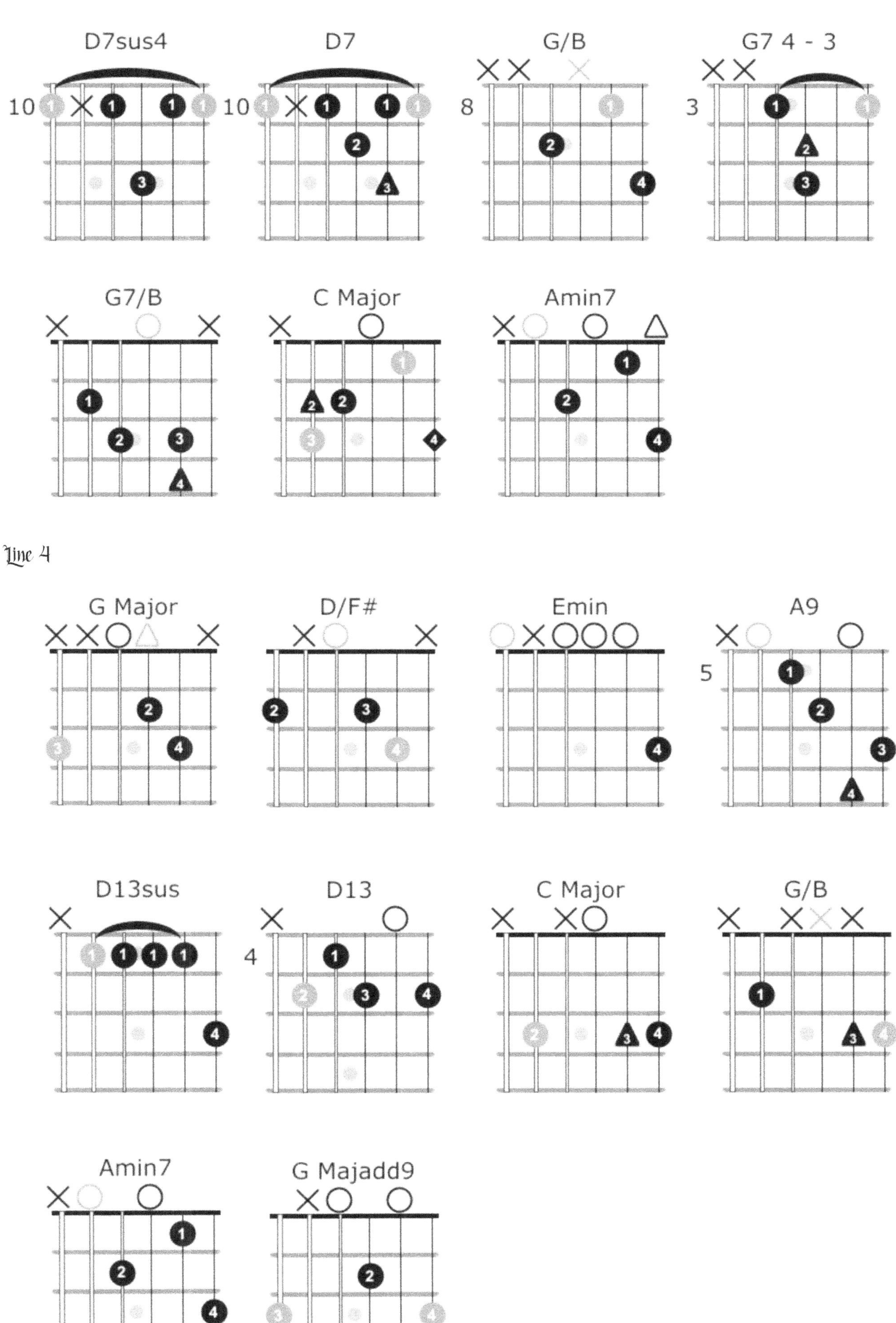

AMAZING GRACE - Advanced

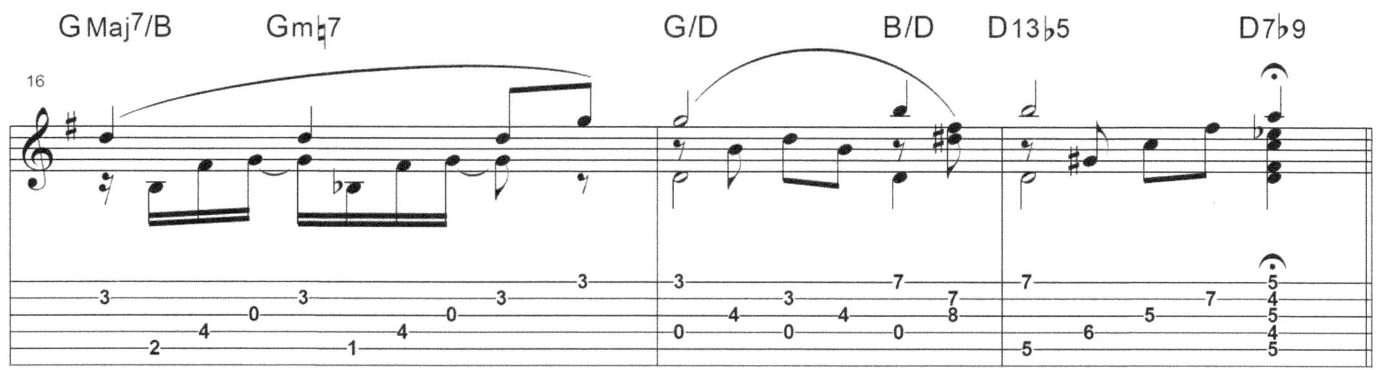

GMaj7/B
Gm♮7
G/D
B/D
D13♭5
D7♭9
16

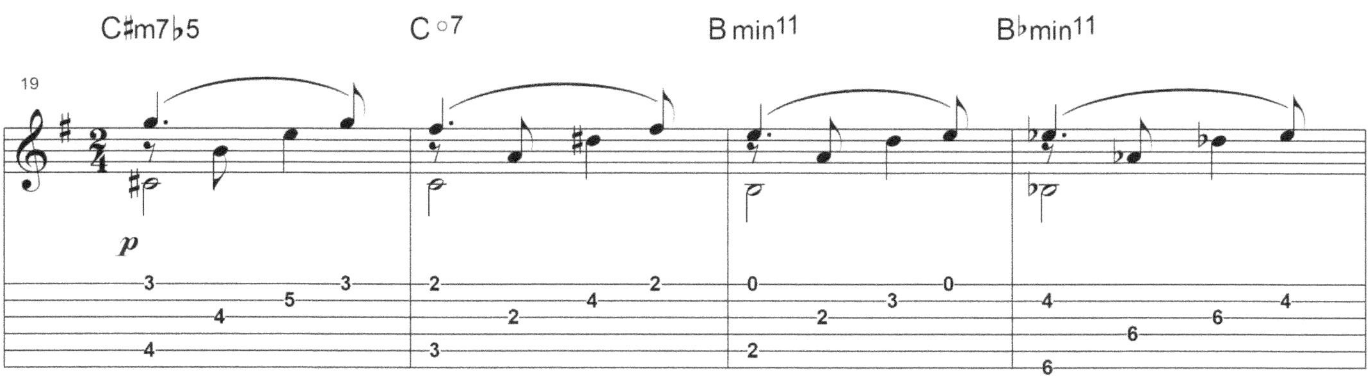

C♯m7♭5
C○7
Bmin11
B♭min11
19
p

Amin11
A♭Majadd9
GMaj♭5
Harmonic played with
right hand index finger.
23
pp
Fine

Chords: Amazing Grace Advanced

Line 1

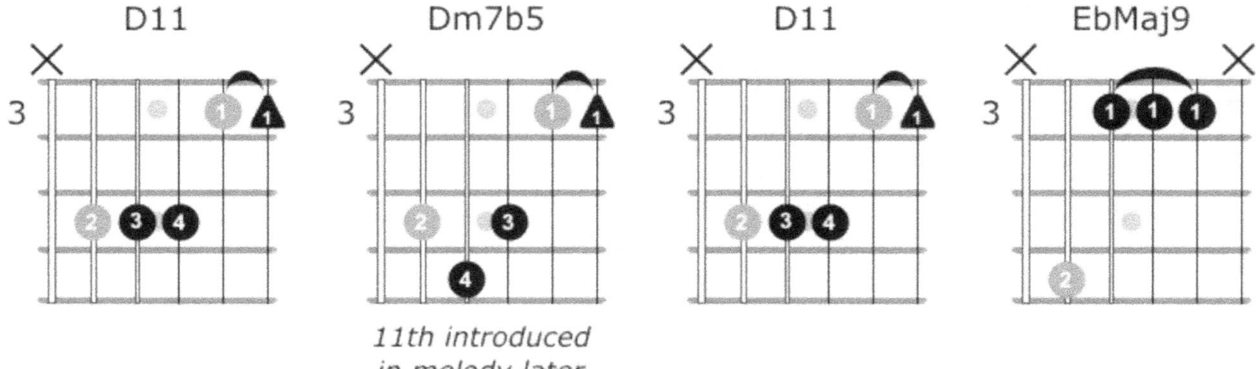

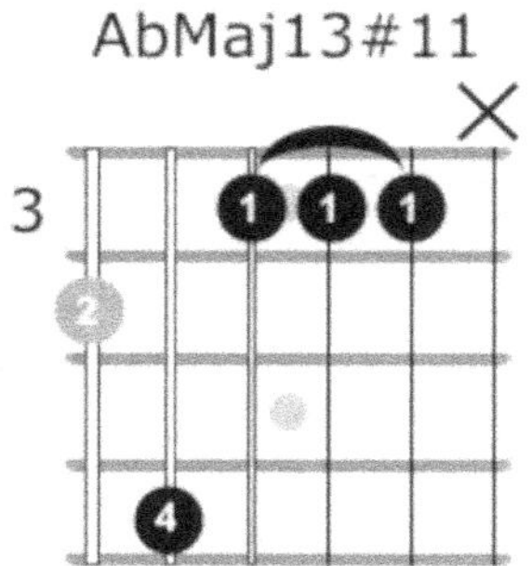

Line 2

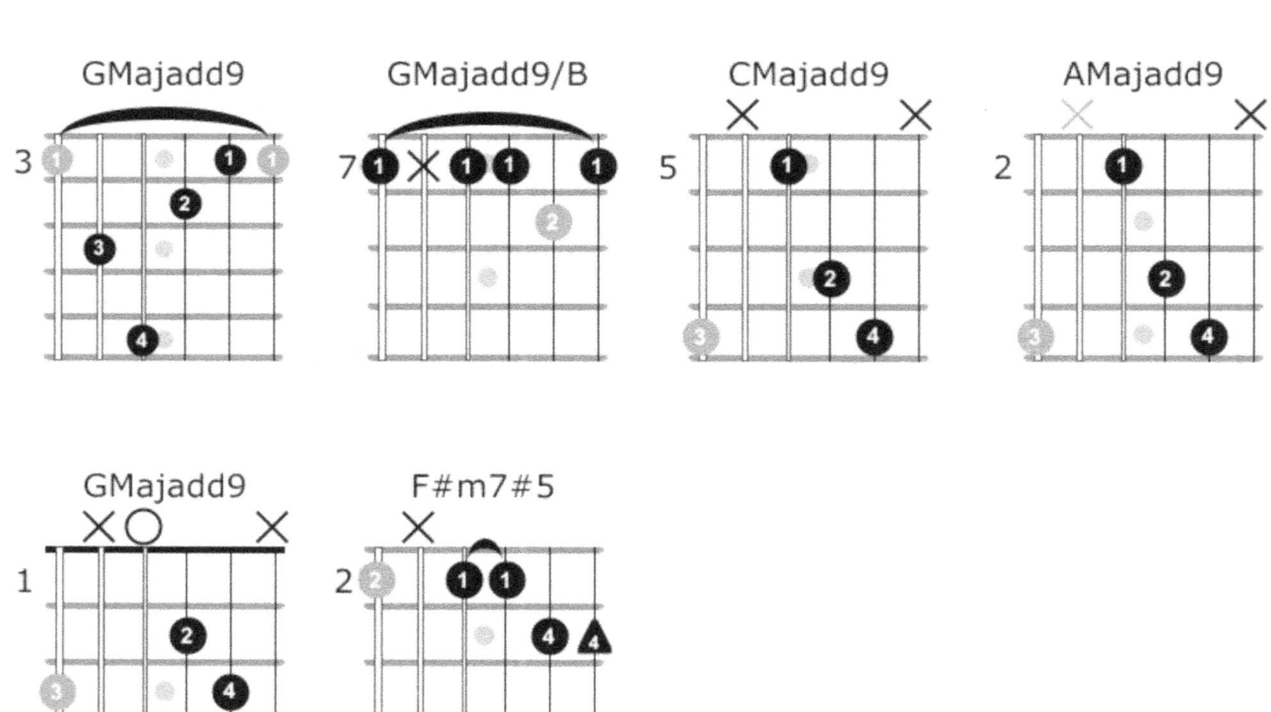

Line 3

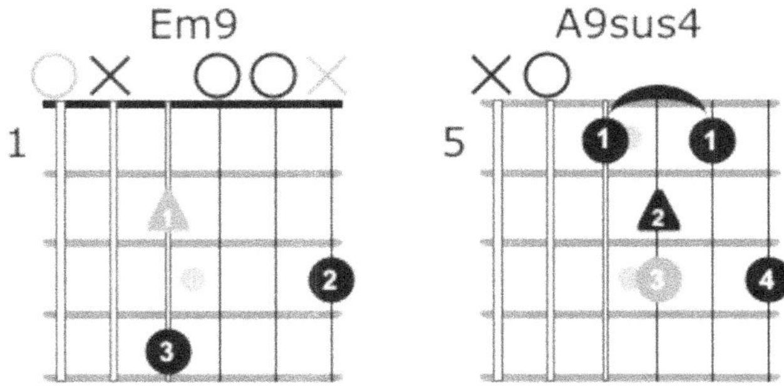

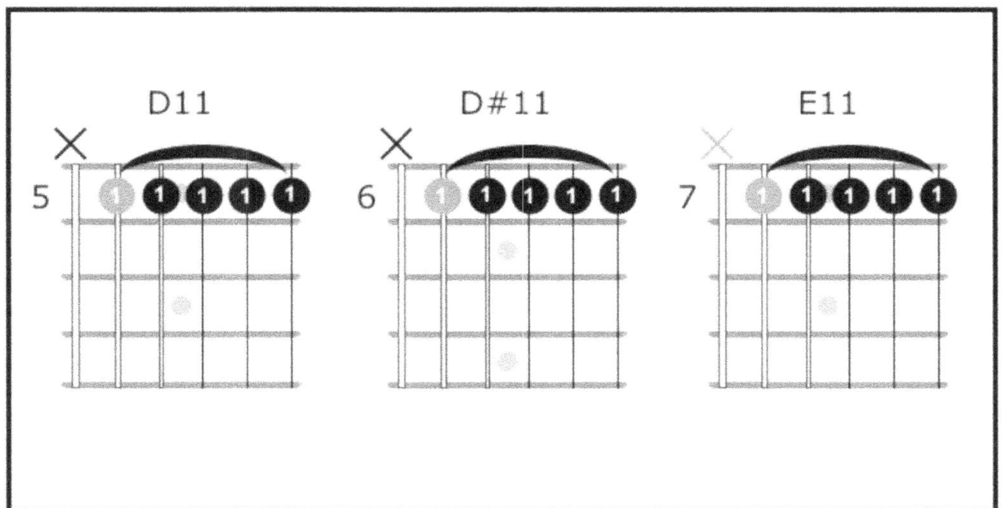

Line 4

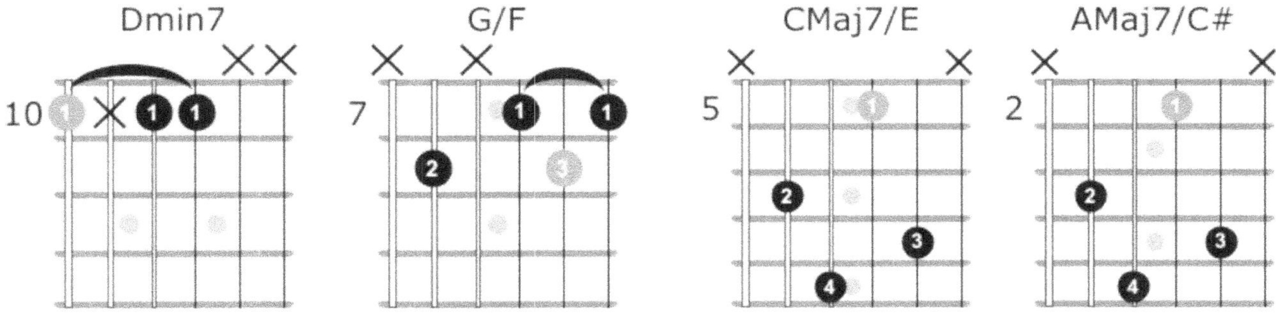

Line 5

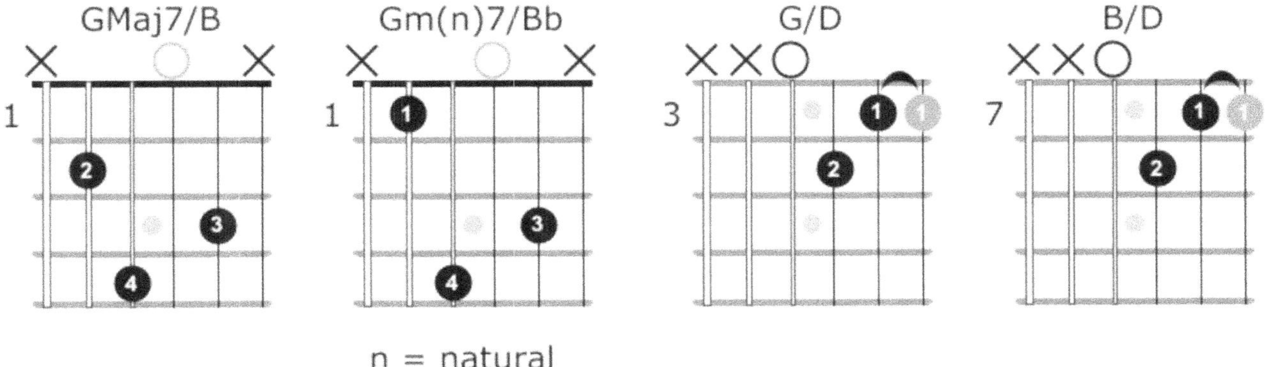

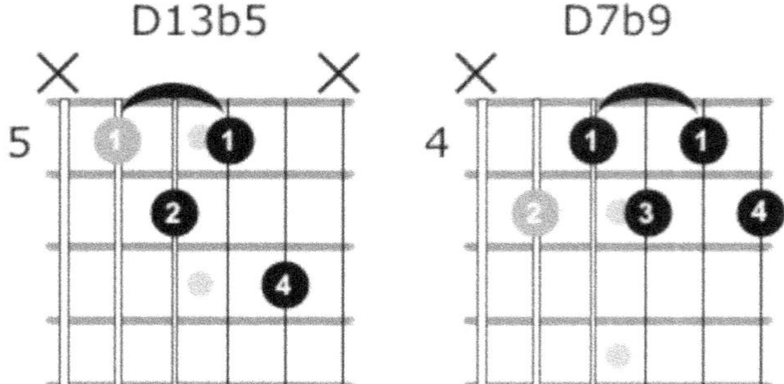

D13b5
D7b9

Line 6

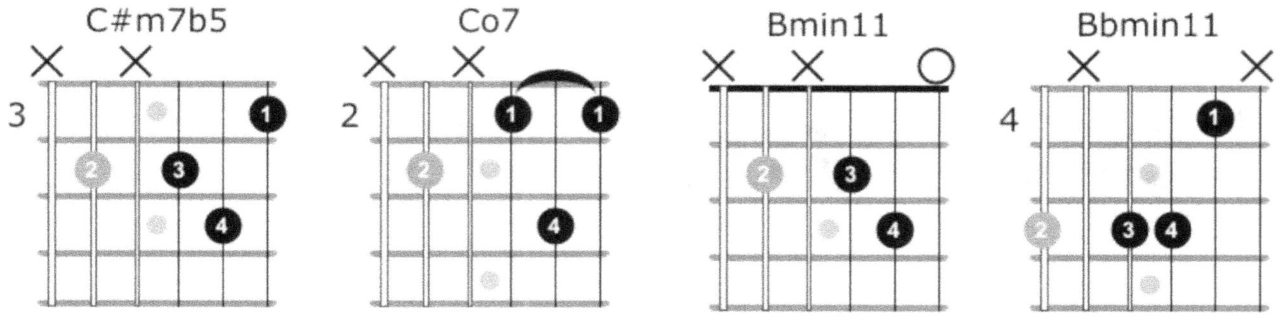

C#m7b5
Co7
Bmin11
Bbmin11

Line7

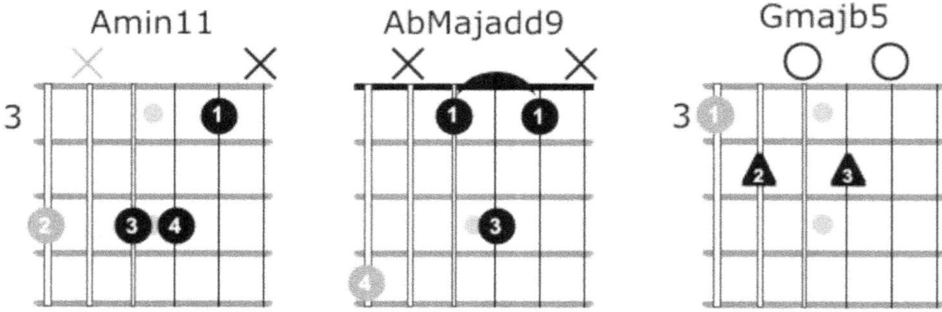

Amin11
AbMajadd9
Gmajb5

Hymn 3
Battle Hymn Of The Republic

Resources

Performance of Intermediate version

Audio Talk through of Intermediate version

Performance of Advanced version

Audio Talk through of Advanced version

Use a QR code reader on your cell/mobile phone or tablet to view and listen to the files above. There's a large selection of completely free QR code reader apps available which work on all operating platforms.

To download all resources and other support files, follow the instructions on page 197 of this publication.

Hymn Notes - Battle Hymn Of The Republic

The melody for Battle Hymn Of The Republic is credited to a man named William Steffe (1830 – 1890) who worked as a bookkeeper and insurance agent. Surprisingly, this rousing tune is the only piece of music ever attributed to Mr Steffe. The melody, however, is more widely considered as the song "John Brown's Body" or "John Brown's Song" which was used as a troop marching song in the American civil war. There are also links and references to an older song, "Canaan's Happy Shore".

Few women feature as creatives in this book, but Julia Ward Howe (1819 – 1910) is one of them. Julia wrote the lyrics to the melody in 1861.

The lyrics on their own, give a cold literal account of what Julia Ward Howe was living through at the time of writing. The overriding impression is that no quarter would be given in what was to be the first major conflict in world history fought with repeating weapons such as the Gatling gun and Henry repeating rifle. The misery that was about to unfold in America due in part to these new weapons was a harbinger of even greater slaughter in two global wars in the following century.

William Steffe　　*Julia Ward Howe*

Lyrics

Verse 1

Mine eyes have seen the glory of the coming of the Lord

He is trampling out the vintage where the grapes of wrath are stored

He hath loosed the fateful lightning of His terrible swift sword

His truth is marching on

Chorus

Glory! Glory! Hallelujah!

Glory! Glory! Hallelujah!

Glory! Glory! Hallelujah!

His truth is marching on

Verse 2

I have seen Him in the watchfires of a hundred circling camps

They have builded Him an altar in the evening dews and damps

I can read His righteous sentence by the dim and flaring lamps

His day is marching on

Chorus

Verse 3 (often missed out)

I have read his fiery gospel writ in rows of burnished steel

As ye deal with my condemners so with you my grace shall deal

let the Hero born of woman crush the serpent with the heel

since God is marching on

Chorus

Verse 4 (sometimes verse 3)

He has sounded forth the trumpet that shall never call retreat

He is sifting out the hearts of men before His judgement seat

Oh, be swift, my soul, to answer him be jubilant, my feet

Our God is marching on

Chorus

Verse 5

In the beauty of the lilies Christ was born across the sea

With a glory in His bosom that transfigures you and me

As He died to make men holy let us die to make men free

While God is marching on

Chorus

BATTLE HYMN OF THE REPUBLIC - Starter

Victoriously

Music by William Steffe
Lyrics by Julia Ward Howe

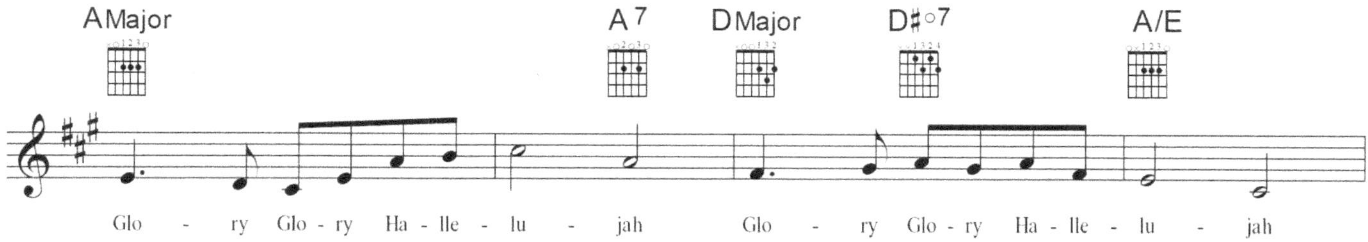

Chorus

BATTLE HYMN OF THE REPUBLIC - Starter alternate key

Chords: Battle Hymn Of The Republic Starter

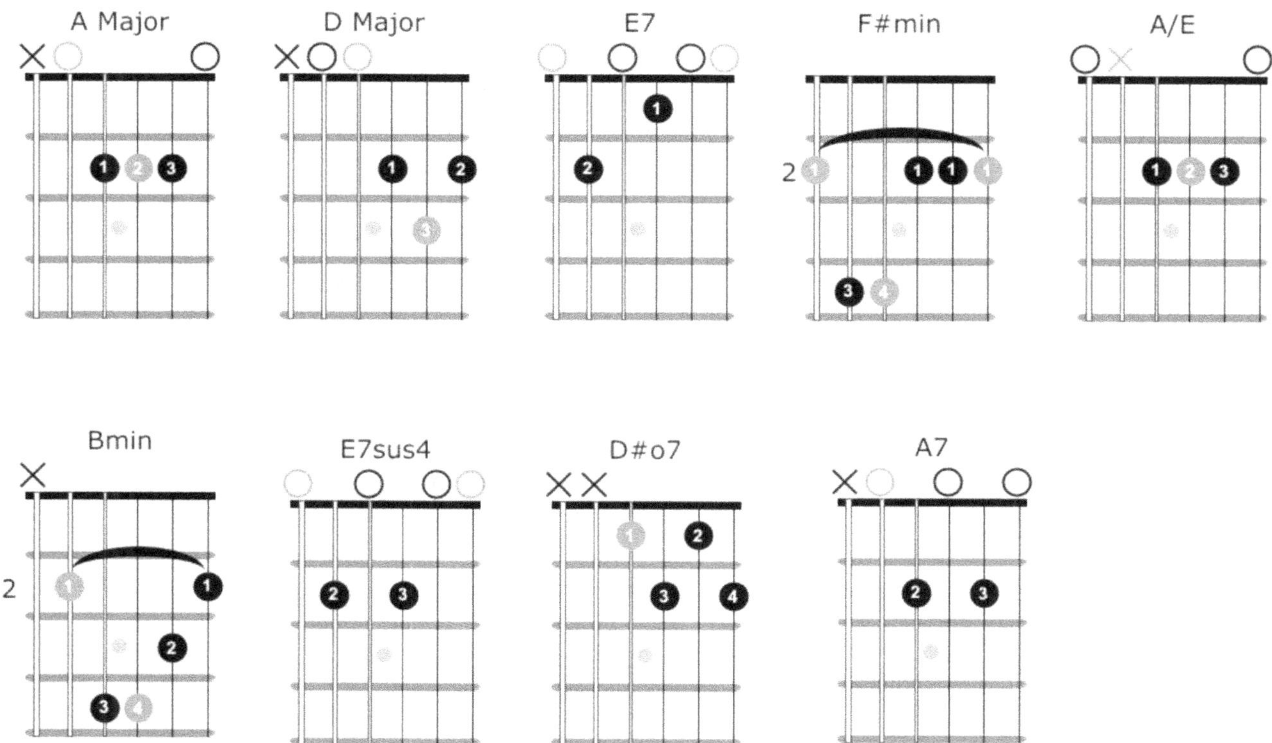

Chords: Battle Hymn Of The Republic Starter Alternate Key

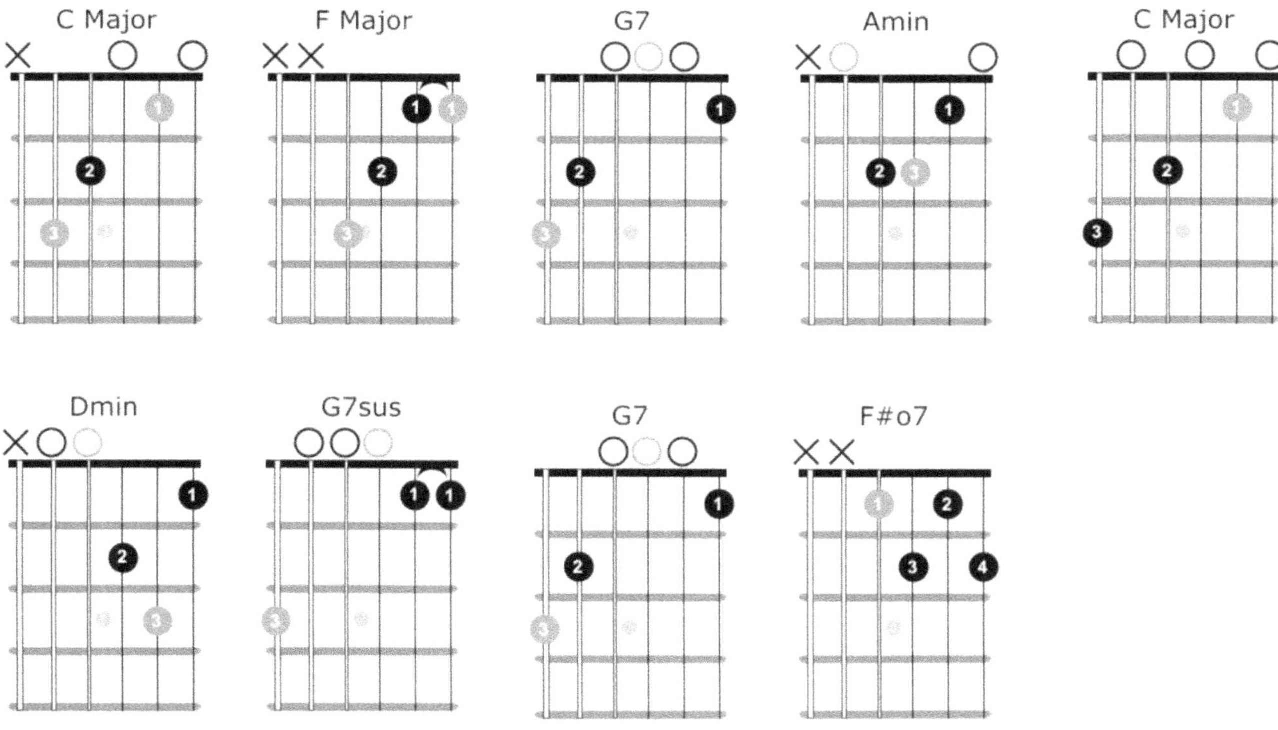

Battle Hymn Of The Republic play along

bpm = 116

Swing feel

Abide With Me + Melody
Abide With Me Backing Track

Count of 3 then play

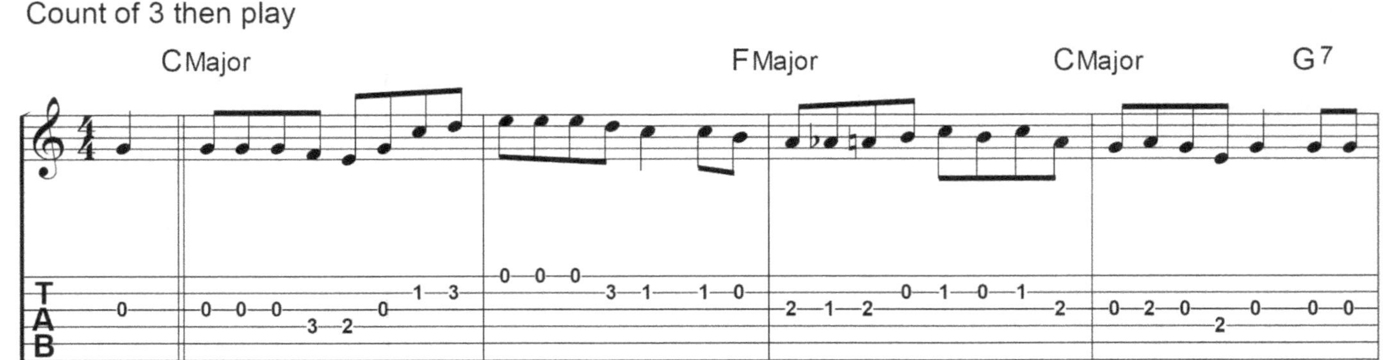

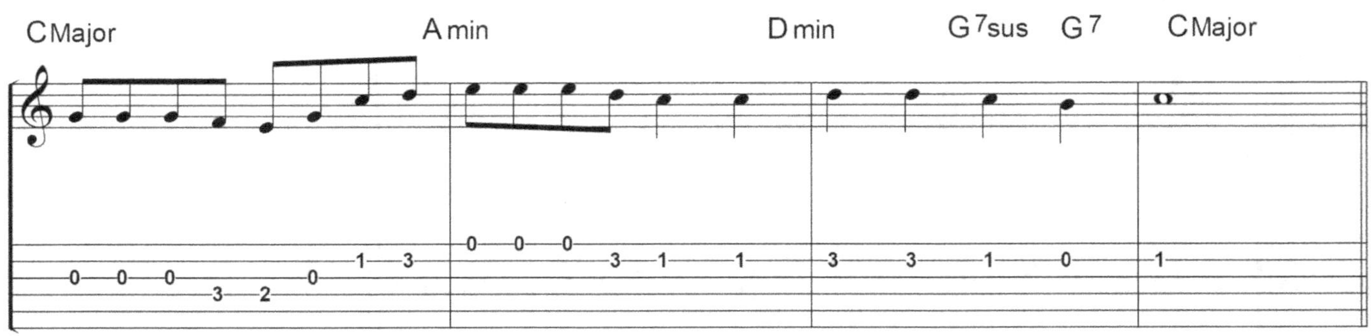

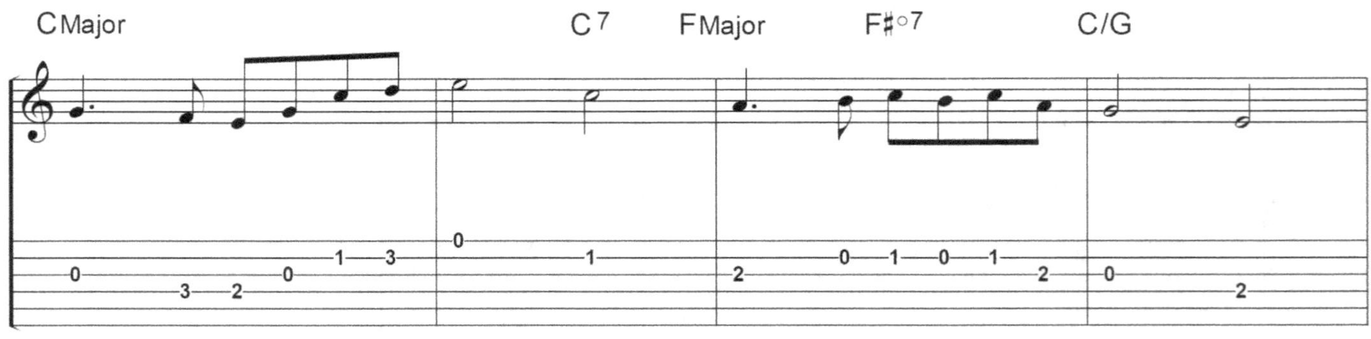

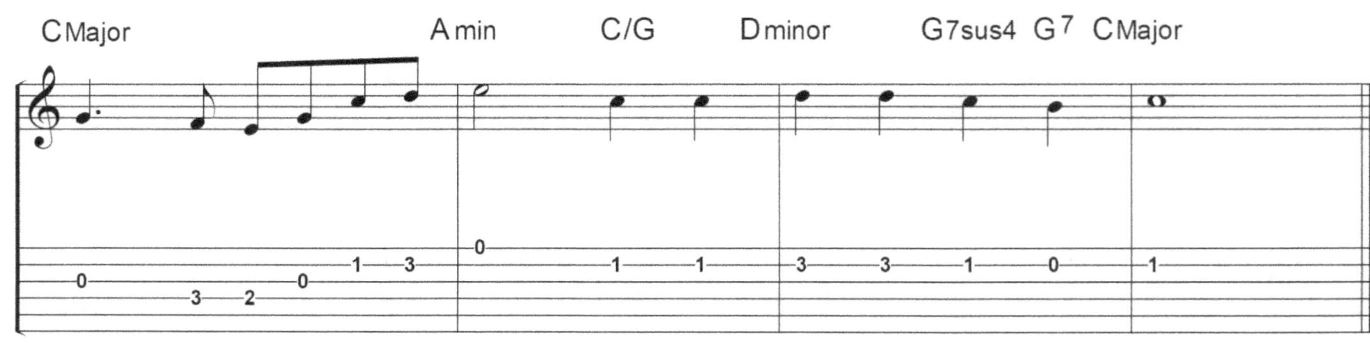

BATTLE HYMN OF THE REPUBLIC - Intermediate

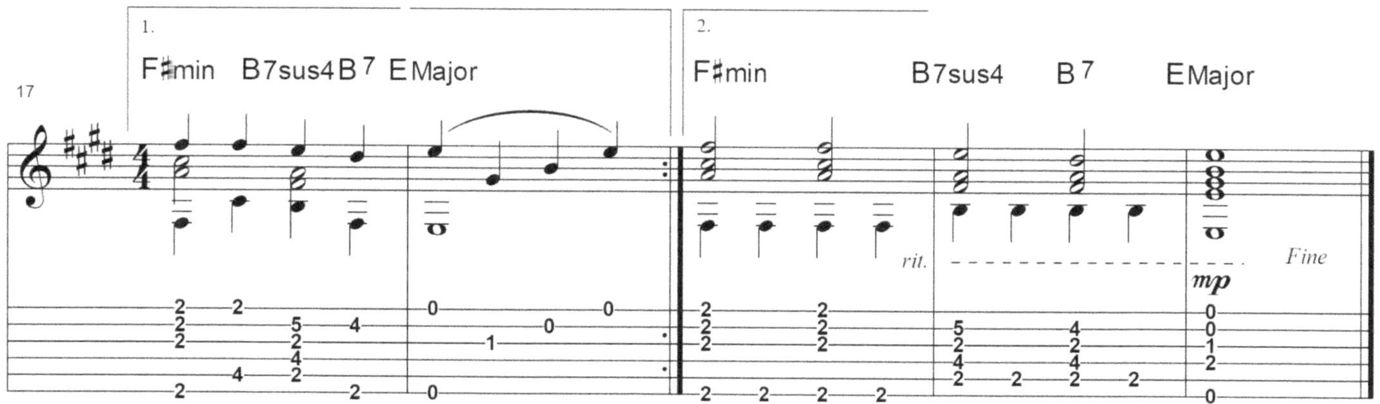

Chords: Battle Hymn Of The Republic Intermediate

Line 1

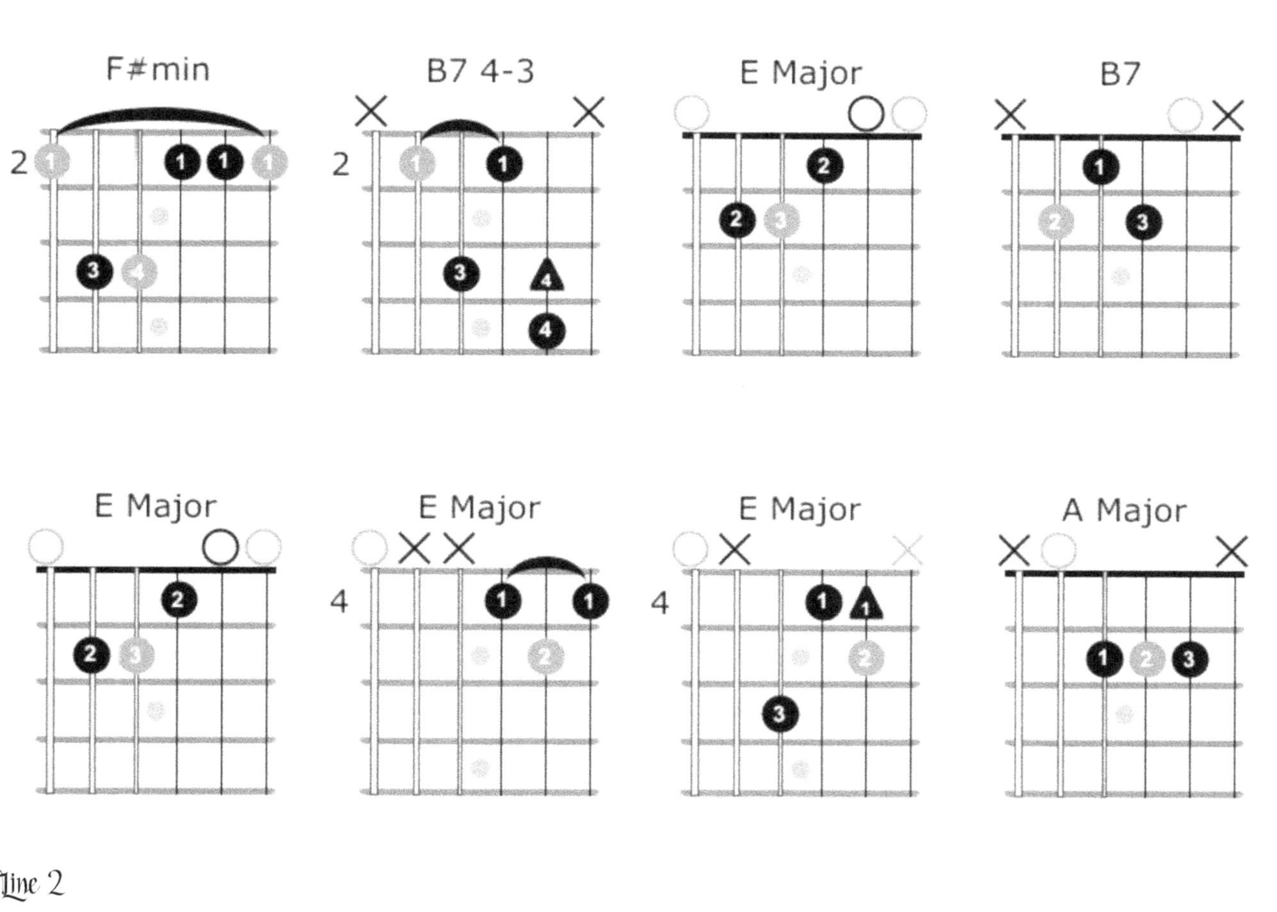

Line 2

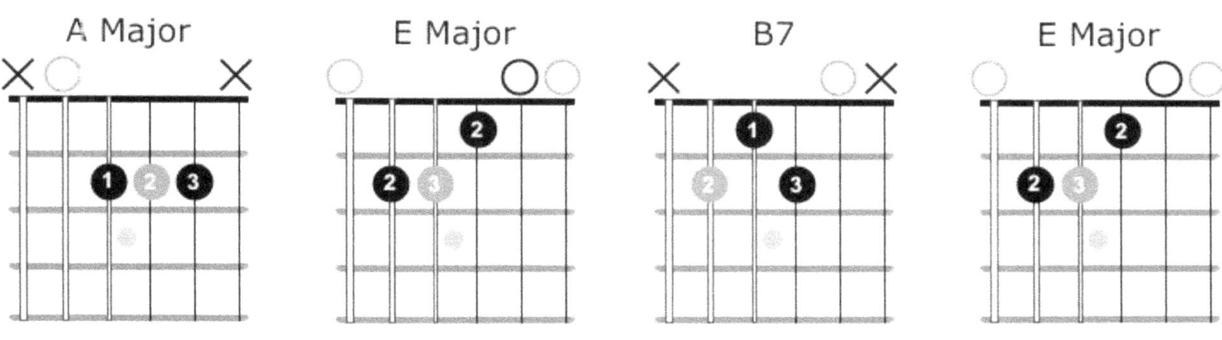

G#7
C#min

Line 3

F#min
B7 4-3
E Major
B7
E Major
E Major
E Major
A Major

Line 4

A Major
E Major
G#7
C#min

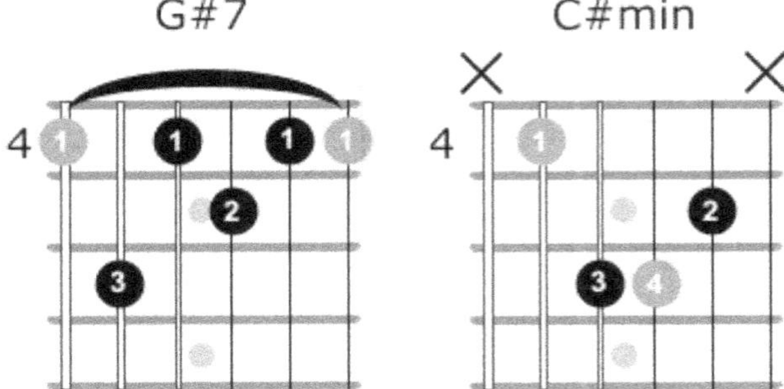

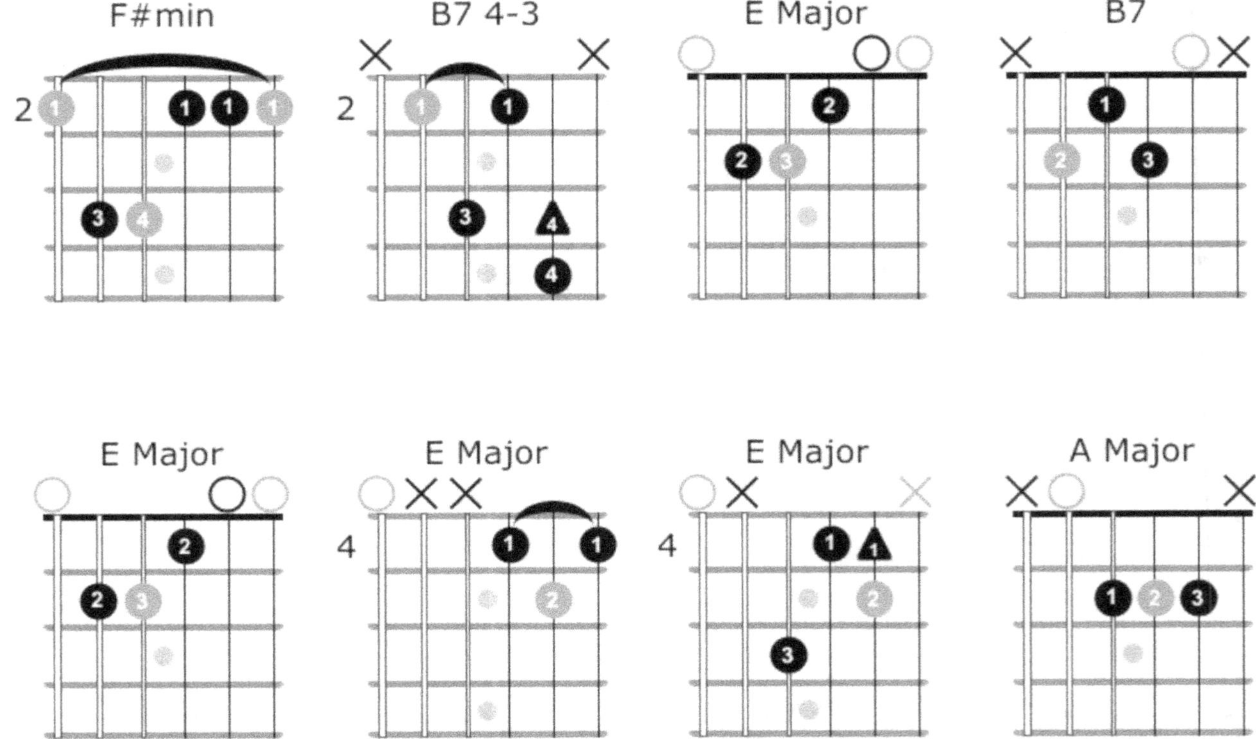

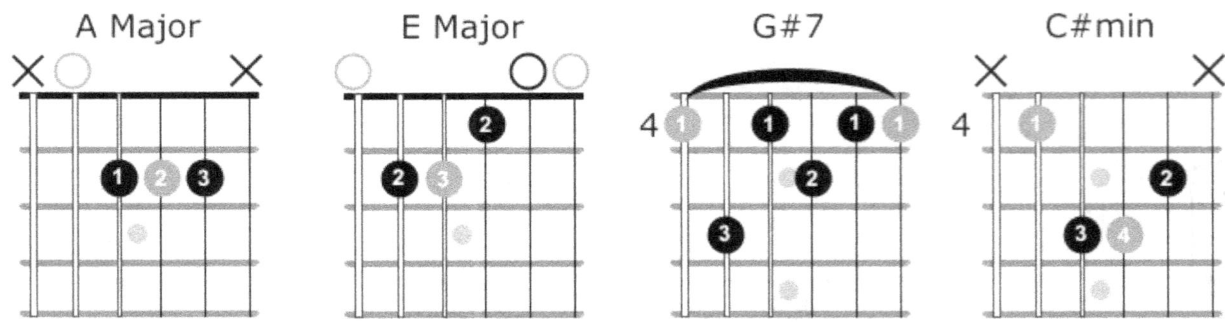

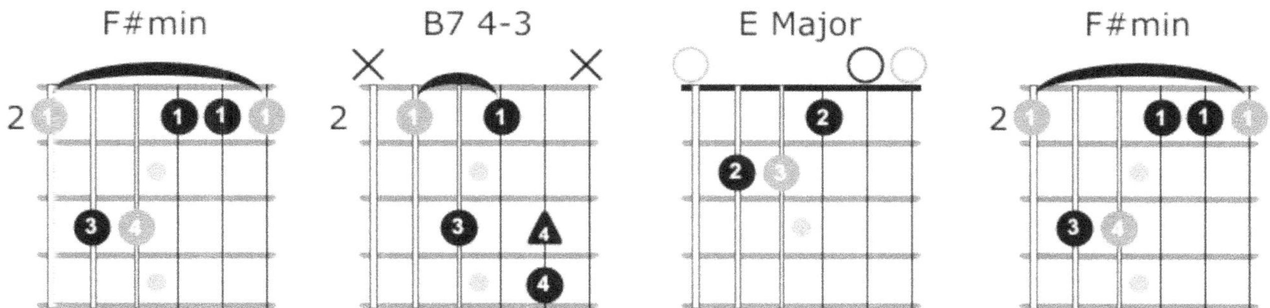

F#min
B7 4-3
E Major
F#min

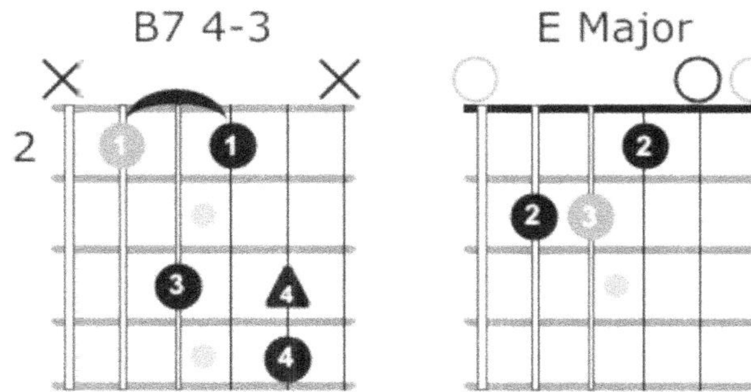

B7 4-3
E Major

BATTLE HYMN OF THE REPUBLIC - Advanced

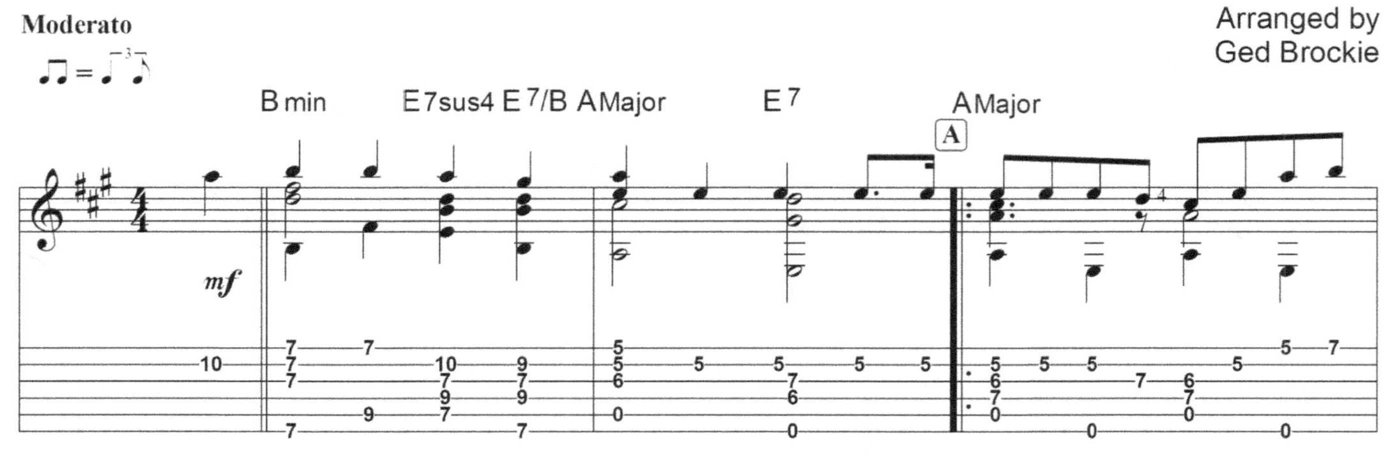

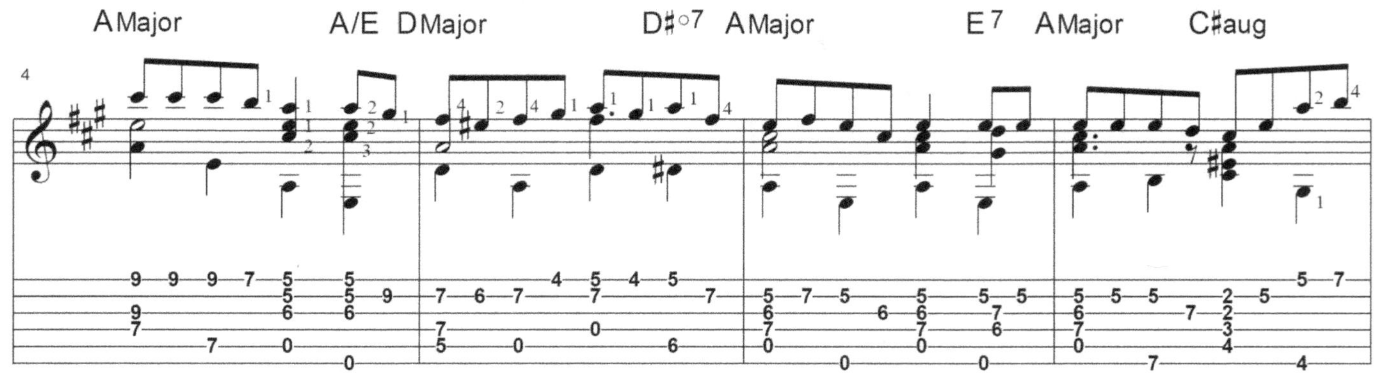

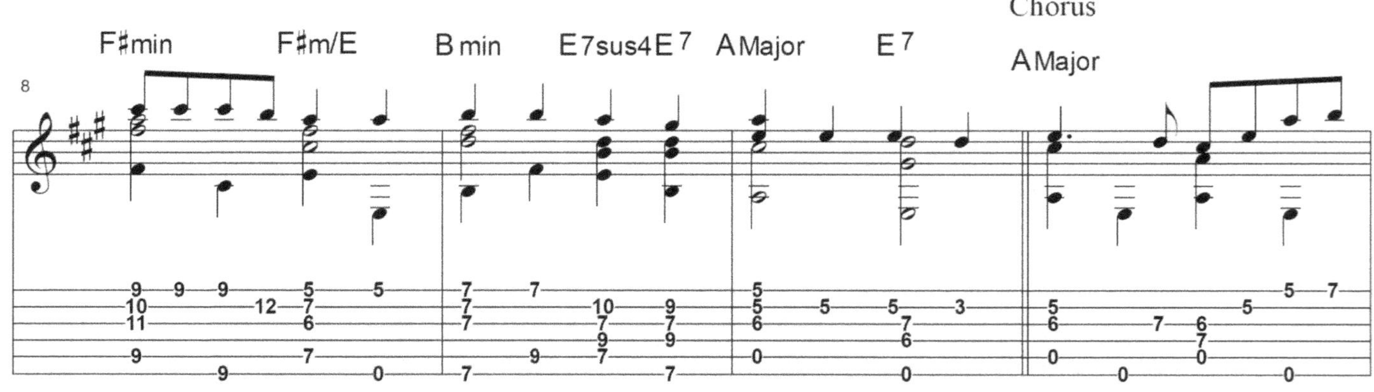

F#min
F#m/E
B min
E7sus4
E 7
1. A Major
E 7
16

2. A Major
F#7
B
B Major
E Major
E#o7
19
f

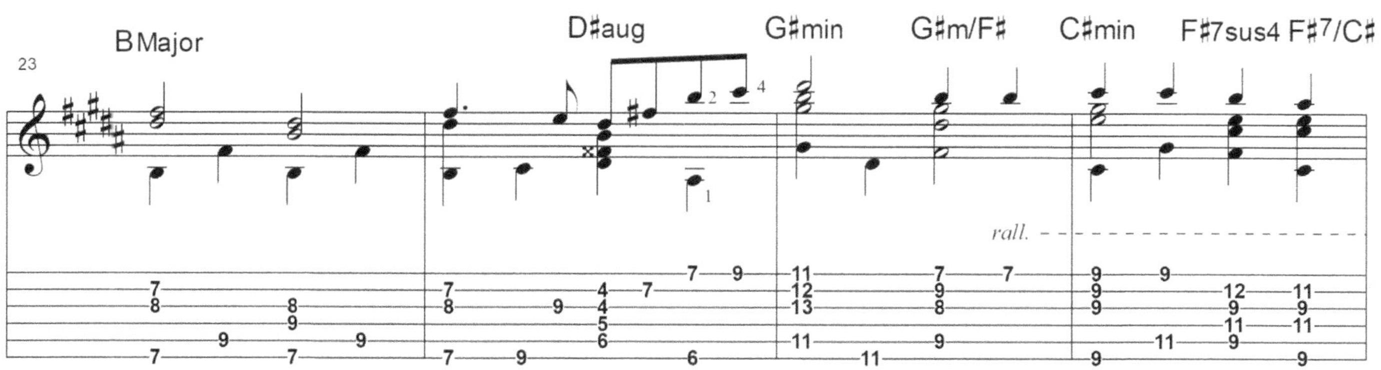

B Major
D#aug
G#min
G#m/F#
C#min
F#7sus4 F#7/C#
23
rall. - - -

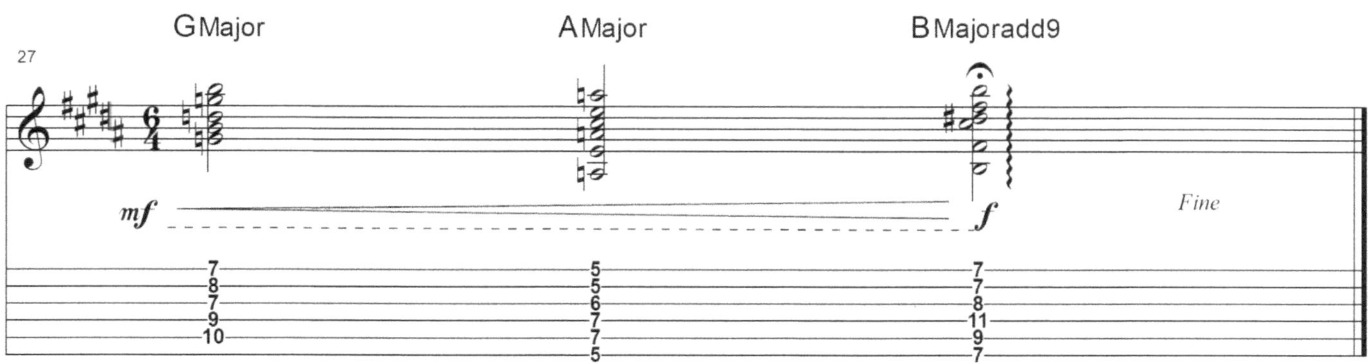

G Major
A Major
B Major add9
27
mf
f
Fine

Chords: Battle Hymn Of The Republic Advanced

Line 1

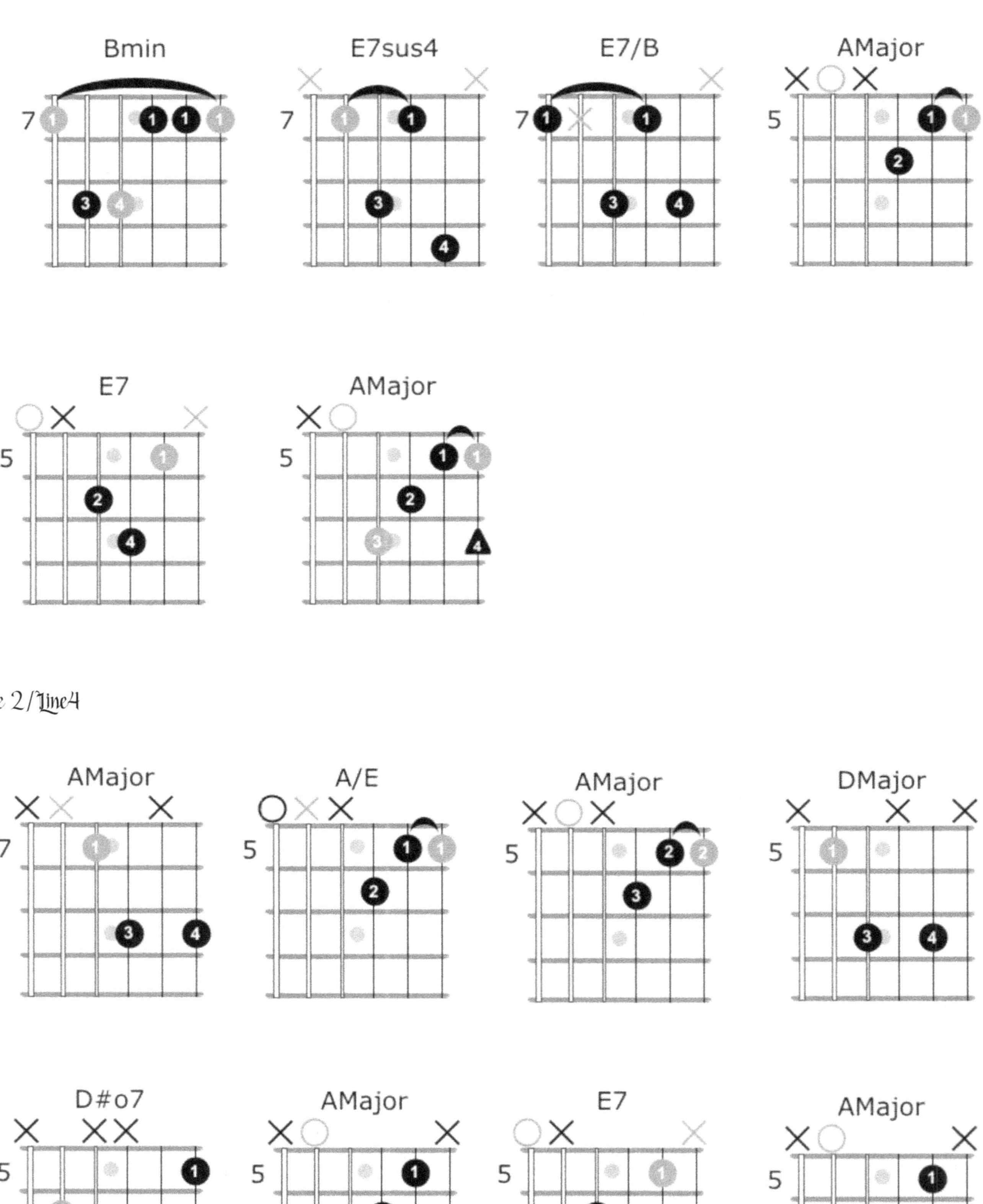

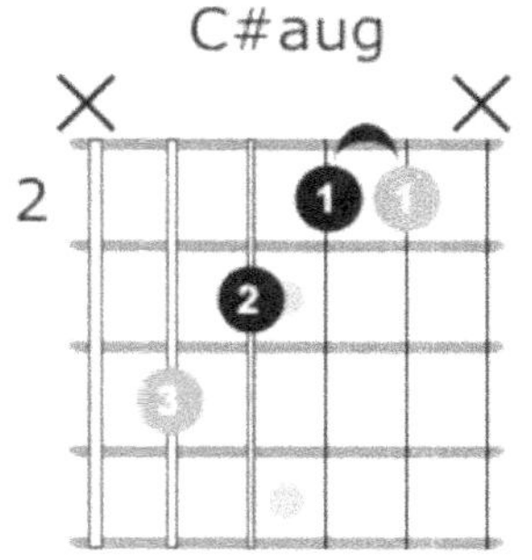

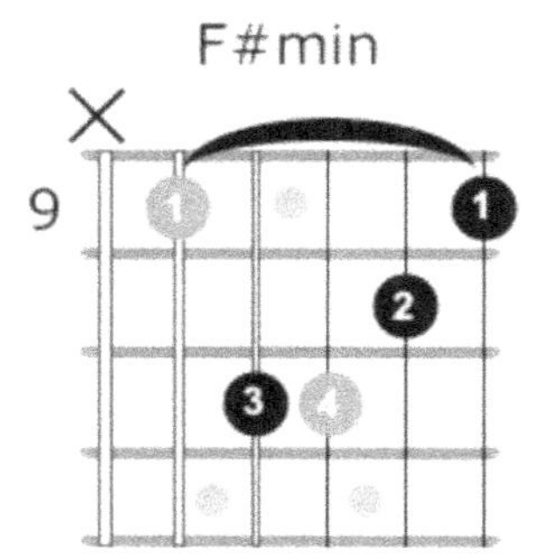

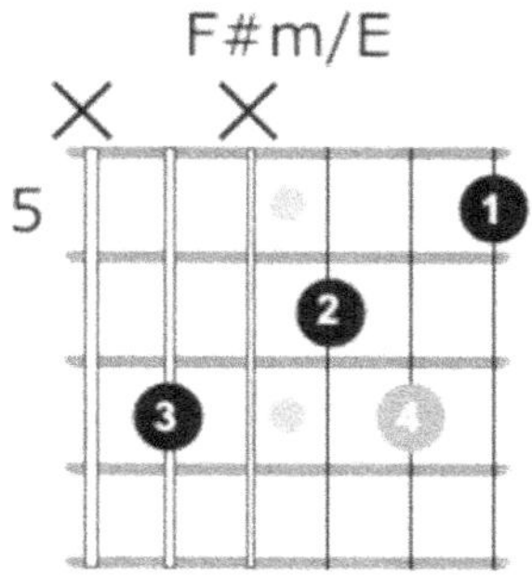

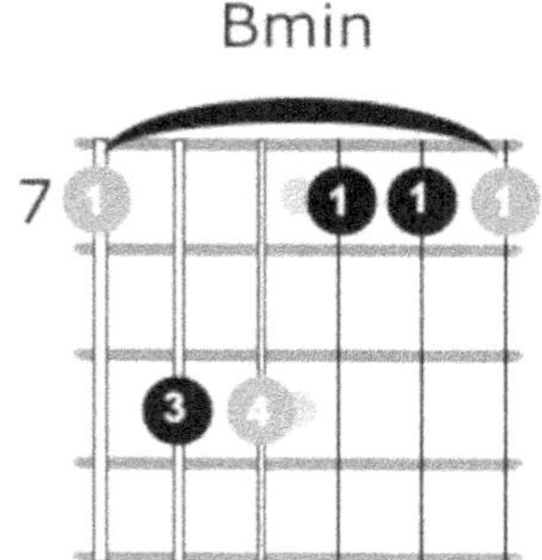

AFTER E7/B GO BACK TO BEGINNING & PLAY FROM 6th CHORD. ON REPEAT MISS THESE 2 CHORDS OUT & PLAY THE CHORDS IN BOX TO RIGHT.

1st Time Ending chords. Play from the 6th chord on previous page for repeat.

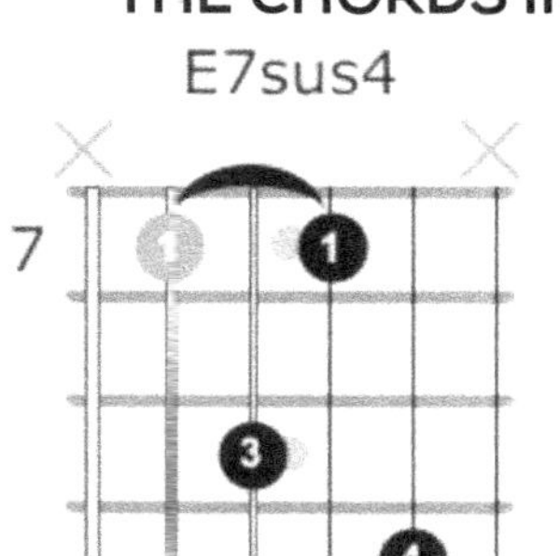

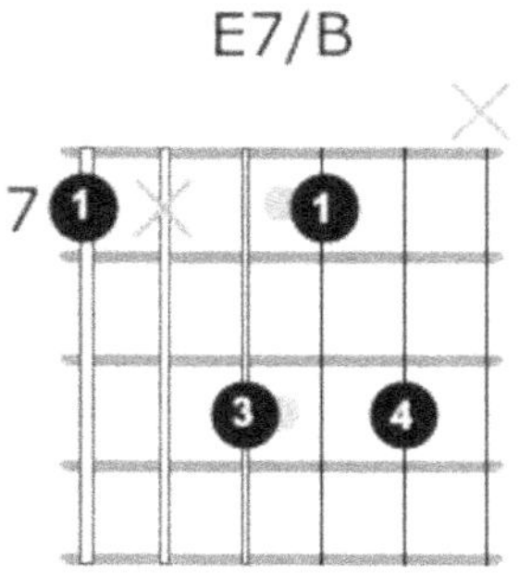

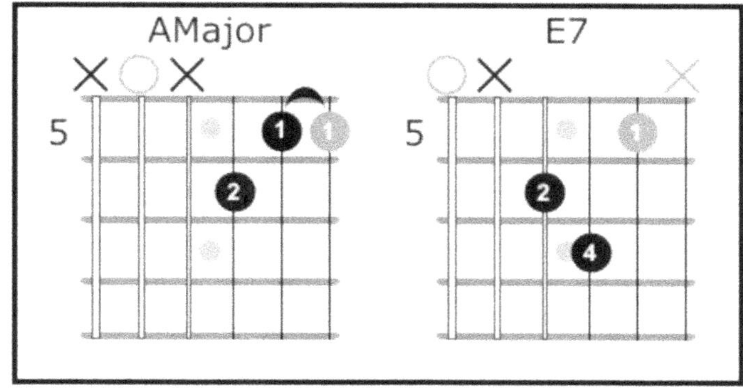

Line 6

2nd Time Ending chords.

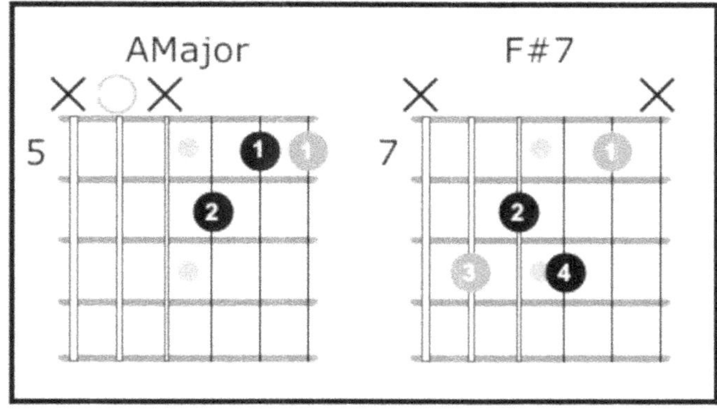

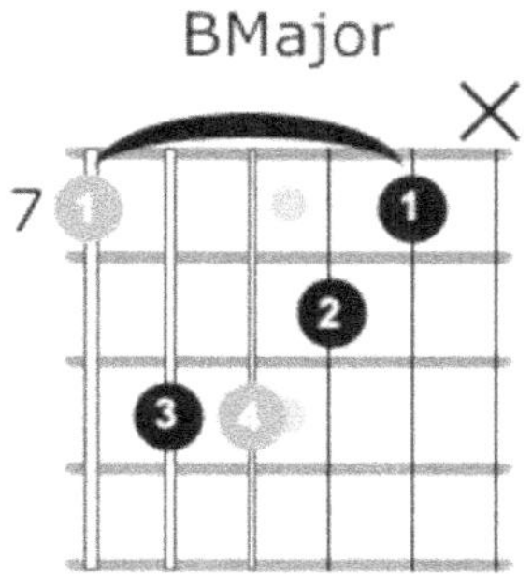

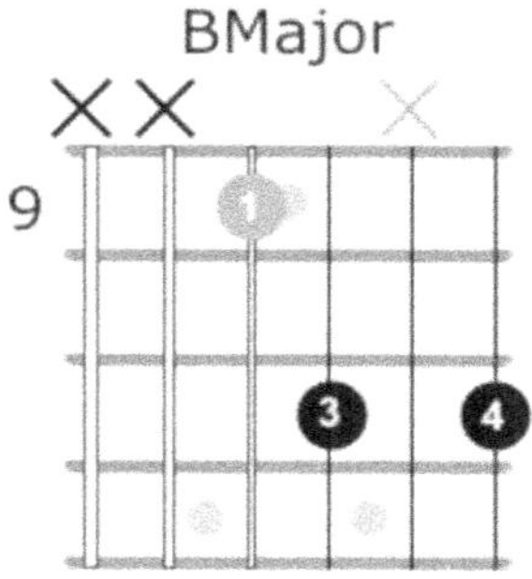

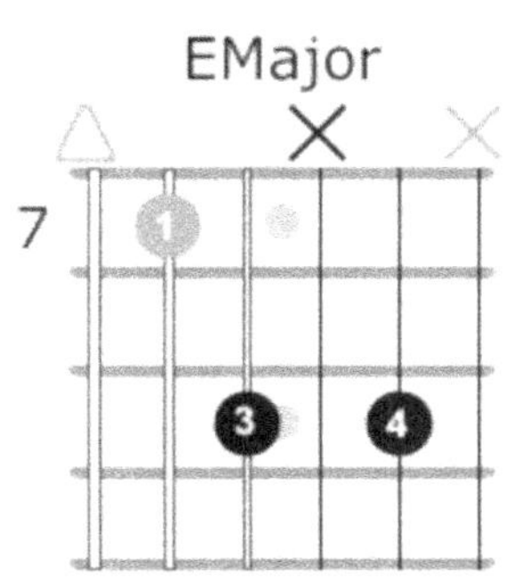

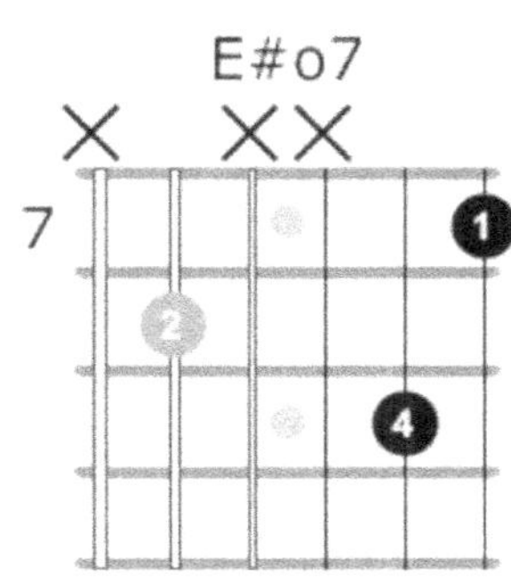

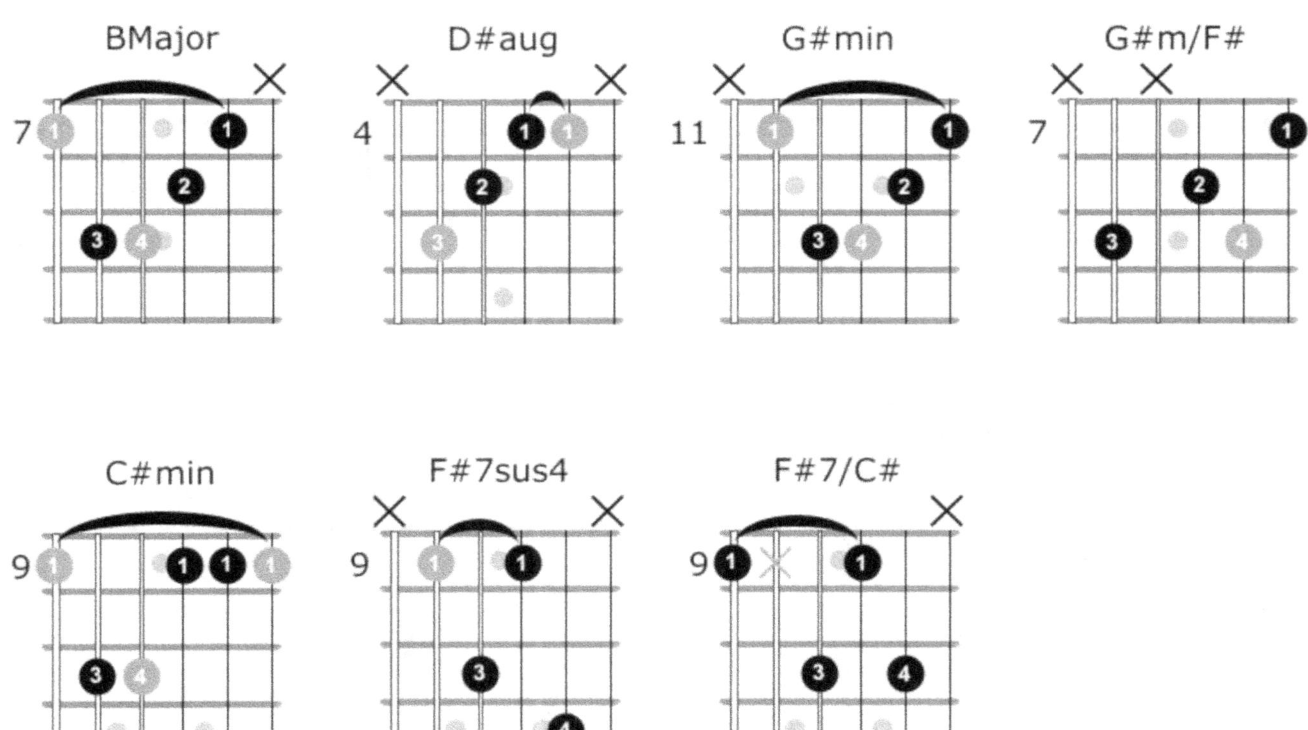

BMajor
D#aug
G#min
G#m/F#
7
4
11
7
C#min
F#7sus4
F#7/C#
9
9
9

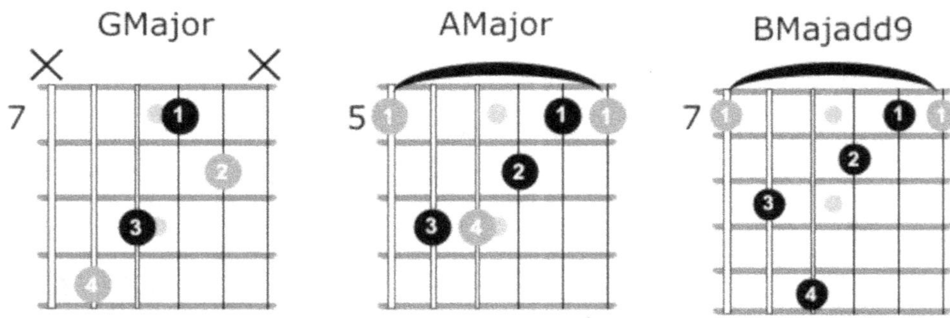

GMajor
AMajor
BMajadd9
7
5
7

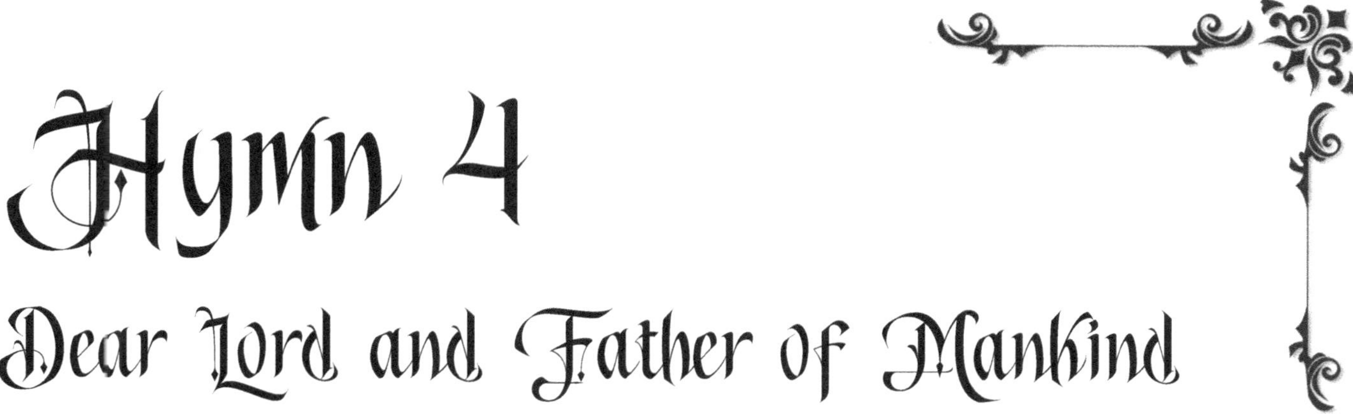

Hymn 4
Dear Lord and Father of Mankind

Resources

Performance of Intermediate version

Audio Talk through of Intermediate version

Performance of Advanced version

Audio Talk through of Advanced version

Use a QR code reader on your cell/mobile phone or tablet to view and listen to the files above. There's a large selection of completely free QR code reader apps available which work on all operating platforms.

To download all resources and other support files, follow the instructions on page 197 of this publication.

Hymn Notes - Dear Lord & Father Of Mankind

John Greenleaf Whittier (1807 – 1892) was the writer of the words to this hymn. They were taken from his poem "The Brewing of Soma".

Mr Whittier, who was a Quaker, was a man who had a caring spirit and an advocate of abolishing slavery as well as promoting women authors. It was said that as a poet, he was heavily influenced by Scottish writer Robert Burns, however, his own poetry seems to have received only look warm reviews.

The music that has been used in this arrangement of the song is the English version set to the melody "Repton" written by Hubert Parry (1848 – 1918) who also wrote the unofficial English national anthem "Jerusalem".

Hubert Parry   *John Greenleaf Whittier*

For anyone reading this in America, the song that you will most probably be familiar with in reference to these lyrics is "Rest" by Frederick Charles Maker. I hope you agree with me that the choice of the English musical version, on this occasion, helps elevate the spirit to a place of reflection and consideration when reading the words below.

Lyrics

Verse 1

Dear Lord and Father of mankind,

Forgive our foolish ways!

Reclothe us in our rightful mind,

In purer lives Thy service find,

In deeper reverence, praise. (last line in each verse repeated)

Verse 2

In simple trust like theirs who heard

Beside the Syrian sea

The gracious calling of the Lord,

Let us, like them, without a word

Rise up and follow Thee.

Verse 3

O Sabbath rest by Galilee!

O calm of hills above,

Where Jesus knelt to share with Thee

The silence of eternity

Interpreted by love!

Verse 4

With that deep hush subduing all

Our words and works that drown

The tender whisper of Thy call,

As noiseless let Thy blessing fall

As fell Thy manna down.

Verse 5

Drop Thy still dews of quietness,

Till all our strivings cease;

Take from our souls the strain and stress,

And let our ordered lives confess

The beauty of Thy peace.

Verse 6

Breathe through the heats of our desire

Thy coolness and Thy balm;

Let sense be dumb, let flesh retire;

Speak through the earthquake, wind, and fire,

O still, small voice of calm.

Dear Lord and Father of Mankind - Starter

Dear Lord and Father of Mankind - Starter alternate key

Steady tempo

Charles Parry

Chords: Dear Lord and Father of Mankind Starter

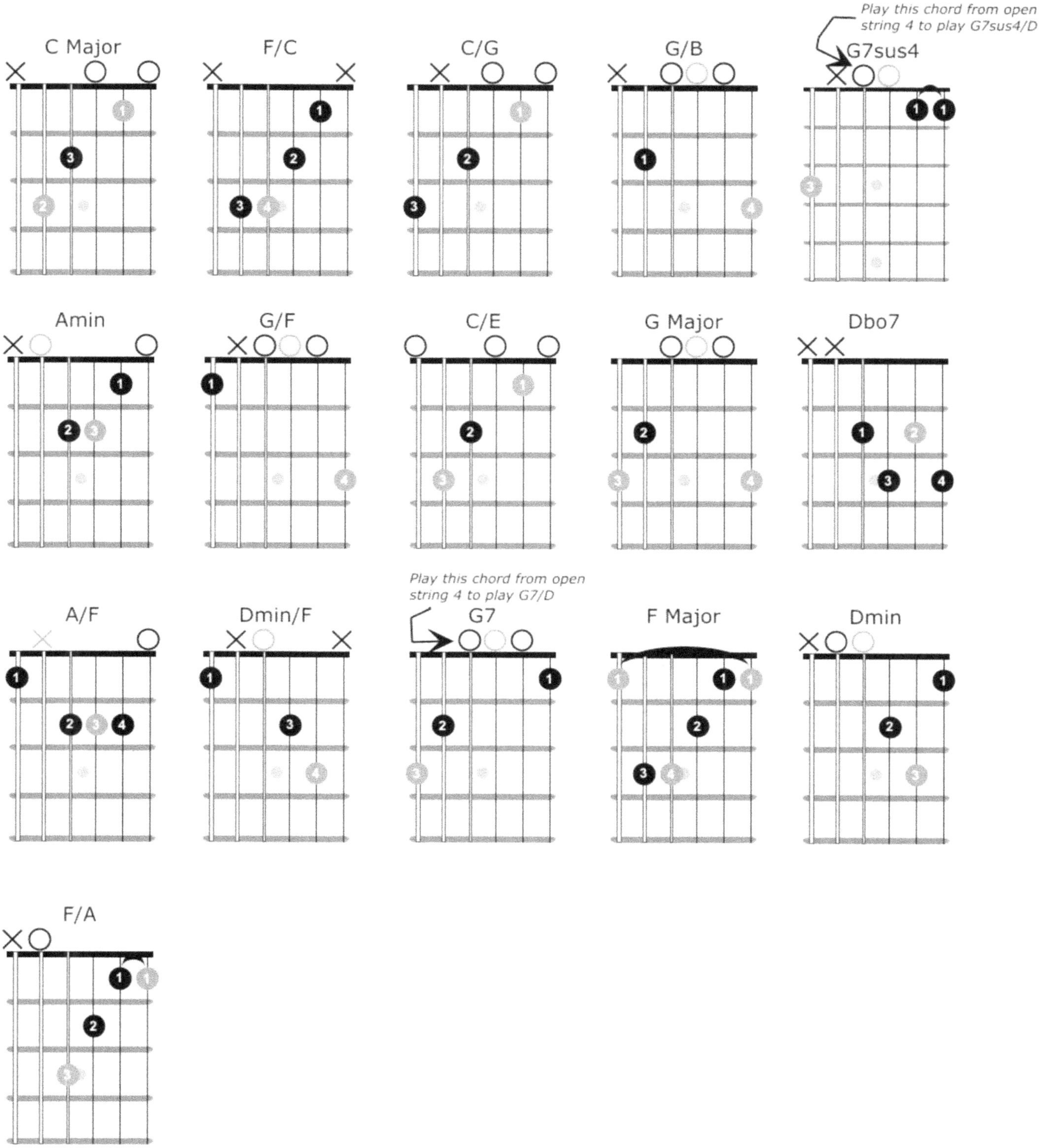

C Major
F/C
C/G
G/B
Play this chord from open string 4 to play G7sus4/D
G7sus4
Amin
G/F
C/E
G Major
Dbo7
A/F
Dmin/F
Play this chord from open string 4 to play G7/D
G7
F Major
Dmin
F/A

Chords: Dear Lord and Father of Mankind Starter Alternate Key

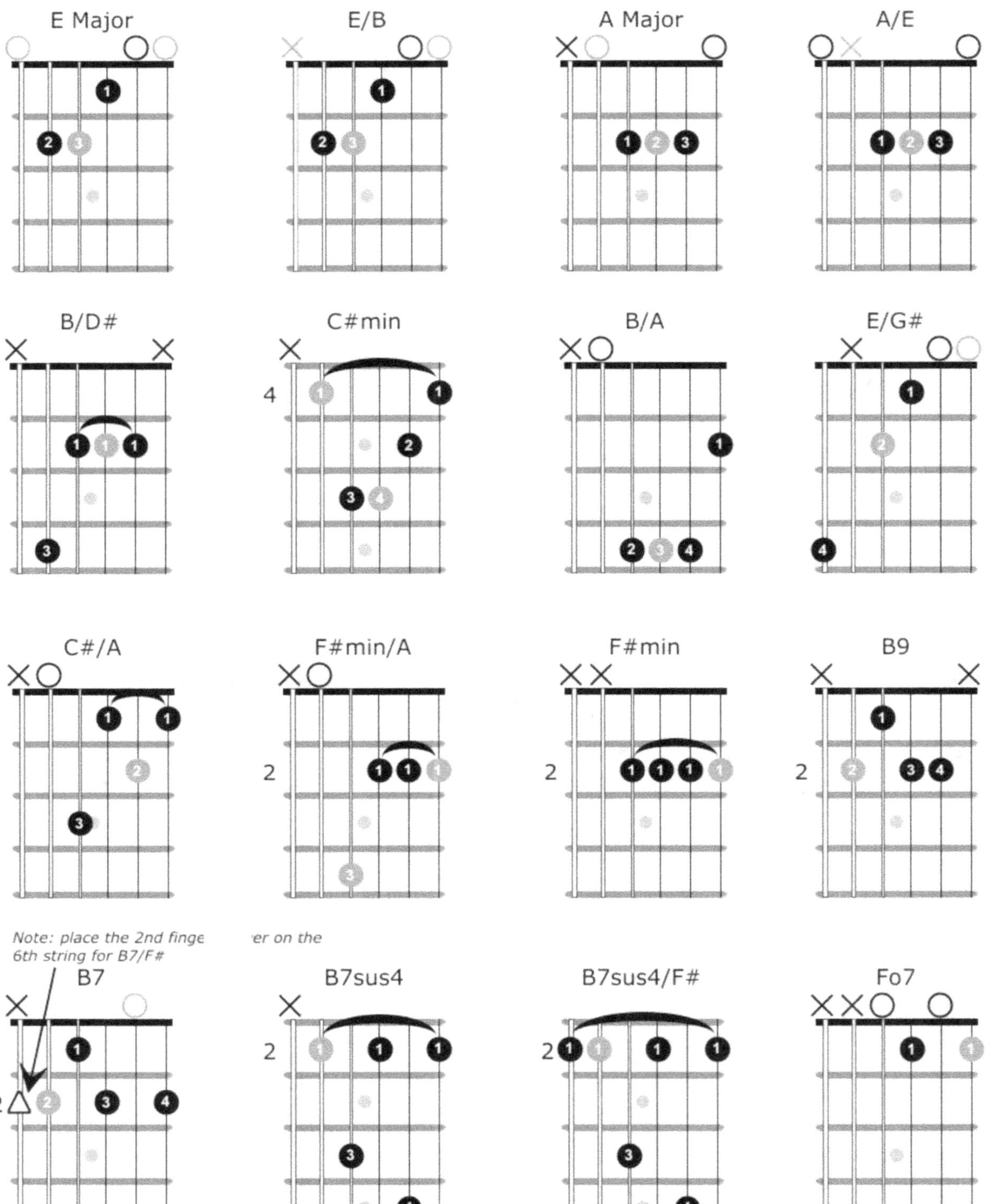

Dear Lord and Father Of Mankind play along

bpm = 80

Abide With Me + Melody
Abide With Me Backing Track

Count of 3 then play

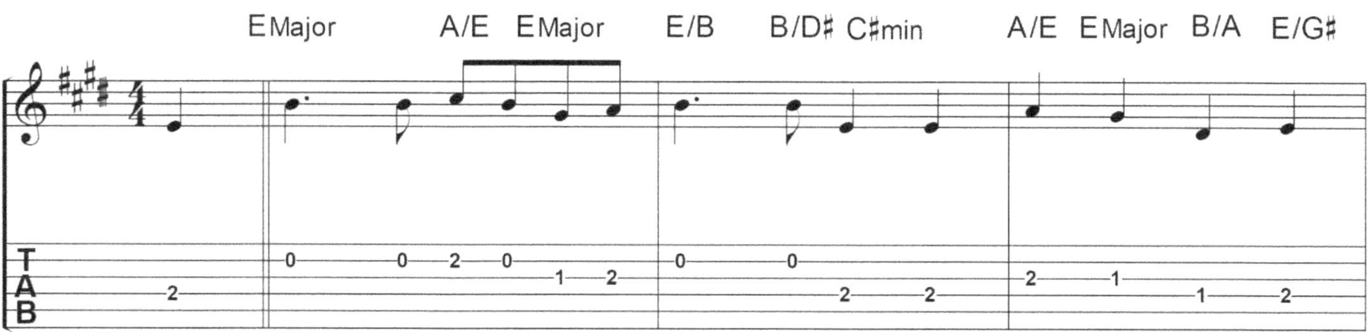

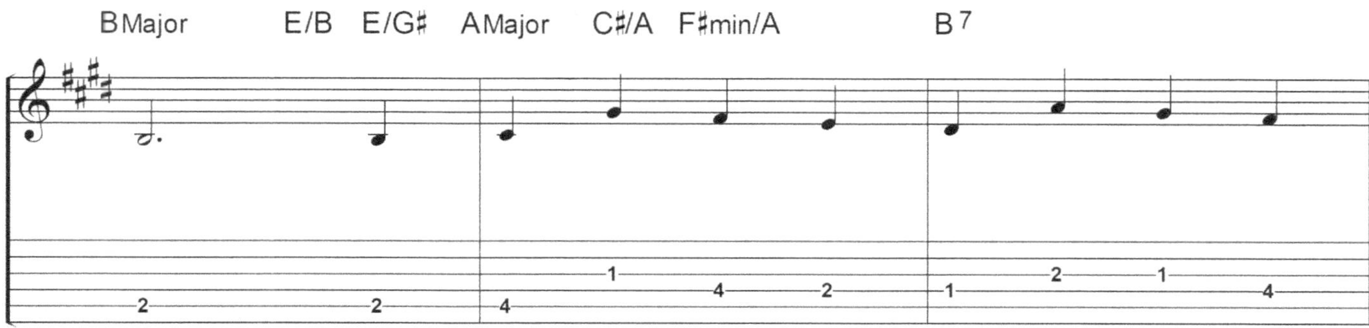

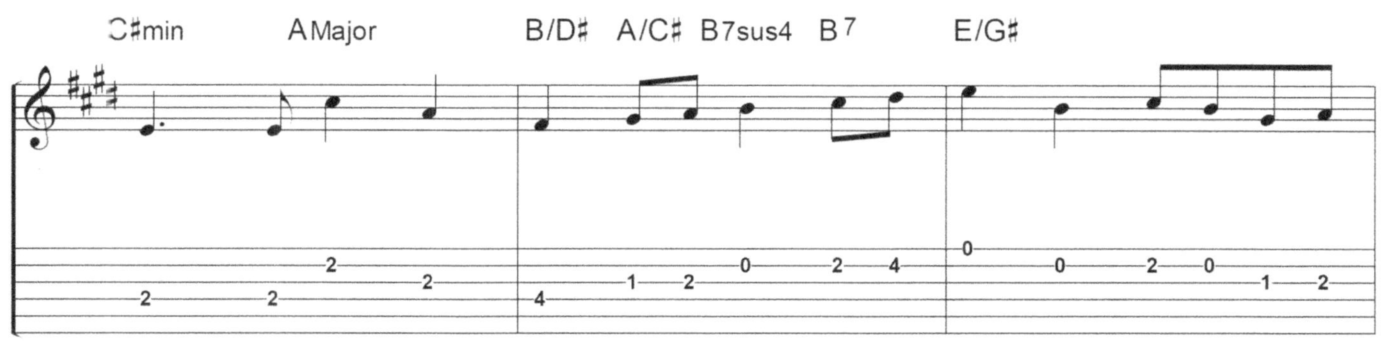

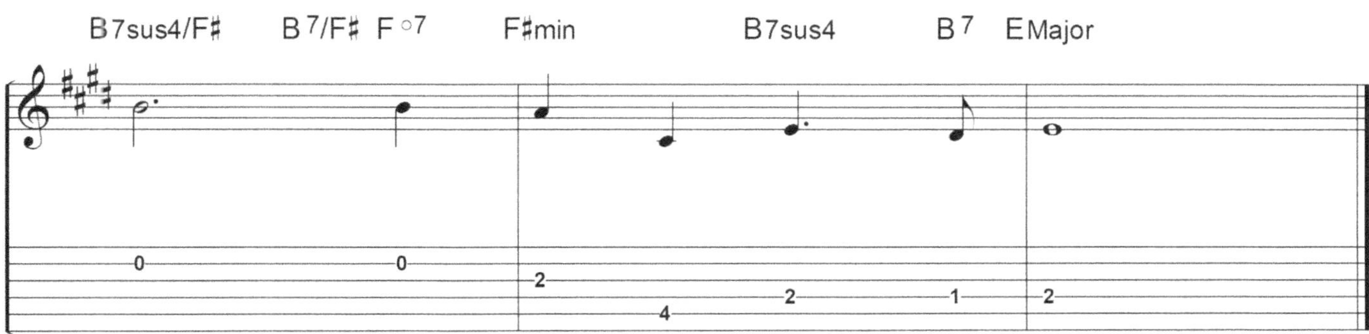

Dear Lord and Father of Mankind - Intermediate

Arranged by
Ged Brockie

Andante

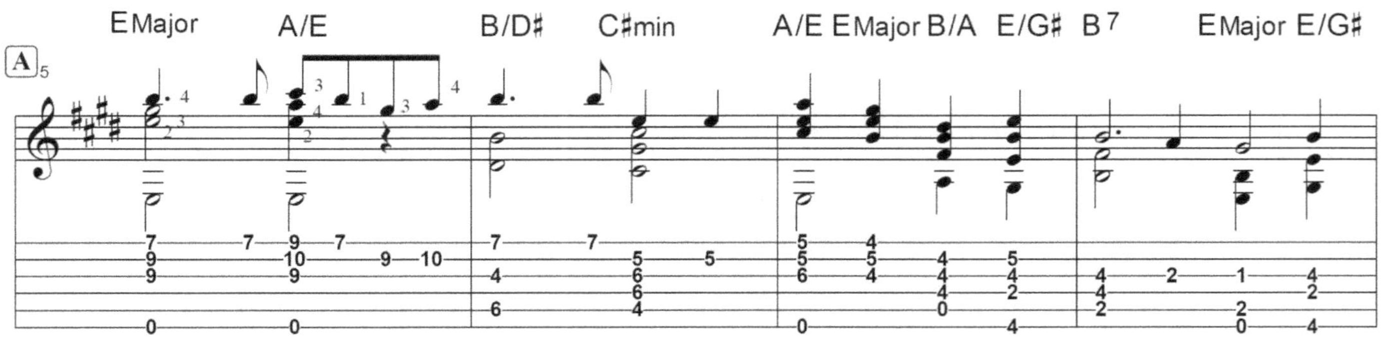

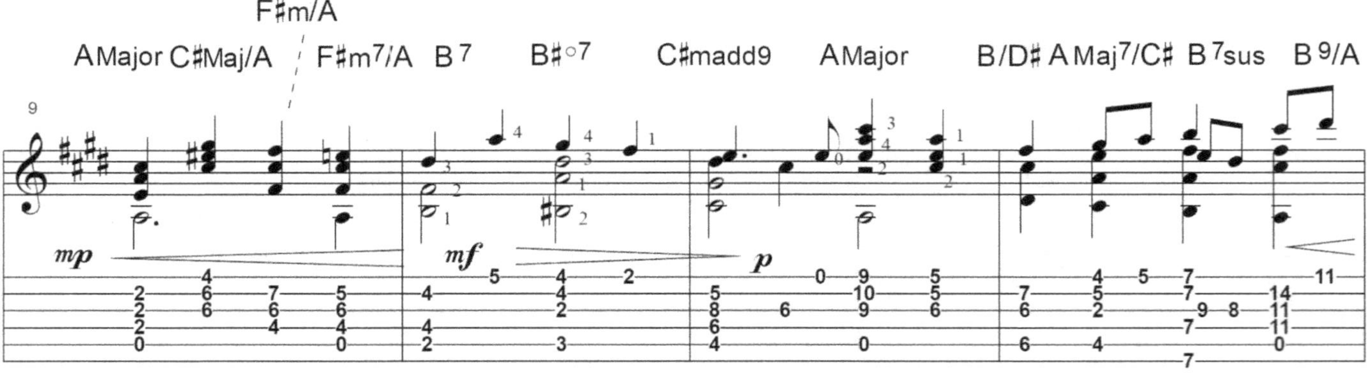

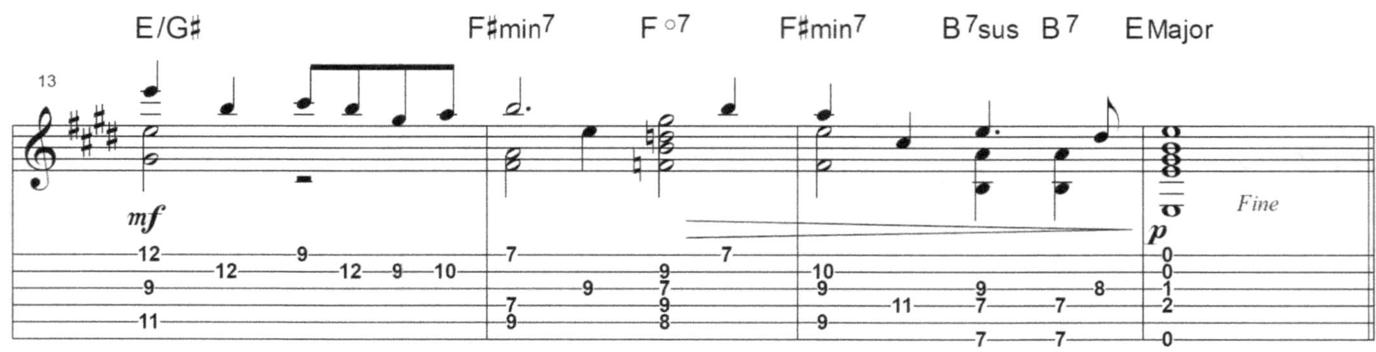

Chords: Dear Lord and Father of Mankind Intermediate

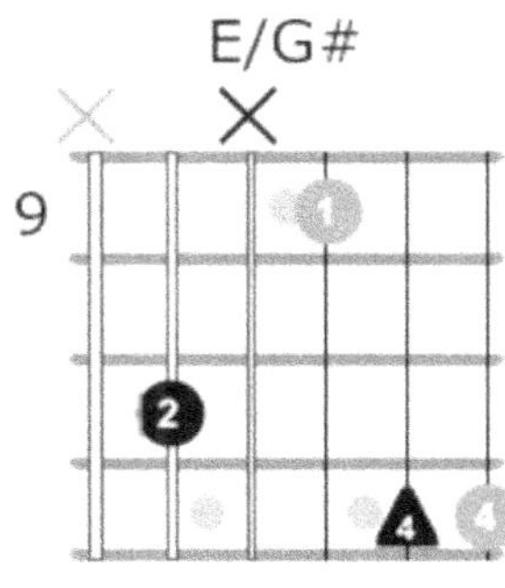

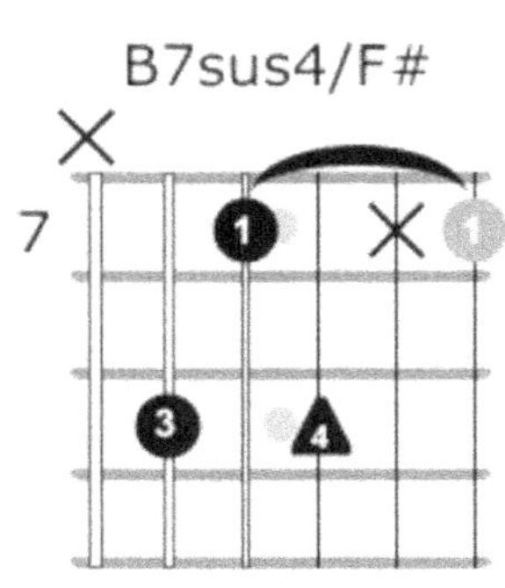

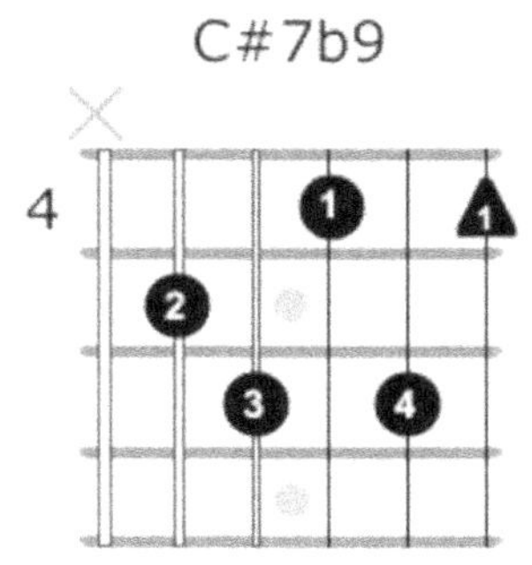

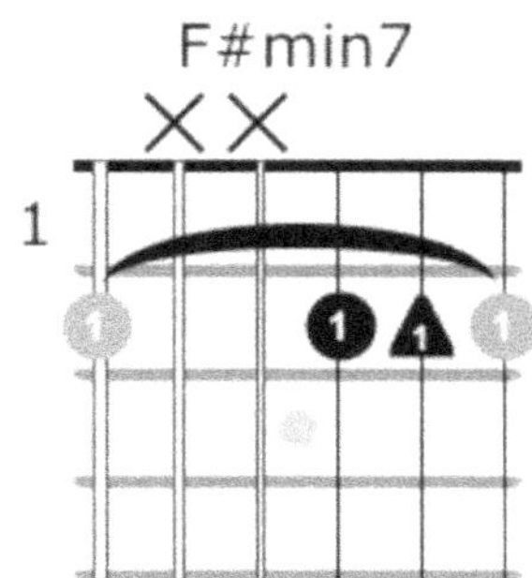

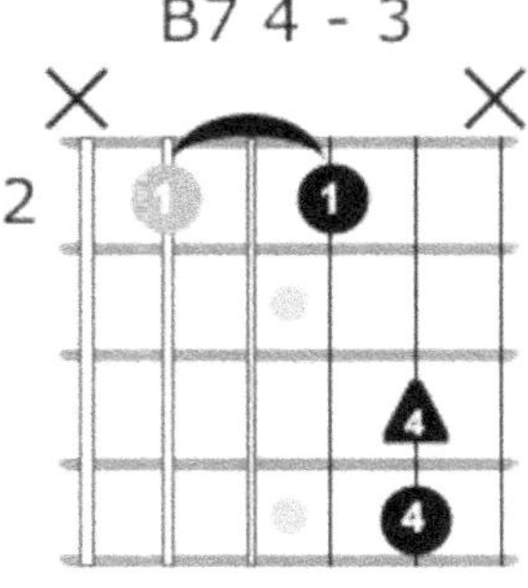

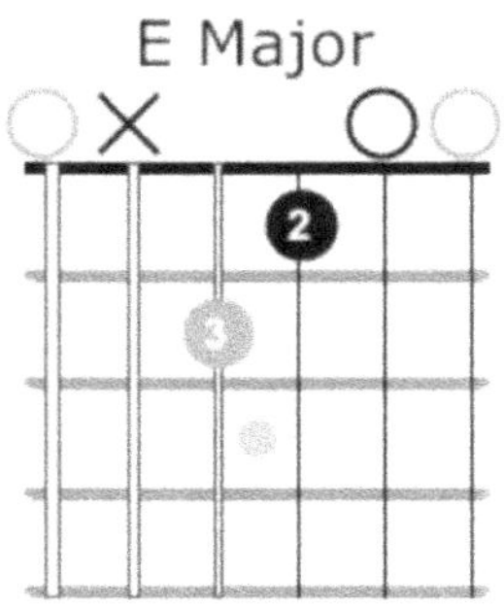

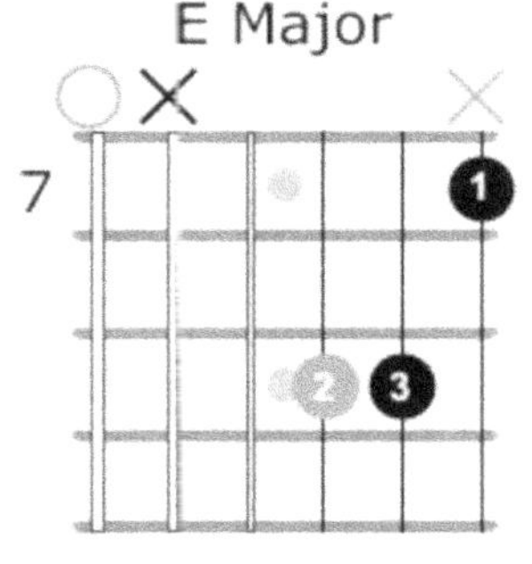

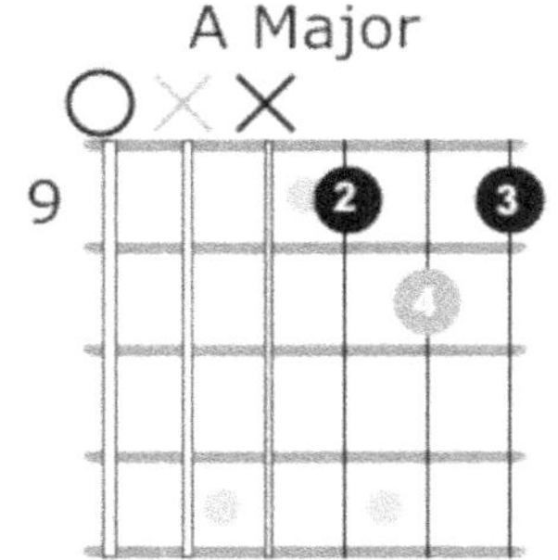

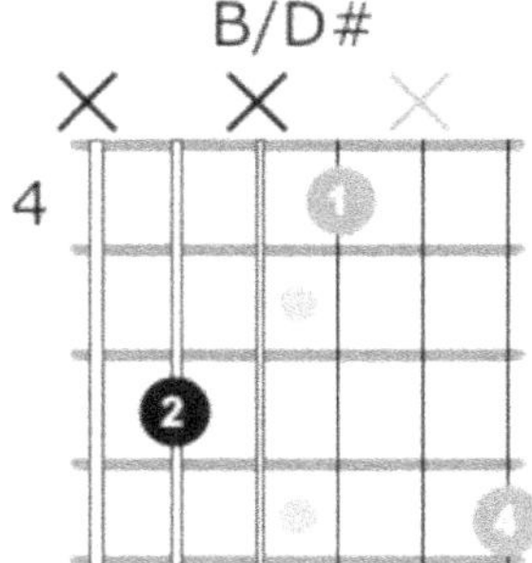

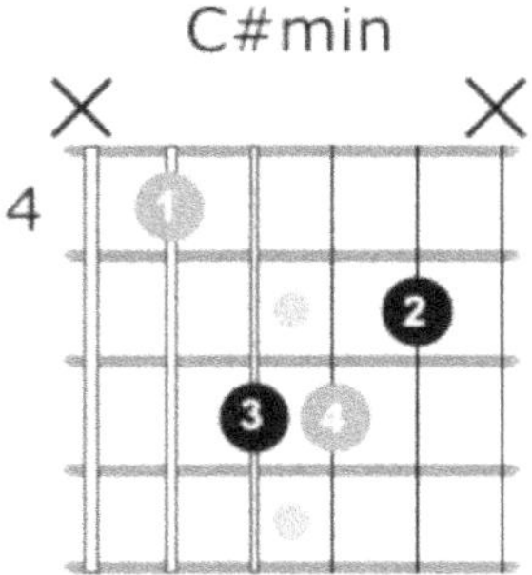

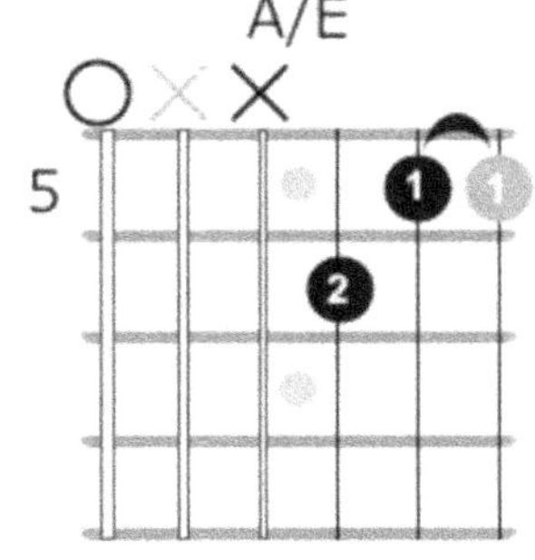

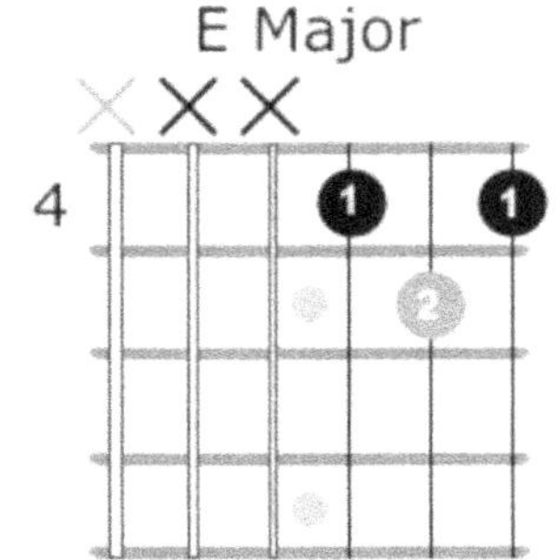

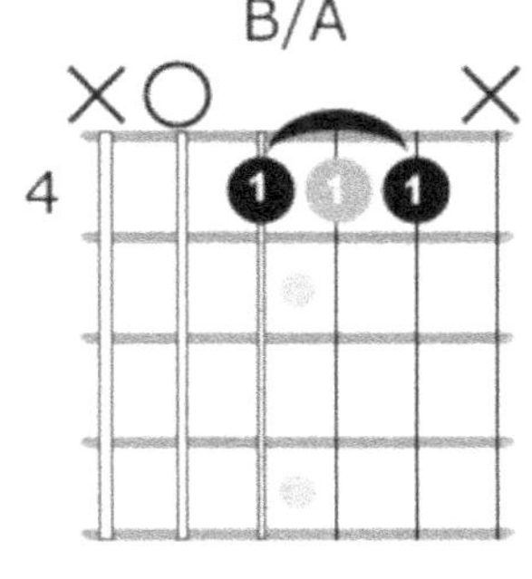

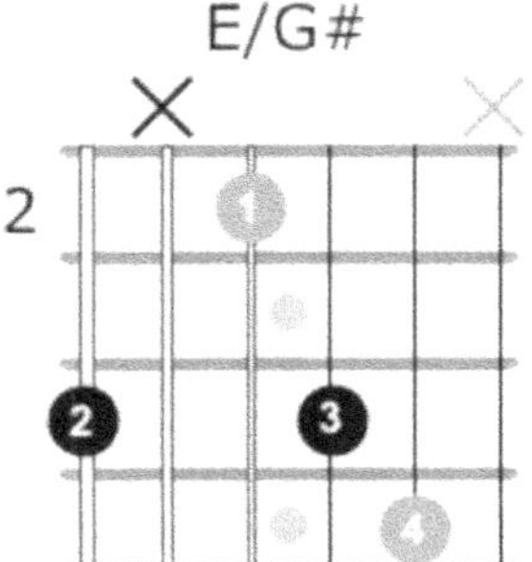

B7 4 - 3 E Major E/G#

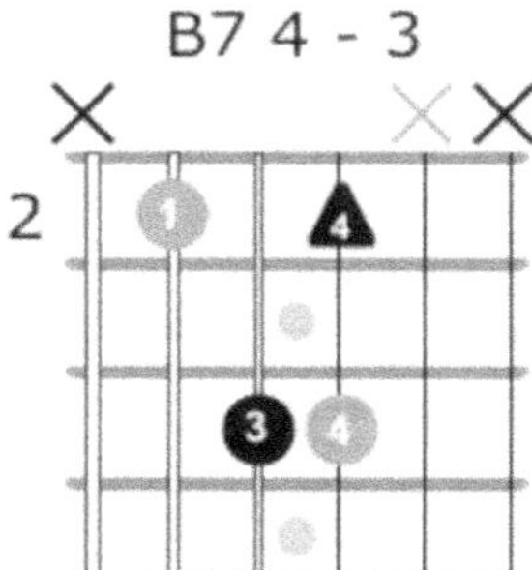 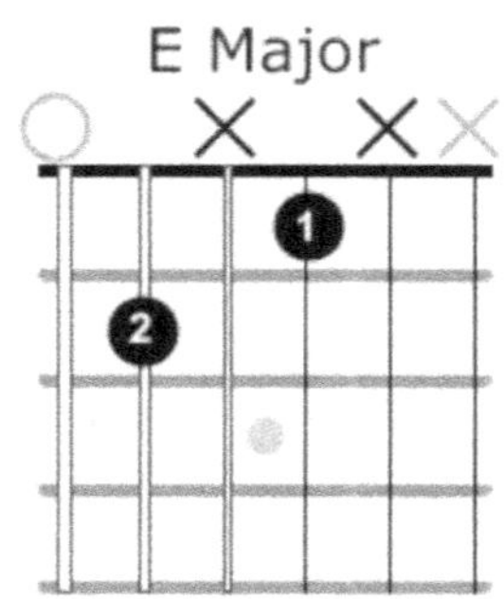 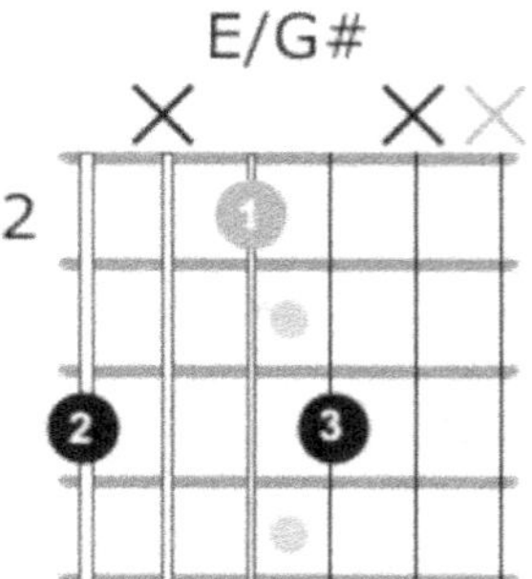

Line 3

A Major C#Maj/A F#min F#min7 (over A)

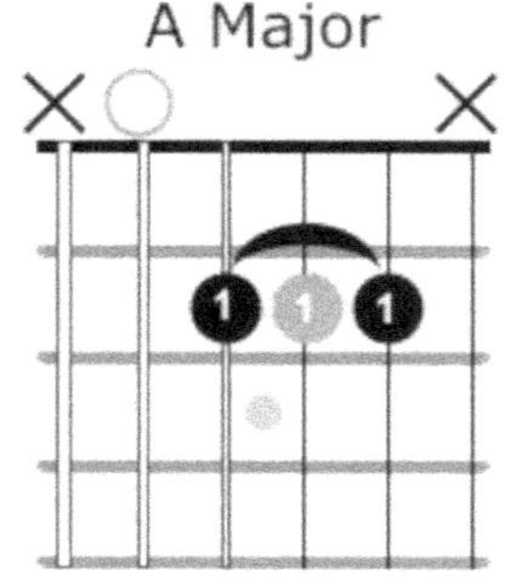 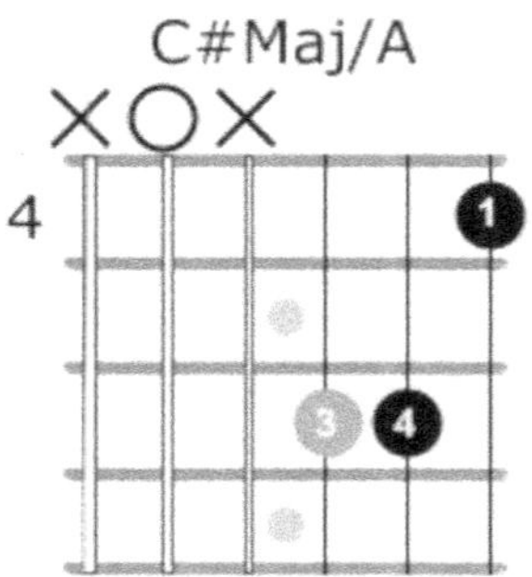 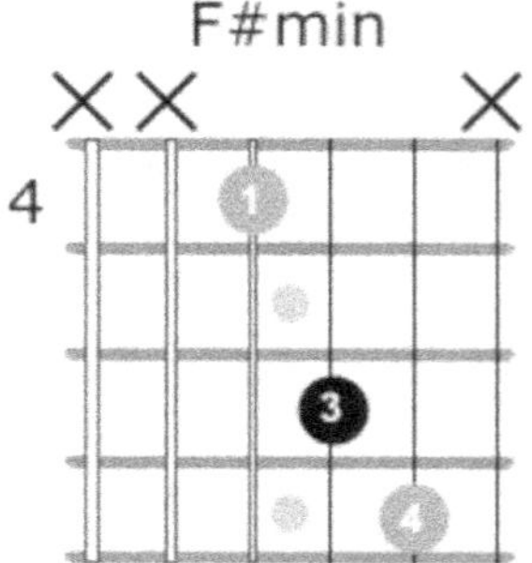 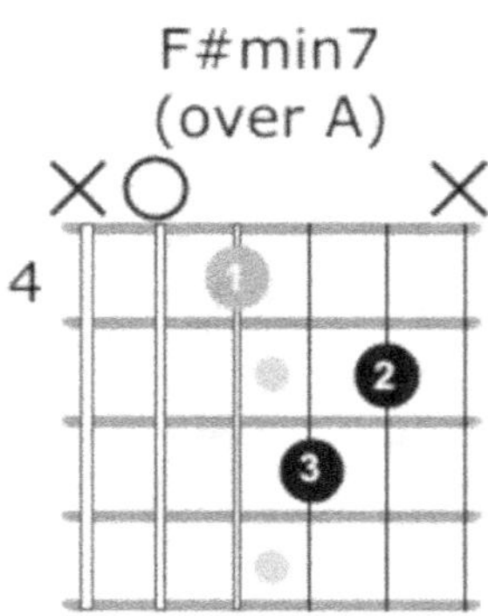

B7 B#o7 C#minadd9 A Major

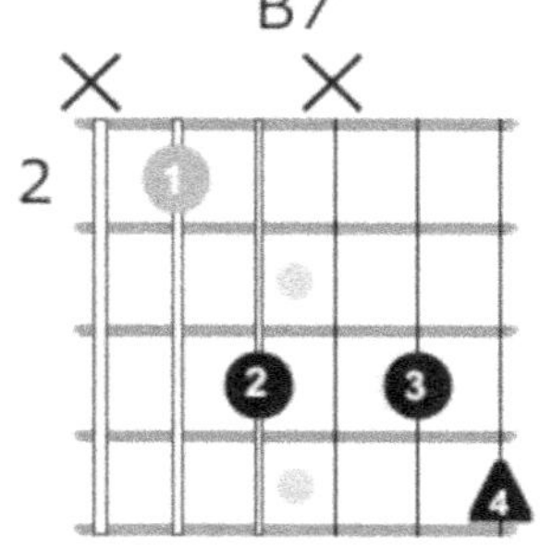 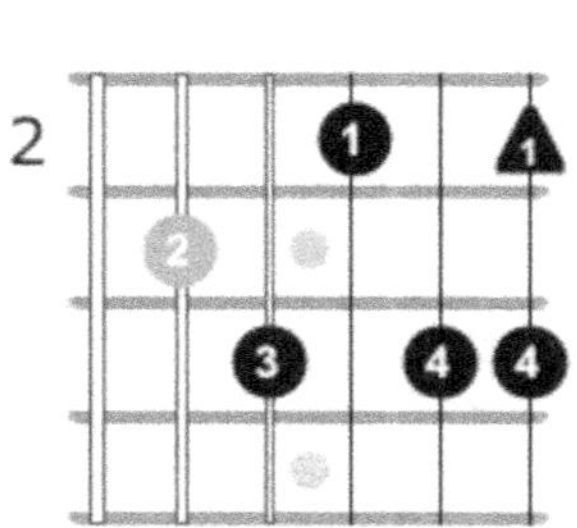 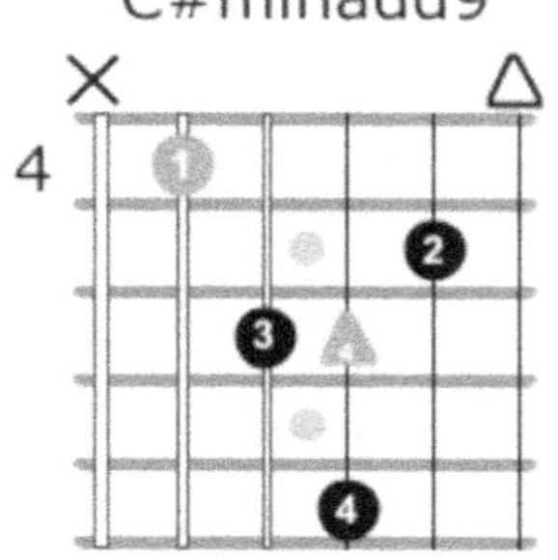 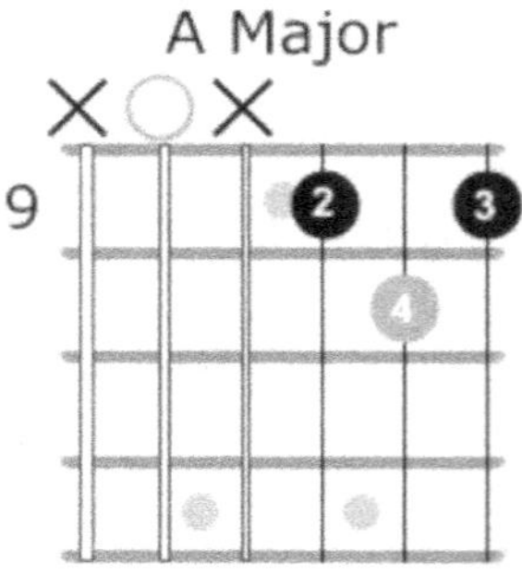

A Major B/D# (with added 9th) A Major/C# B7 4 - 3

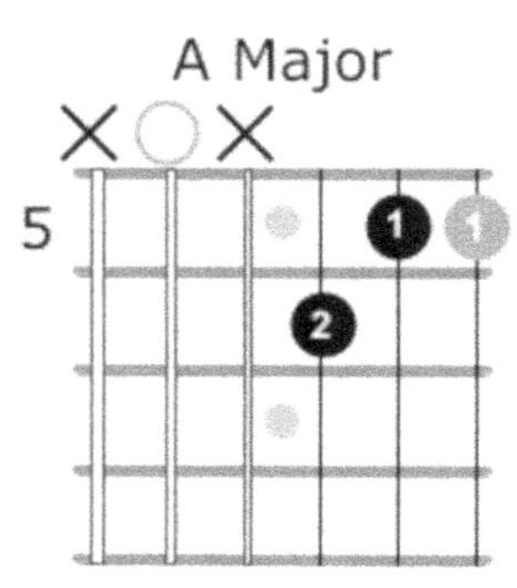 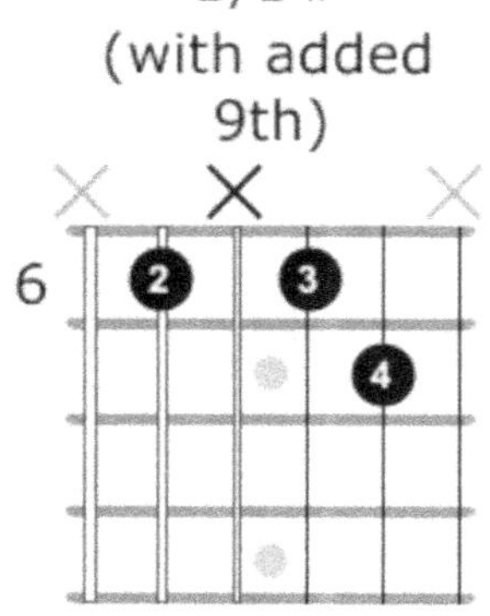 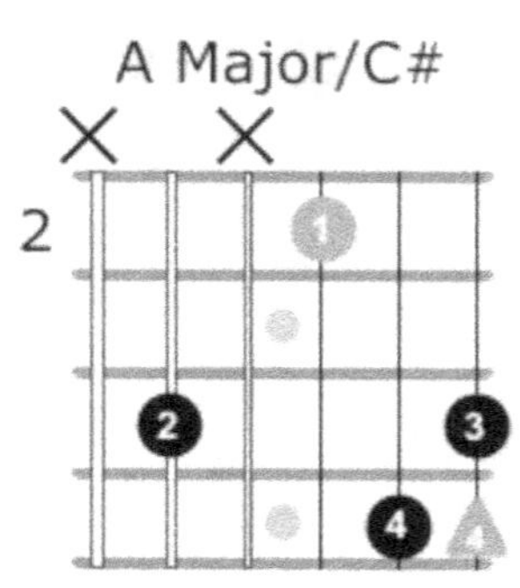 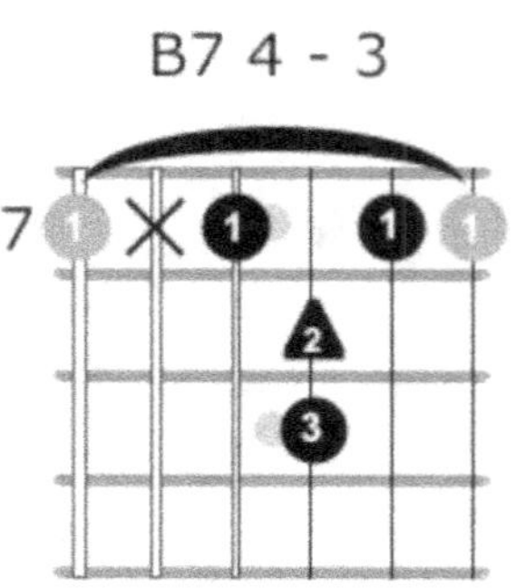

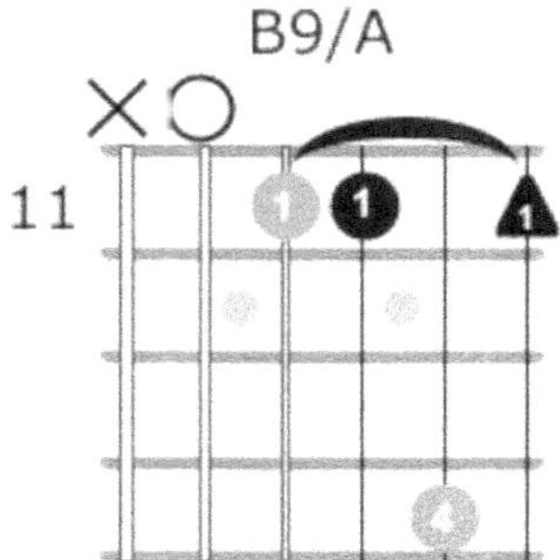

𝕷ine 4

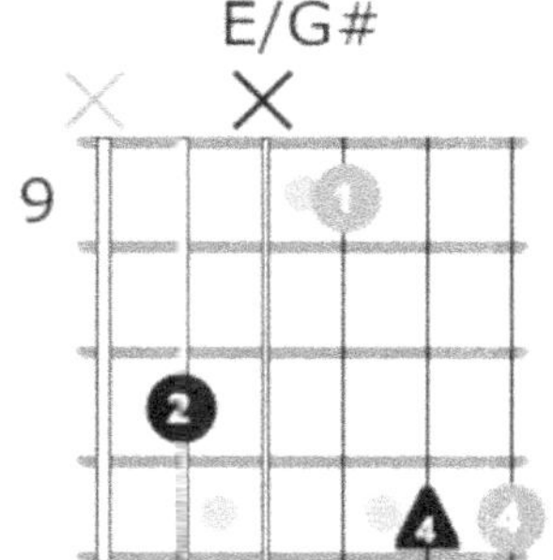

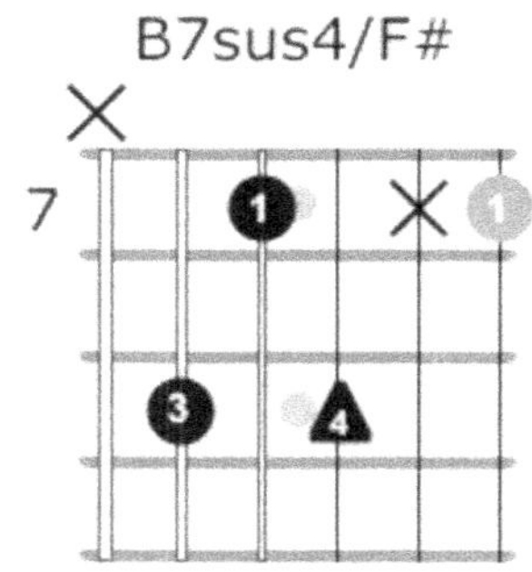

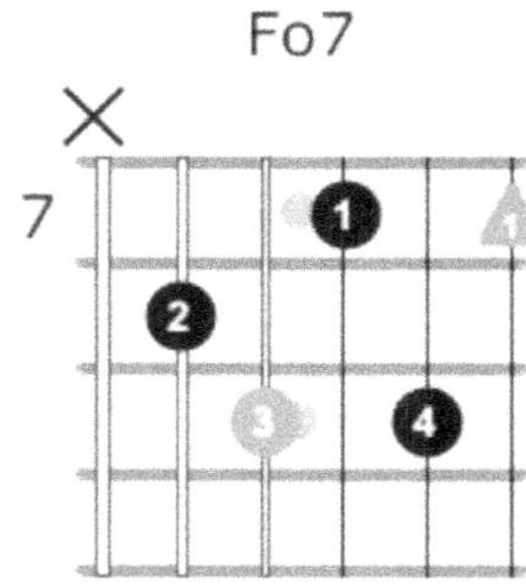

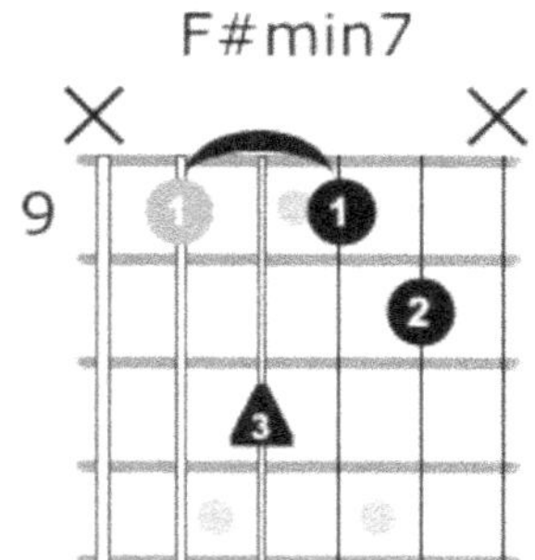

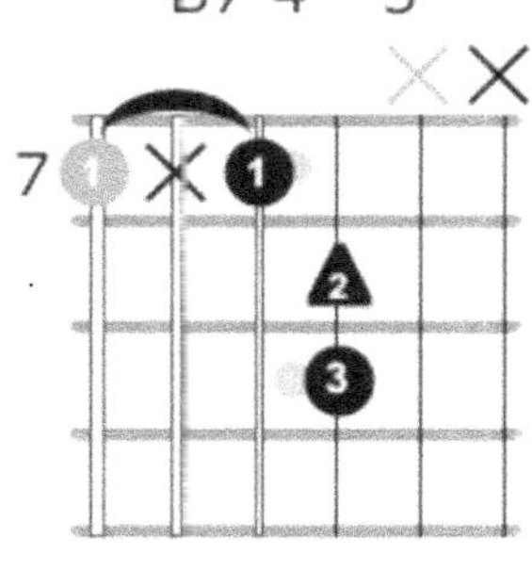

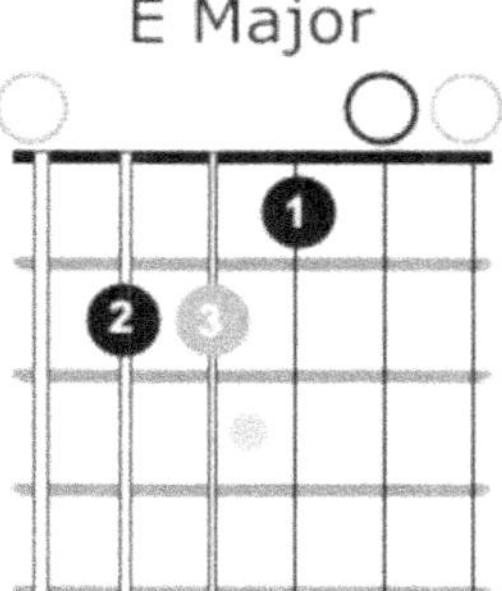

Dear Lord and Father of Mankind - Advanced

Chords: Dear Lord & Father Of Mankind Advanced

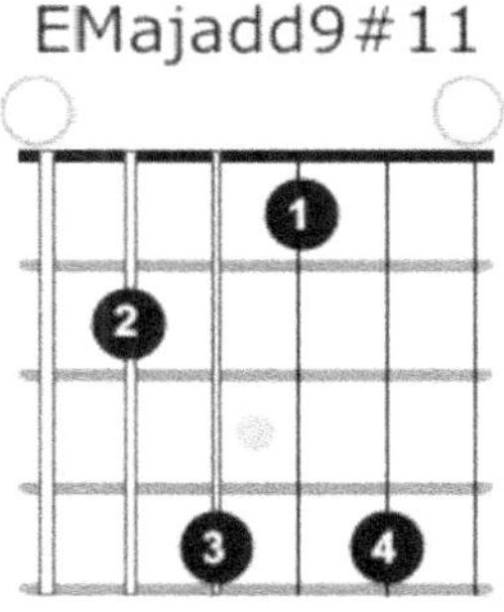 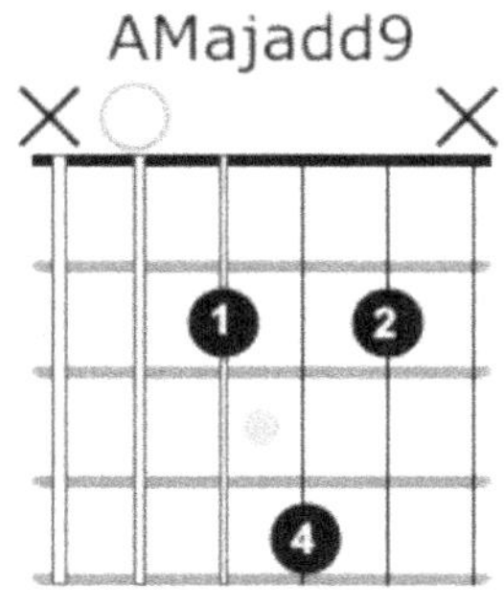 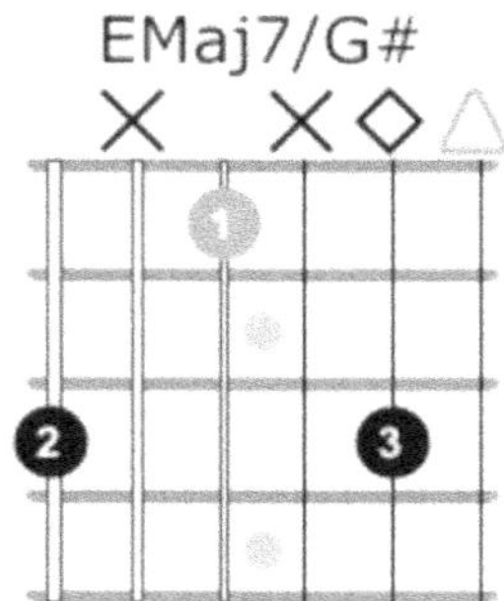 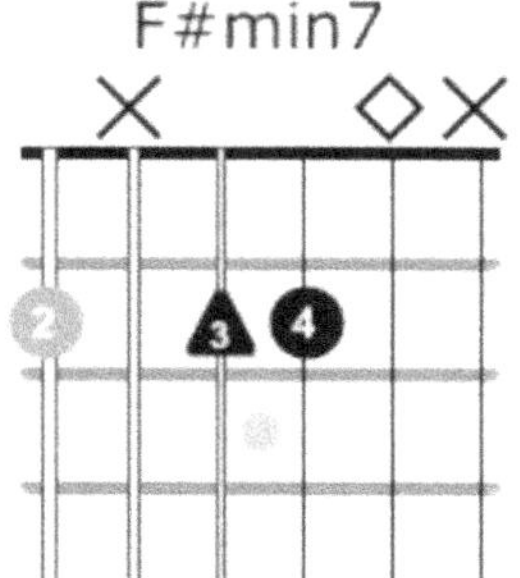

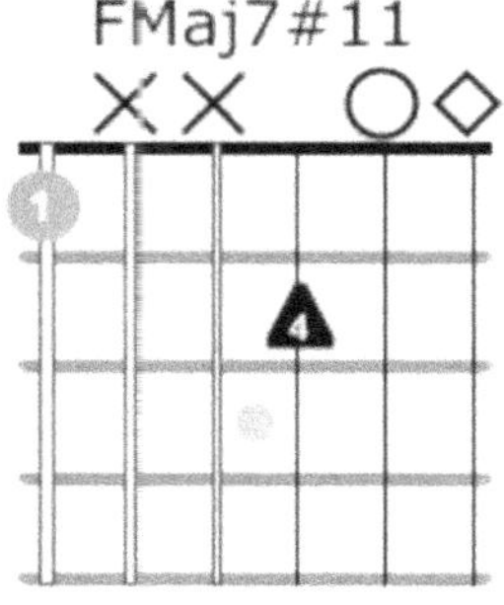 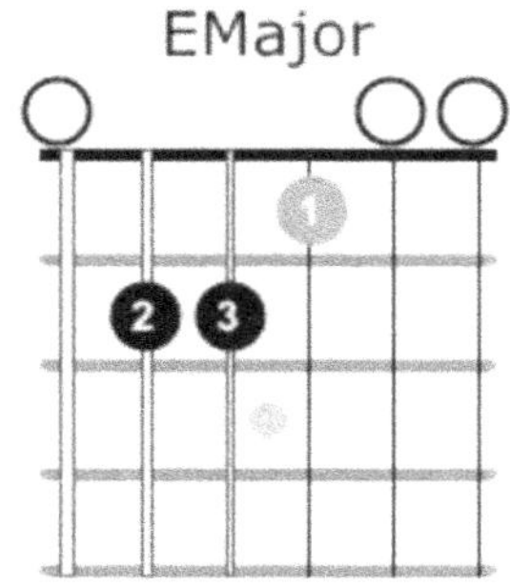

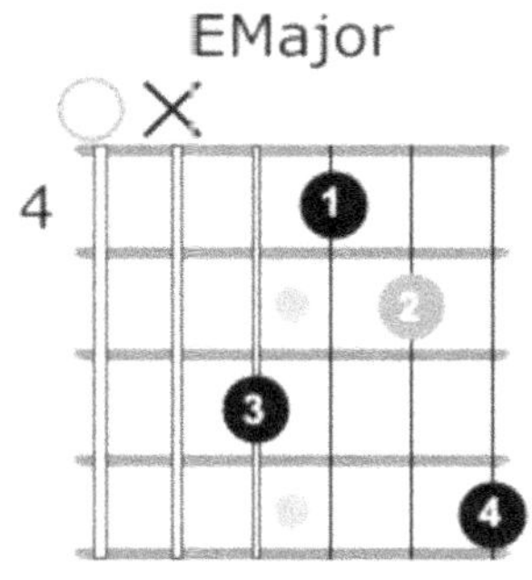 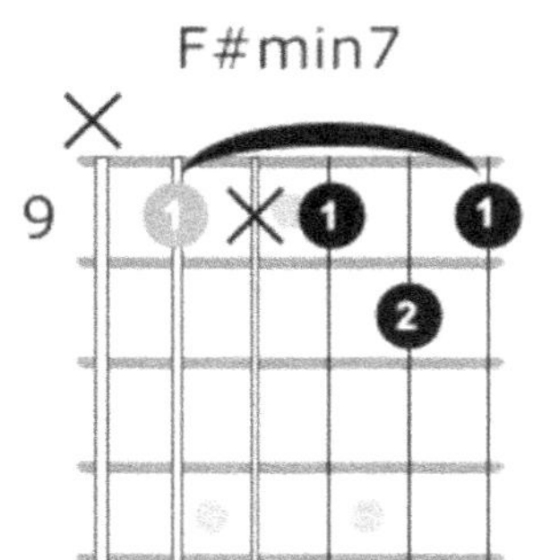  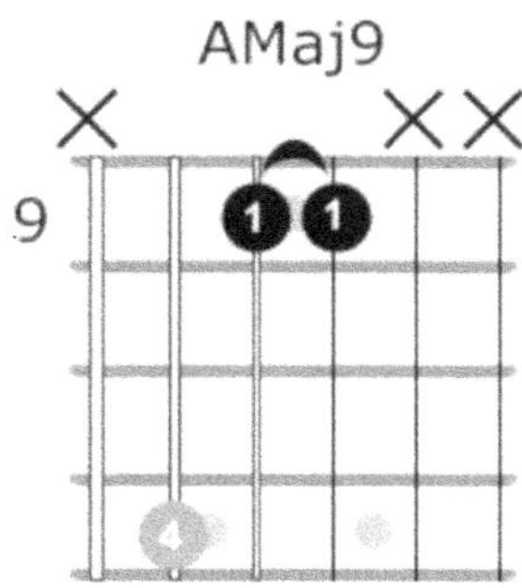

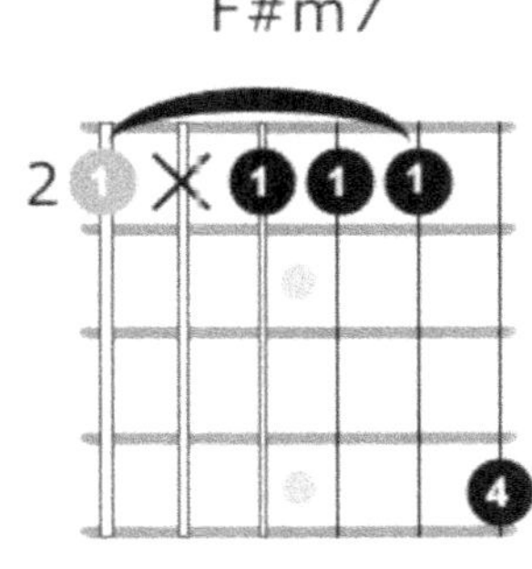 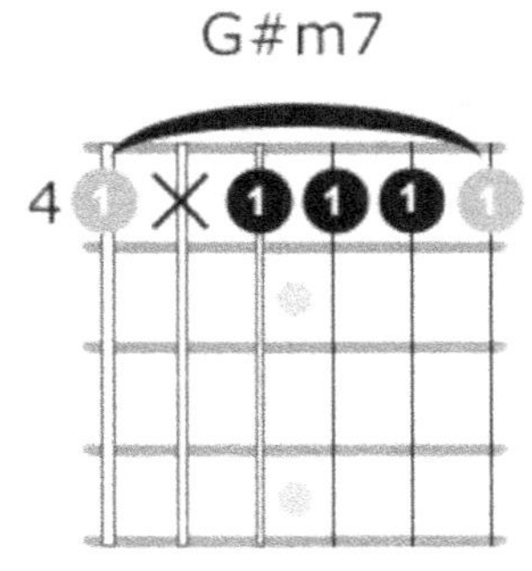 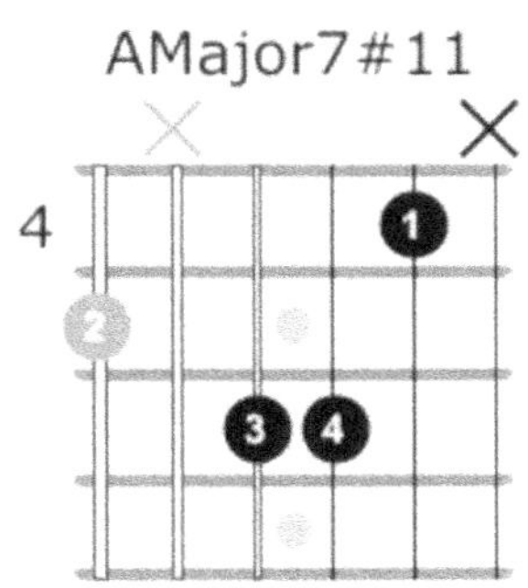 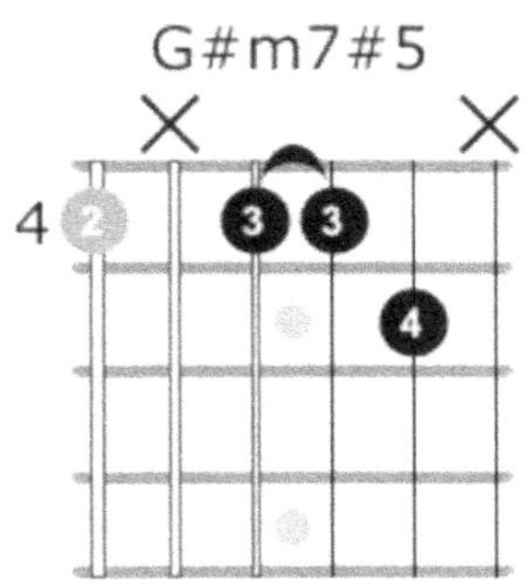

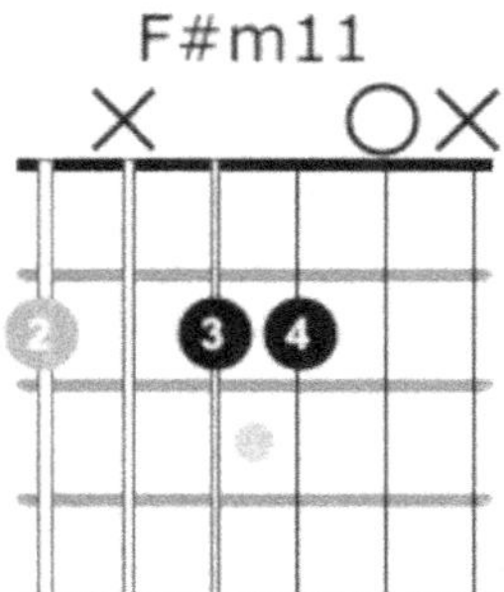

F#m11

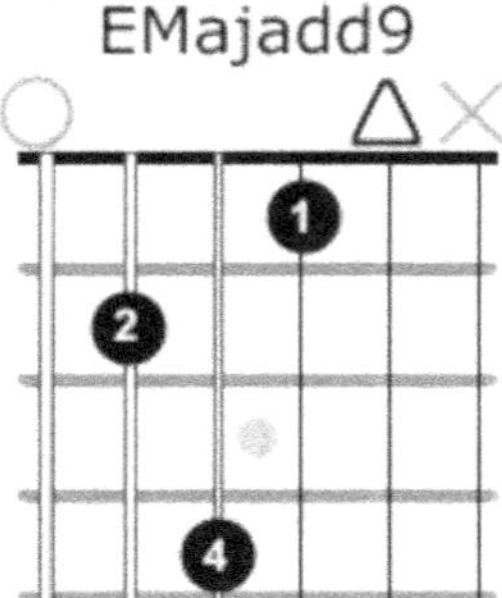

EMajadd9

Line 3

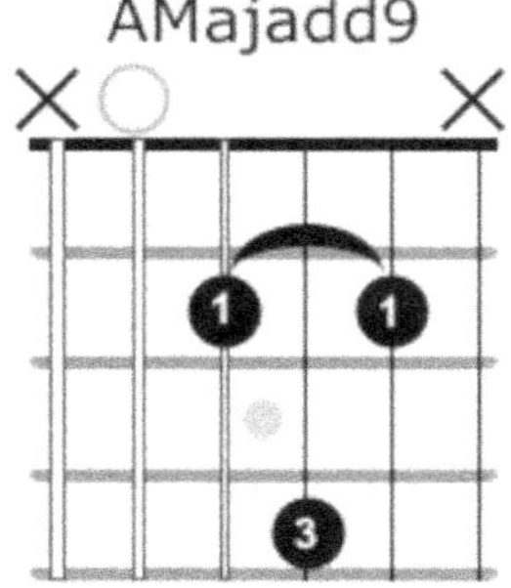

AMajadd9

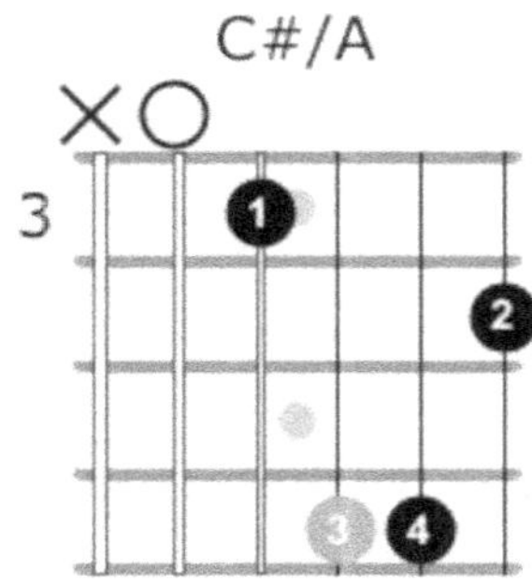

C#/A

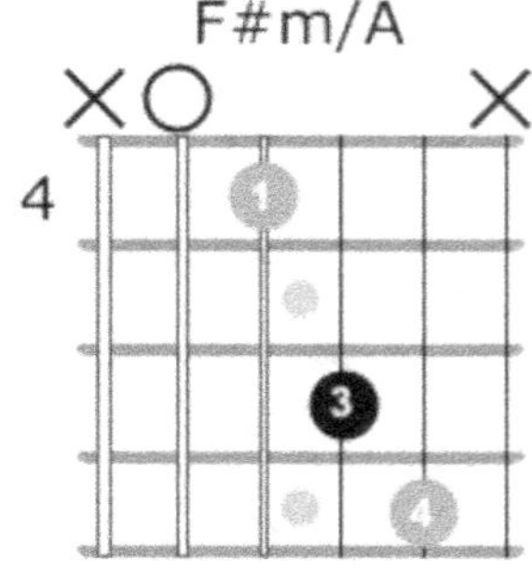

F#m/A

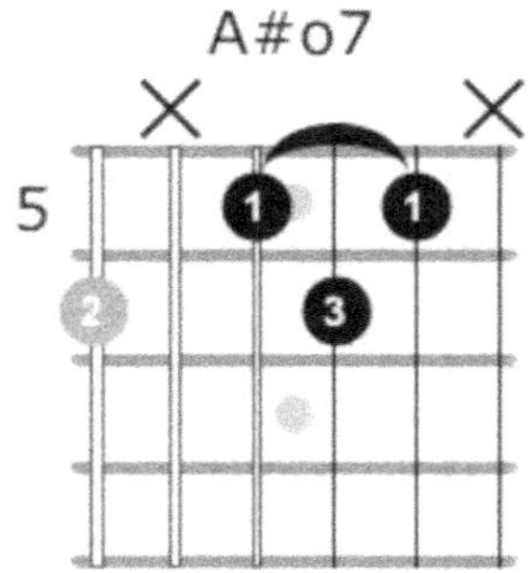

A#o7

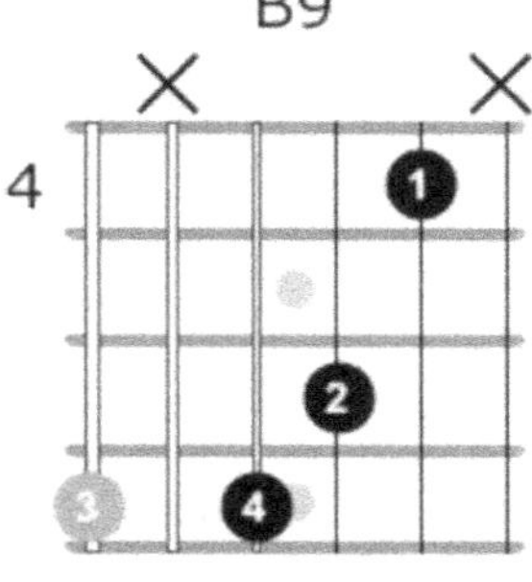

B9

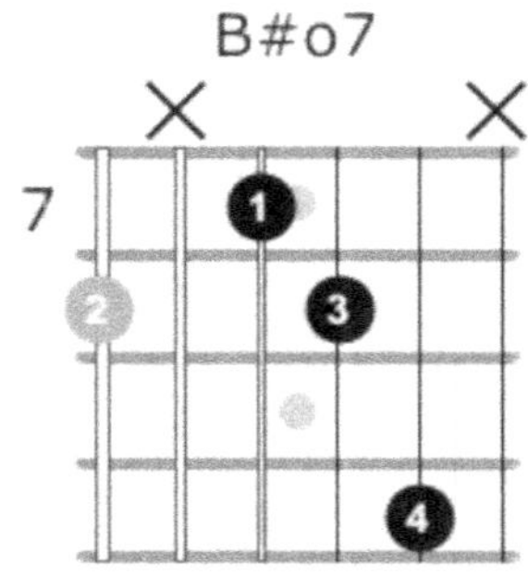

B#o7

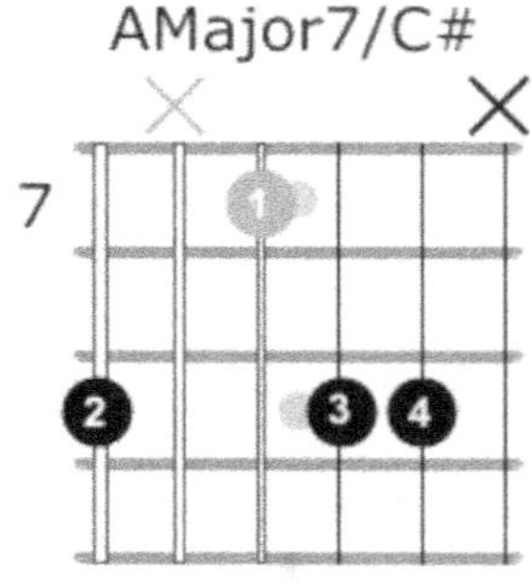

AMajor7/C#

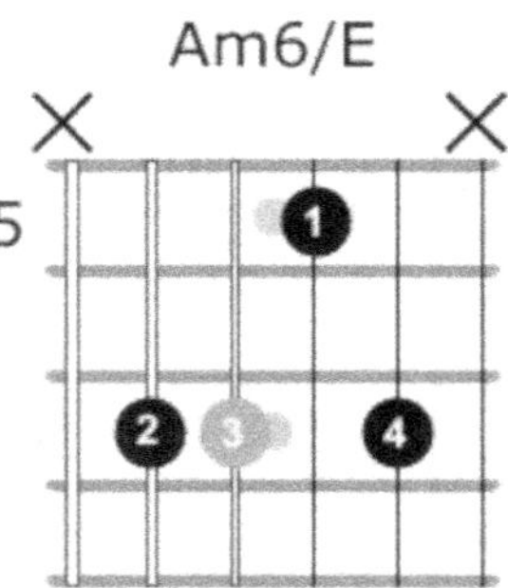

Am6/E

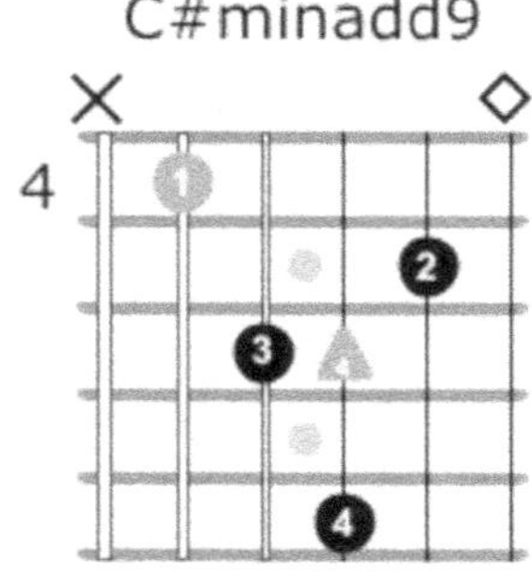

C#minadd9

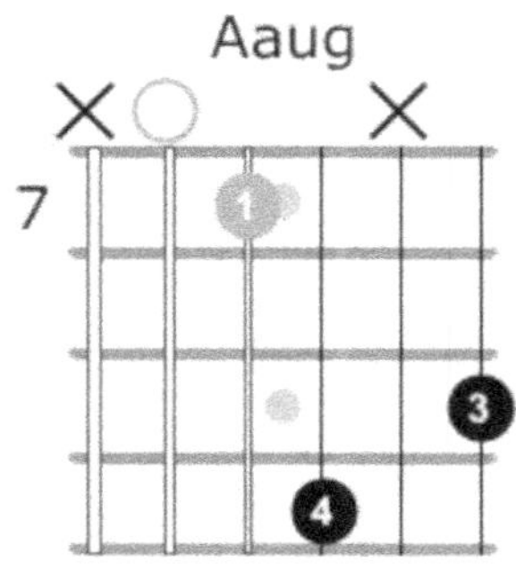

Aaug

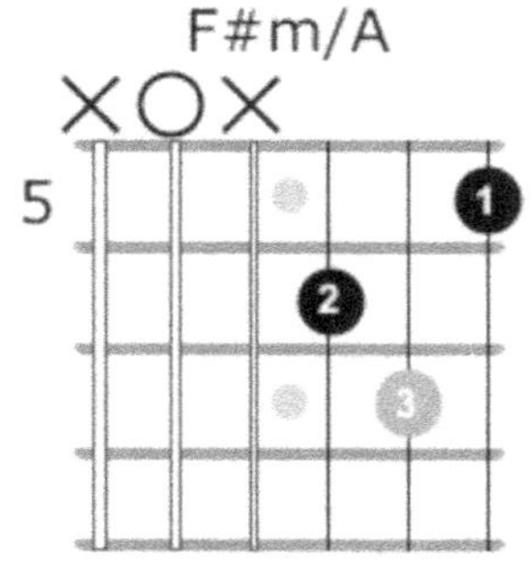

F#m/A

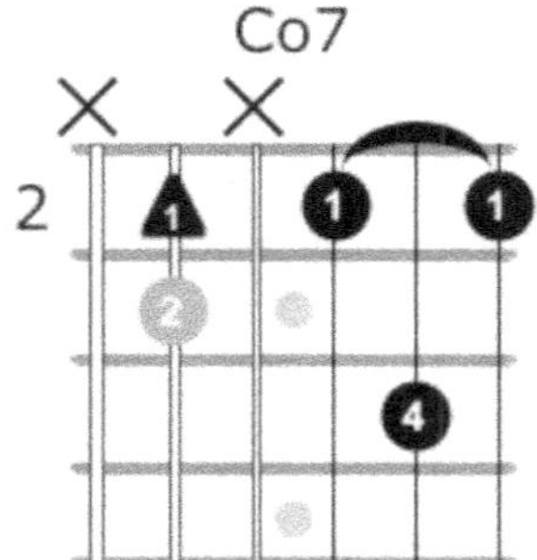

Co7

B/A

EMajadd9/G#

B/A

Line 4

EMajadd9

AMaj6/E

Bm7/F#

C#7/E#

F#min7

F#m(n)7

Note: (n) = natural. Could be notated F#m/E#

F#m/E

B7/D#

EMajadd9

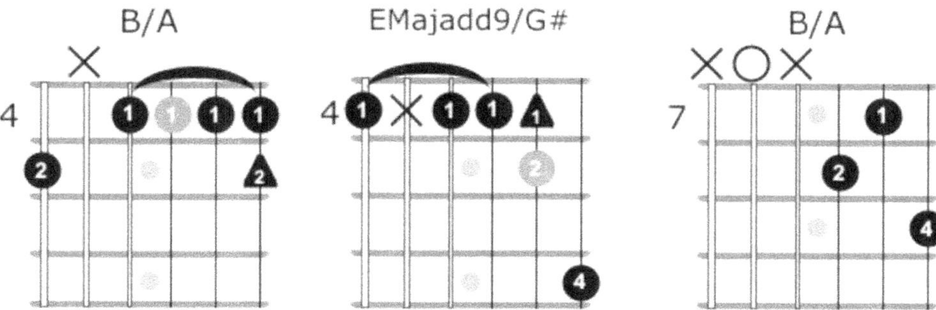

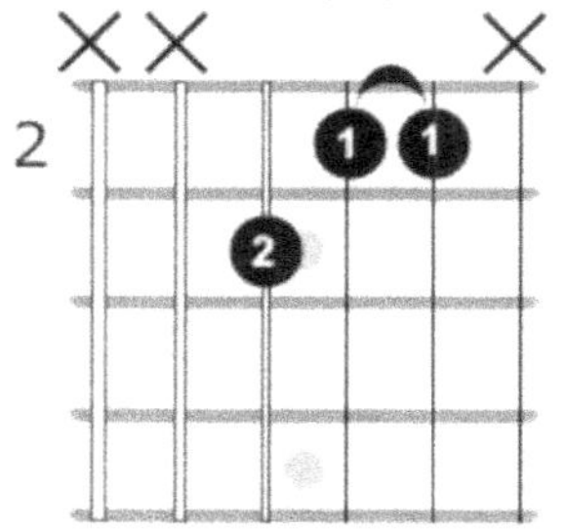

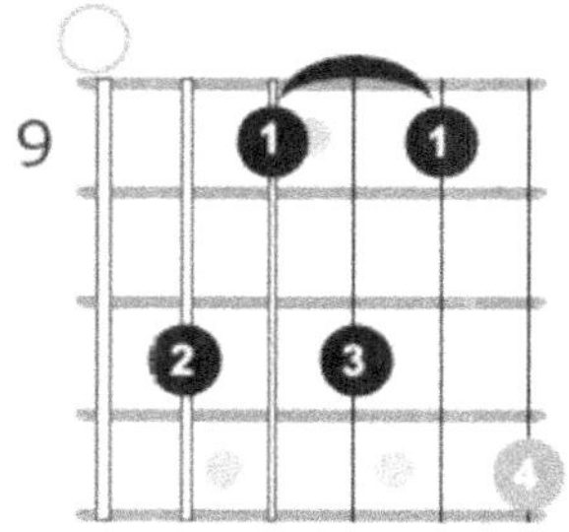

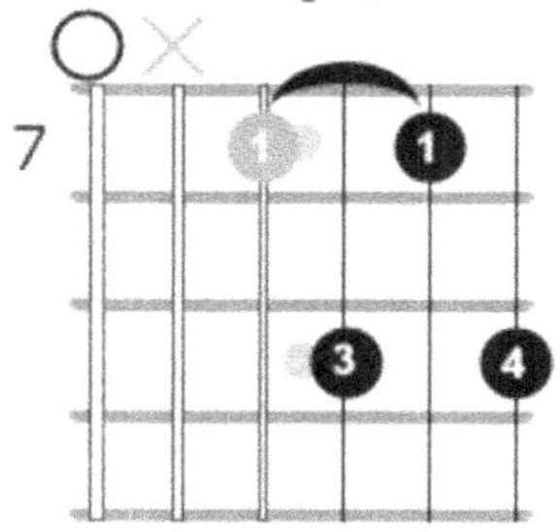

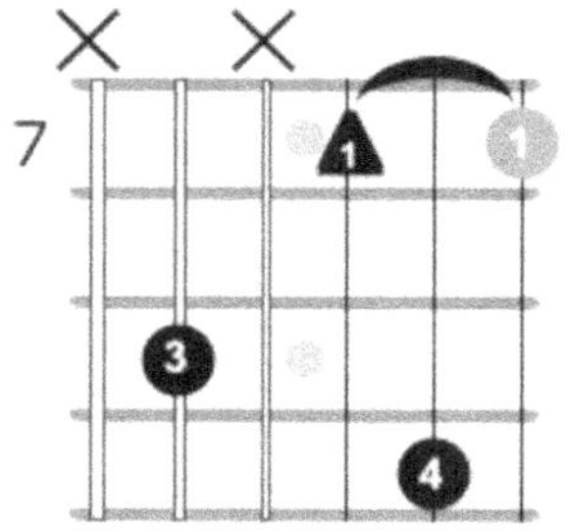

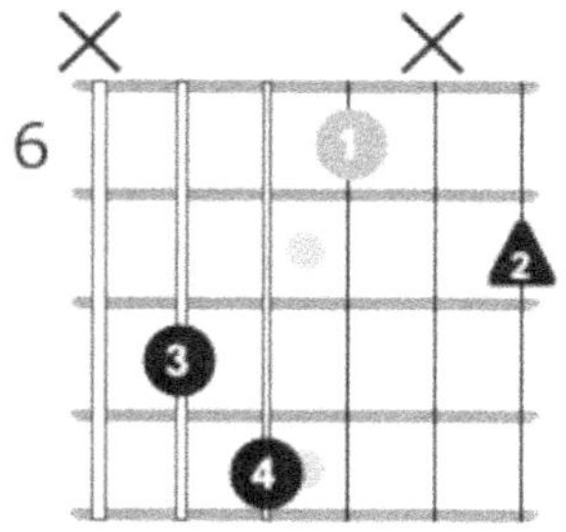

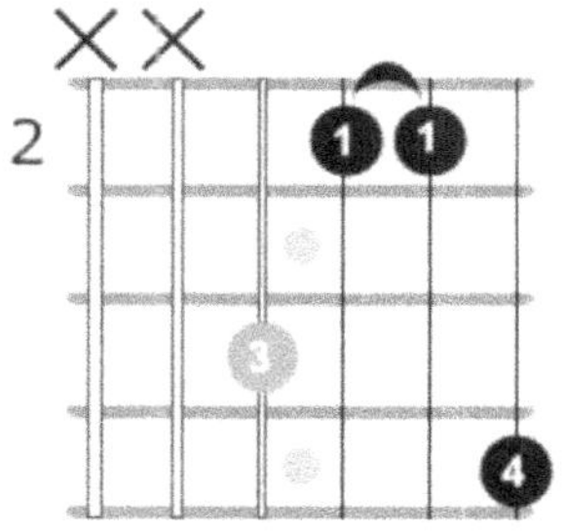

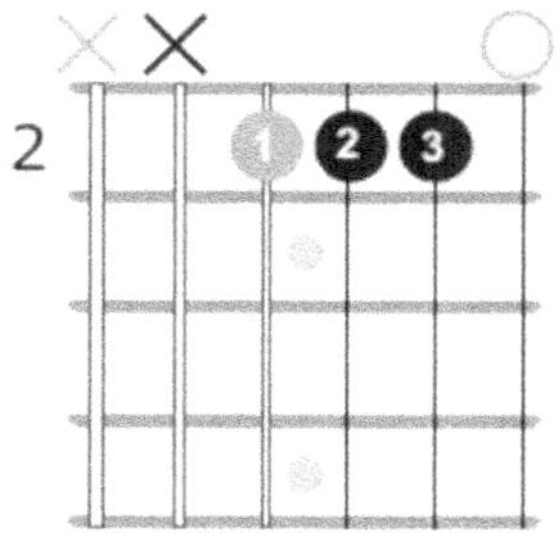

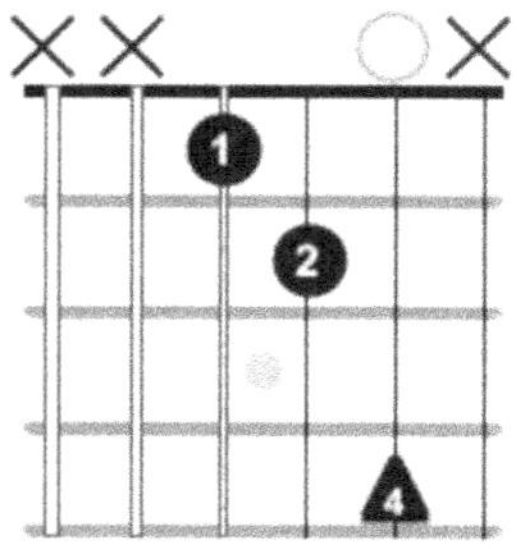

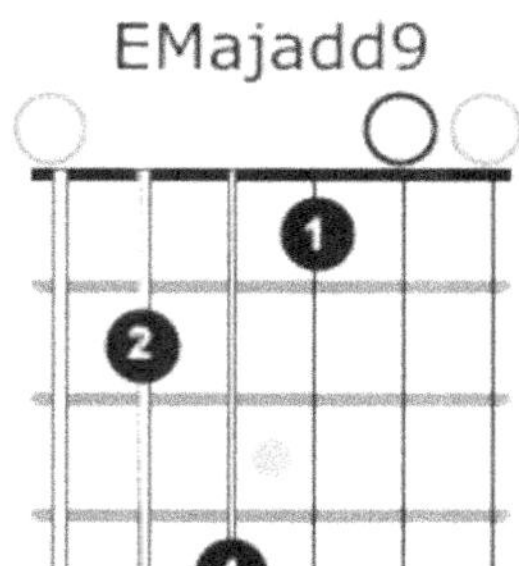

Hymn 5
Great Is Thy Faithfulness

Resources

Performance of Intermediate version

Audio Talk through of Intermediate version

Performance of Advanced version

Audio Talk through of Advanced version

Use a QR code reader on your cell/mobile phone or tablet to view and listen to the files above. There's a large selection of completely free QR code reader apps available which work on all operating platforms.

To download all resources and other support files, follow the instructions on page 197 of this publication.

Hymn Notes - Great Is Thy Faithfulness

Thomas Obidiah Chisholm (1866 – 1960), wrote the words which would become Great Is Thy Faithfulness in 1923. After sending the lyrics to William Runyan, the song was published in the same year. Thomas Chisholm was a prolific writer of sacred poems, writing more than twelve hundred in his lifetime.

William M. Runyan   *Thomas Chisholm*

William M. Runyan (1870 – 1957) was born into a Christian family and his musical talent shone through with his playing the organ as a teenager at services taken by his father the Rev. William White Runyan.

This song generated a lot of radio play, TV and public performance over a long period of time and is a favourite of congregations around the world. The royalties amassed were endowed by Rev. Runyan's granddaughter, Ms. Nancy Price Murrow, to help give assistance to music students who needed financial help at Baker University, Baldwin, Missouri. This act of generosity ensures that Rev. Runyan's legacy, from the music he wrote to the words of Thomas Chisholm, will benefit future generations of musicians for many years to come.

Lyrics

Verse 1

Great is Thy faithfulness, O God my Father

There is no shadow of turning with Thee

Thou changest not, Thy compassions, they fail not

As Thou hast been, Thou forever will be

Chorus

Great is Thy faithfulness

Great is Thy faithfulness

Morning by morning new mercies I see

All I have needed Thy hand hath provided

Great is Thy faithfulness, Lord, unto me

Verse 2

Summer and winter and springtime and harvest

Sun, moon and stars in their courses above

Join with all nature in manifold witness

To Thy great faithfulness, mercy and love

Chorus

Verse 3

Pardon for sin and a peace that endureth

Thine own dear presence to cheer and to guide

Strength for today and bright hope for tomorrow

Blessings all mine with ten thousand beside

Chorus

Great Is Thy Faithfulness - Starter

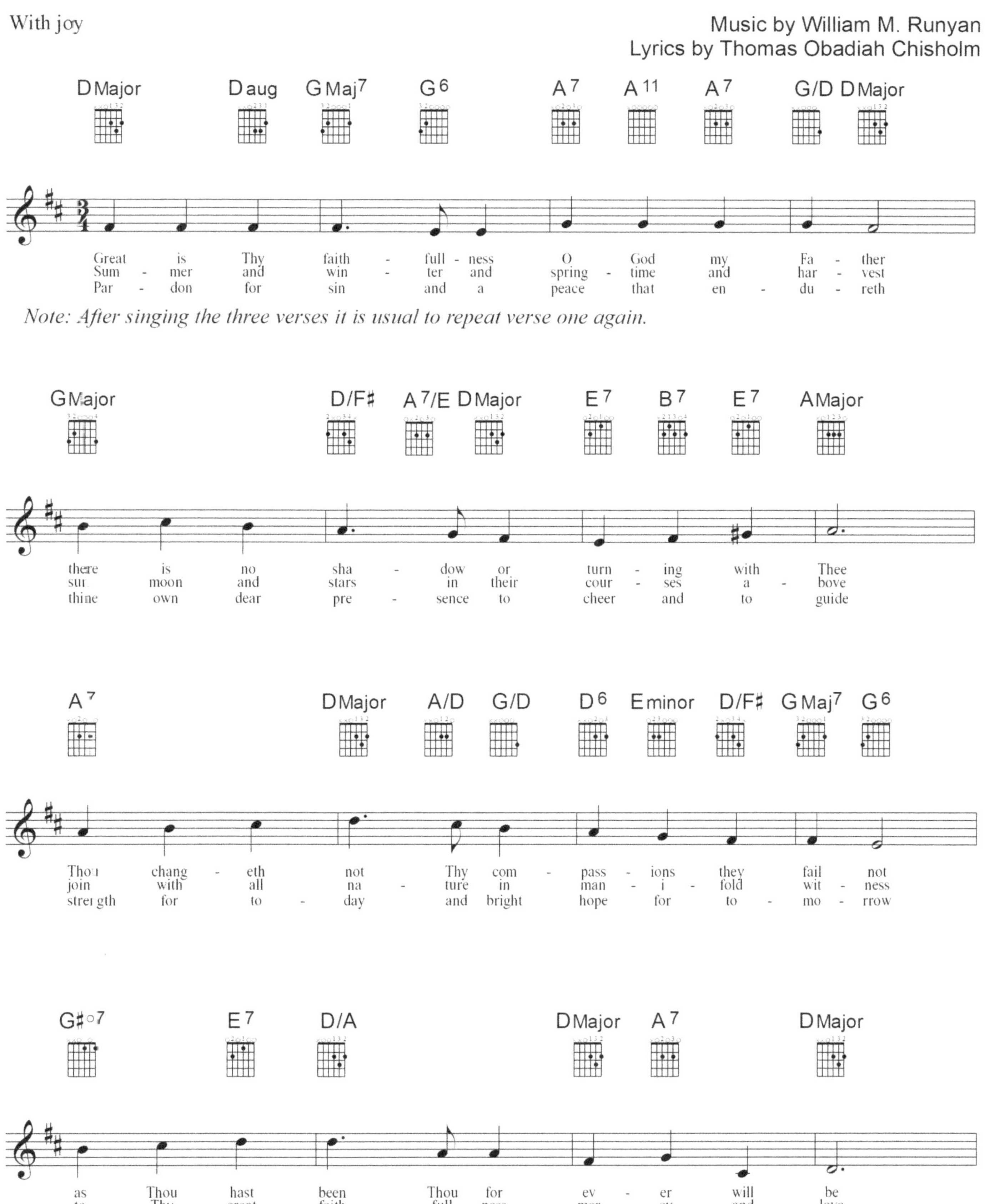

Note: After singing the three verses it is usual to repeat verse one again.

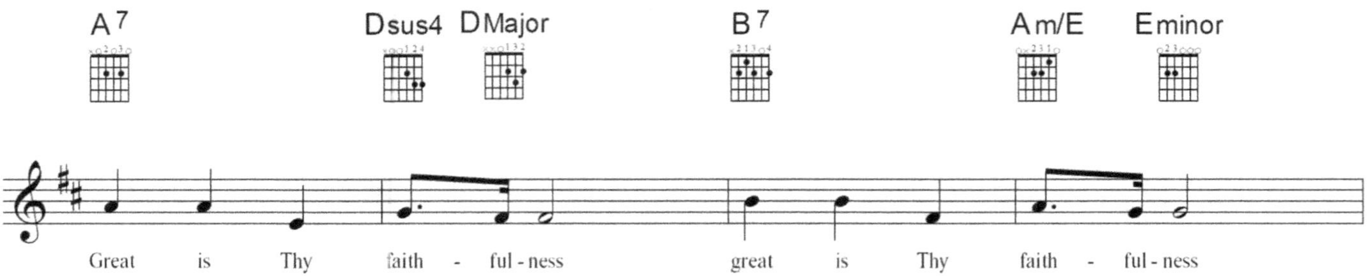

A 7
Dsus4 DMajor
B 7
Am/E Eminor
Great   is   Thy   faith - ful - ness   great   is   Thy   faith - ful - ness

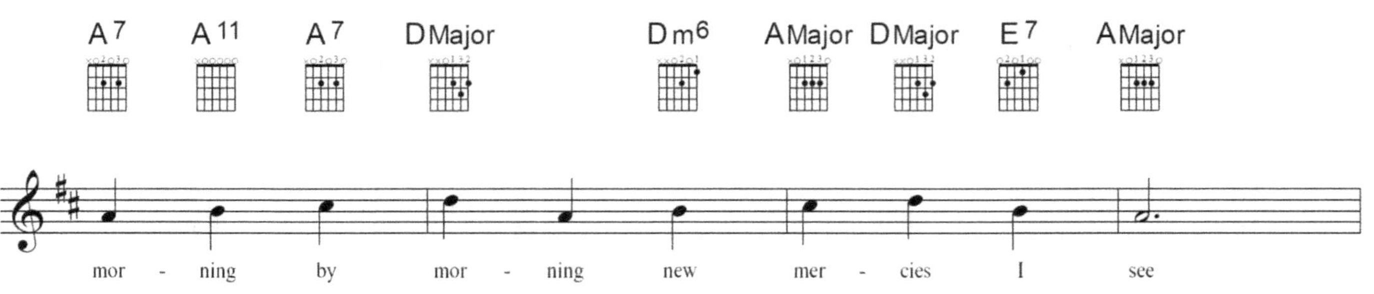

A 7   A 11   A 7   DMajor   Dm6   AMajor DMajor   E 7   AMajor
mor - ning   by   mor - ning   new   mer - cies   I   see

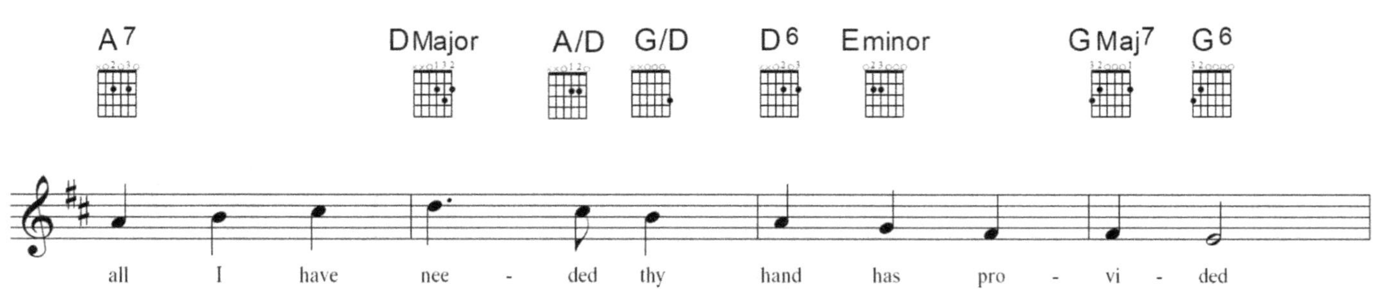

A 7   DMajor   A/D G/D   D 6   Eminor   GMaj7   G 6
all   I   have   nee - ded   thy   hand   has   pro - vi - ded

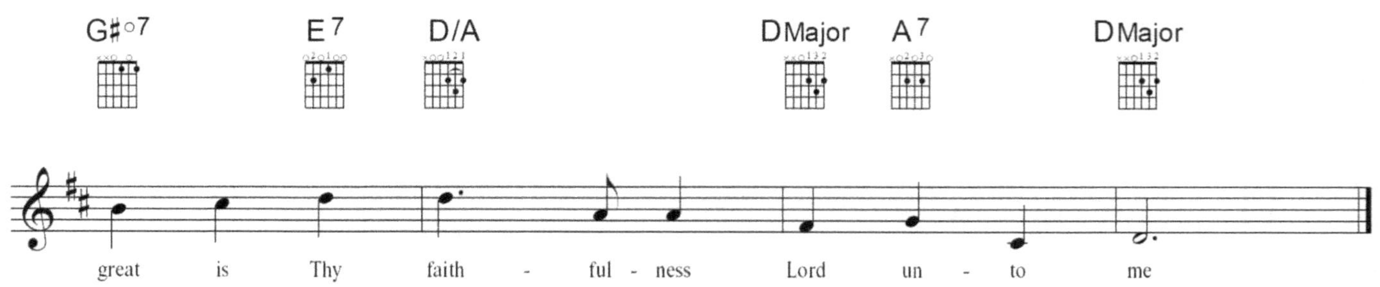

G#o7   E 7   D/A   DMajor   A 7   DMajor
great   is   Thy   faith - ful - ness   Lord   un - to   me

Great Is Thy Faithfulness - Starter alternate key

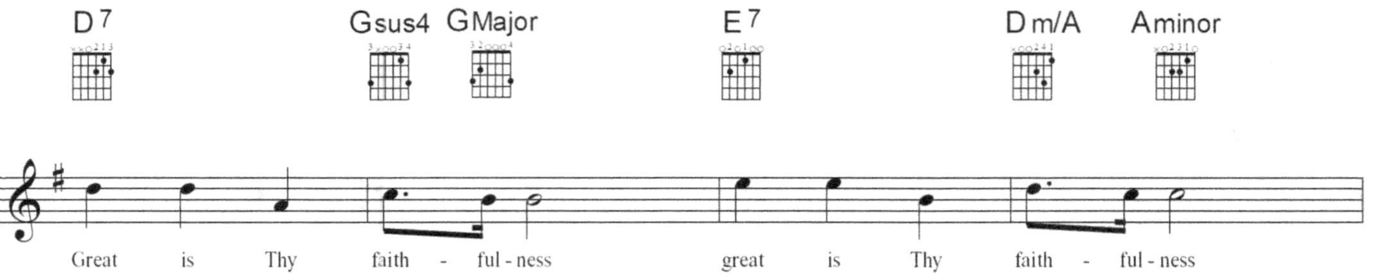

D7   Gsus4 GMajor   E7   Dm/A Aminor
Great is Thy faith - ful - ness great is Thy faith - ful - ness

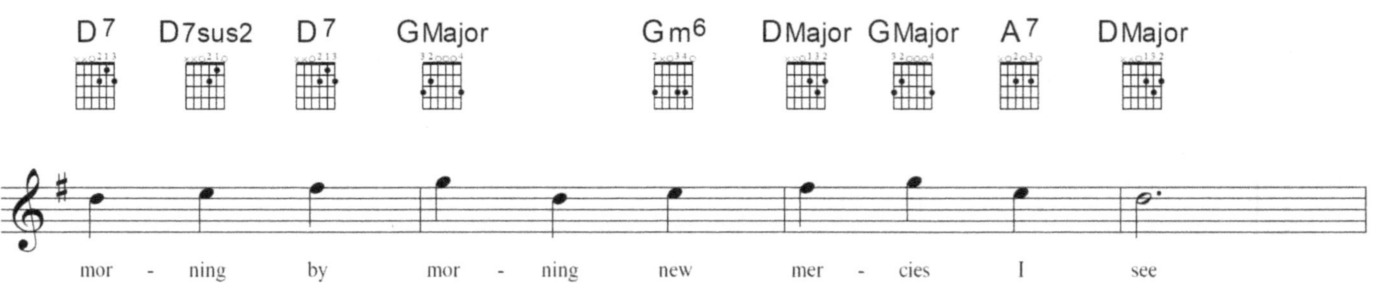

D7 D7sus2 D7 GMajor   Gm6 DMajor GMajor A7 DMajor
mor - ning by mor - ning new mer - cies I see

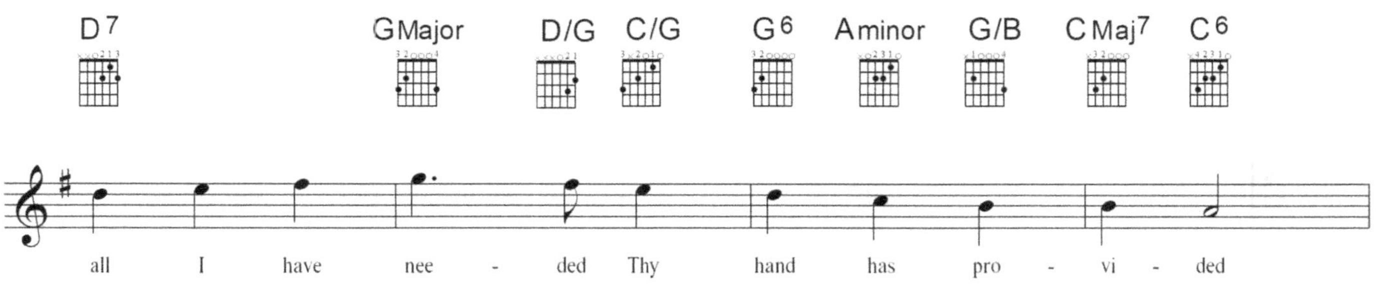

D7   GMajor D/G C/G G6 Aminor G/B CMaj7 C6
all I have nee - ded Thy hand has pro - vi - ded

C#o7   A7 G/D   GMajor D7   GMajor
great is Thy faith - ful - ness Lord un - to me

Chords: Great Is Thy Faithfulness

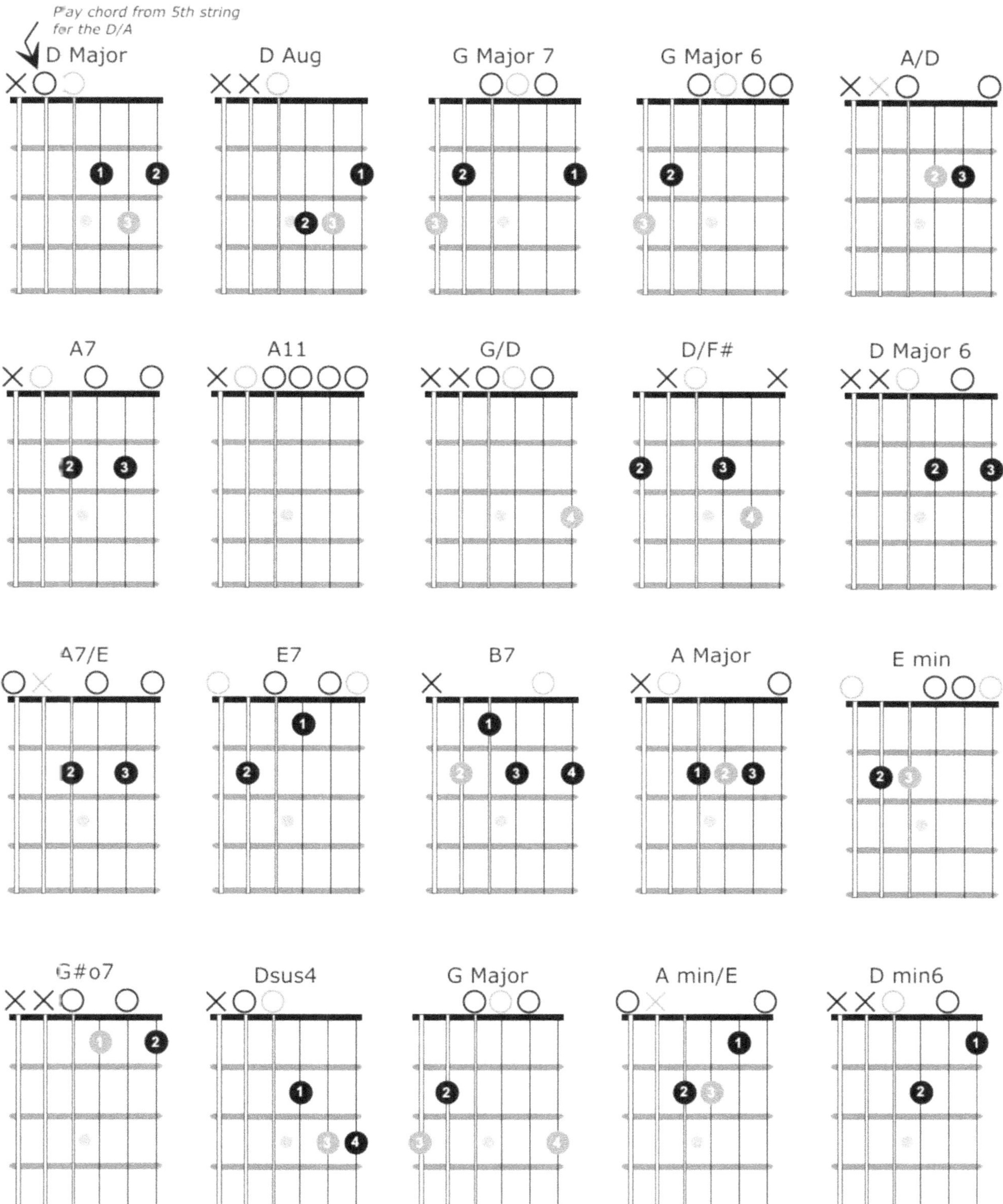

Chords: Great Is Thy Faithfulness Starter Song Alternate Key

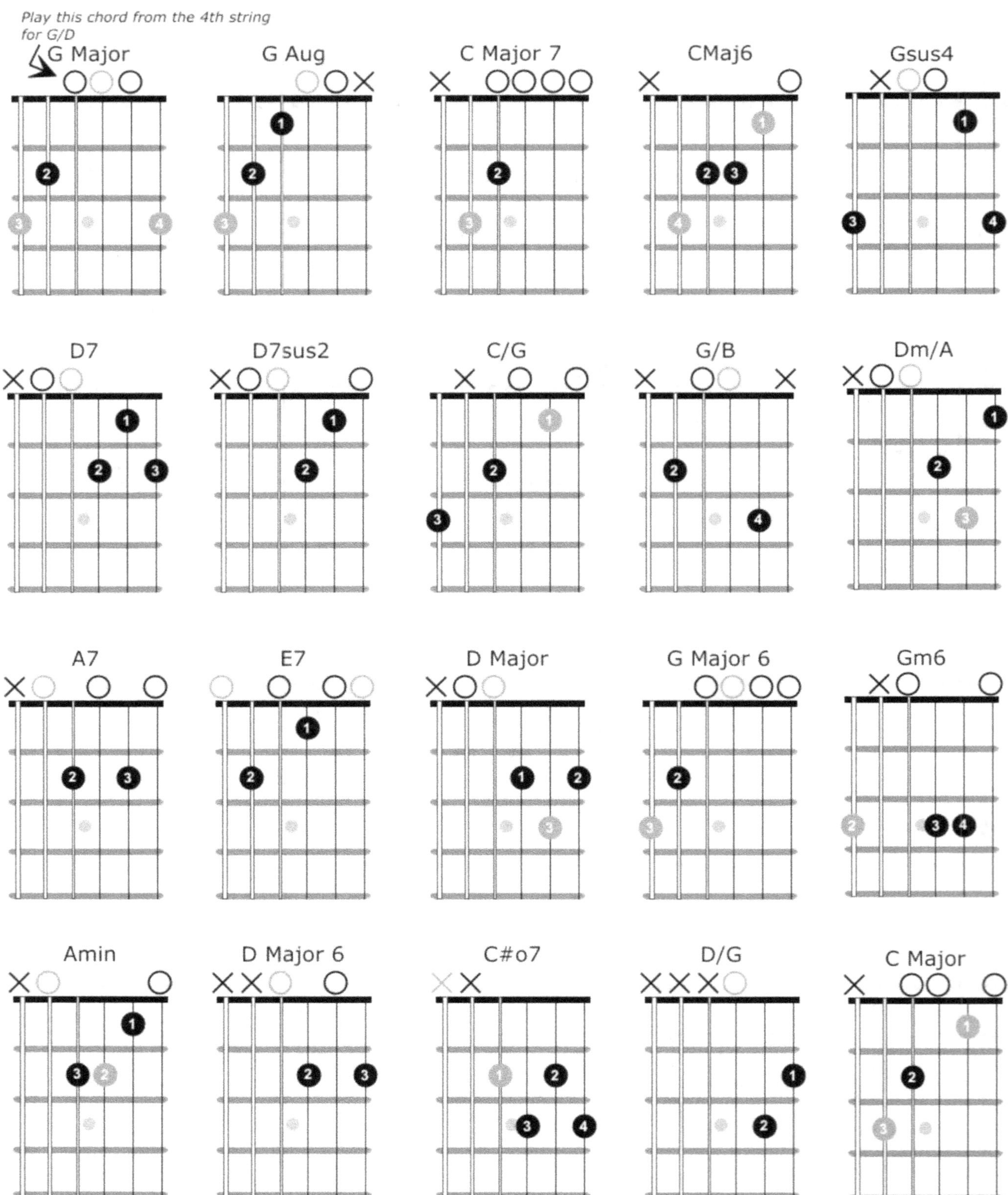

Great Is Thy Faithfulness play along

bpm = 74

Abide With Me + Melody
Abide With Me Backing Track

Count of 3 then play

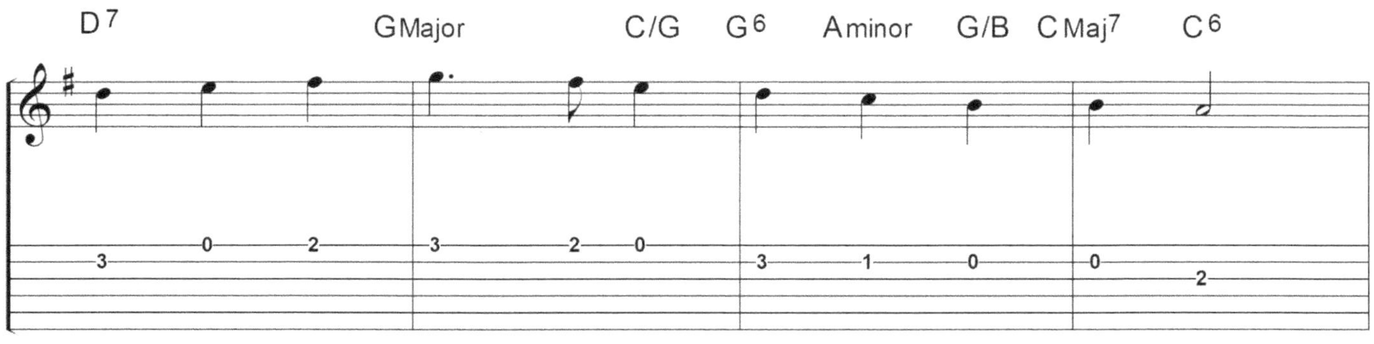

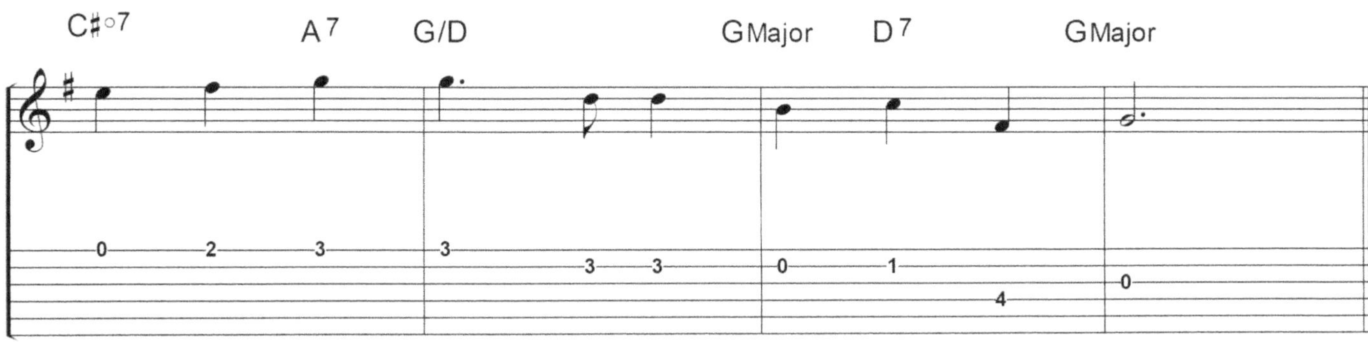

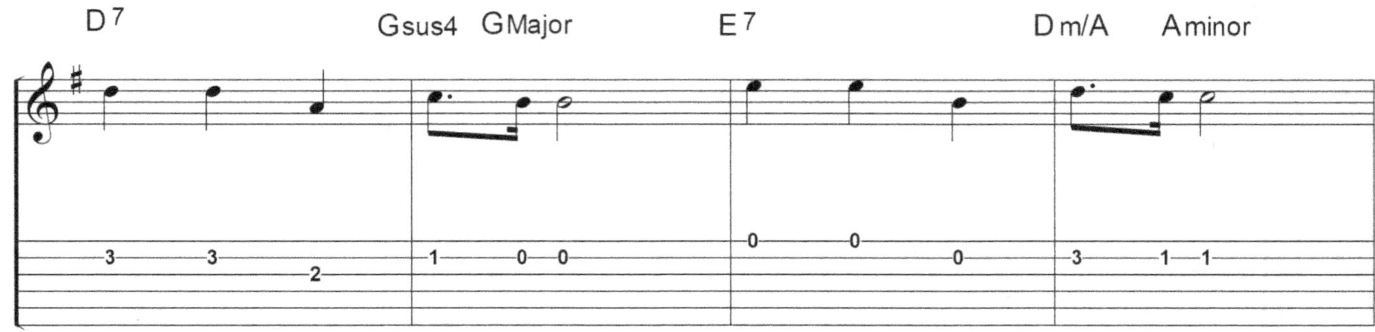

D7
Gsus4 GMajor
E7
Dm/A Aminor

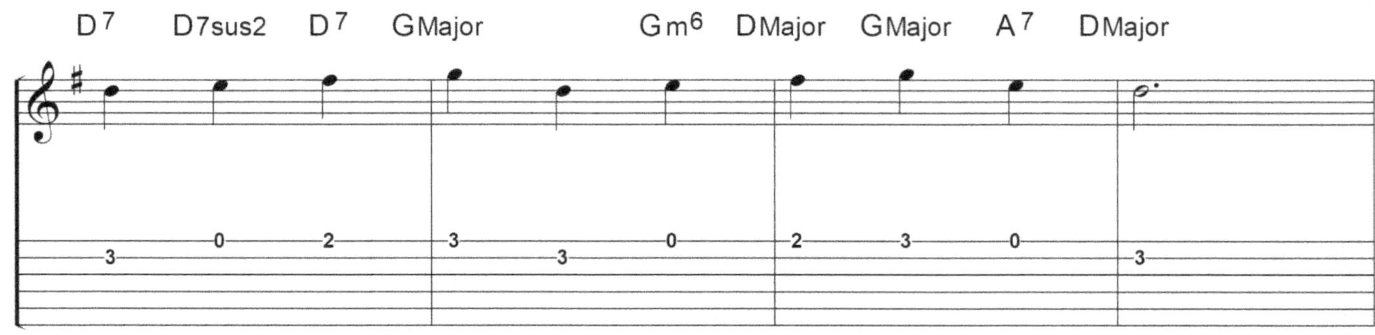

D7 D7sus2 D7 GMajor
Gm6 DMajor GMajor A7 DMajor

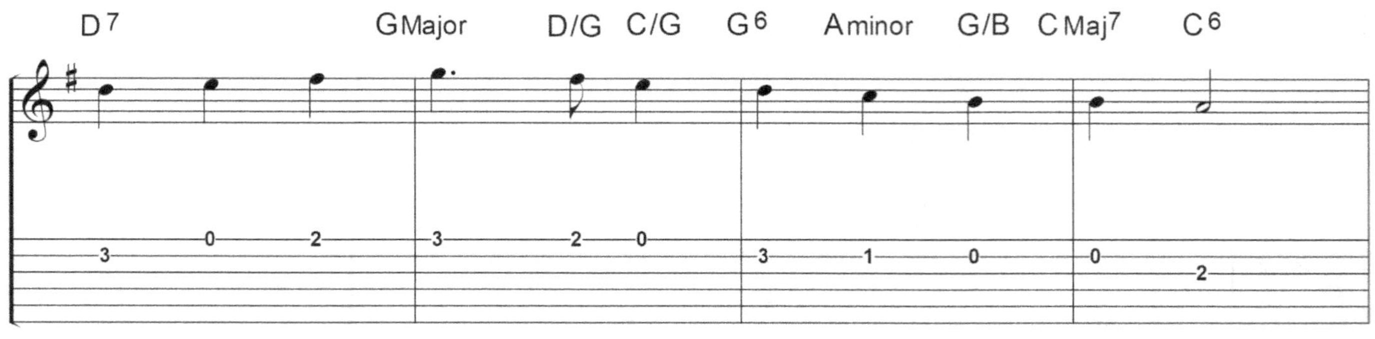

D7
GMajor D/G C/G G6 Aminor G/B CMaj7 C6

C#o7
A7 G/D
GMajor D7 GMajor

Great Is Thy Faithfulness - Intermediate

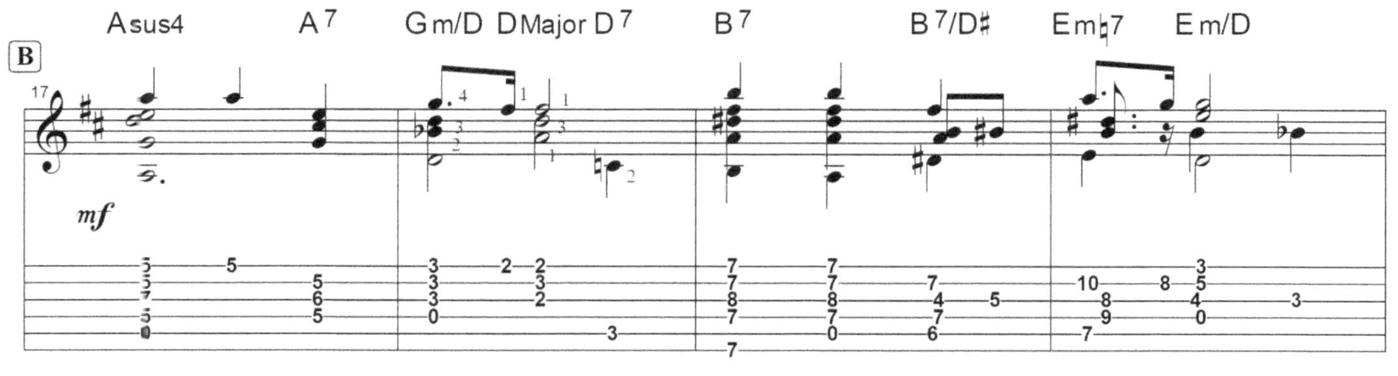

B
17
Asus4   A7   Gm/D DMajor D7   B7   B7/D#   Em7   Em/D
mf

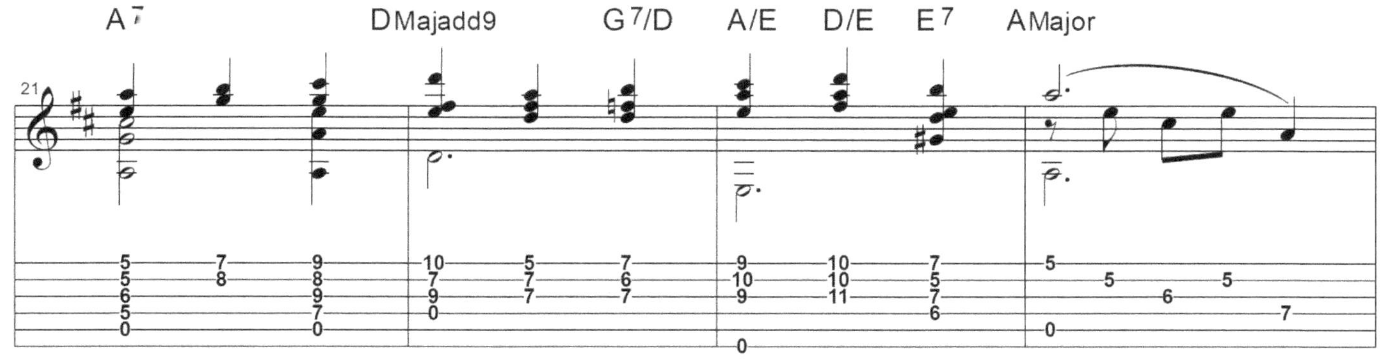

21
A7   DMajadd9   G7/D   A/E   D/E   E7   AMajor

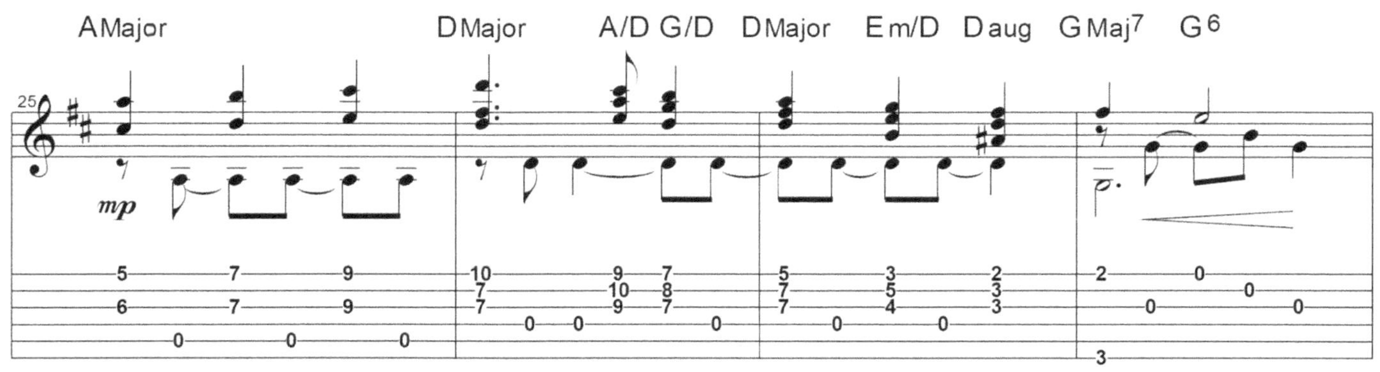

25
AMajor   DMajor   A/D G/D   DMajor   Em/D Daug   GMaj7   G6
mp

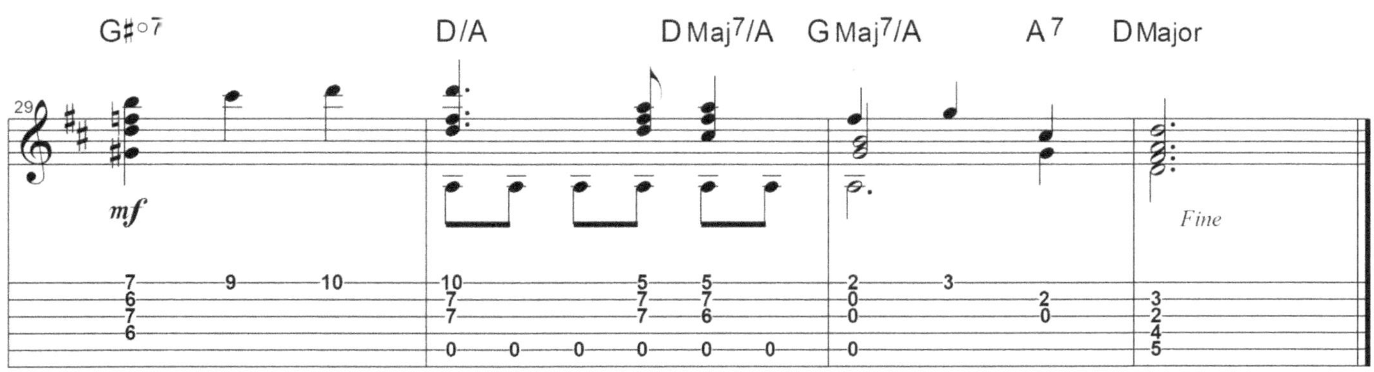

29
G#°7   D/A   DMaj7/A GMaj7/A   A7   DMajor
mf
Fine

Chords: Great Is Thy Faithfulness Intermediate

Line 1

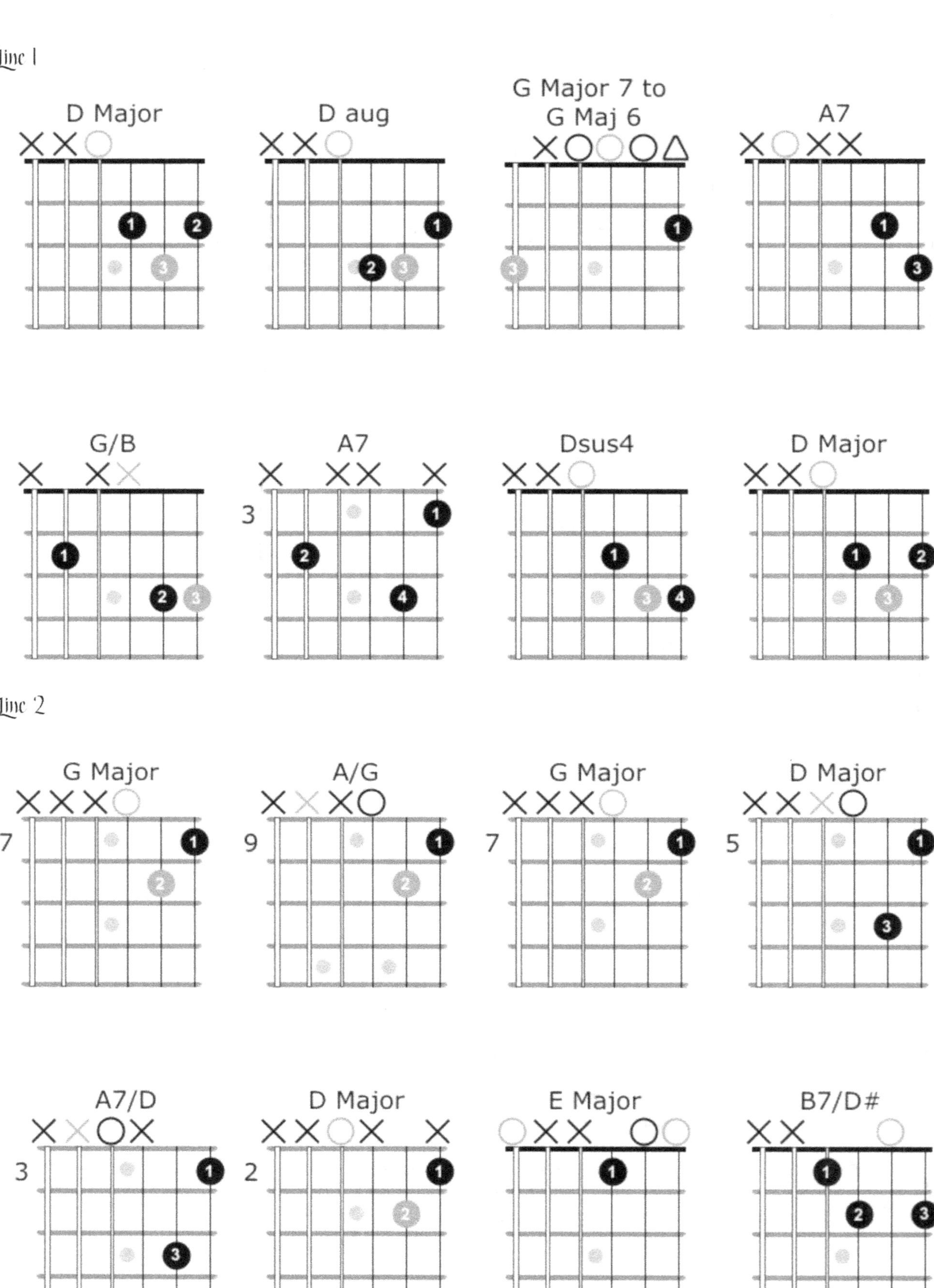

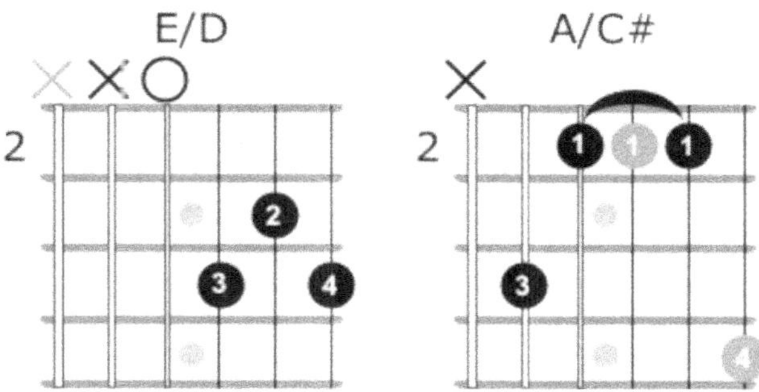

E/D

A/C#

Line 3

A Major

A Major

A Major

D Major

A/D

G/D

D Major

Em/D

D aug

G Major 7 to
G Maj 6

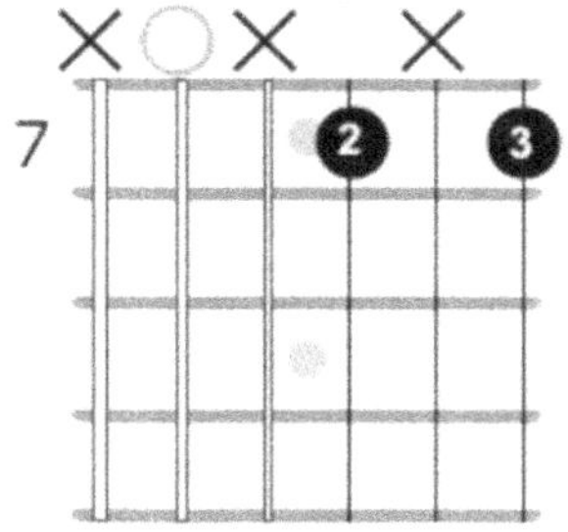

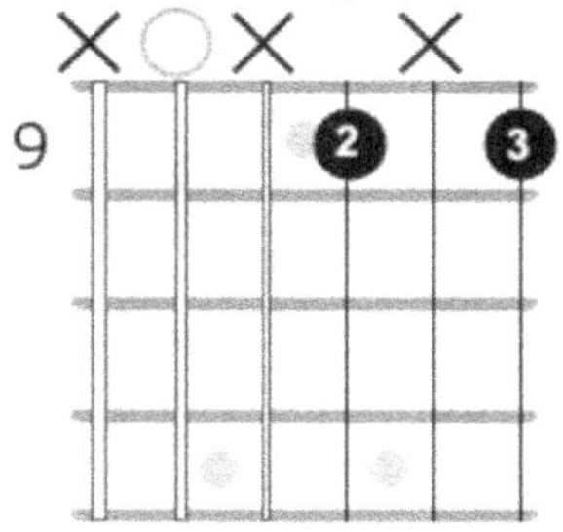

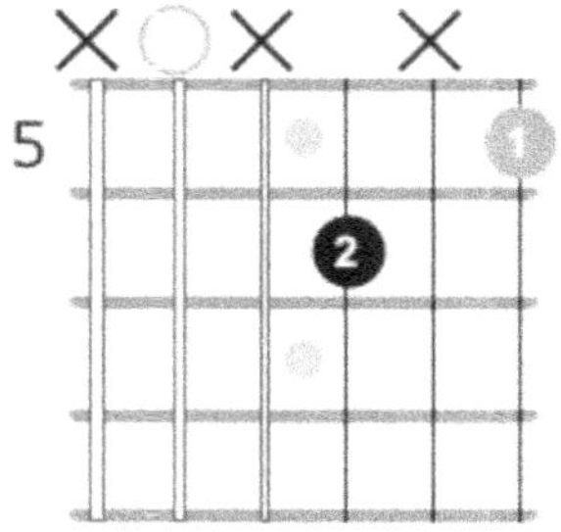

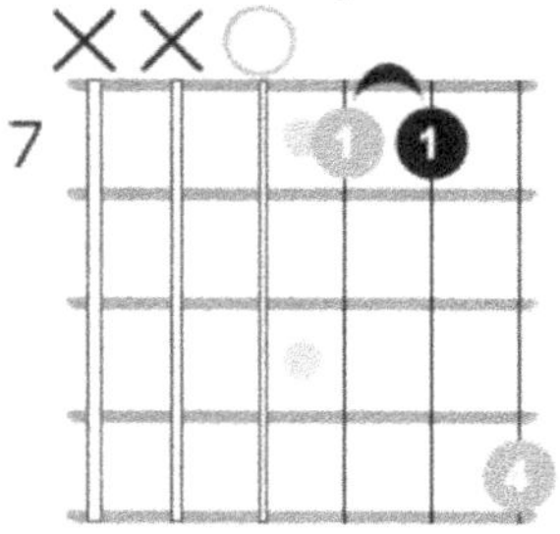

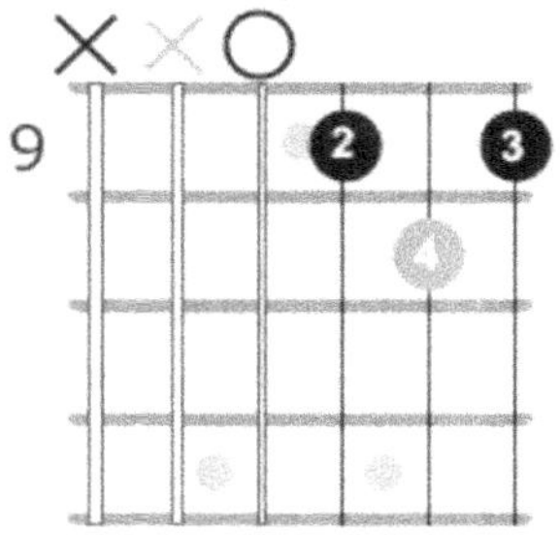

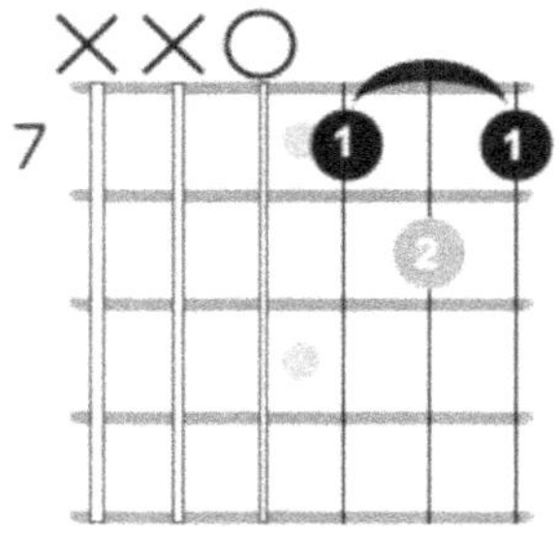

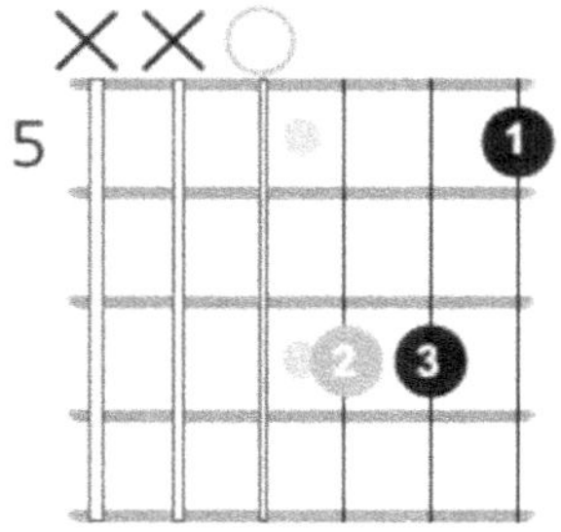

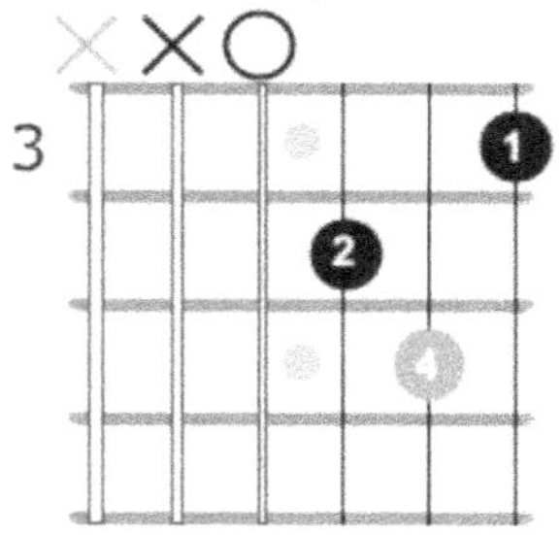

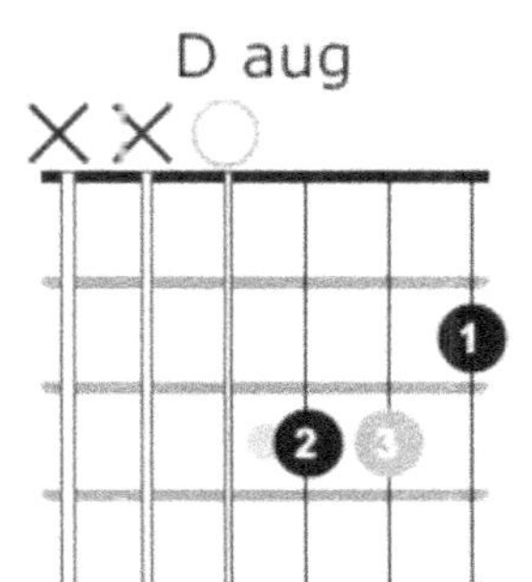

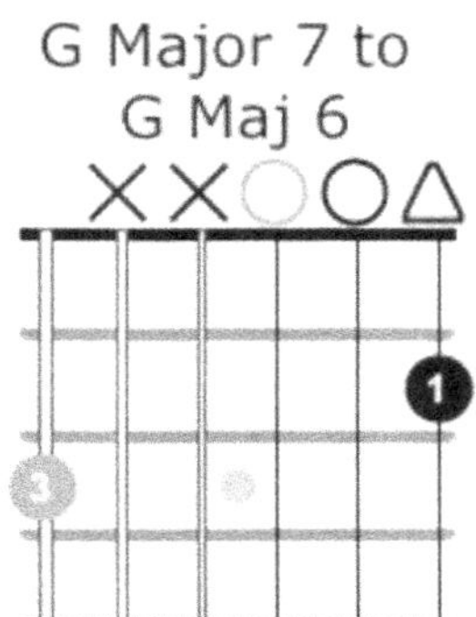

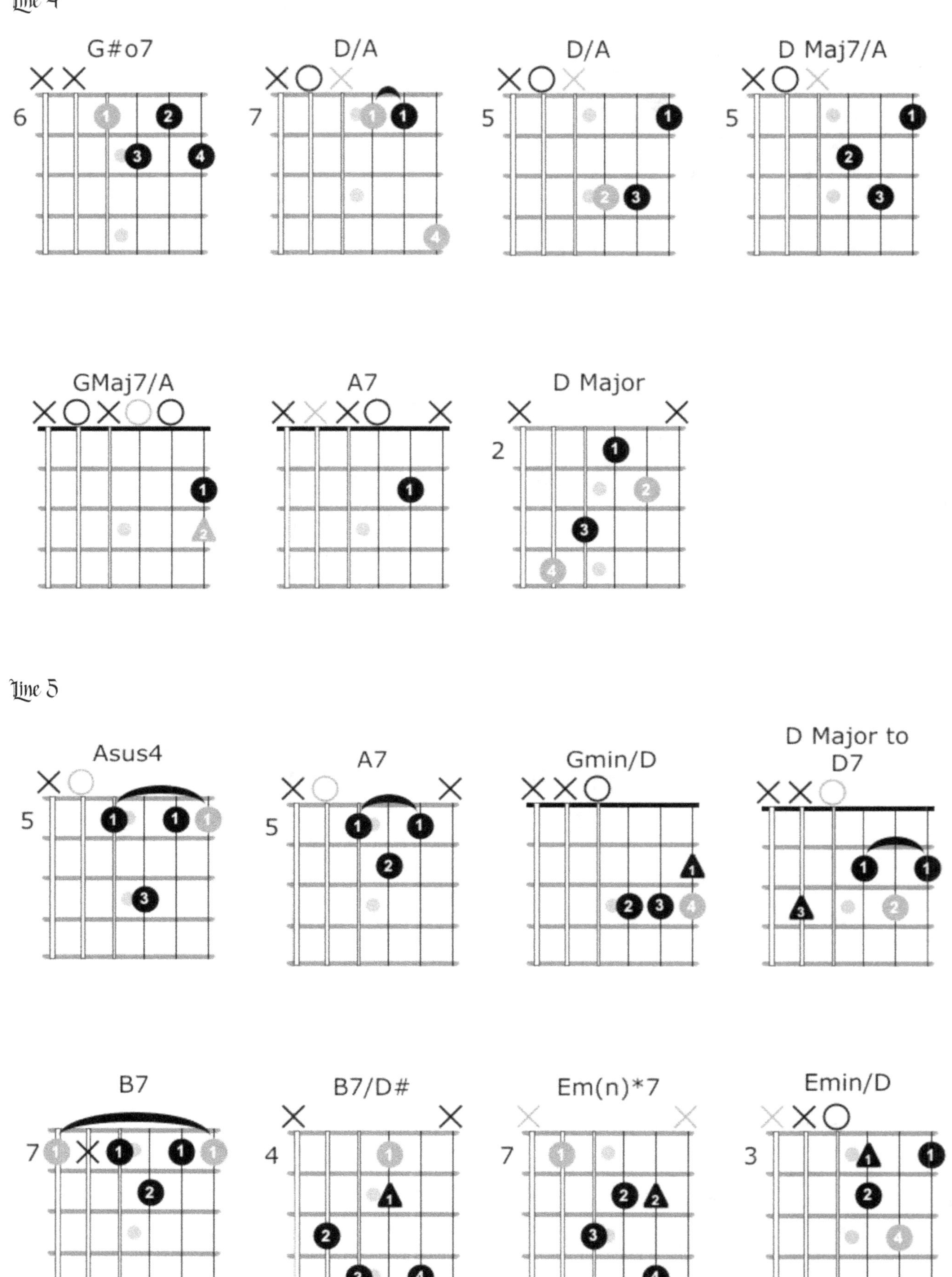

Line 4
G#o7
D/A
D/A
D Maj7/A
GMaj7/A
A7
D Major
Line 5
Asus4
A7
Gmin/D
D Major to D7
B7
B7/D#
Em(n)*7
Emin/D
* = natural

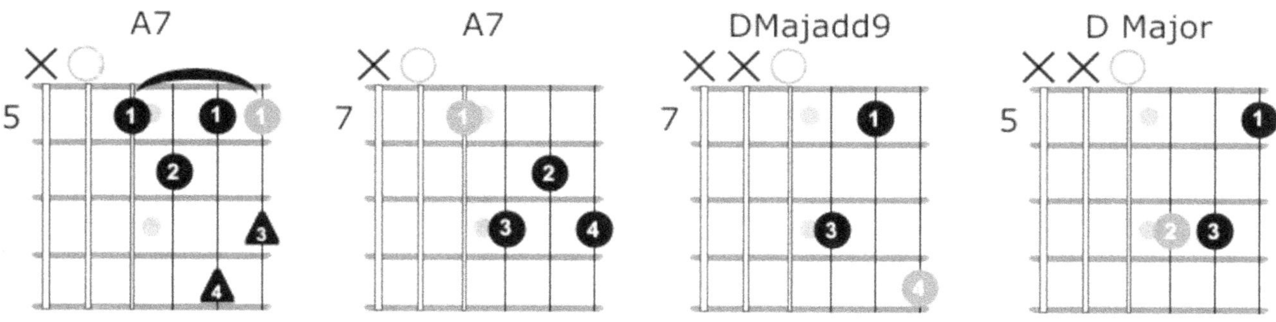

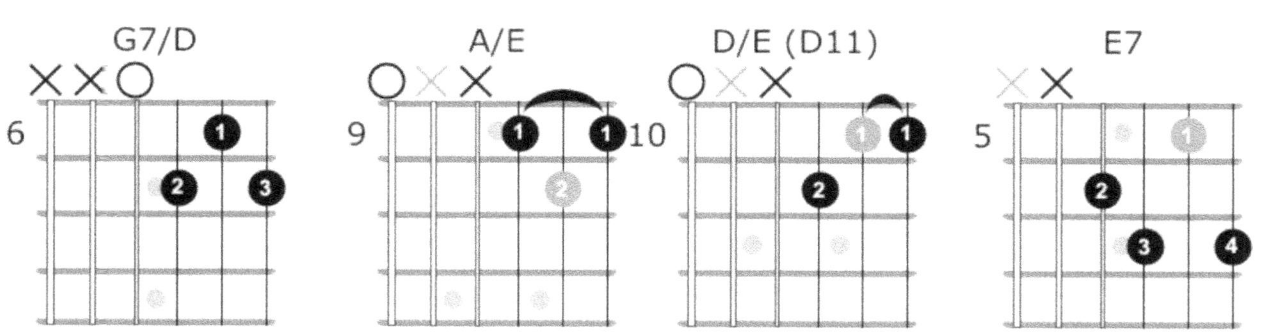

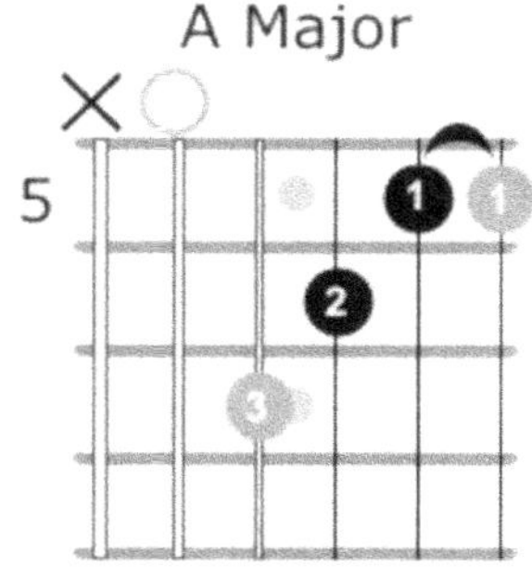

A Major

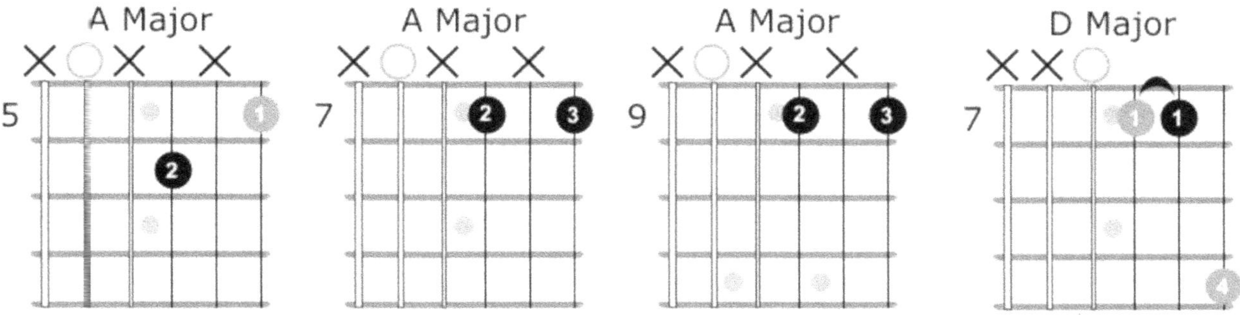

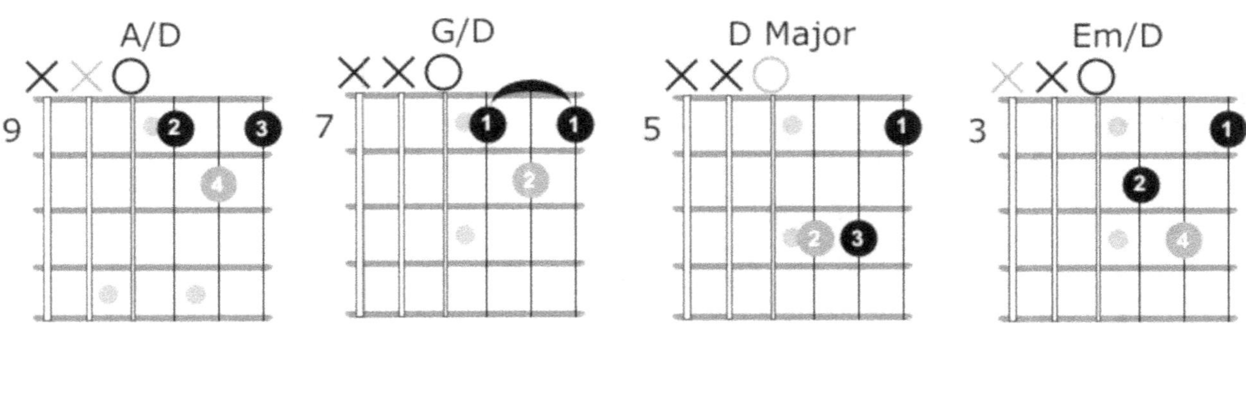

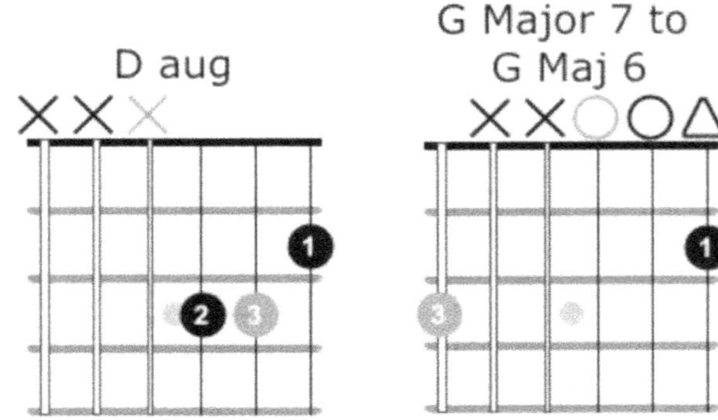

Line 8

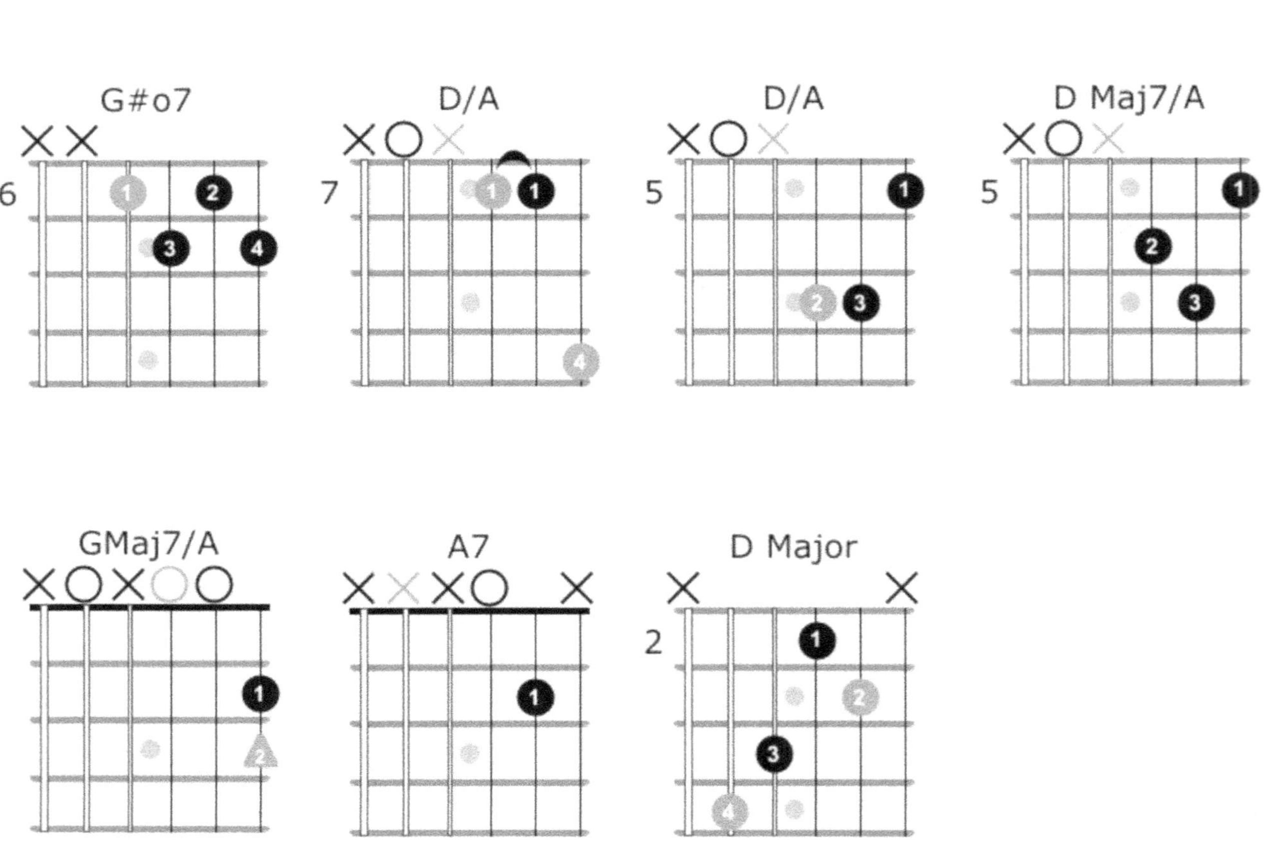

Great Is Thy Faithfulness - Advanced

D6/9   Emin13 A9#5   Ab7#5b9   Gb13b9   B7b9   Emin11 GMaj13
14

G#o7   DMajadd9/A   D6/9/A B/A   A13sus   A11b9 A7b9
17   (B7)
p

DMaj7/A   A11   EbMaj#11/A A7b9   Eb/A Daug/A   DMajor   Co7
20   B
mf

B7sus B7#5   B/A Emin11b7 A7/E   A11   A13   A7#5
23

Bmin7 F#min7 FMaj9#11 E13sus F13 E13b9/D A7b9
26
N.H.
F/A B/A F#/A AbMaj13#11 GMaj13#11 CMaj13 EbMaj13#11 DbMaj13#11 CMaj13#11
29
Em9b7 GMaj7 C#min7/G# G#o7 D/A
32
mp
A13sus Eb/A A7b9 BbMaj6 DMaj
35
rall.
p
Fine

Chords: Great Is Thy Faithfulness Advanced

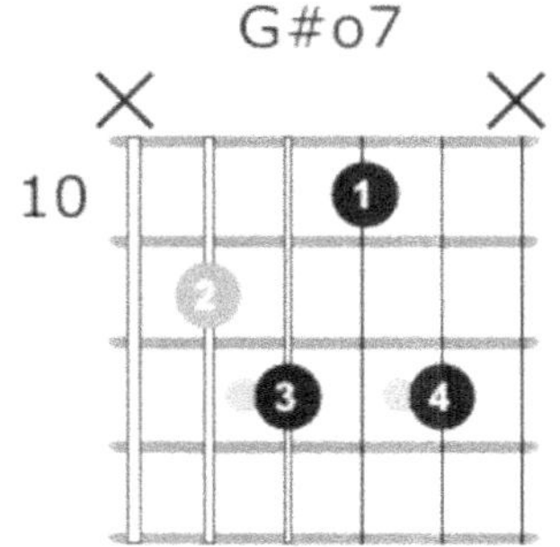

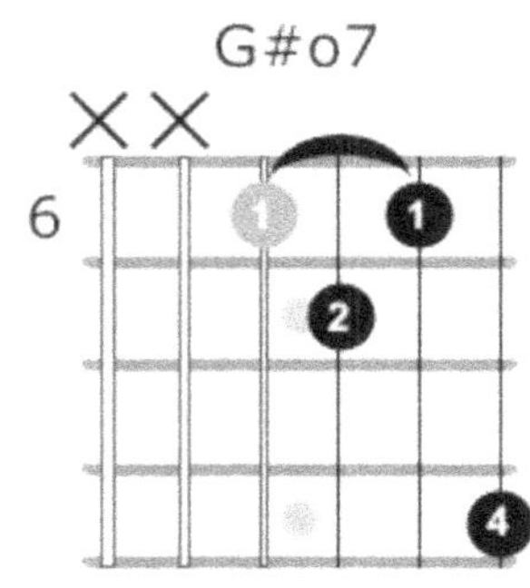

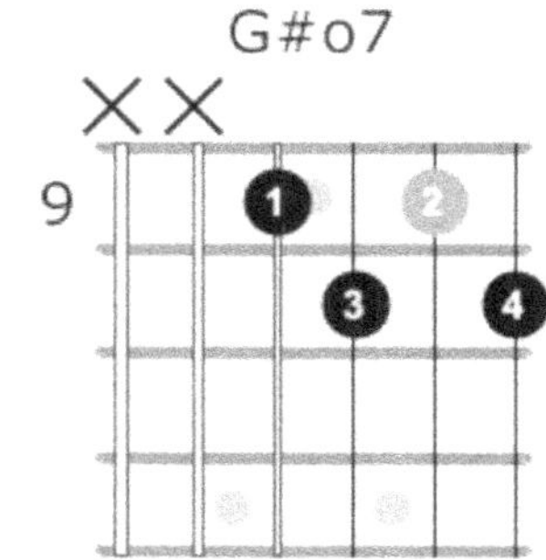

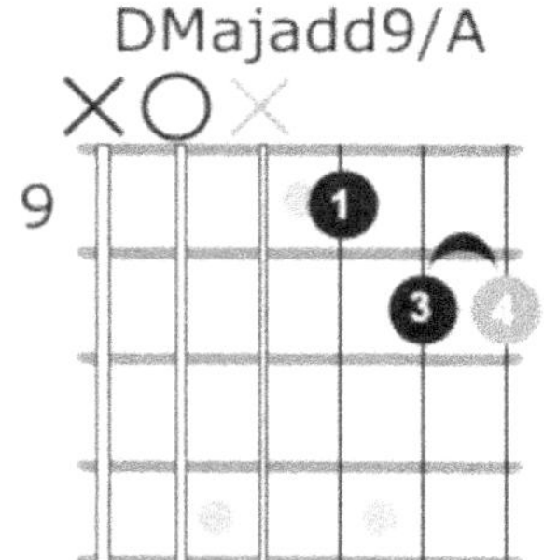

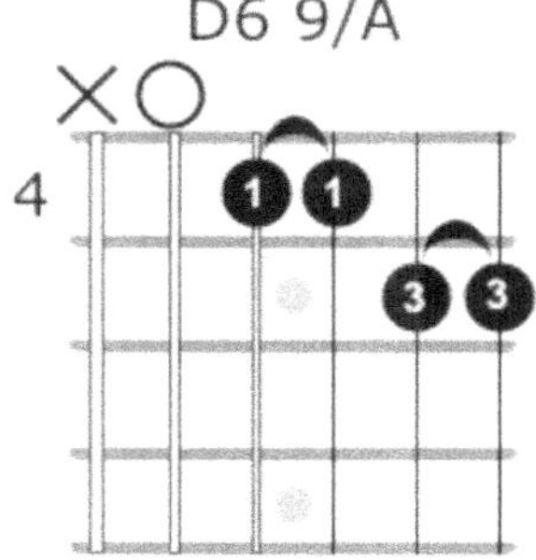

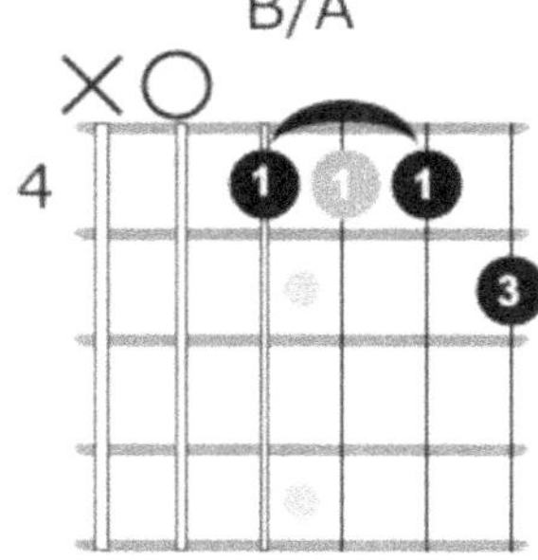

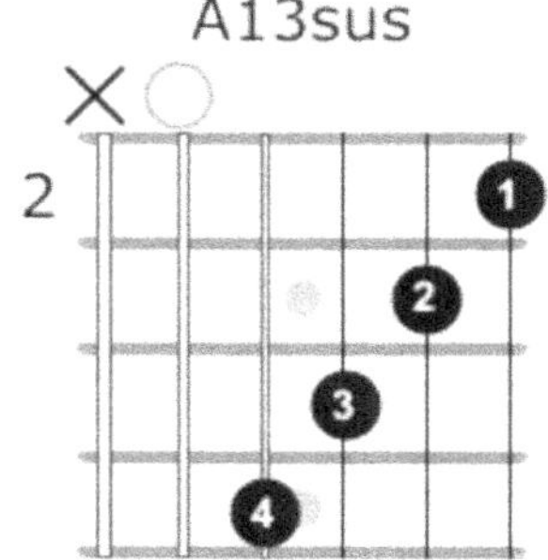

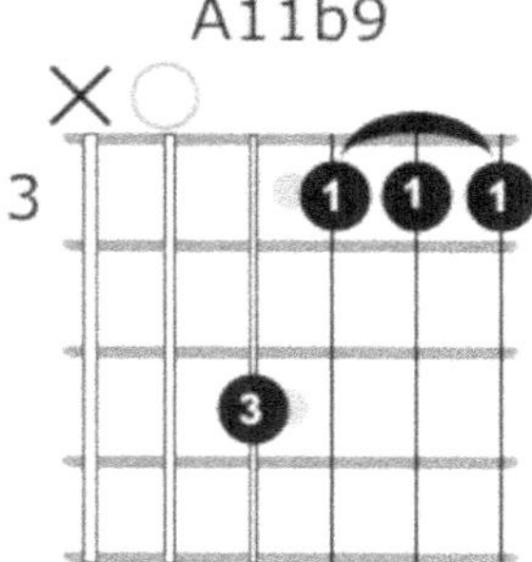

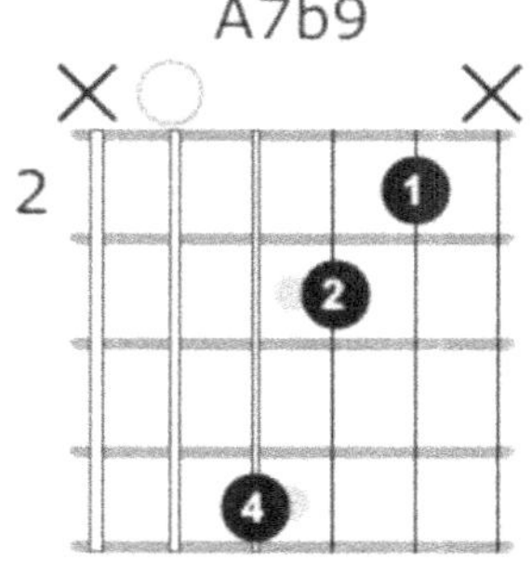

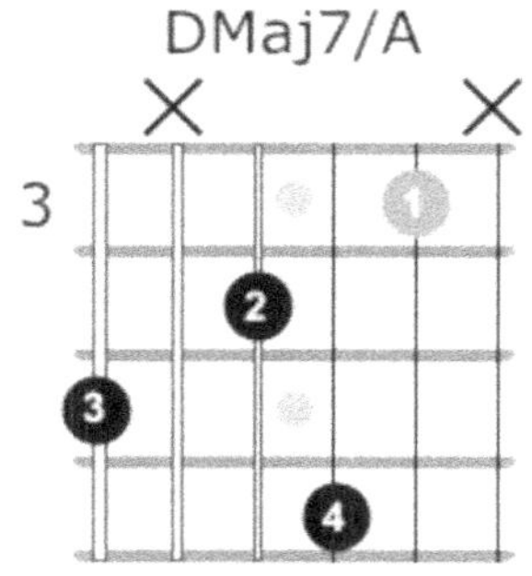

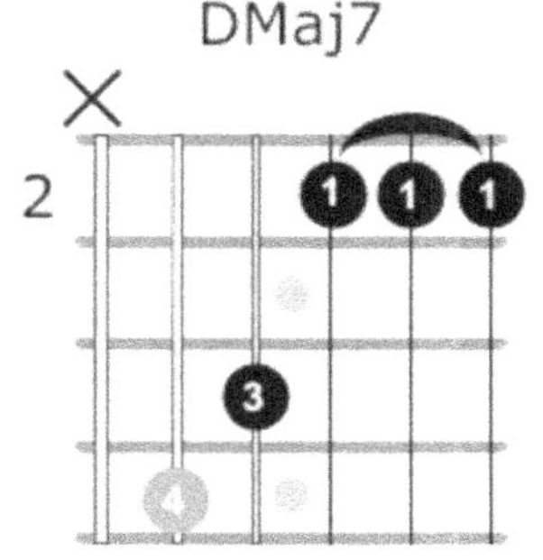

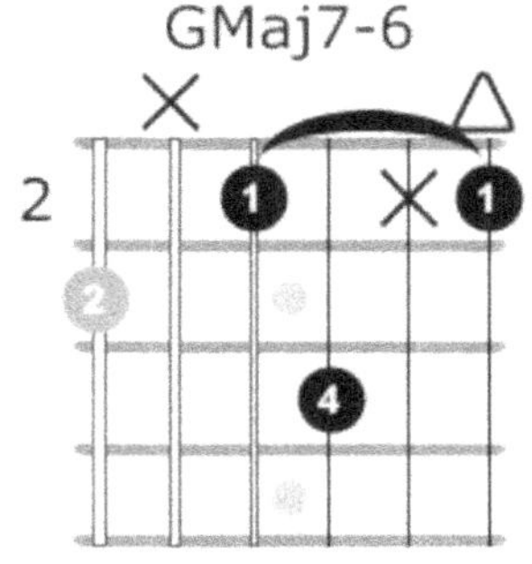

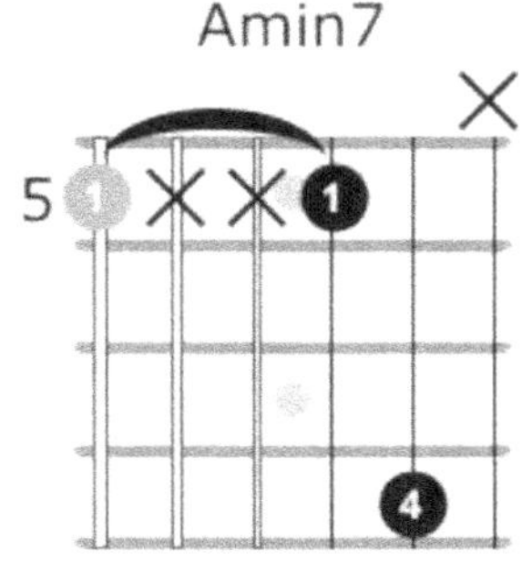

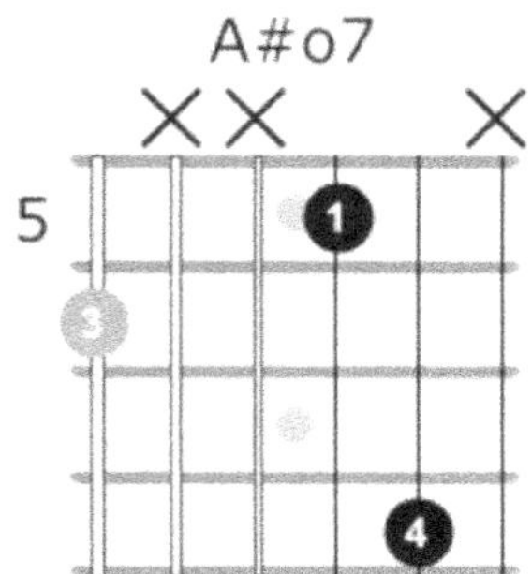

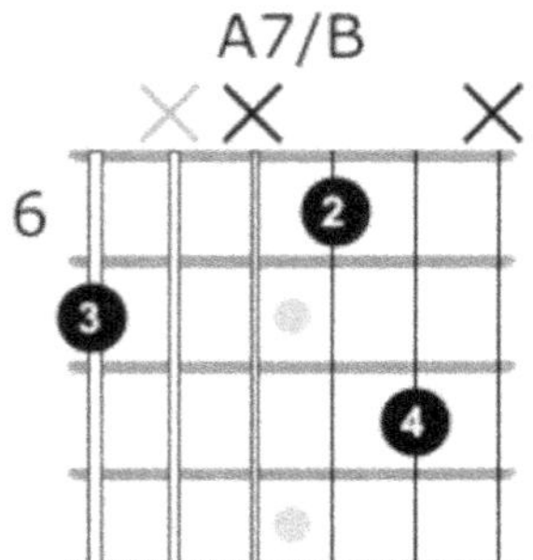

A7/B

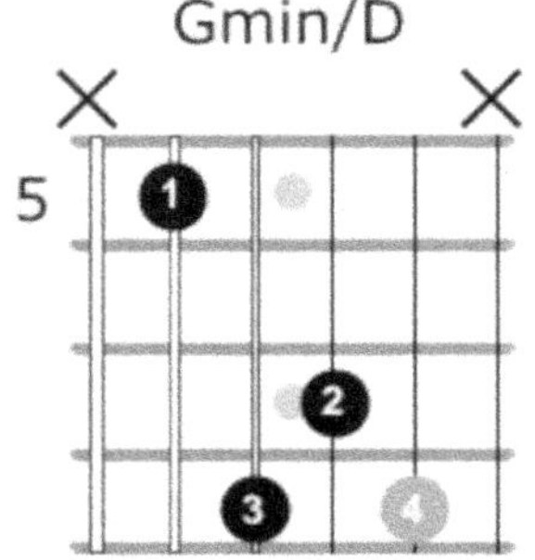

Gmin/D

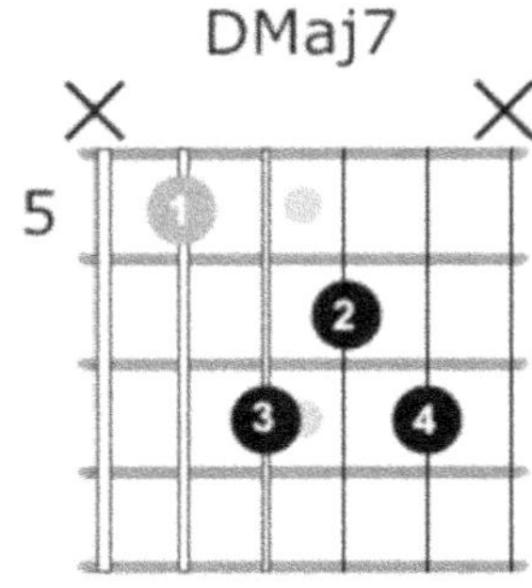

DMaj7

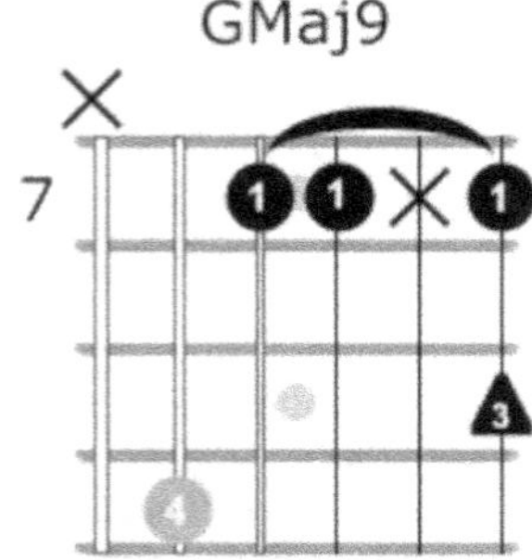

GMaj9

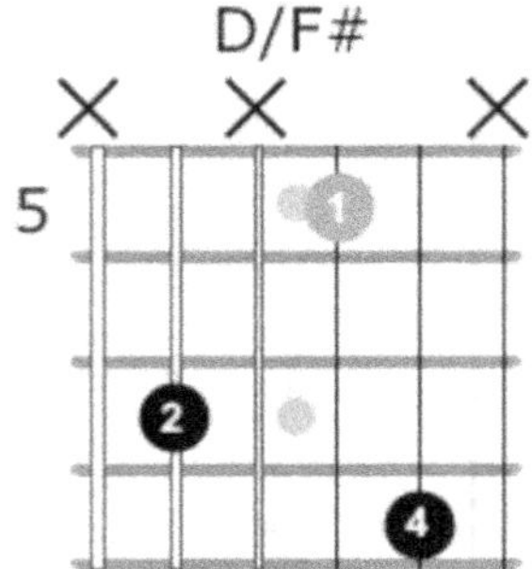

D/F#

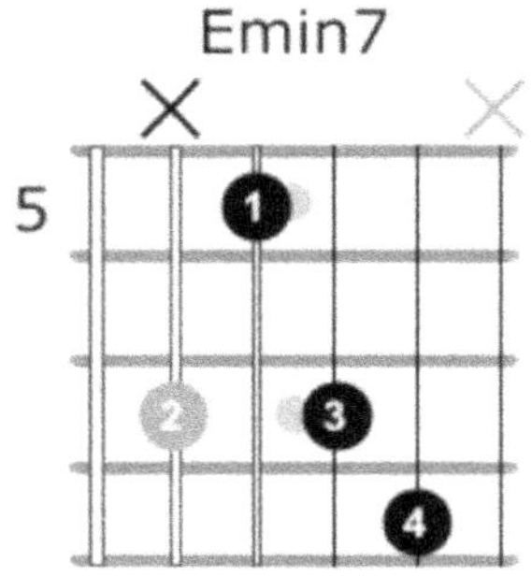

Emin7

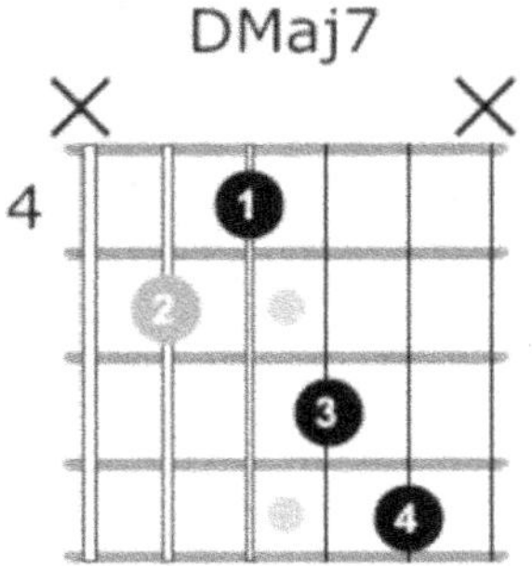

DMaj7

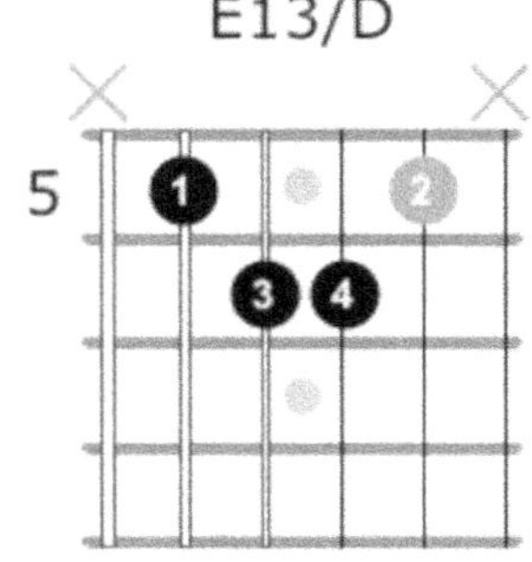

E13/D

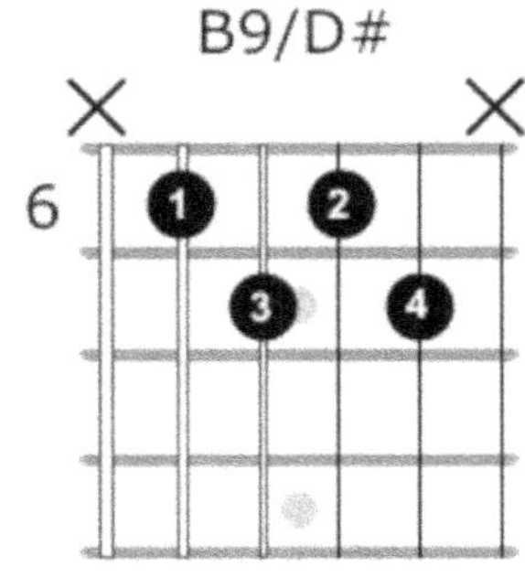

B9/D#

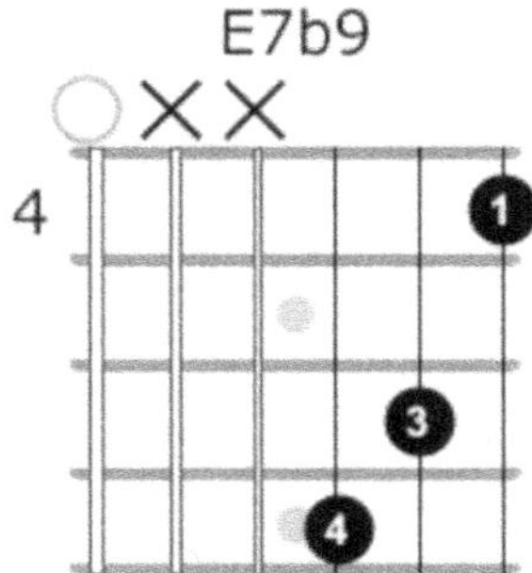

E7b9

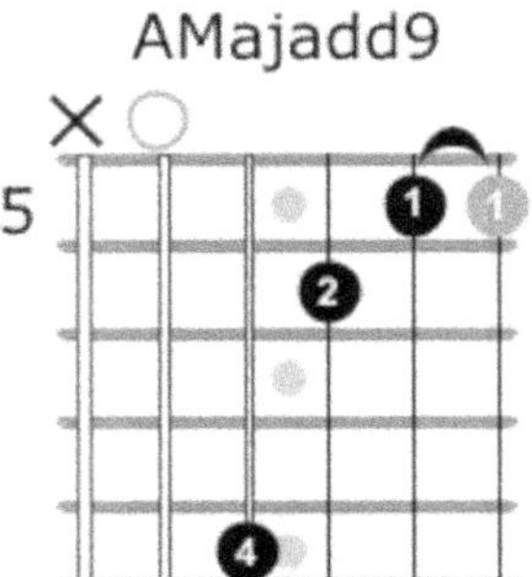

AMajadd9

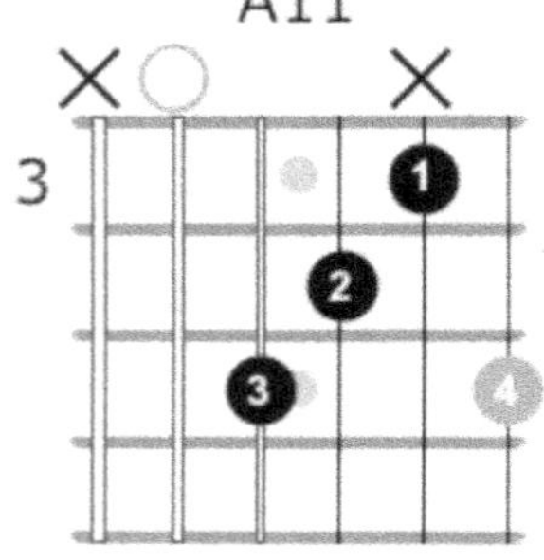

A11

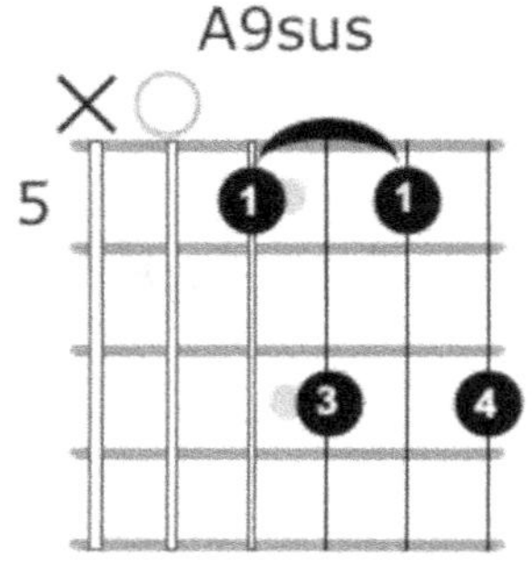

A9sus

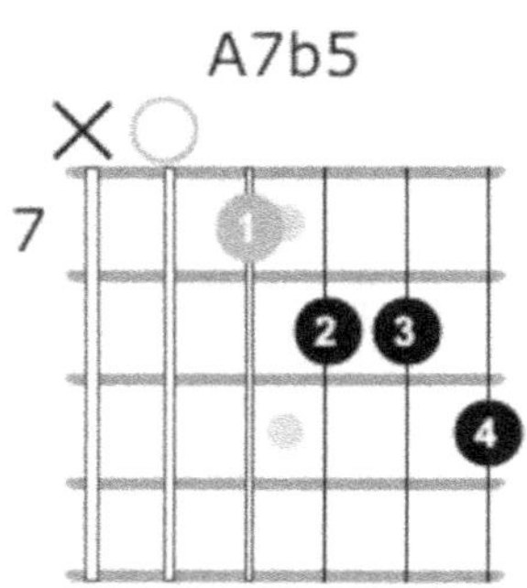

A7b5

Line 5

D6 9 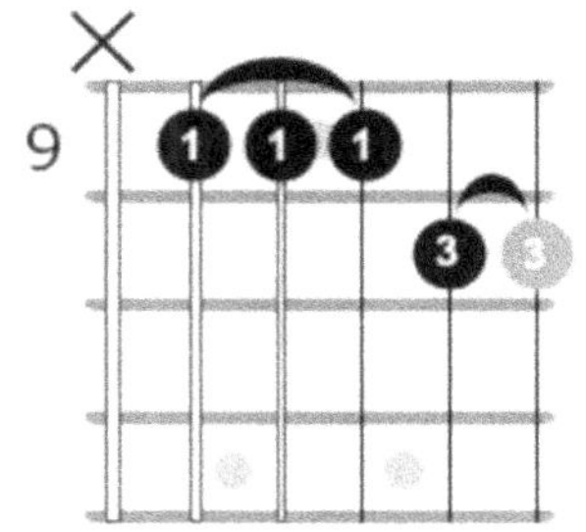
Emin13 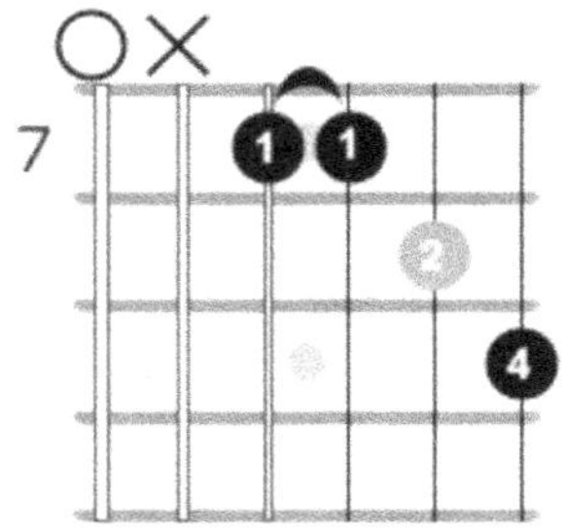
A9#5 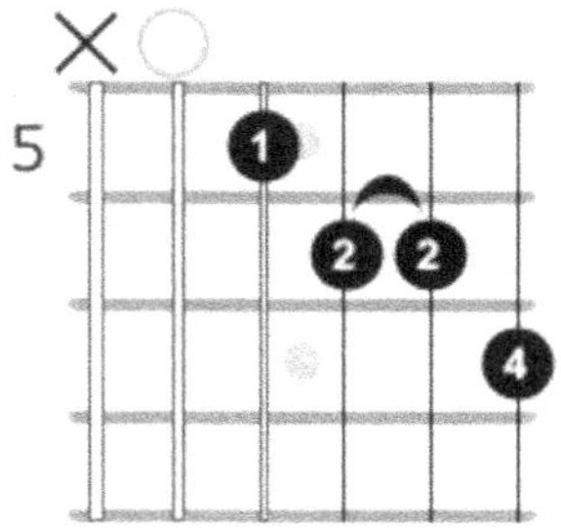
Ab7#5b9

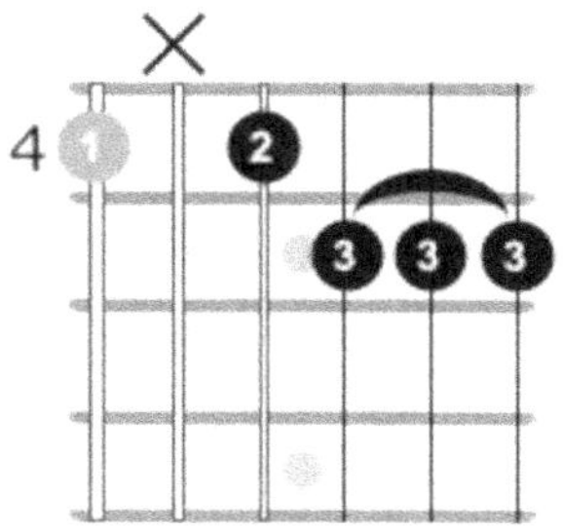

Gb13b9 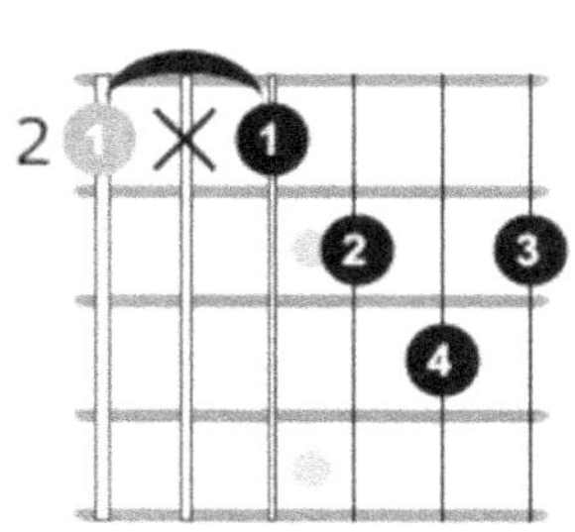
B7b9 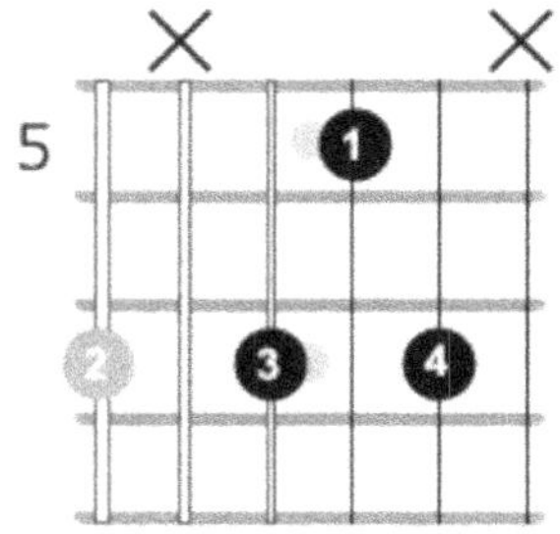
Emin11 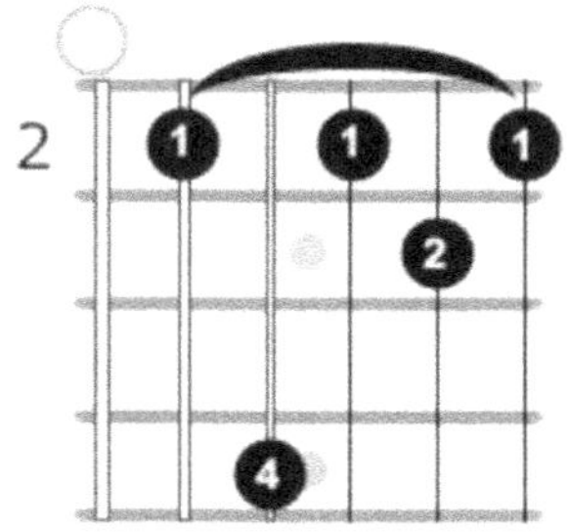
GMaj13

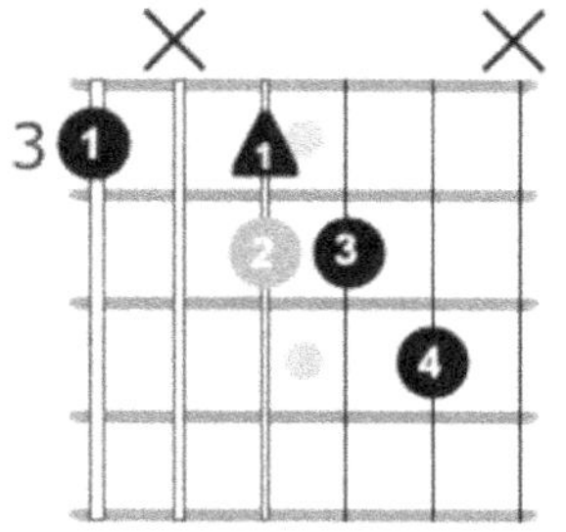

Line 6

G#o7 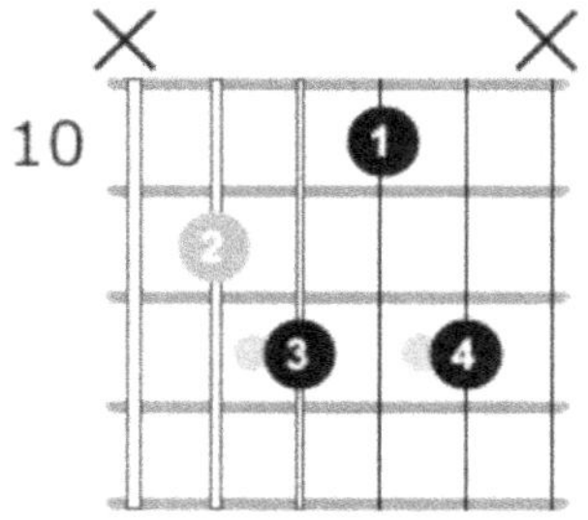
G#o7 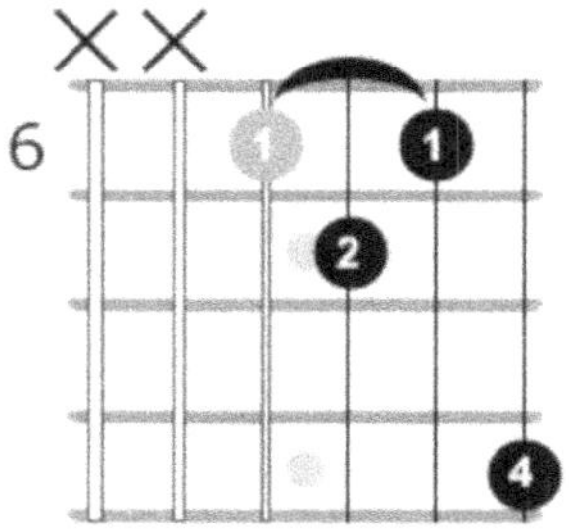
G#o7 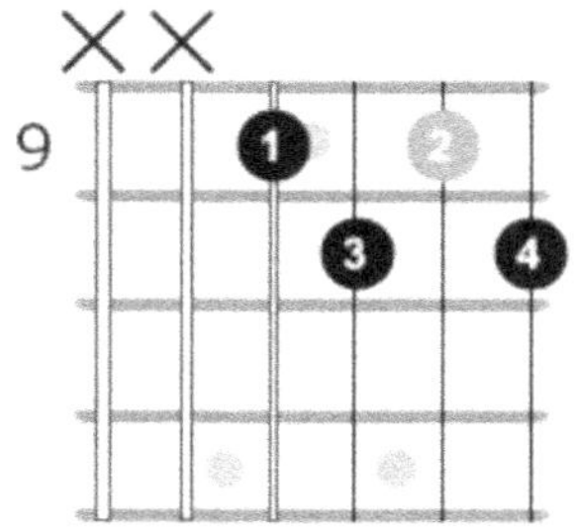
DMajadd9/A

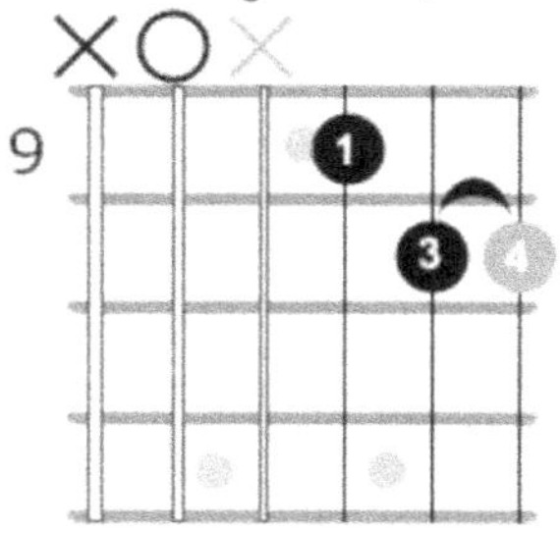

D6 9/A 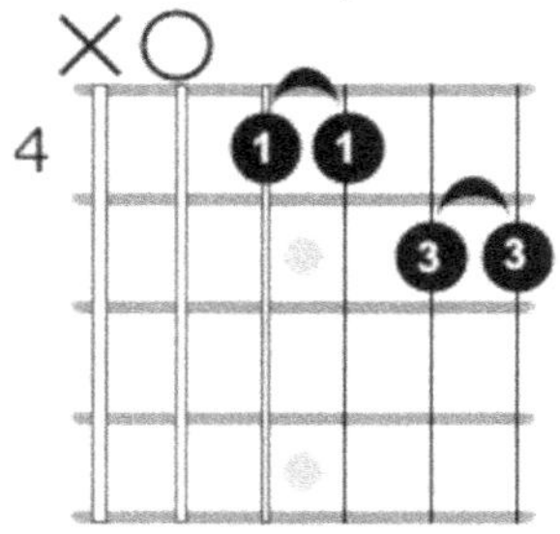
B/A (B7) 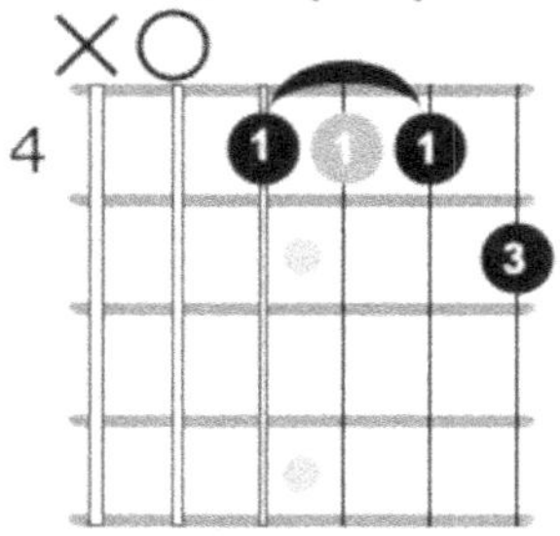
A13sus 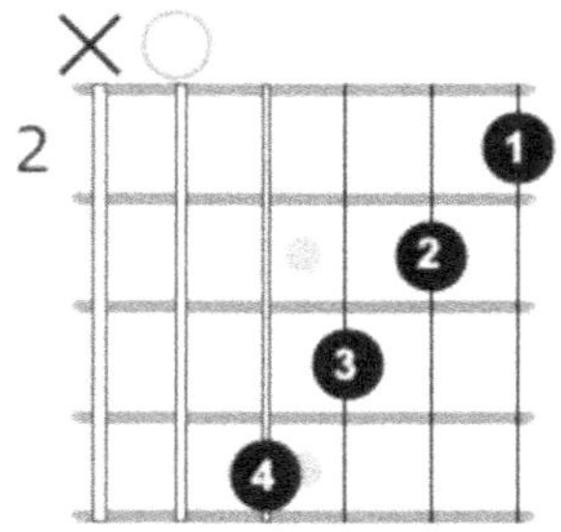
A11b9

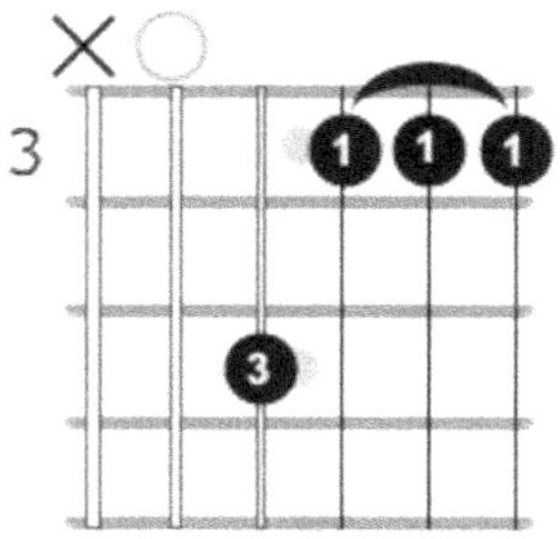

A7b9

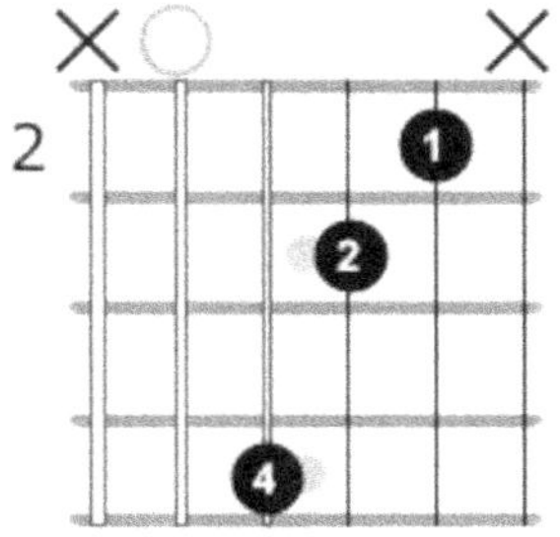

Line 7

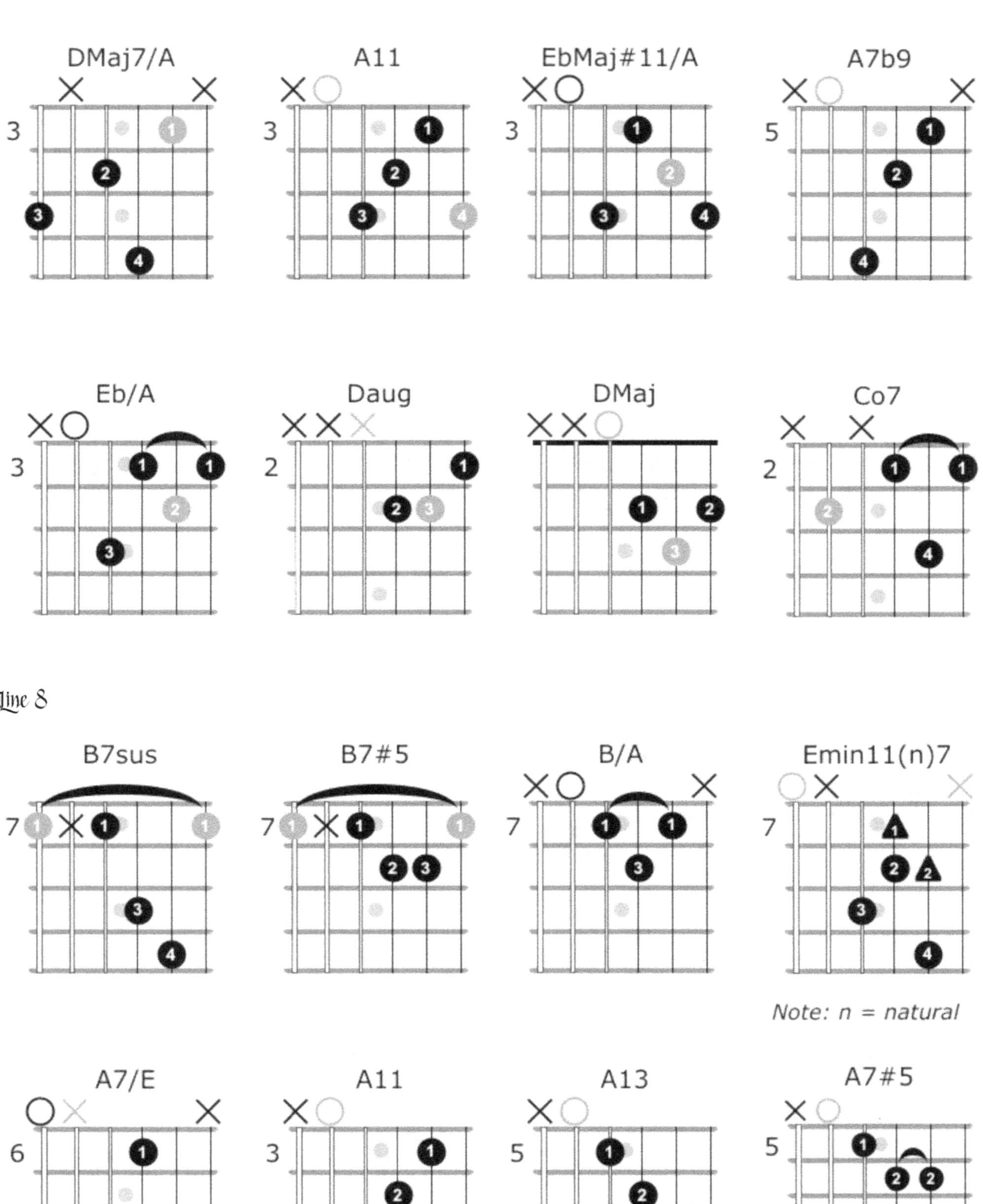

DMaj7/A
A11
EbMaj#11/A
A7b9
Eb/A
Daug
DMaj
Co7
Line 8
B7sus
B7#5
B/A
Emin11(n)7
Note: n = natural
A7/E
A11
A13
A7#5

Line 9
Bmin7
F#min7
FMaj9#11
E13sus
F13
E13b9/D
A7b9
Line 10
F/A
B/A
F#/A
AbMaj13#11
GMaj13#11
CMaj13
EbMaj13#11
DbMaj13#11
CMaj13#11

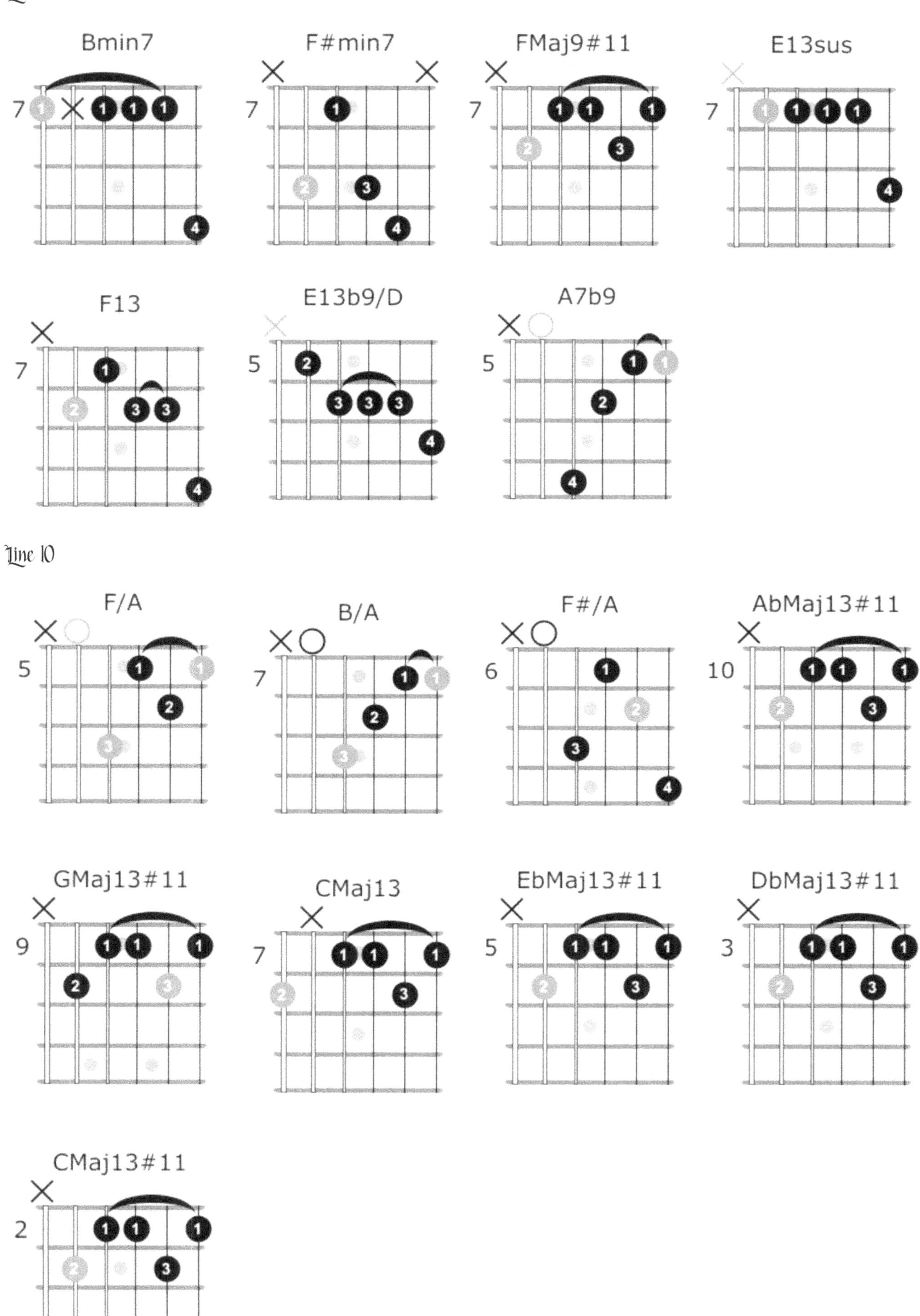

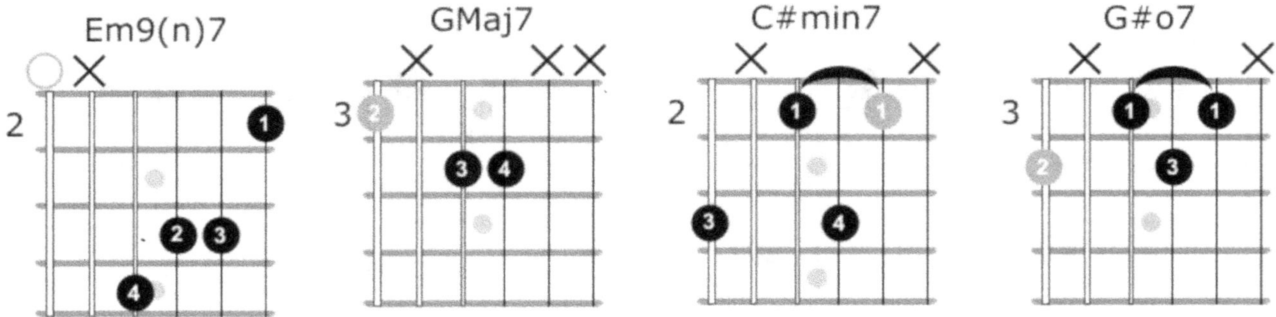

Note: n = natural

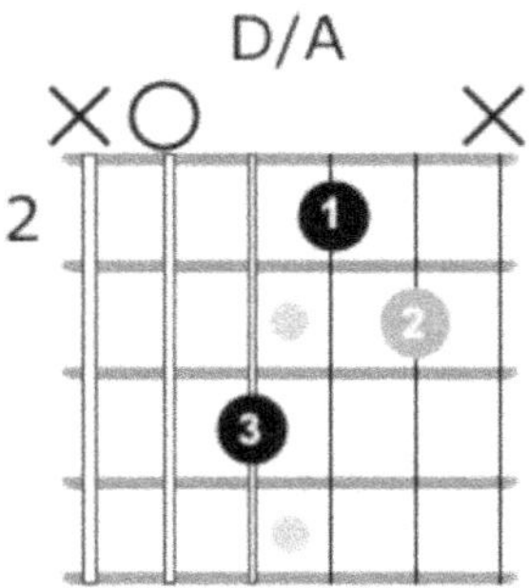

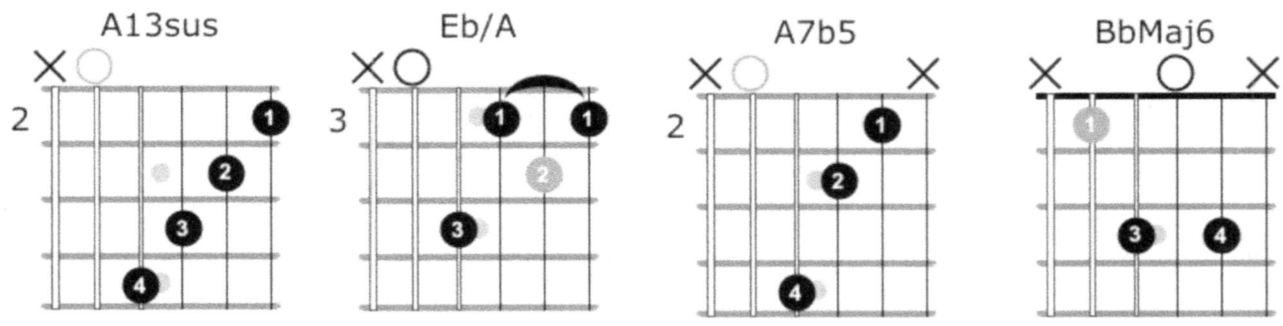

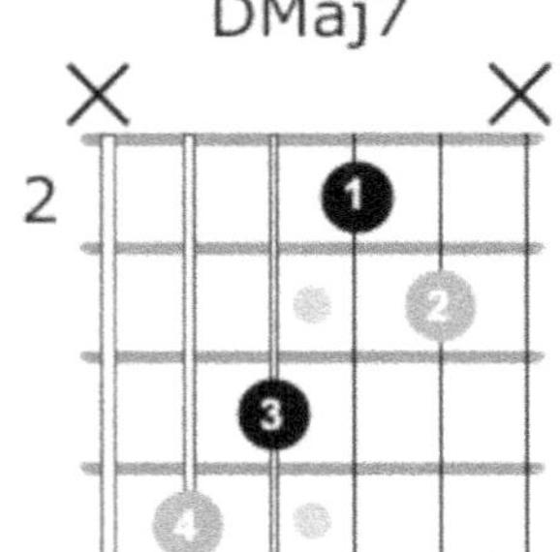

Hymn 6
How Great Thou Art

Resources

Performance of Intermediate version

Audio Talk through of Intermediate version

Performance of Advanced version

Audio Talk through of Advanced version

Use a QR code reader on your cell/mobile phone or tablet to view and listen to the files above. There's a large selection of completely free QR code reader apps available which work on all operating platforms.

To download all resources and other support files, follow the instructions on page 197 of this publication.

Hymn Notes - How Great Thou Art

Swedish poet and lay minister Carl Gustav Boberg (1859 – 1940) was inspired to write the words of "O Store God" (O great God) from which we eventually arrived at the English language version "How Great Thou Art".

Carl was walking back from church and observed a violent storm come over the hills and lake. It subdued quickly and by the time he got home the sun was shining and an idyll of peace presented itself. He gave a detailed account of this happening which had a great emotional effect on him and wrote the words for this hymn. This event was documented by J. Irving Erickson.

The words were set to a traditional Swedish song and Carl originally gave the song nine verses. The song rates very highly with congregations around the world and has been translated into many other languages besides English.

Carl Boberg

Carl Boberg wrote more than sixty hymns and gospel songs and in addition to his lay ministry, was also a serving member of the Swedish parliament between 1912 and 1931.

Lyrics

Verse 1

Oh Lord, my God

When I, in awesome wonder

Consider all the worlds Thy hands have made

I see the stars, I hear the rolling thunder

Thy power throughout the universe displayed

Chorus

Then sings my soul, my Savior God to Thee

How great Thou art, how great Thou art

Then sings my soul, my Savior God to Thee

How great Thou art, how great Thou art

Verse 2

When thru the woods and forest glades I wander

And hear the birds sing sweetly in the trees,

When I look down from lofty mountain grandeur

And hear the brook and feel the gentle breeze,

Verse 3

And when I think that God, His Son not sparing

Sent Him to die, I scarce can take it in

That on the cross, my burden gladly bearing

He bled and died to take away my sin

Chorus

Verse 3

When Christ shall come, with shout of acclamation

And take me home, what joy shall fill my heart

Then I shall bow, in humble adoration

And then proclaim, my God, how great Thou art

Chorus

How Great Thou Art - Starter

How Great Thou Art - Starter alternate key

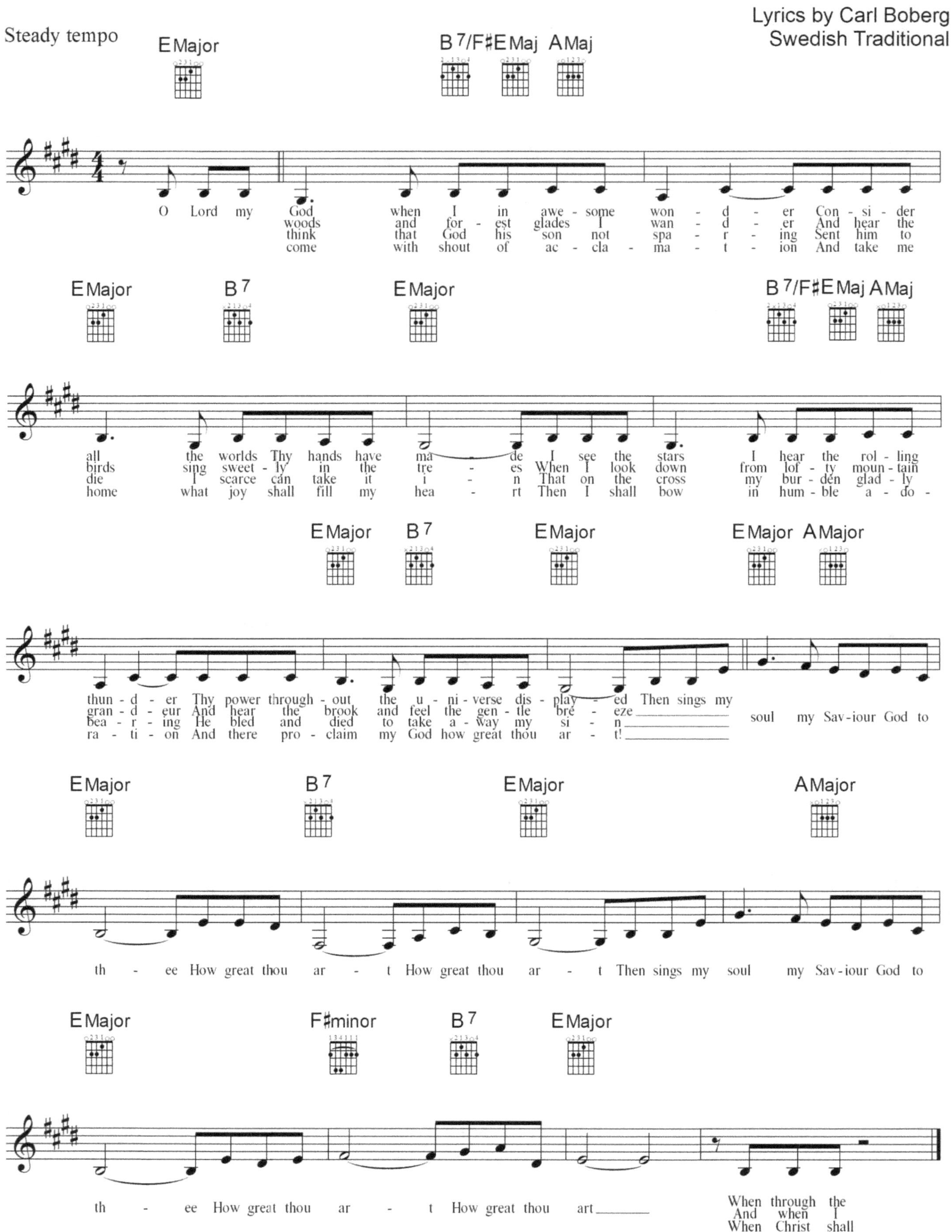

100

Chords: How Great Though Art

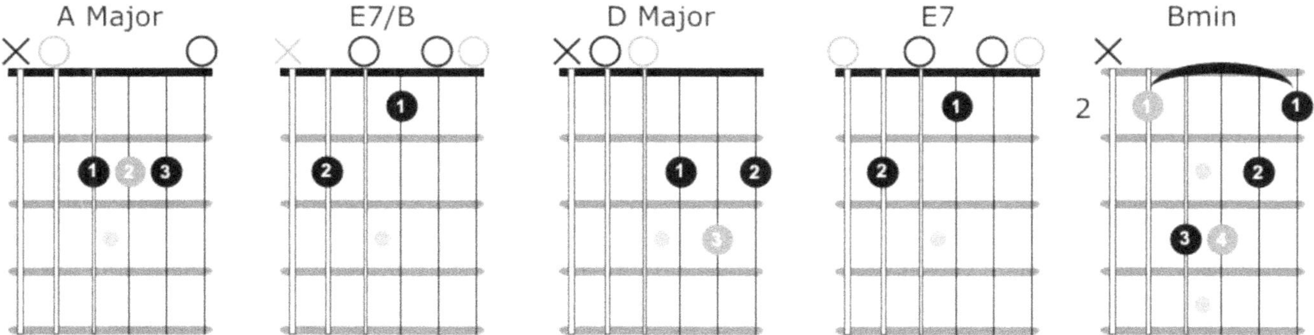

Chords: How Great Though Art Starter Song Alternate Key

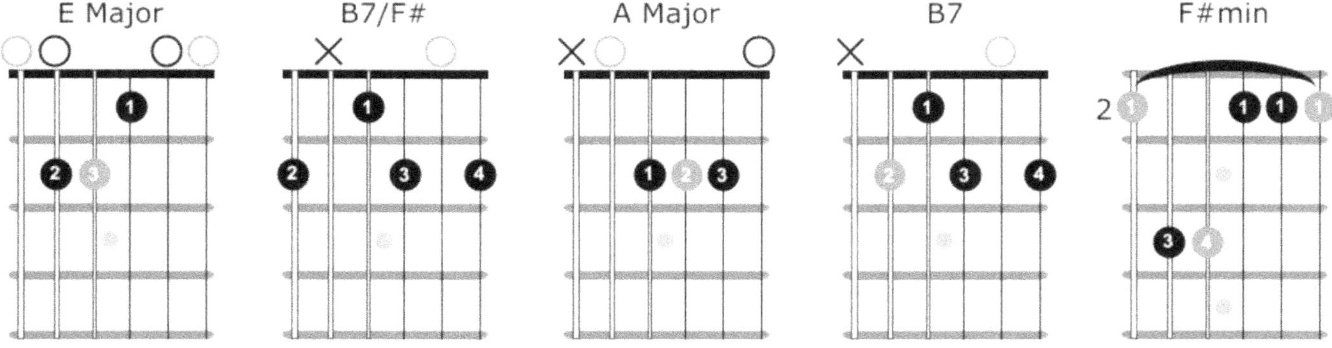

How Great Thou Art play along

bpm = 82

Abide With Me + Melody
Abide With Me Backing Track

Count of 3 then play

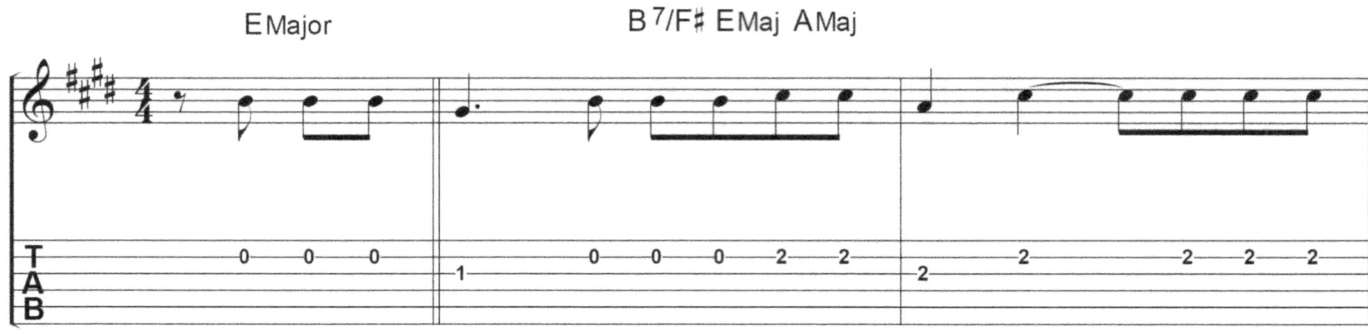

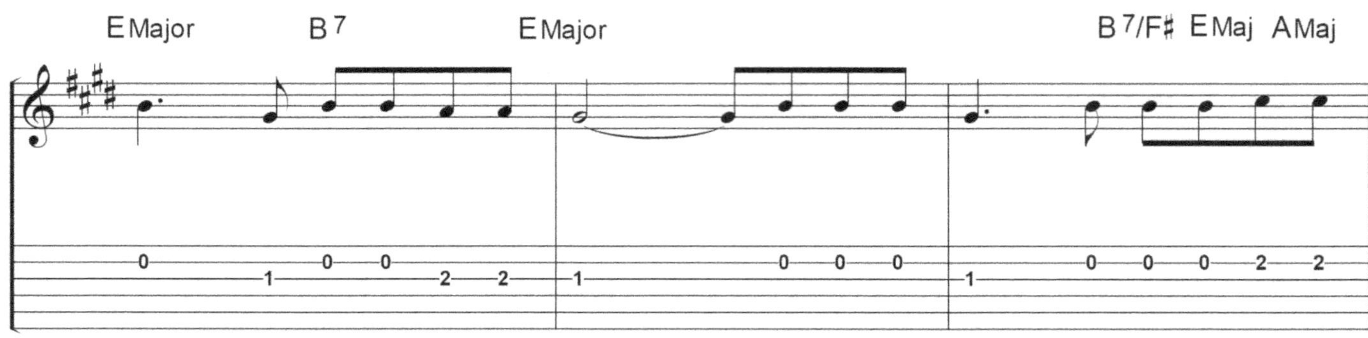

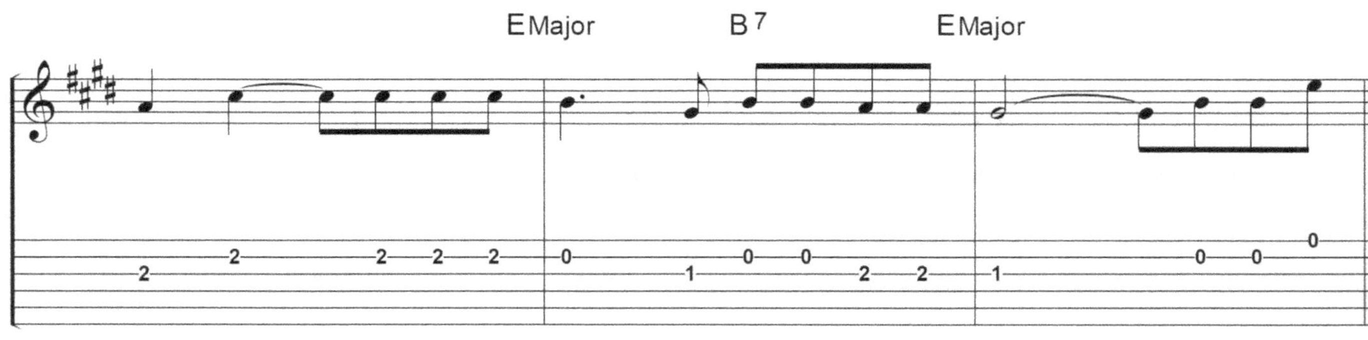

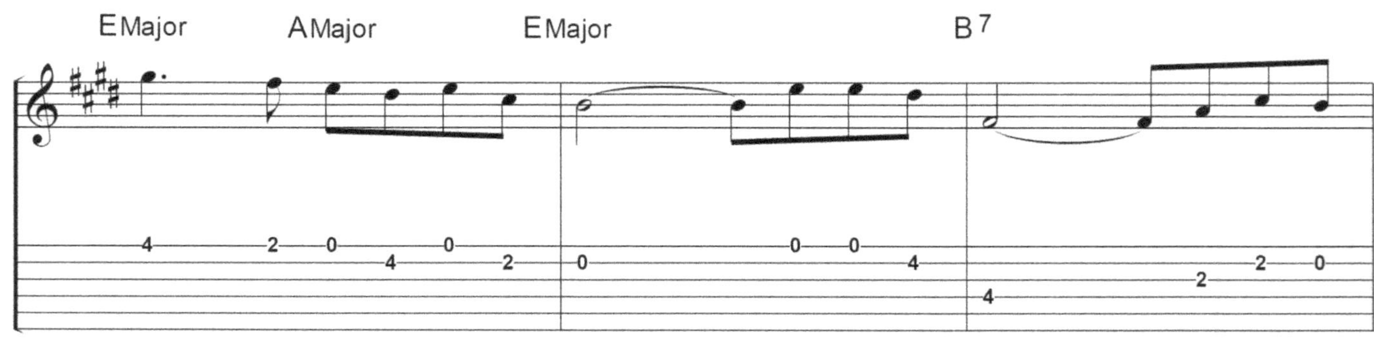

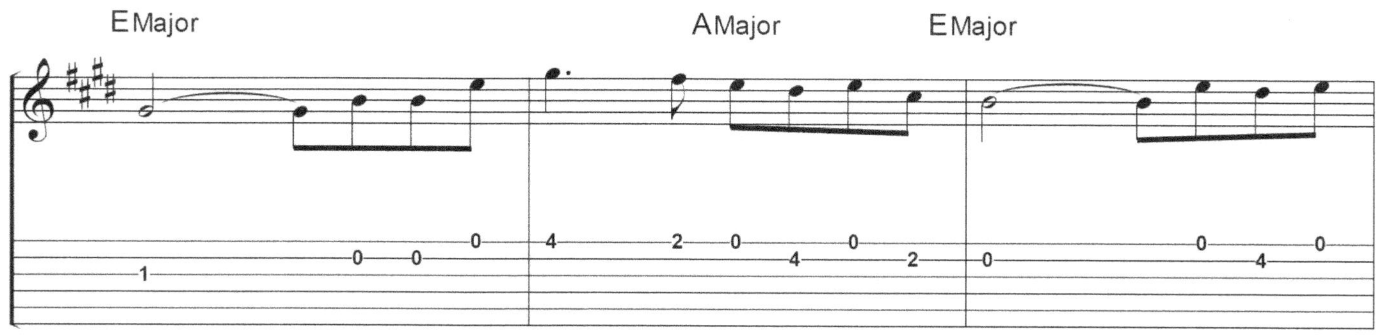

E Major
A Major
E Major

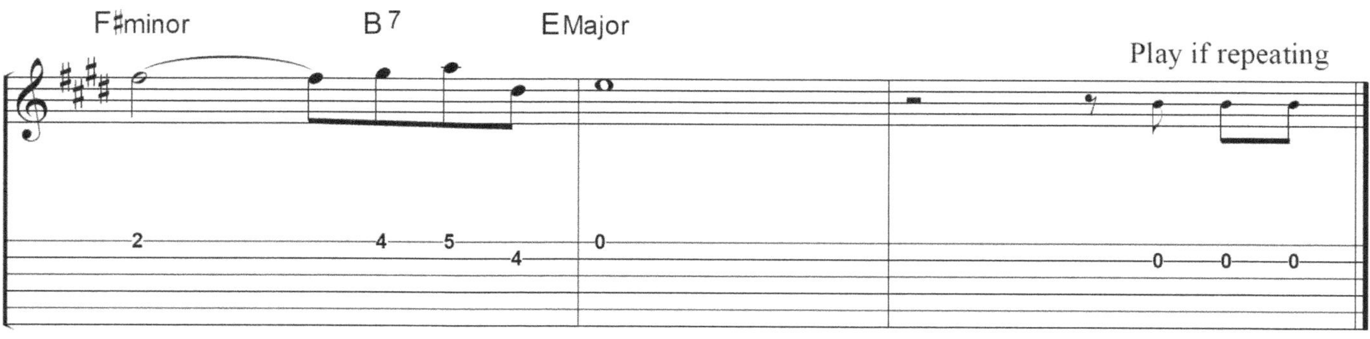

F#minor
B 7
E Major
Play if repeating

How Great Thou Art - Intermediate

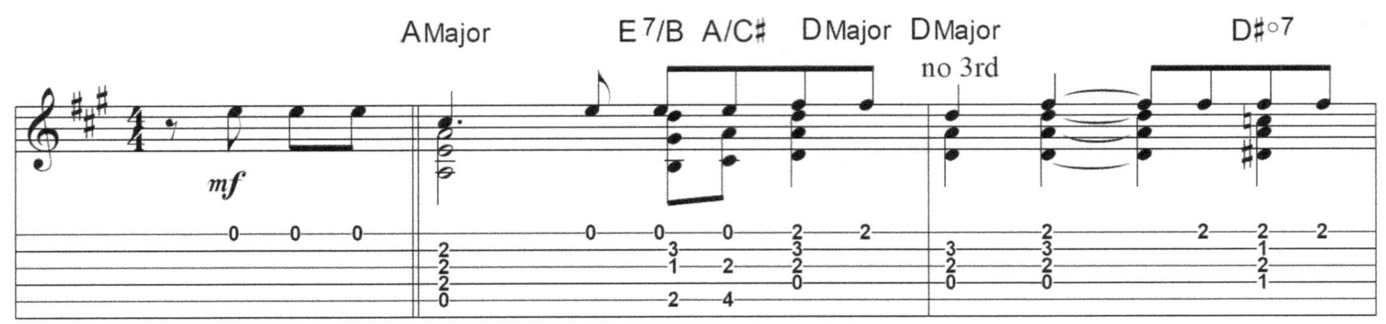

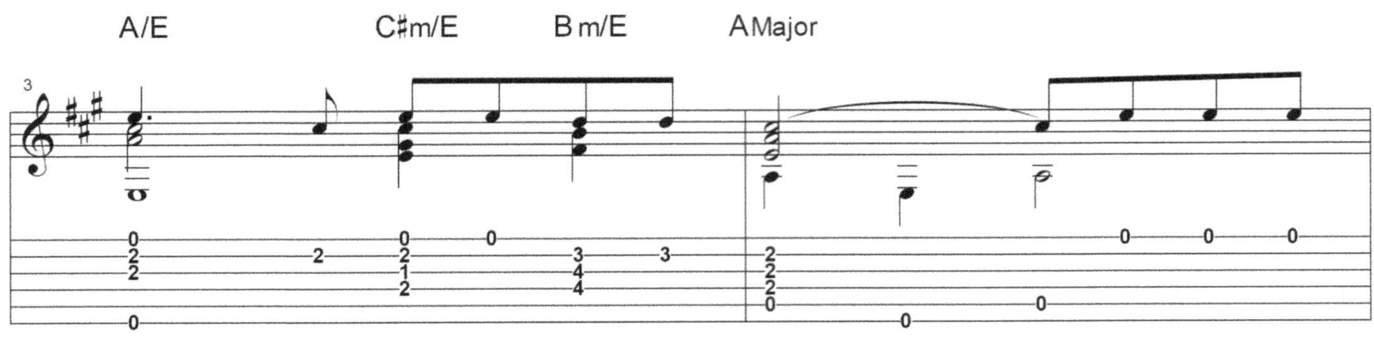

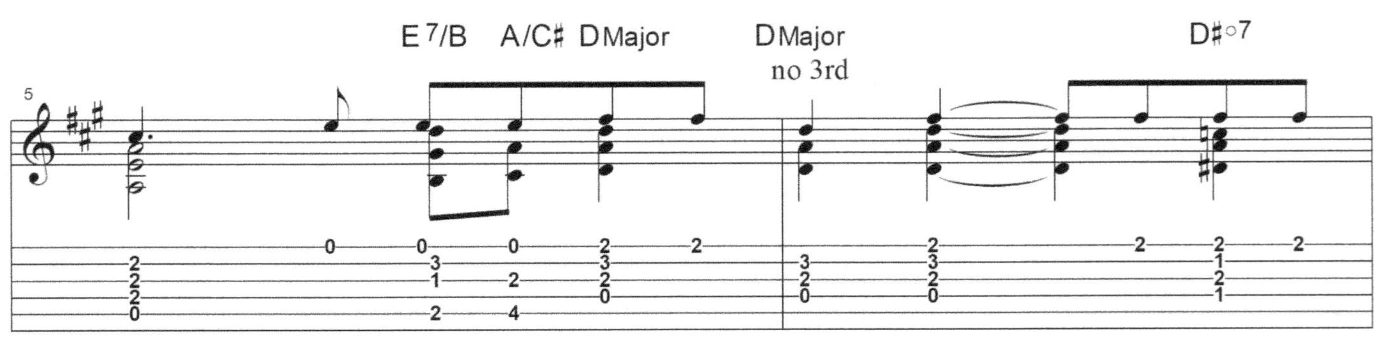

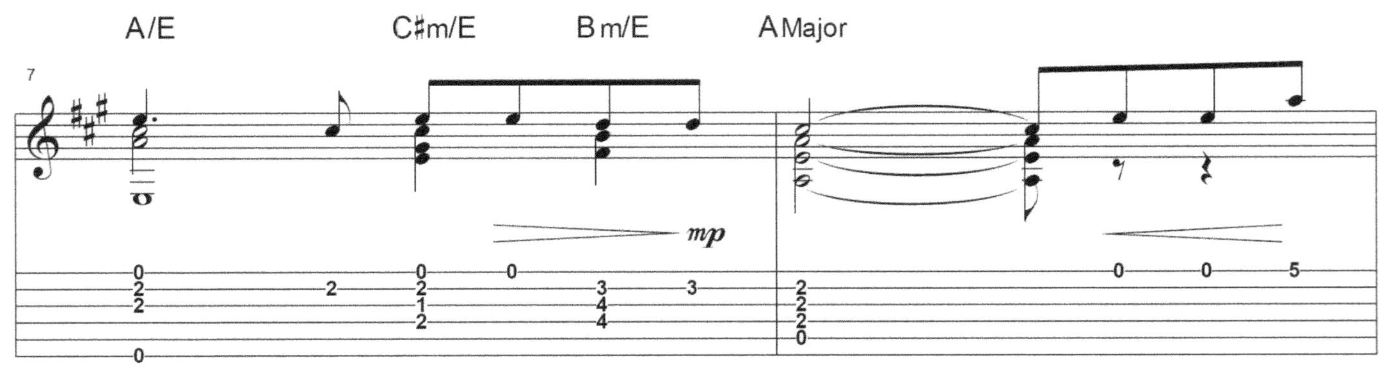

A 9 DMajor D○ DMajor AMajor A/E EMajor
9
mf
mp

E 7 D/E E 7 AMajor
11

A 9 DMajor D○ DMajor AMajor E 7/B A/C♯
13
mf

D 6 A 7/D Bminor E 7 AMajor
15
ritardando
mp
Fine

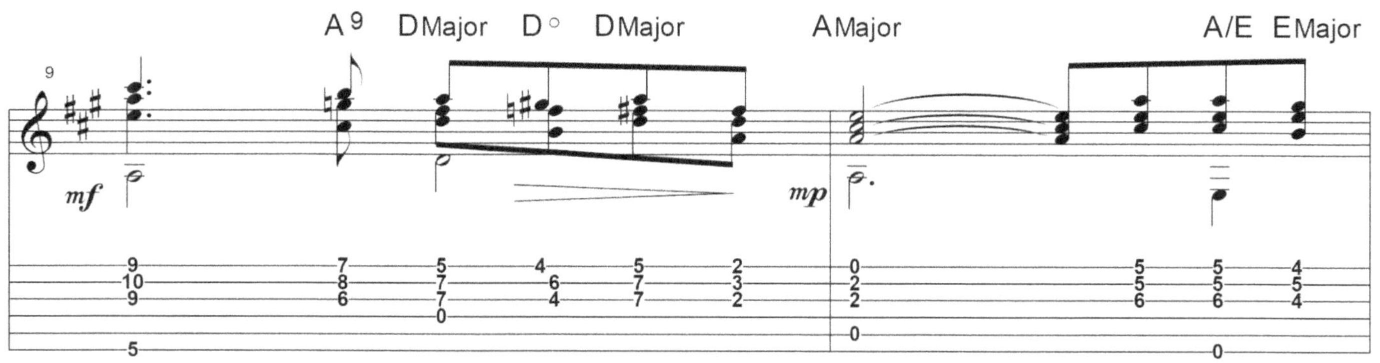

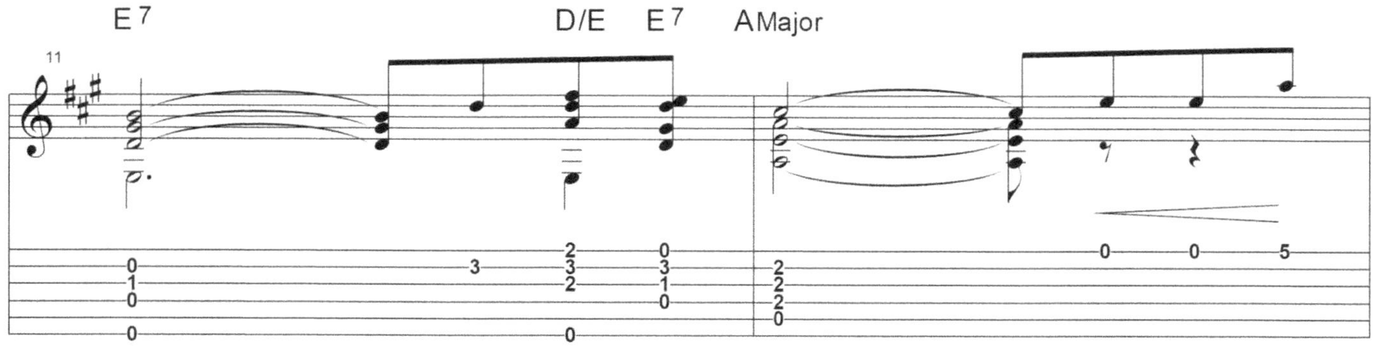

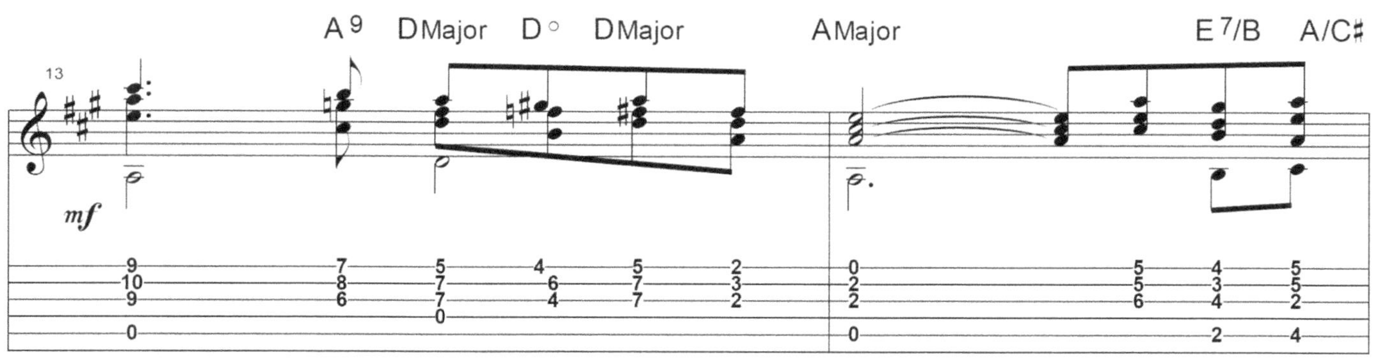

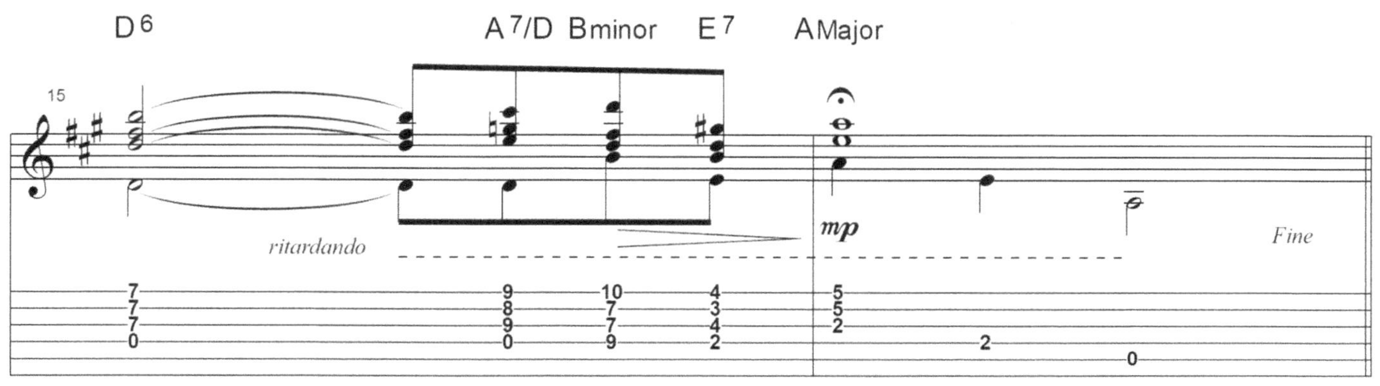

105

Chords: How Great Thou Art Intermediate

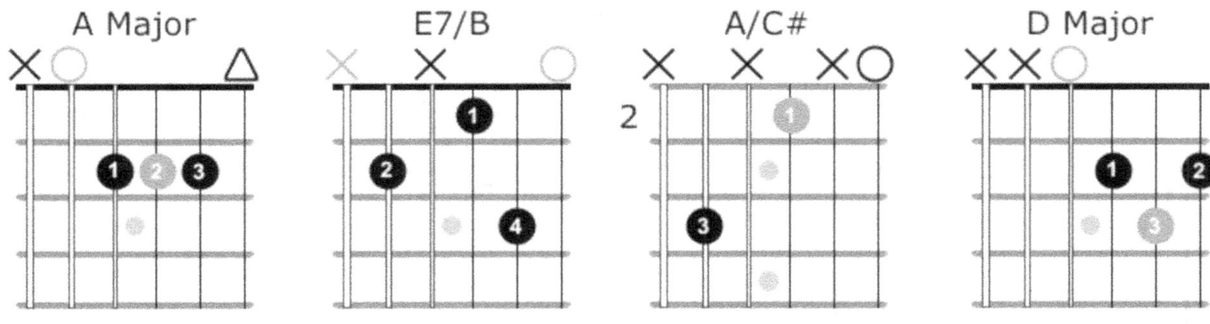

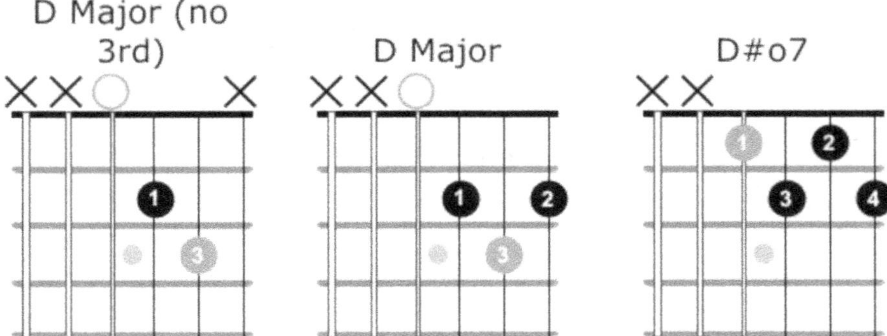

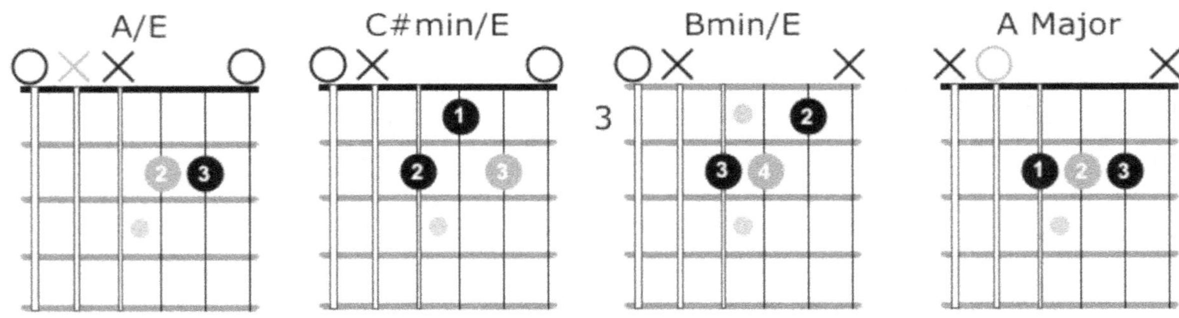

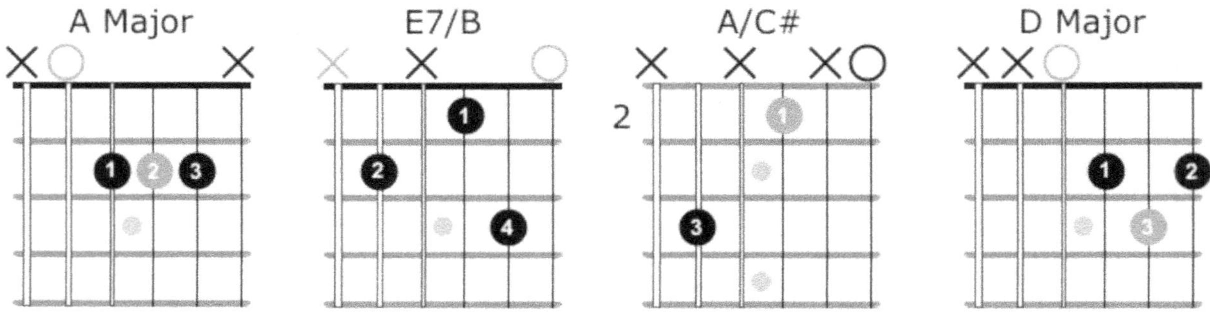

D Major

D Major

D#o7

Line 4

A/E

C#min/E

Bmin/E
3

A Major

Line 5

A Major
9

A9
6

D Major
5

Do
4

D Major
5

D Major

A Major

A Major
5

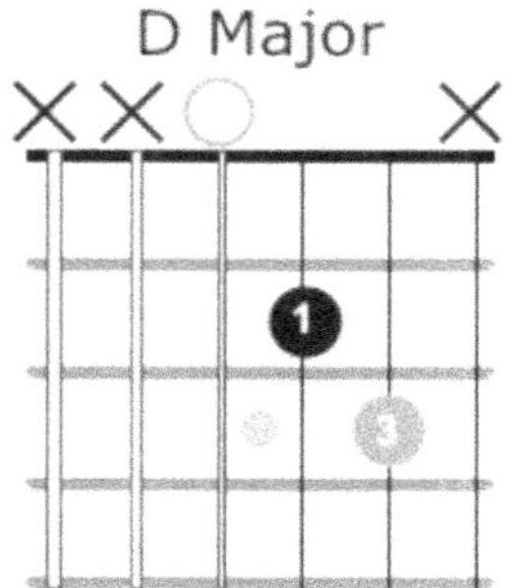

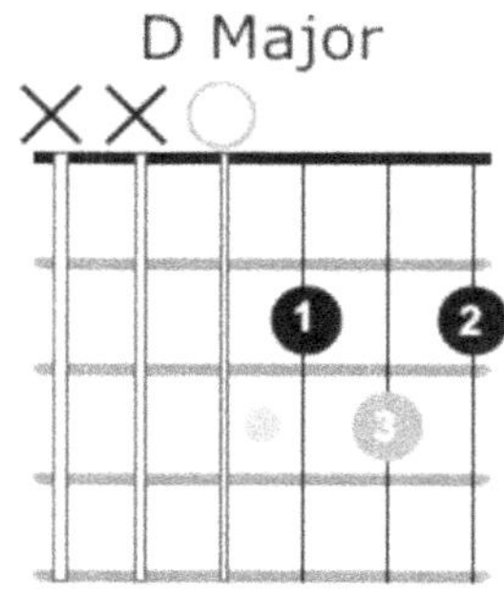

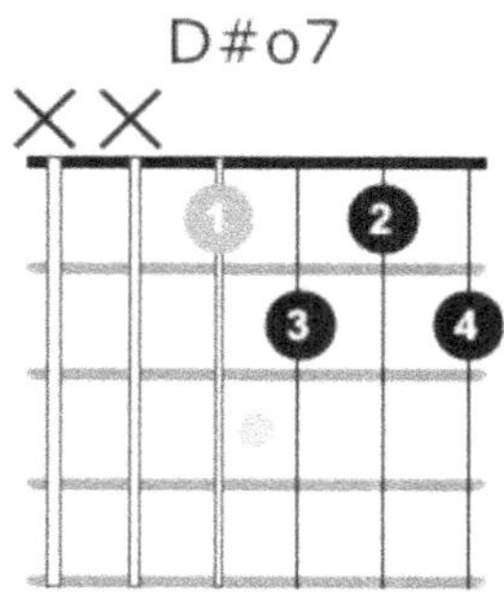

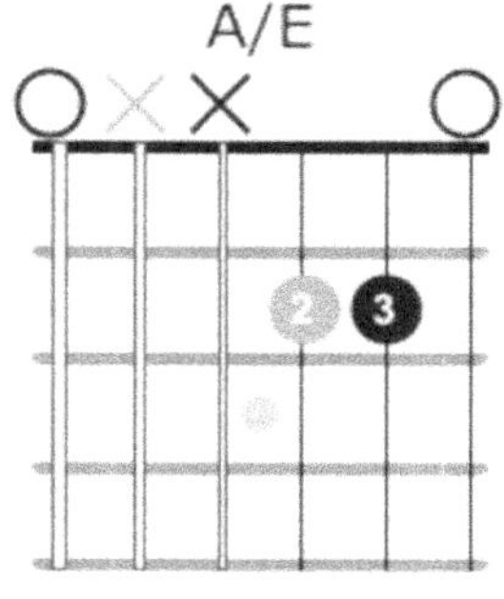

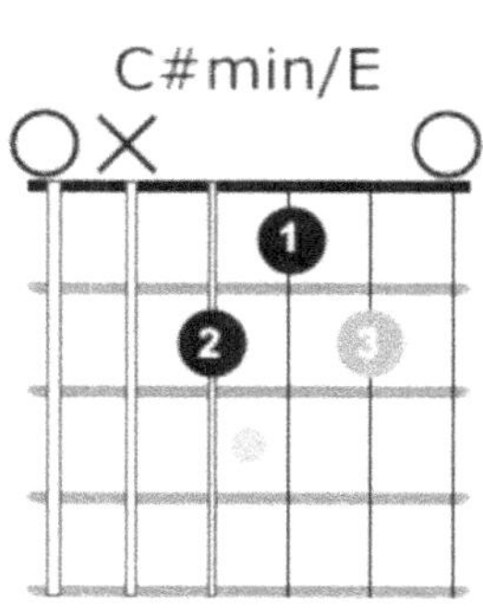

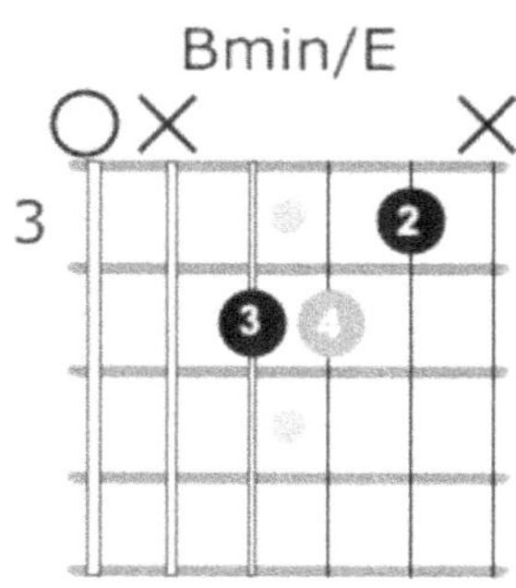

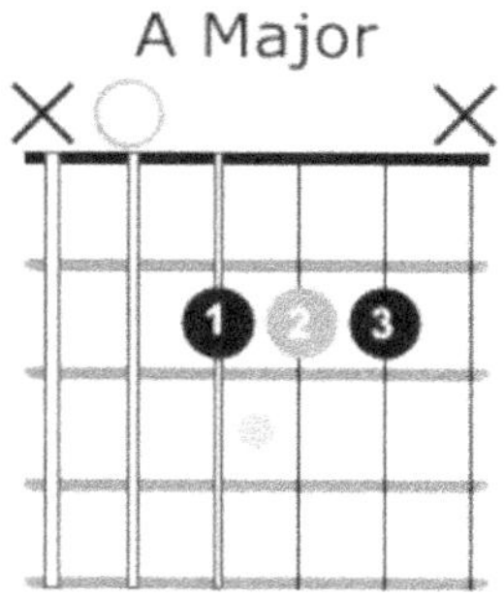

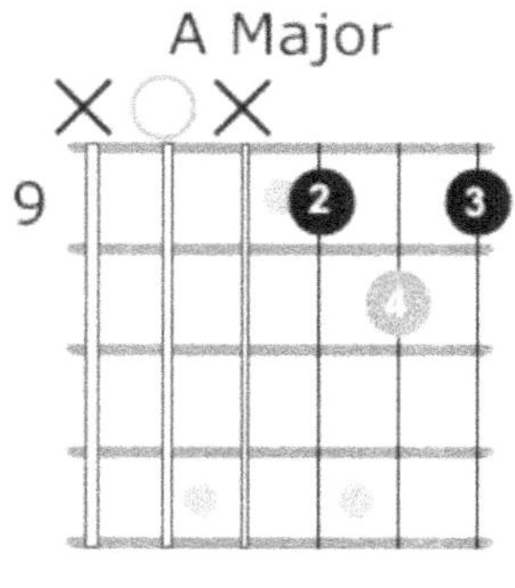

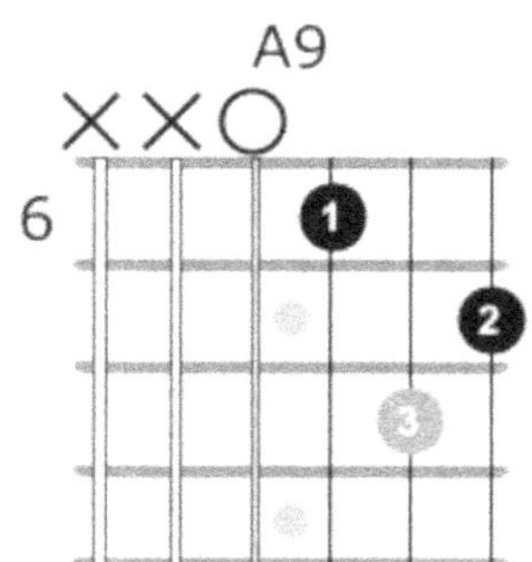

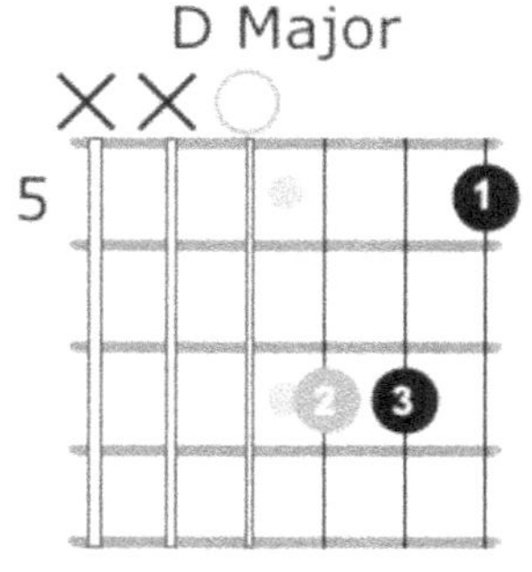

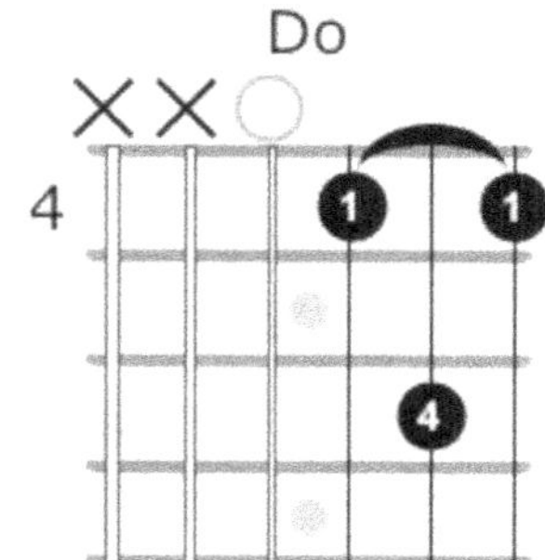

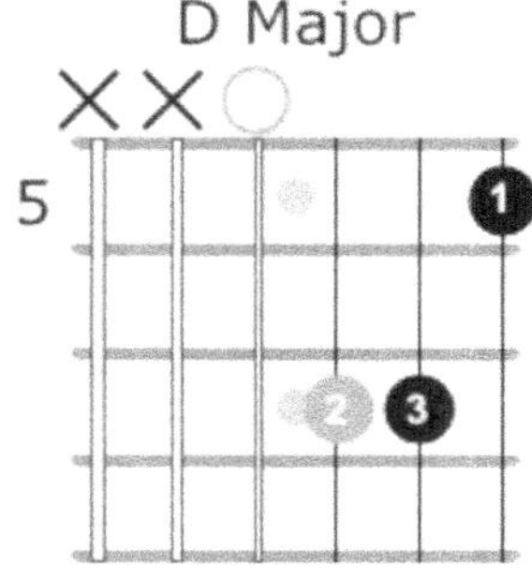

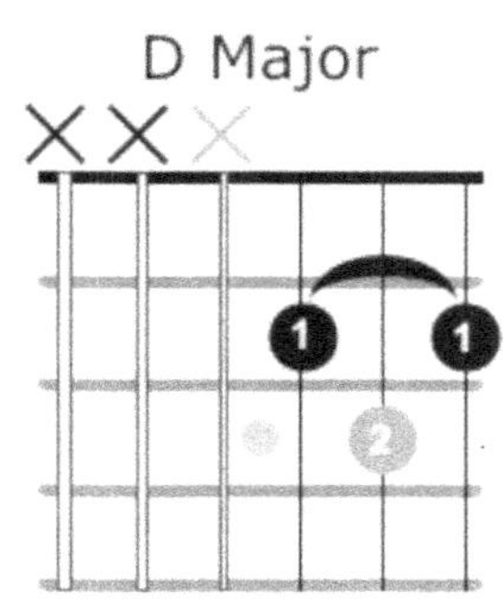

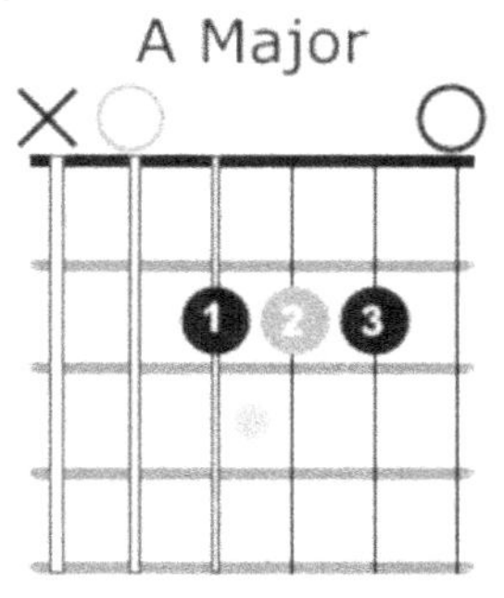

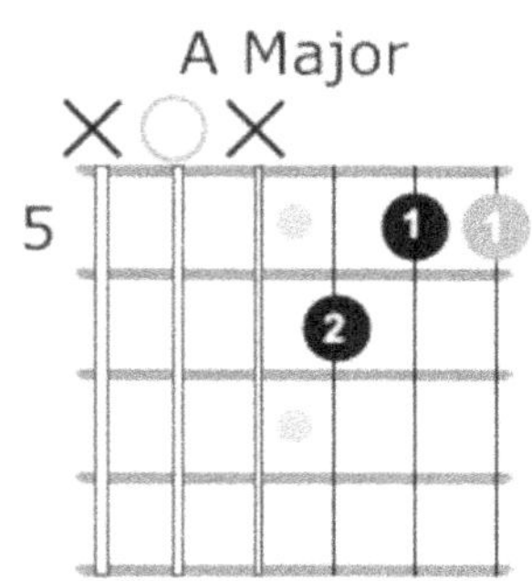

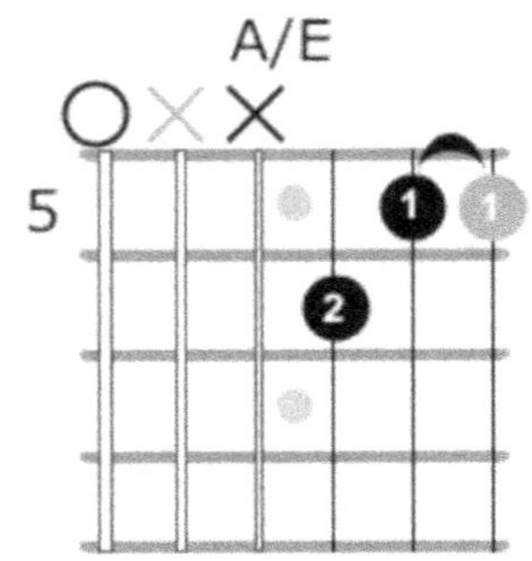

A/E

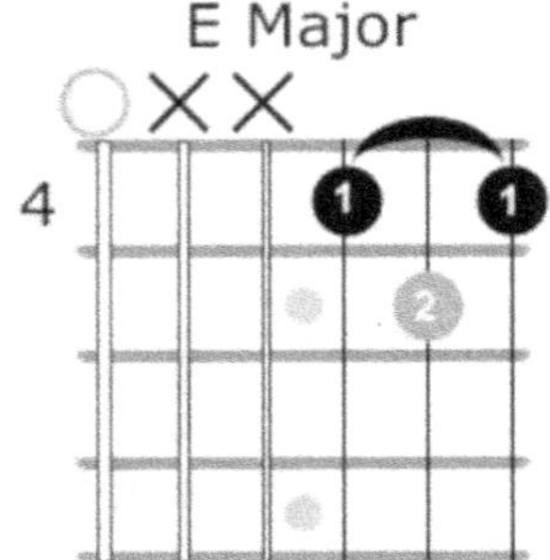

E Major

Line 6

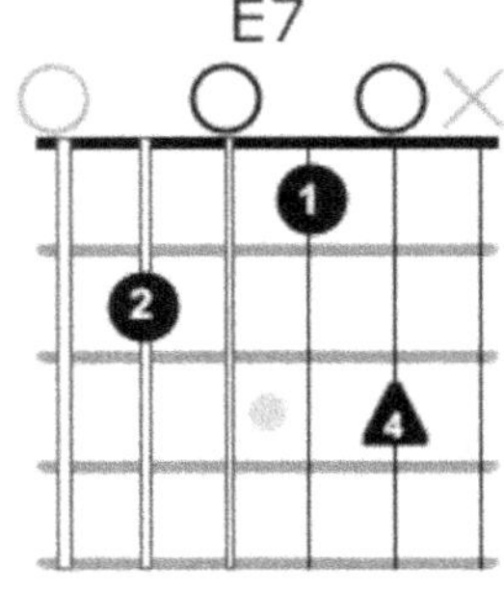

E7

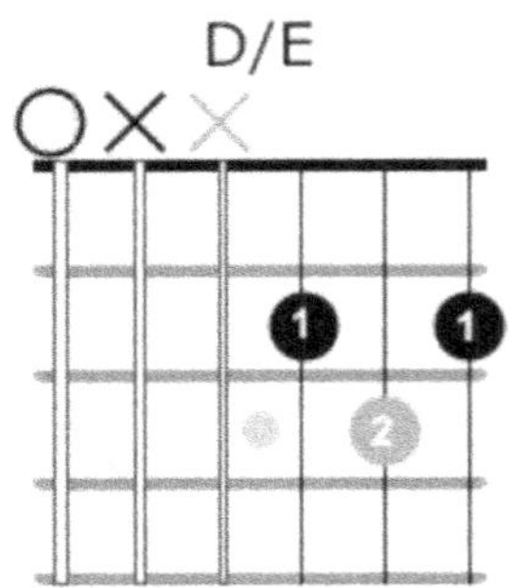

D/E

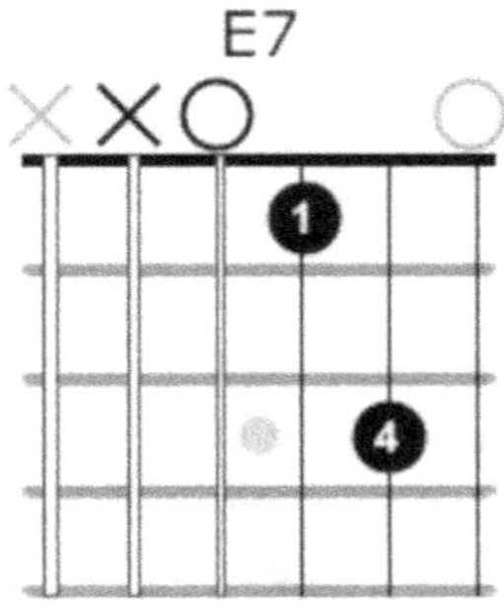

E7

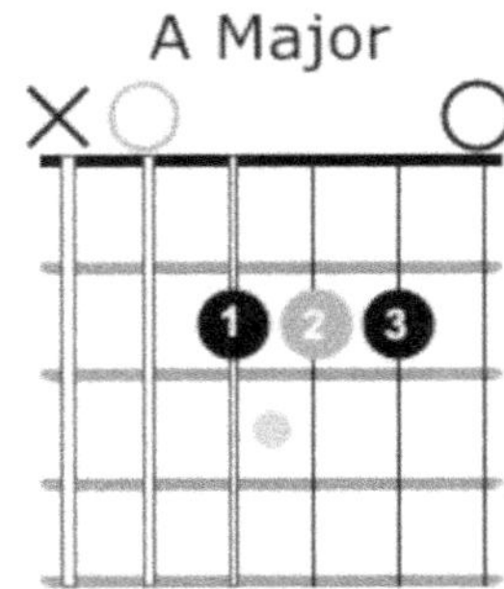

A Major

Line 7

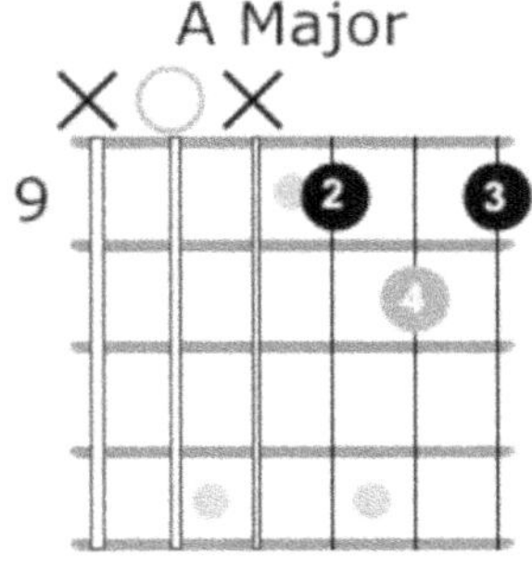

A Major

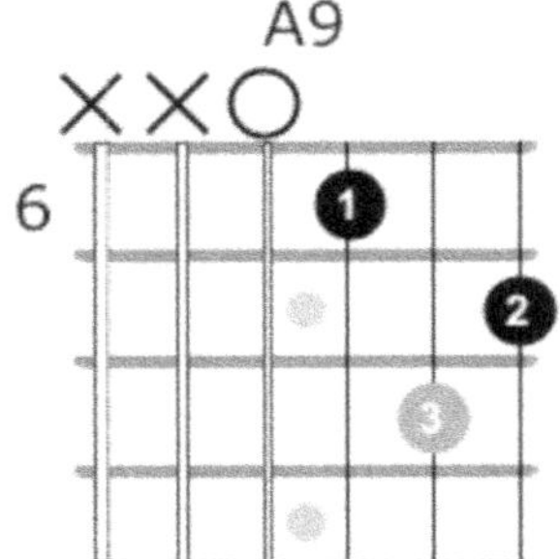

A9

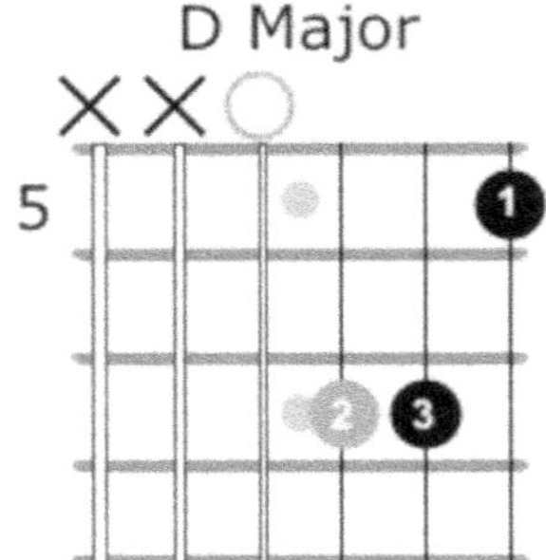

D Major

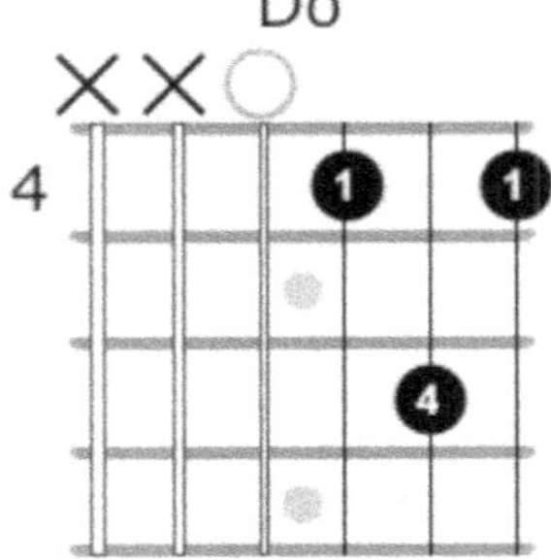

Do

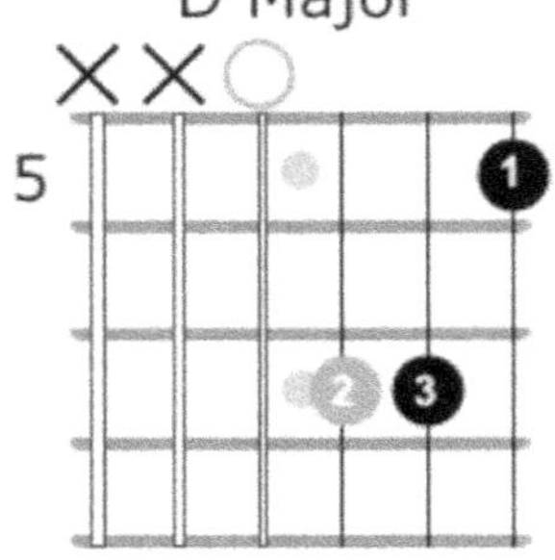

D Major

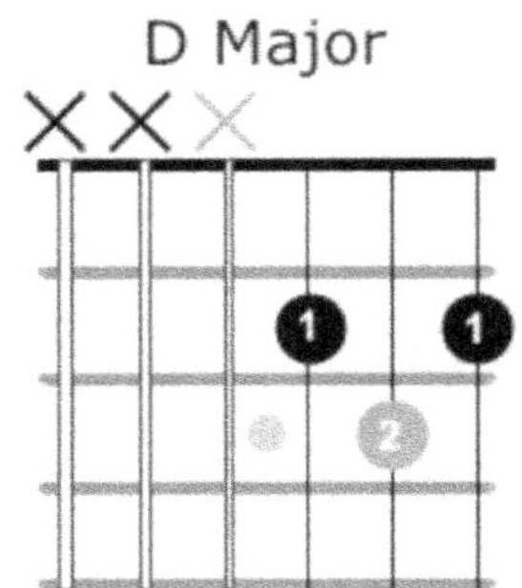

D Major

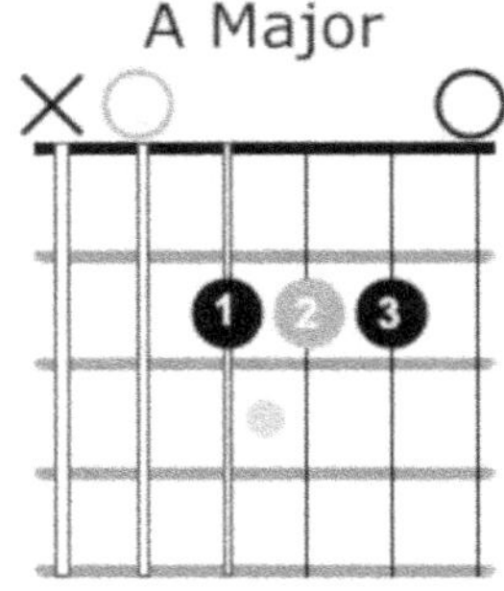

A Major

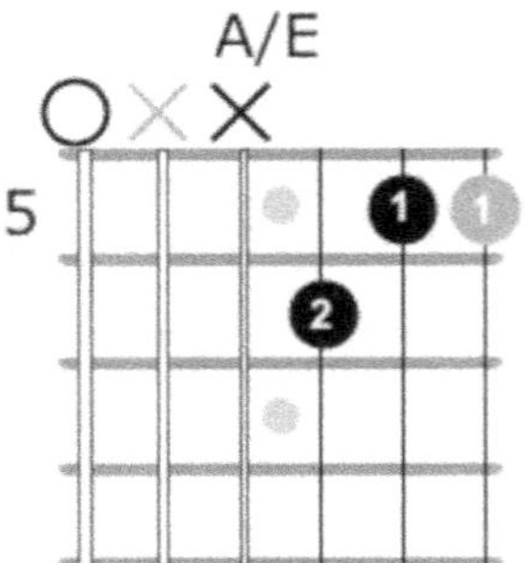

A/E

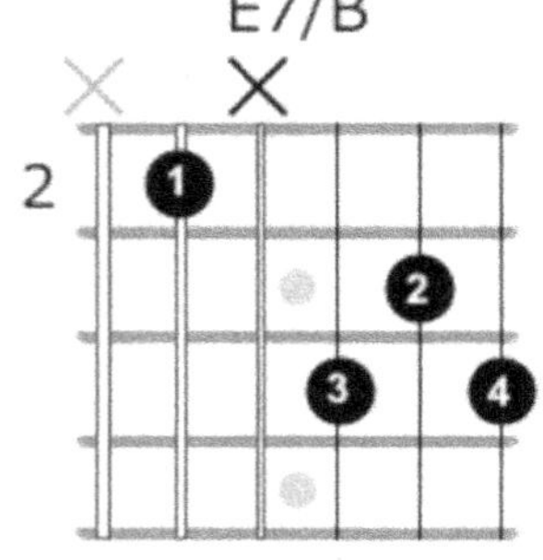

E7/B

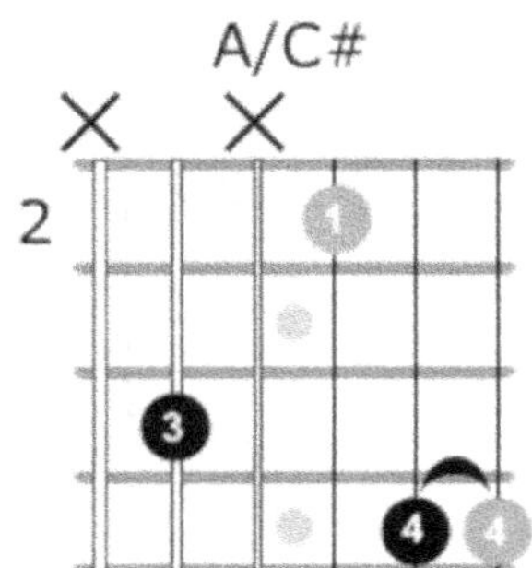

A/C#

108

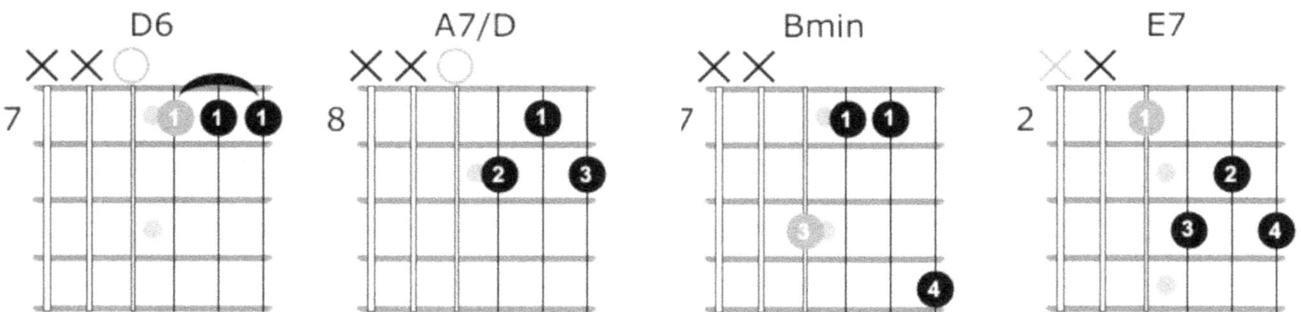

D6
A7/D
Bmin
E7

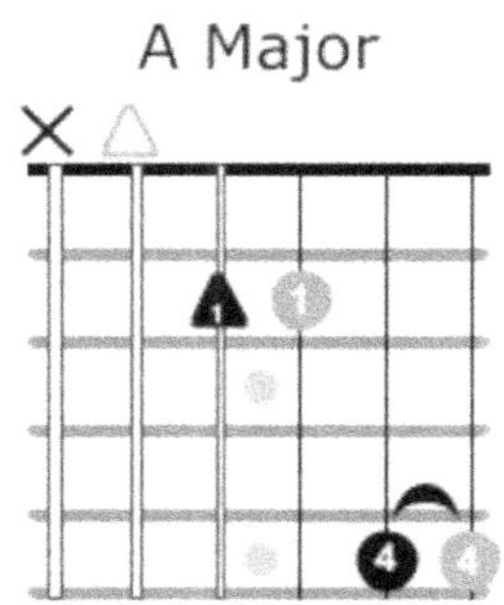

A Major

How Great Thou Art - Advanced

Arranged by
Ged Brockie

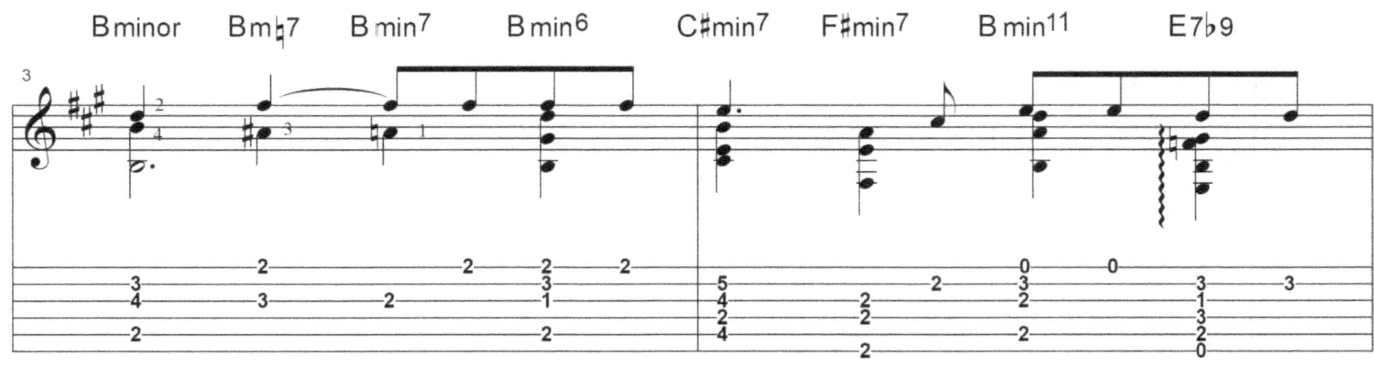

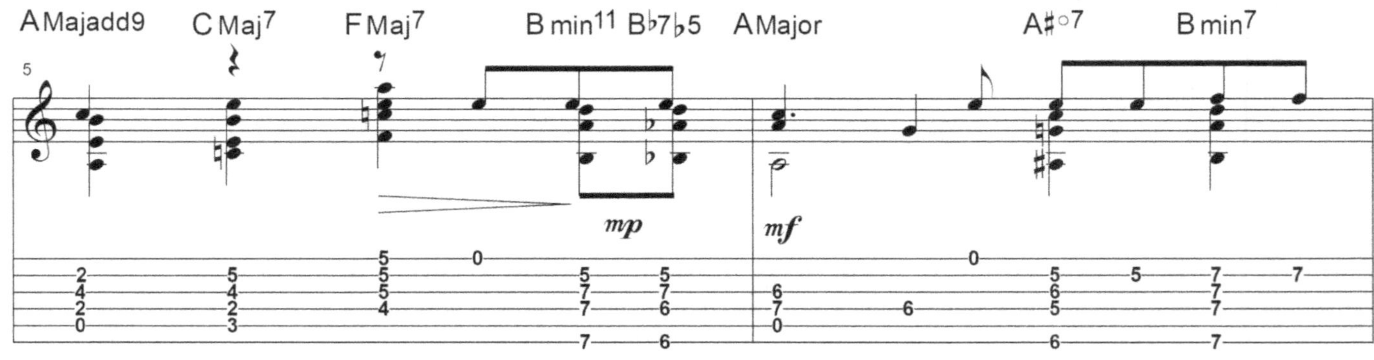

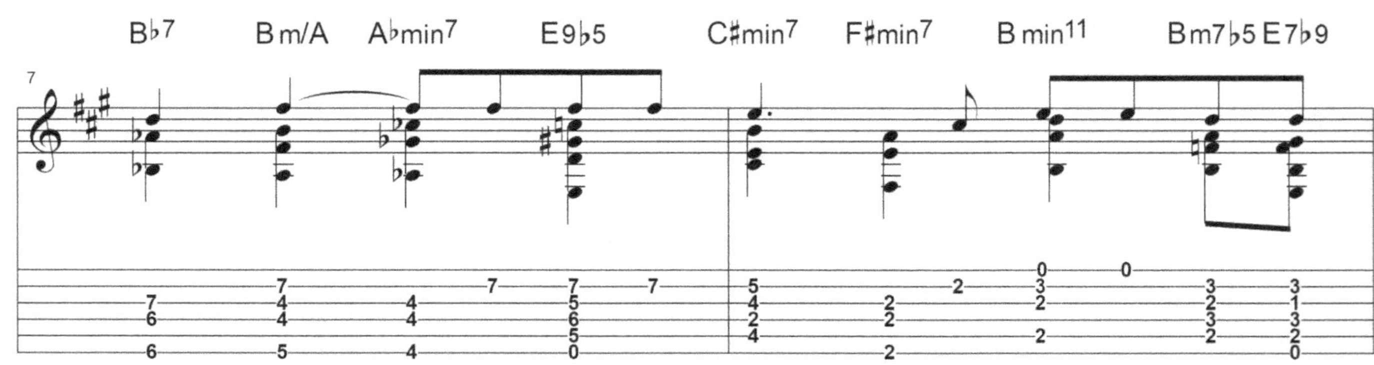

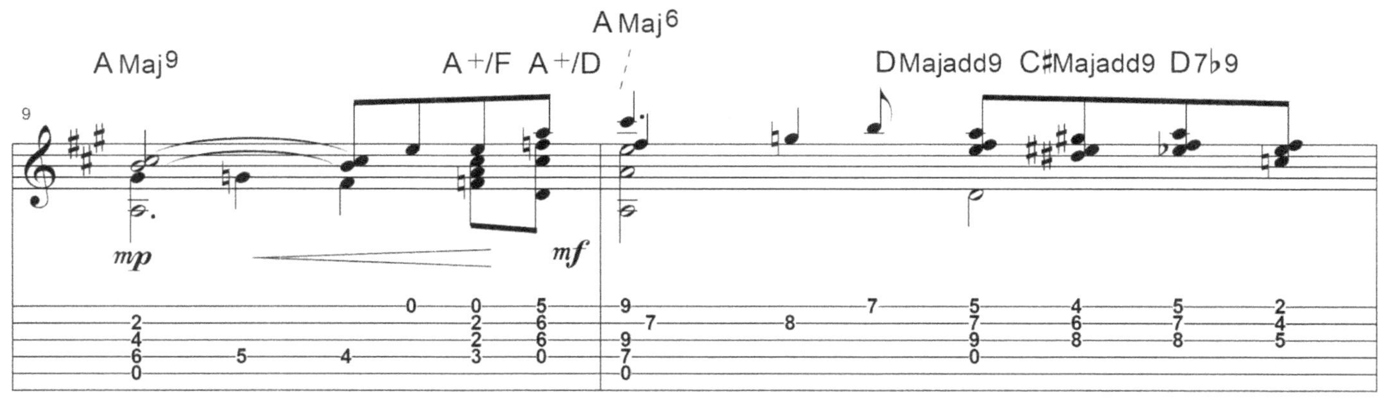

A Maj9
A+/F A+/D
A Maj6
D Majadd9 C#Majadd9 D7b9
9
mp
mf

A Majadd9
C#min7
F#min F#m7 F#min9 E7sus4
E7b9
E11
E7
(no 3rd)
11
mp

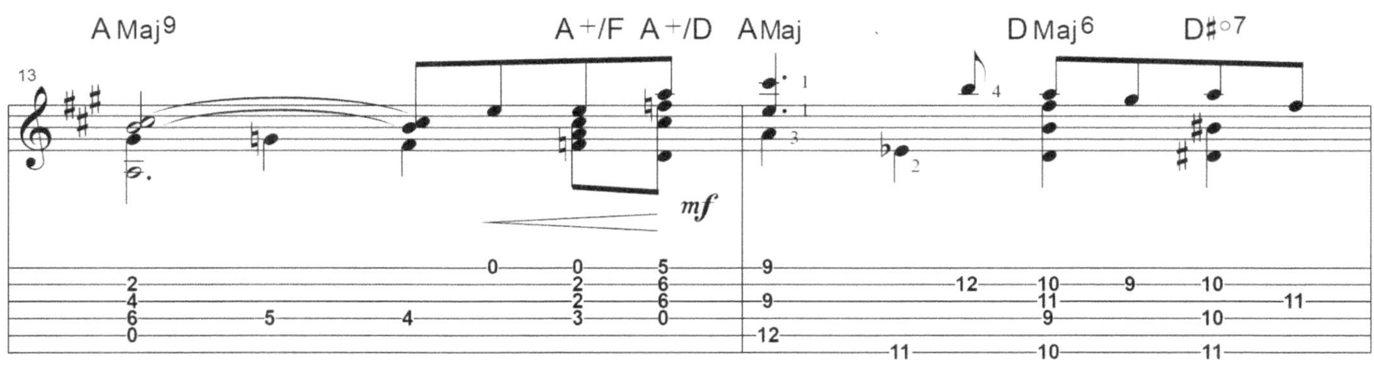

A Maj9
A+/F A+/D A Maj
D Maj6
D#°7
13
mf

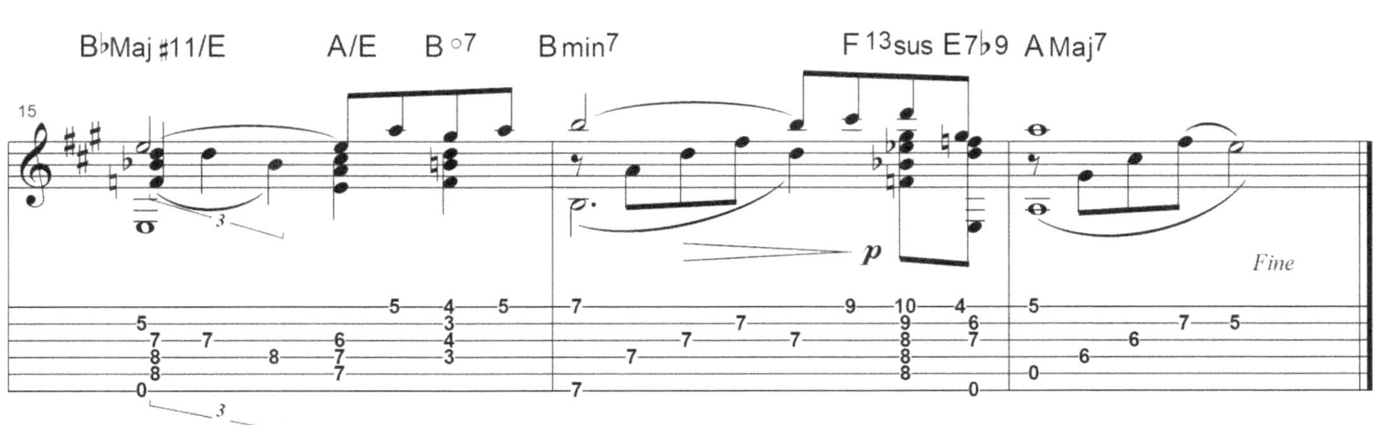

BbMaj#11/E
A/E B°7
B min7
F13sus E7b9 A Maj7
15
p
Fine

Chords: How Great Thou Art Advanced

Line 1

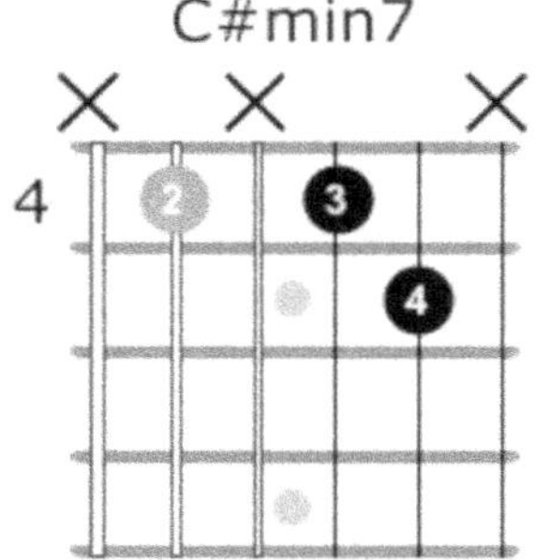

C#min7

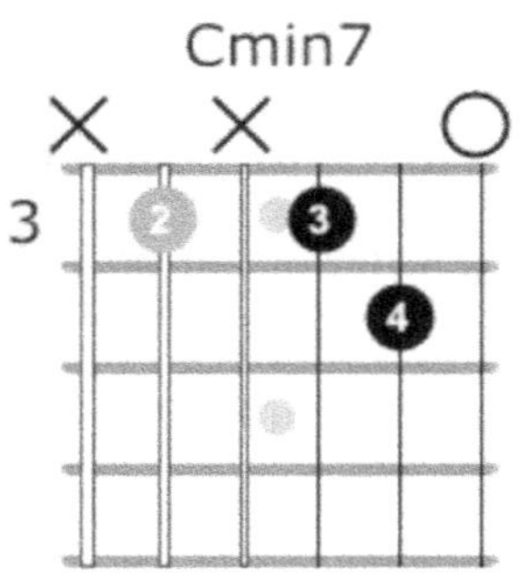

Cmin7

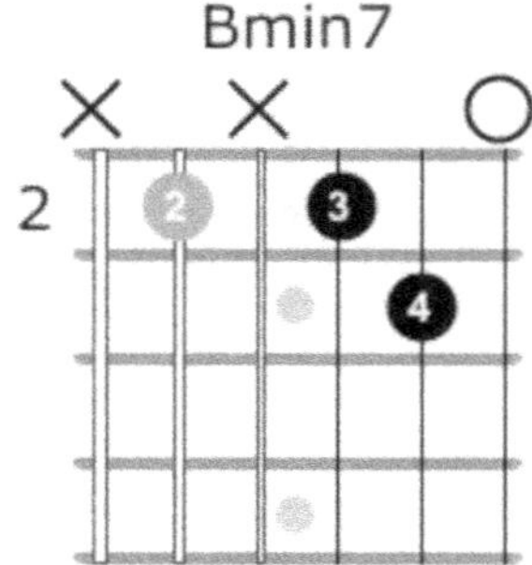

Bmin7

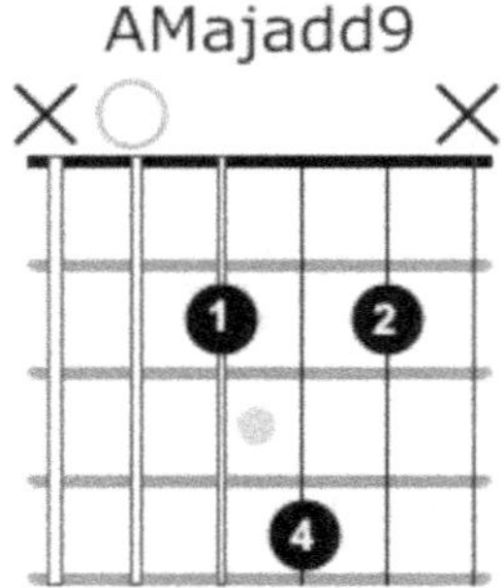

AMajadd9

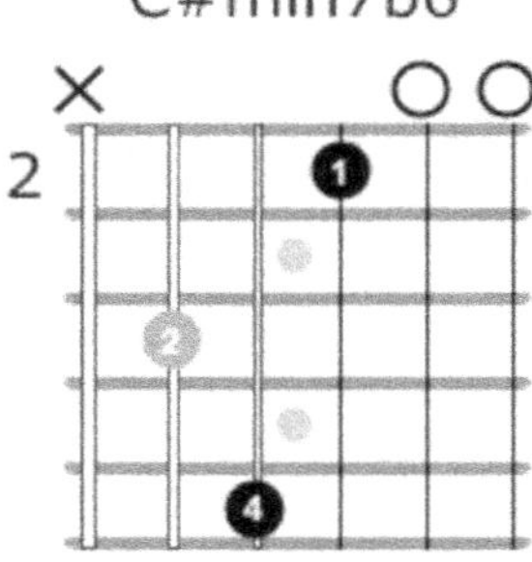

C#min7b6

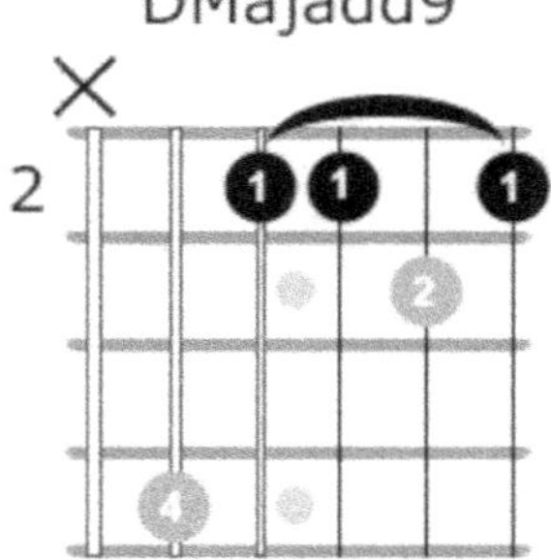

DMajadd9

Line 2

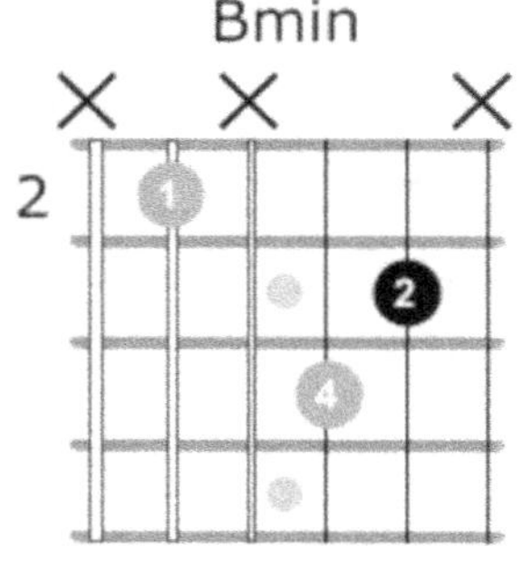

Bmin

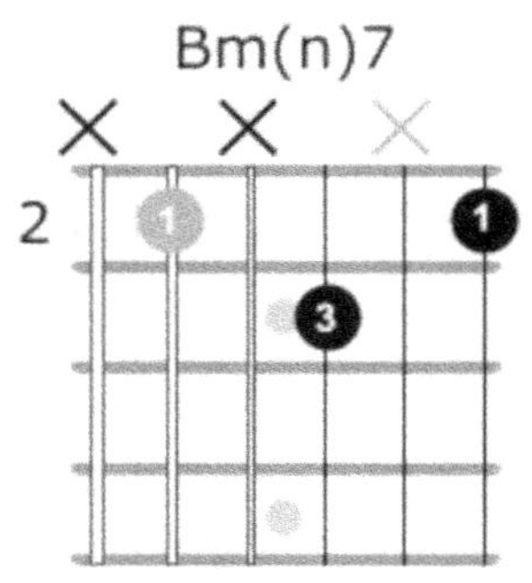

Bm(n)7

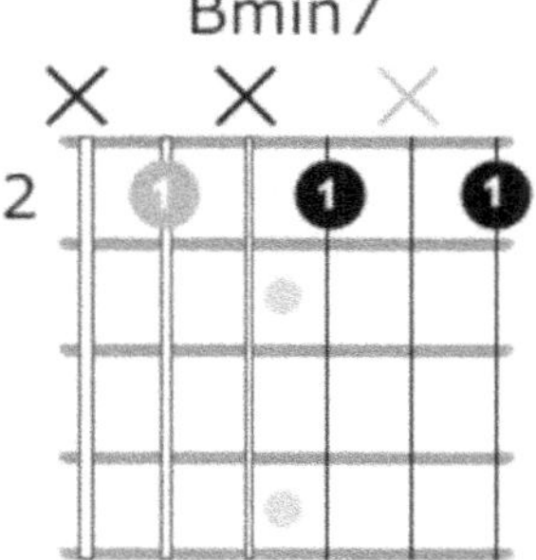

Bmin7

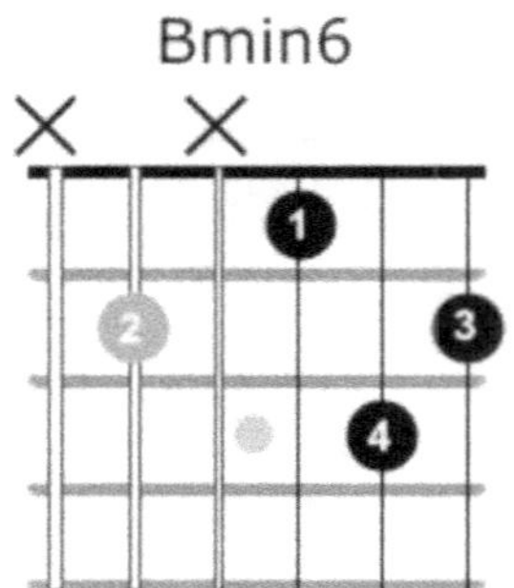

Bmin6

Note: n = natural

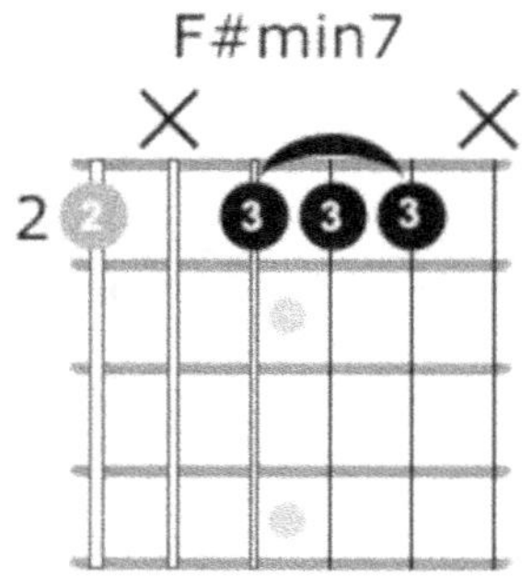

C#min7

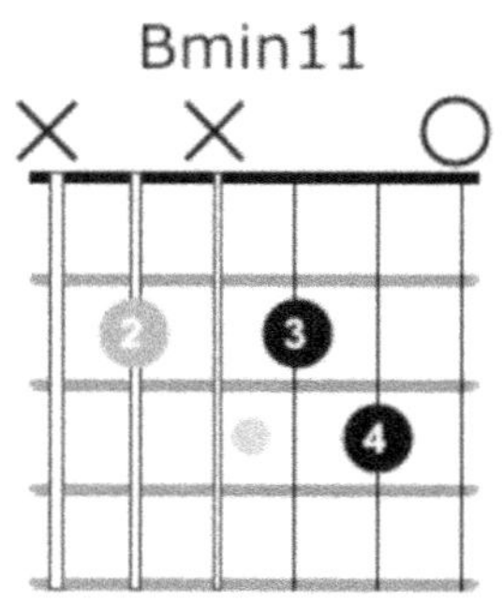

F#min7

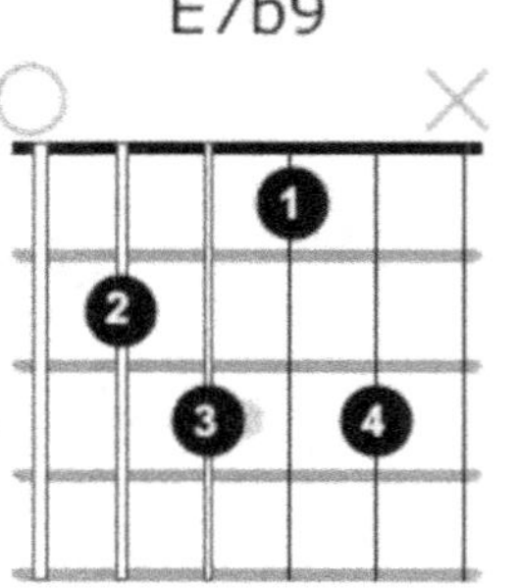

Bmin11

E7b9

Line 3

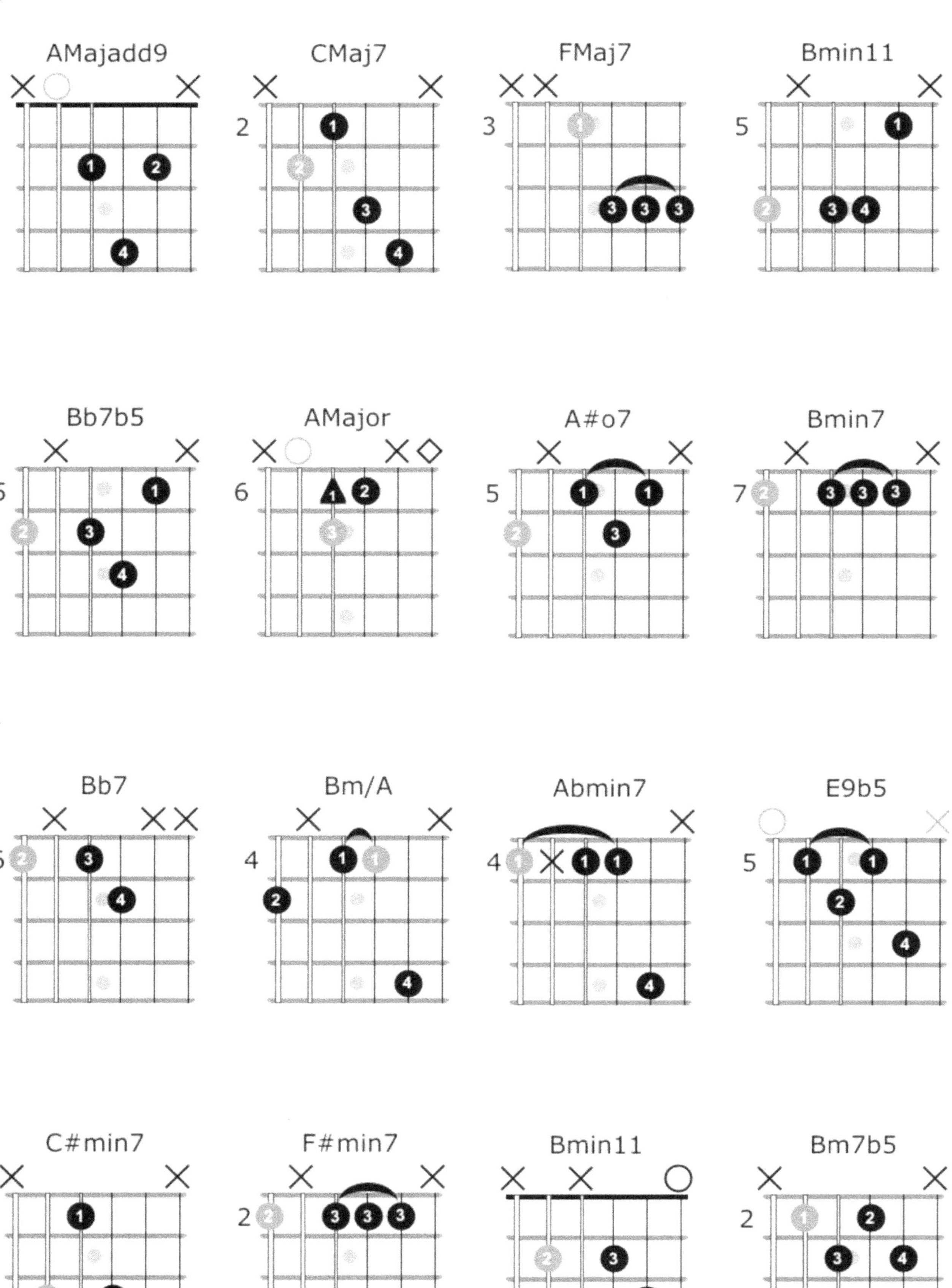

AMajadd9
CMaj7
FMaj7
Bmin11
Bb7b5
AMajor
A#o7
Bmin7
Line 4
Bb7
Bm/A
Abmin7
E9b5
C#min7
F#min7
Bmin11
Bm7b5

E7b9

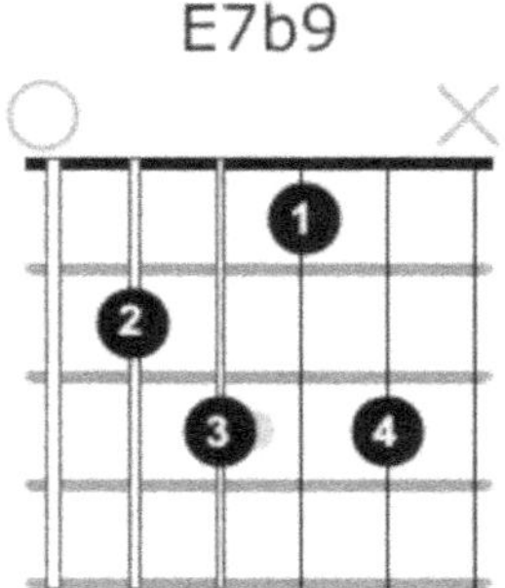

Line 5

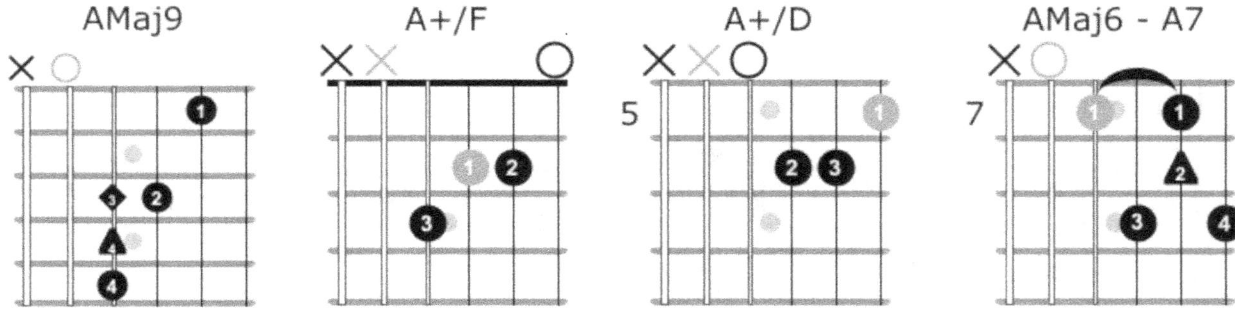

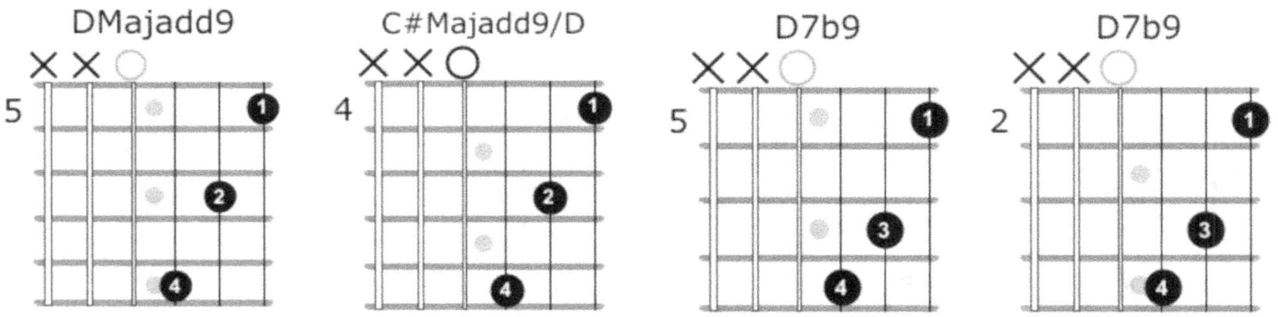

Line 6

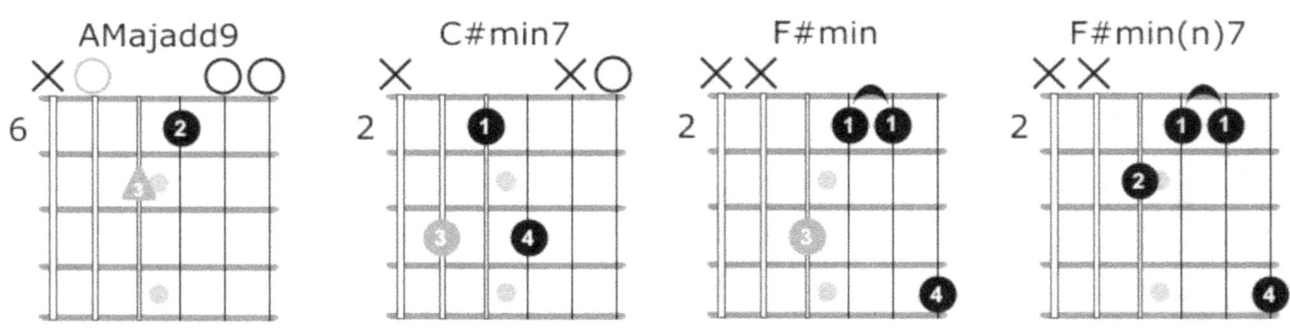

Note: n = natural

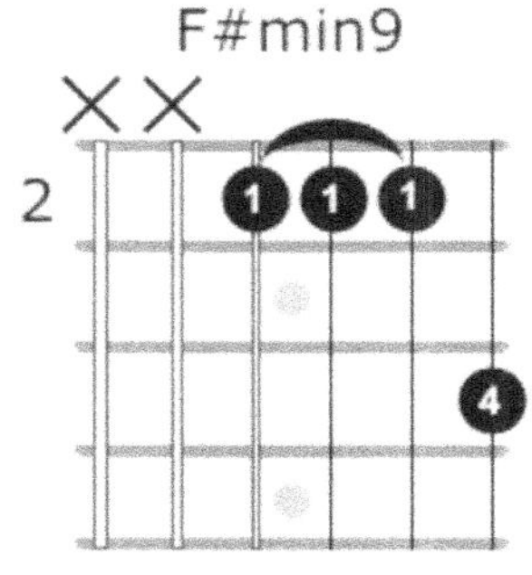

F#min9

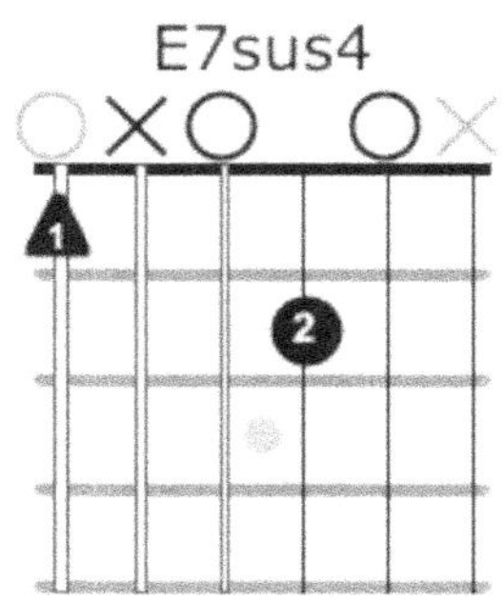

E7sus4

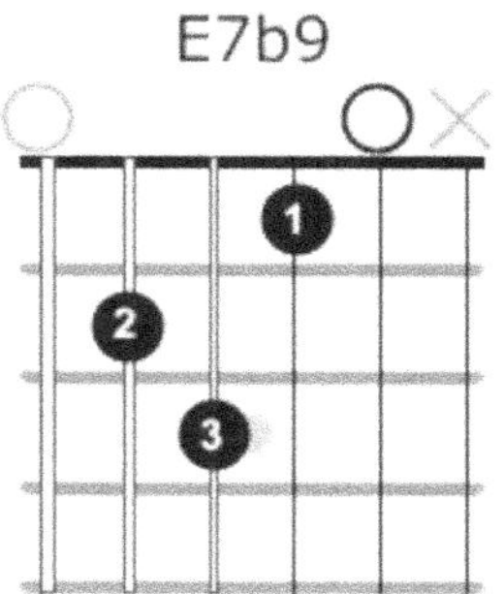

E7b9

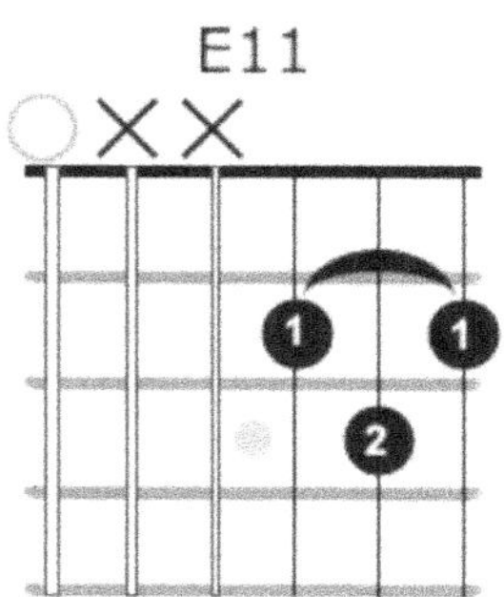

E11

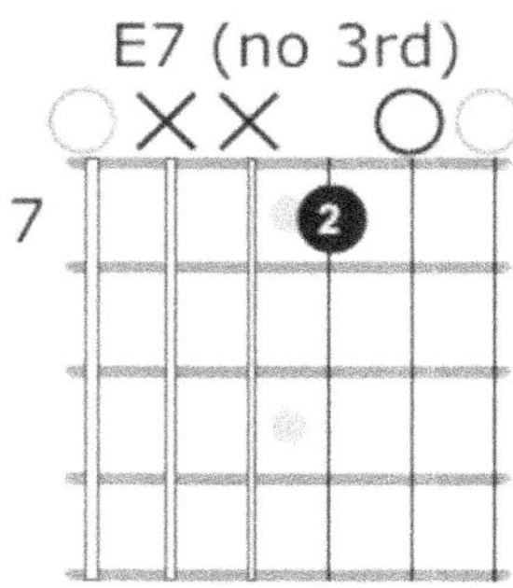

E7 (no 3rd)

Line 7

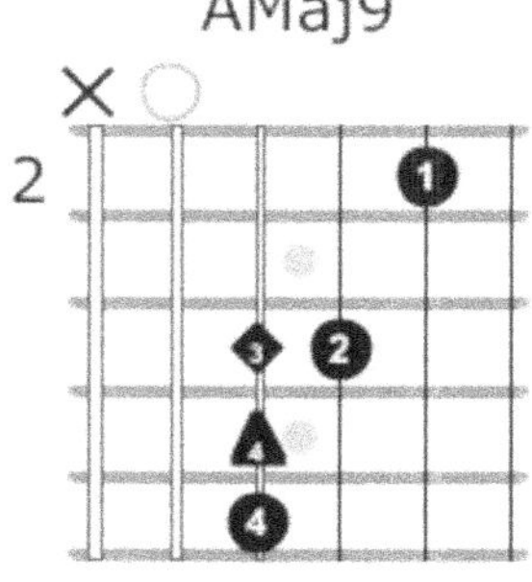

AMaj9

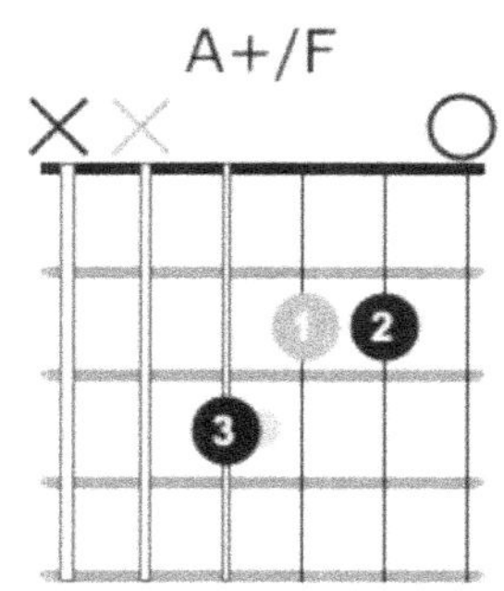

A+/F

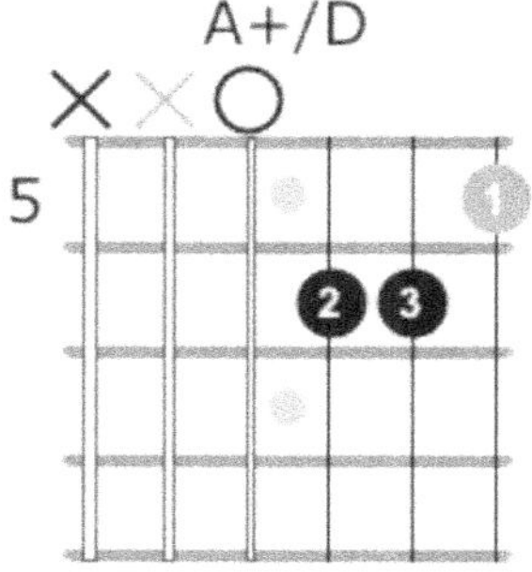

A+/D

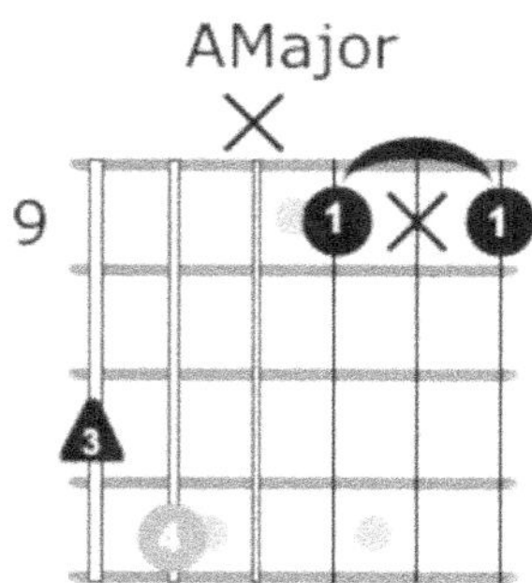

AMajor

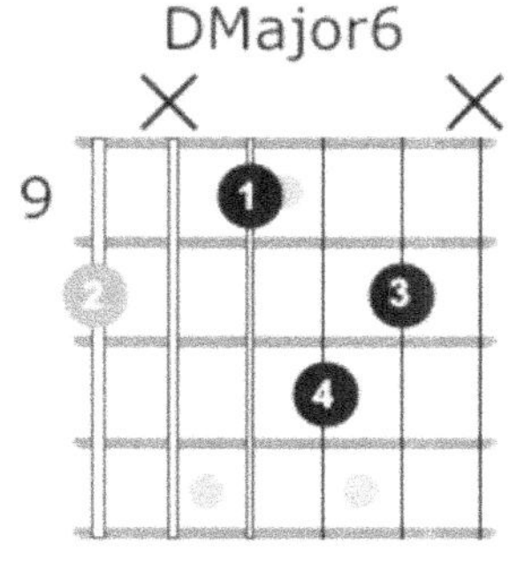

DMajor6

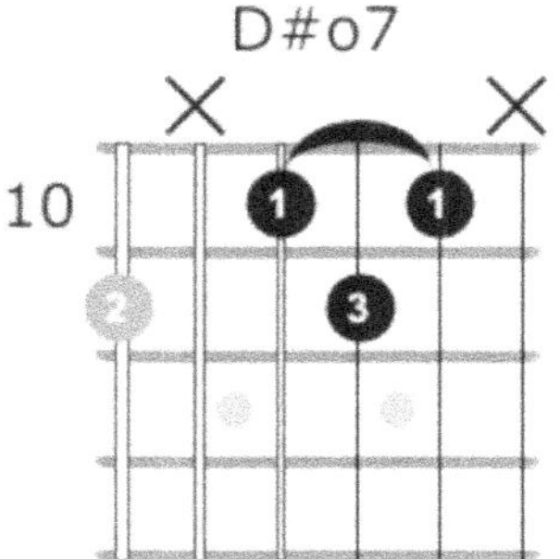

D#o7

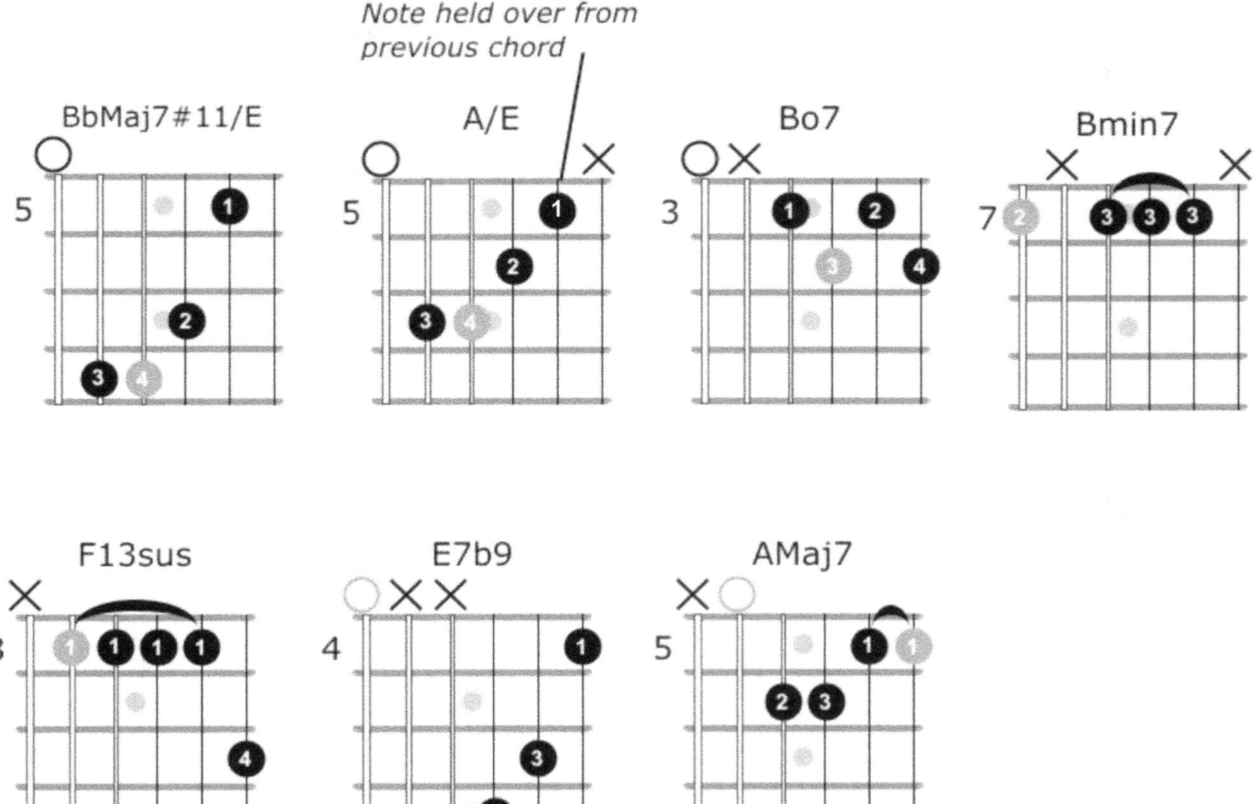

Note held over from previous chord
BbMaj7#11/E
A/E
Bo7
Bmin7
F13sus
E7b9
AMaj7

Hymn 7
O Love That Will Not Let Me Go

Resources

Performance of Intermediate version

Audio Talk through of Intermediate version

Performance of Advanced version

Audio Talk through of Advanced version

Use a QR code reader on your cell/mobile phone or tablet to view and listen to the files above. There's a large selection of completely free QR code reader apps available which work on all operating platforms.

To download all resources and other support files, follow the instructions on page 197 of this publication.

Hymn Notes - O Love That Will Not Let Me Go

George Matheson (1842 – 1906) waw born in Glasgow Scotland, and his life story certainly has a tinge of sadness attached to it. Engaged to be married aged twenty, his fiance, on being told he was going blind, withdrew from the marriage proposal. He never married.

This hymn was composed on the evening of his sister's marriage and one can't but consider these words in relation to his own life experience. The lines *"My heart restores its borrowed ray"* and *"I trace the rainbow through the rain"* are surely some of the most heartfelt words ever composed for a hymn. The word *"climb"* instead of trace as in *"...trace the rainbow"* was originally penned but the Church of Scotland intervened thinking it ridiculous that a rainbow could be climbed. Matheson was completely blind at this point...

Albert L. Peace   *George Matheson*

The music to accompany the lyrics was quickly composed by English organist and composer Albert L. Peace (1844 – 1912). Peace had recently been the organist at the university of Glasgow. A prolific and talented musician, he had eighty one works published and played throughout the United Kingdom.

Lyrics

Verse 1

O Love that will not let me go

I rest my weary soul in thee

I give thee back the life I owe

That in thine ocean depths its flow

May richer fuller be

Verse 2

O Light that foll'west all my way

I yield my flick'ring torch to thee

My heart restores its borrowed ray

That in thy sunshine's blaze its day

May brighter fairer be

Verse 3

O Joy that seekest me through pain

I cannot close my heart to thee

I trace the rainbow through the rain

And feel the promise is not vain

That morn shall tearless be

Verse 4

O Cross that liftest up my head

I dare not ask to fly from thee

I lay in dust life's glory dead

And from the ground there blossoms red

Life that shall endless be

O Love That Will Not Let Me Go - Starter

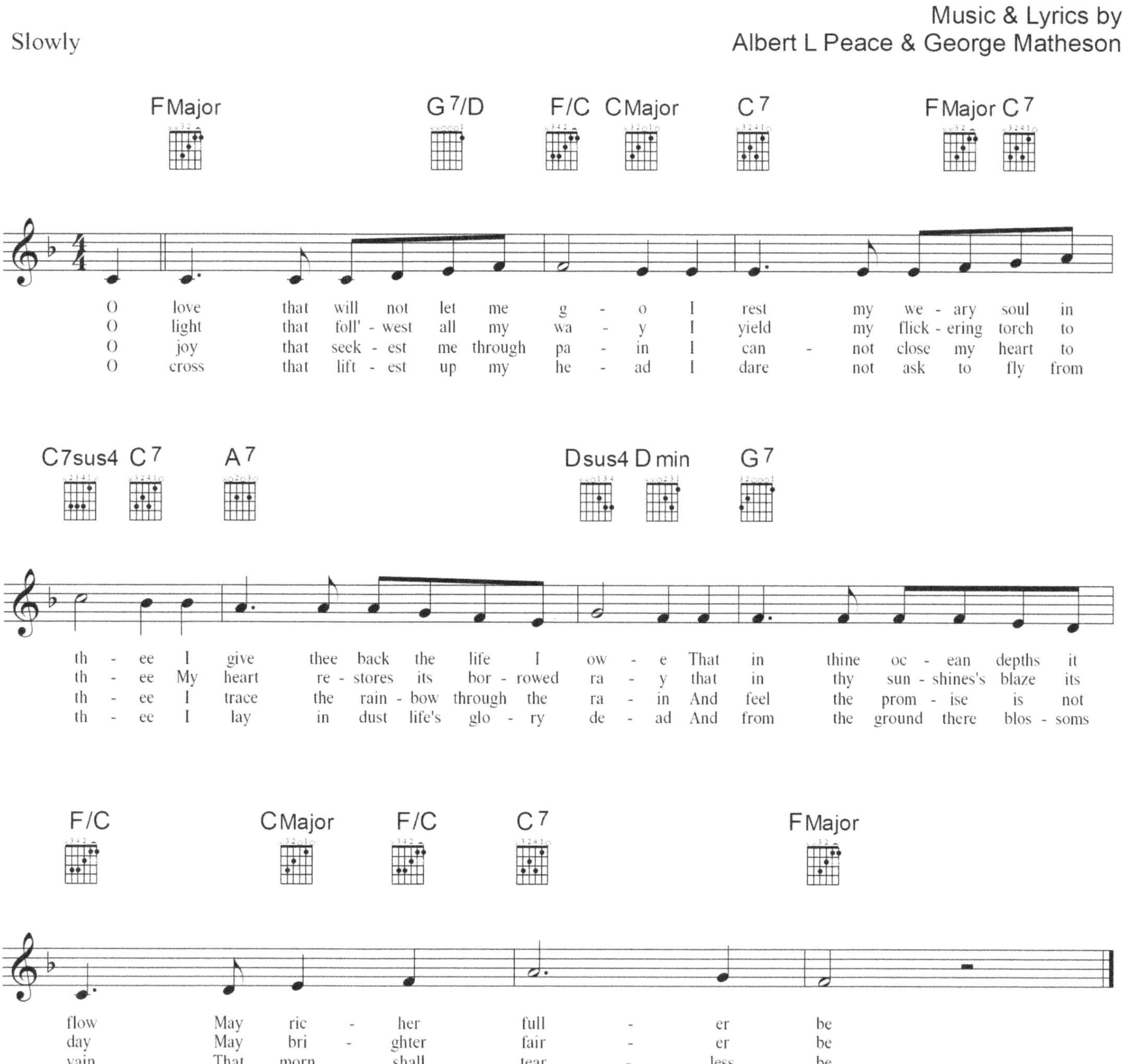

O Love That Will Not Let Me Go - Starter alternate key

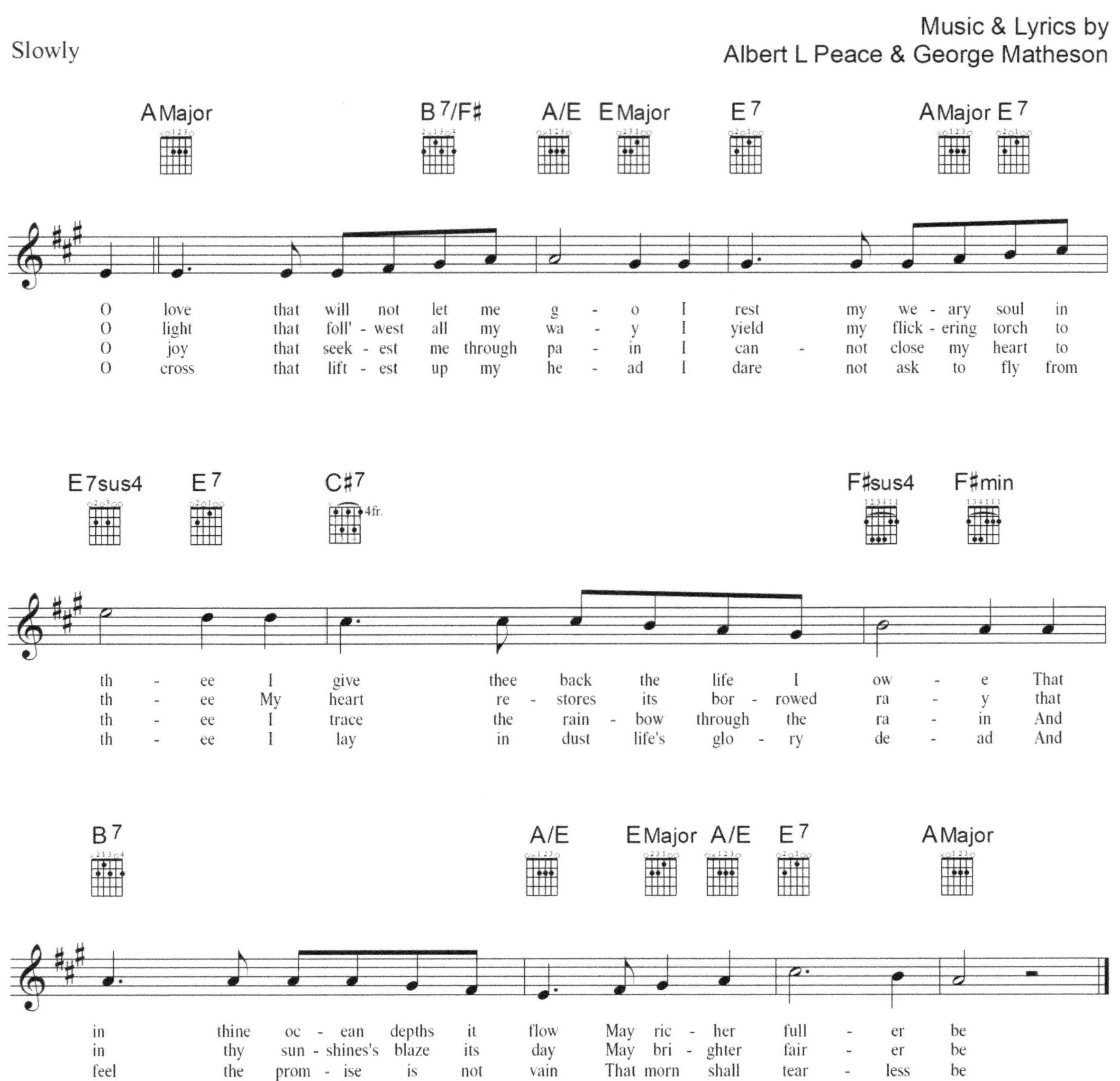

Chords: O Love That Will Not Let Me Go

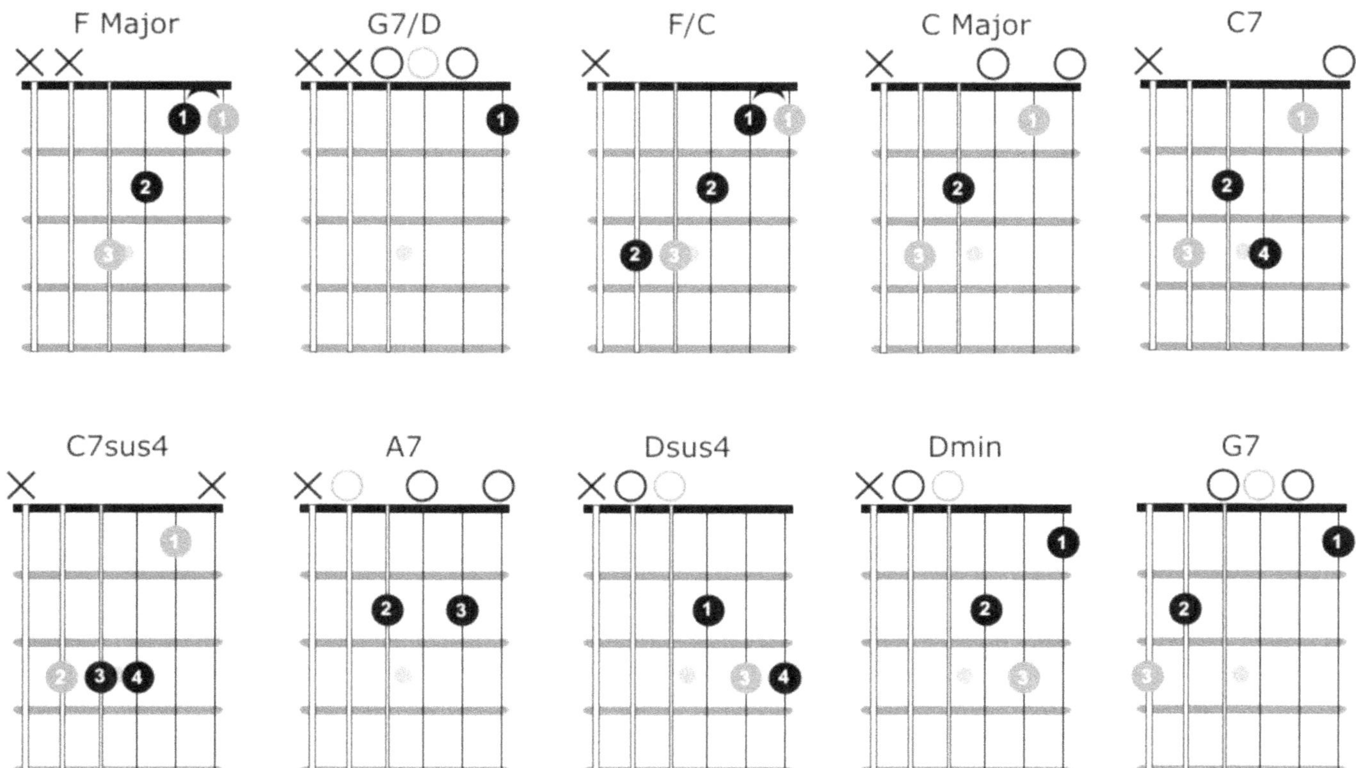

Chords: O Love That Will Not Let Me Go Starter Song Alternate Key

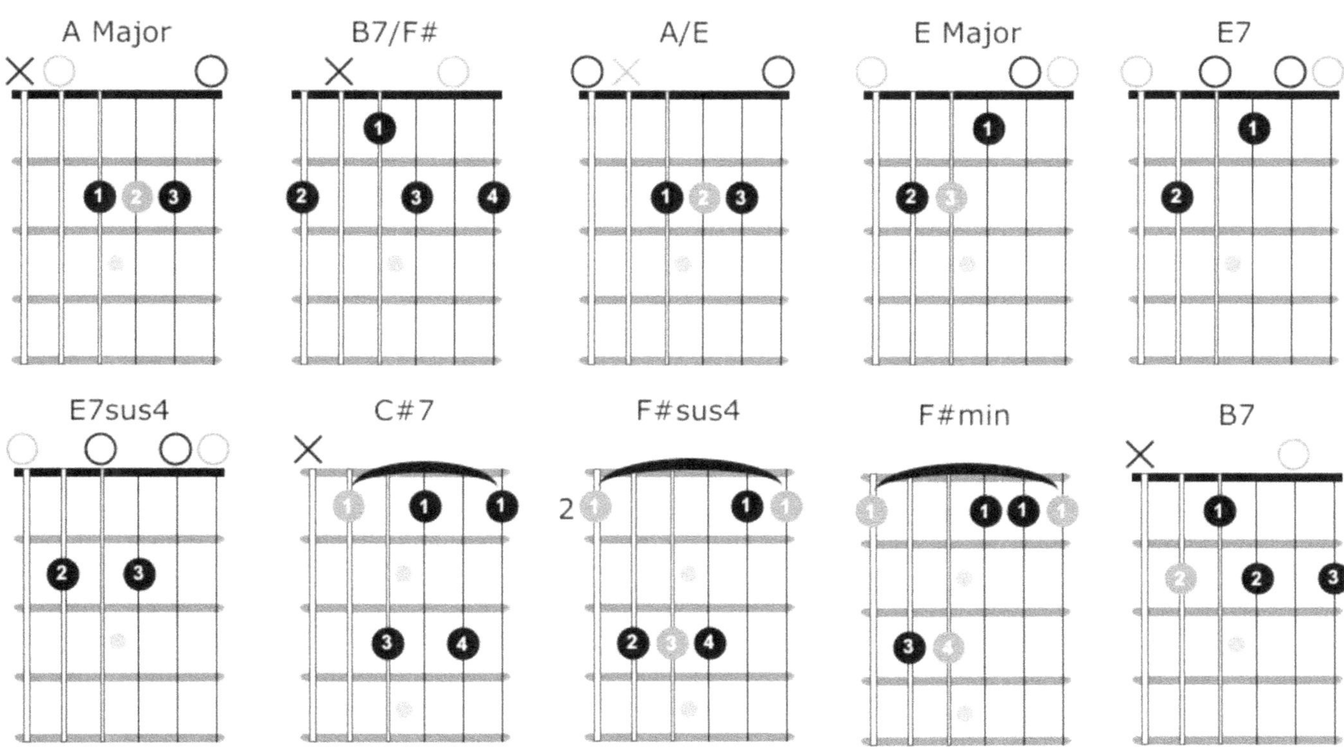

O Love That Will Not Let Me Go play along

bpm = 70

Abide With Me + Melody
Abide With Me Backing Track

Count of 3 then play

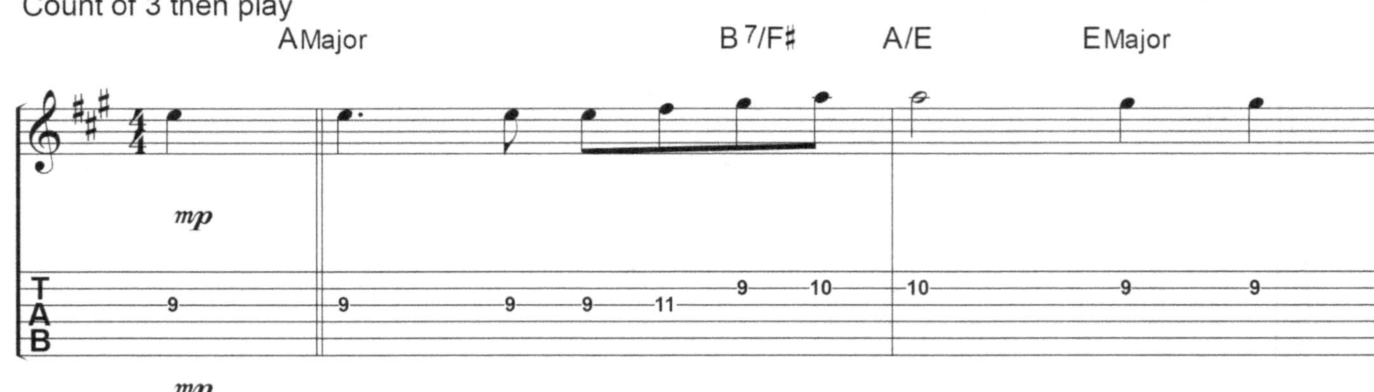

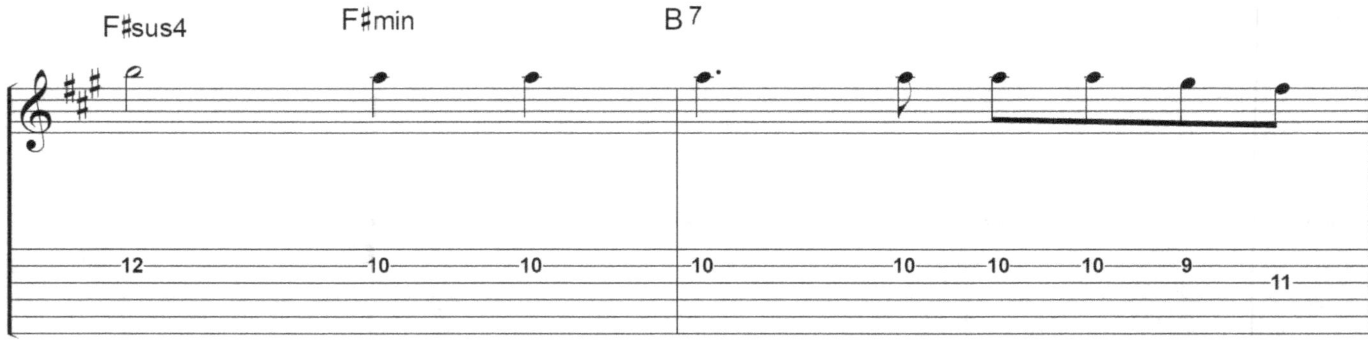

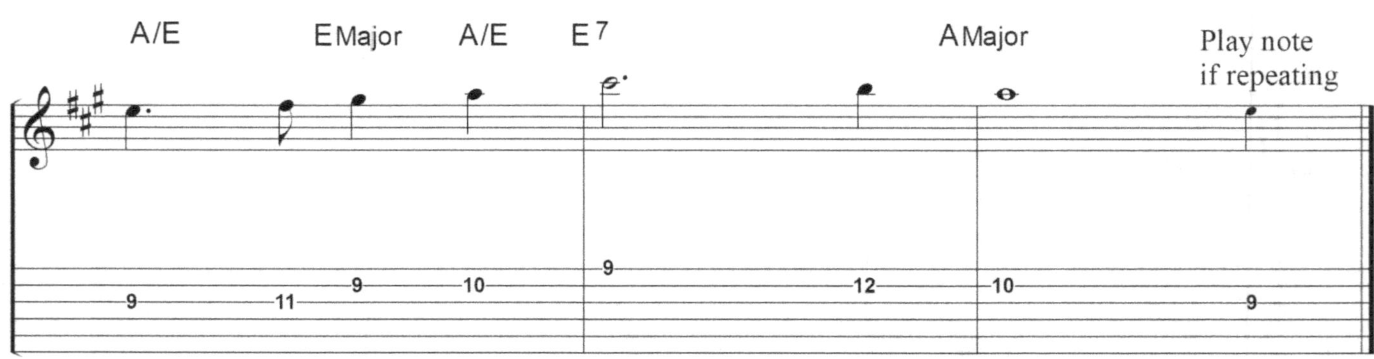

O Love That Will Not Let Me Go - Intermediate

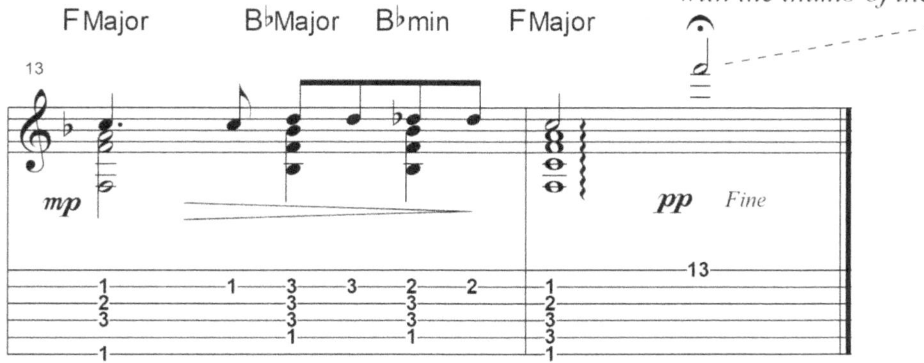

123

Chords: O Love That Will Not Let Me Go Intermediate

Fsus4 Fsus2 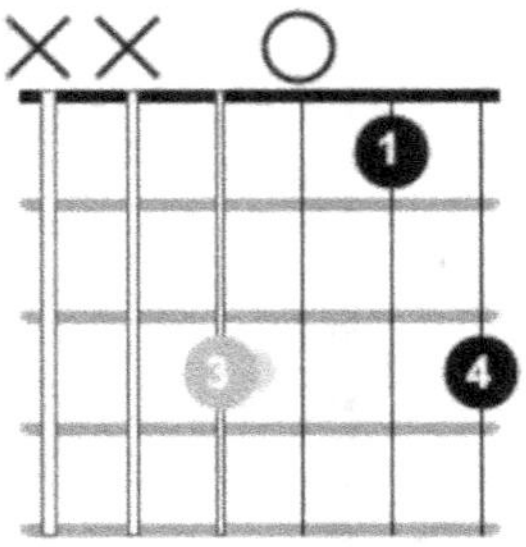 F Major (Bb is a passing note) 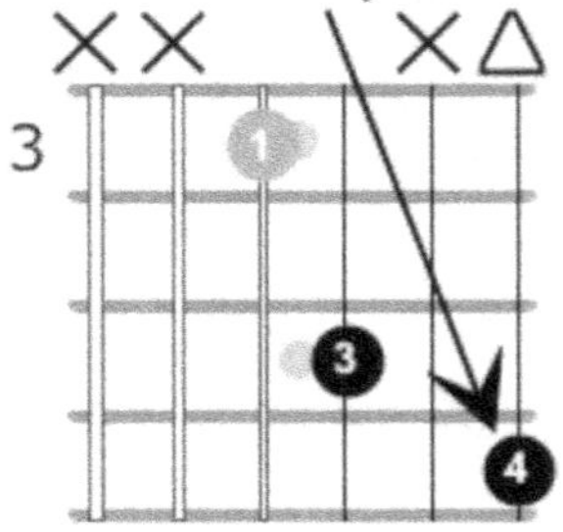 C7sus4

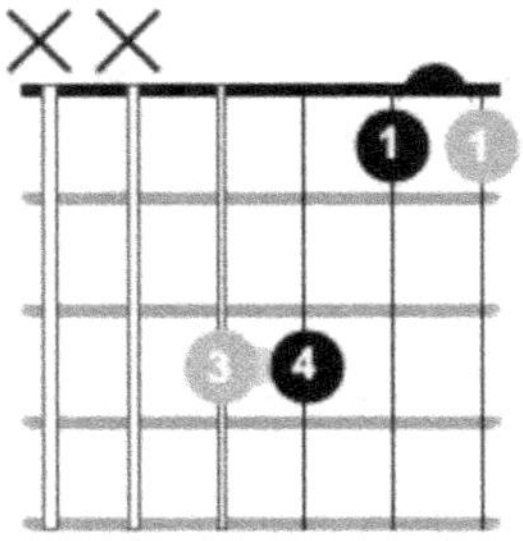

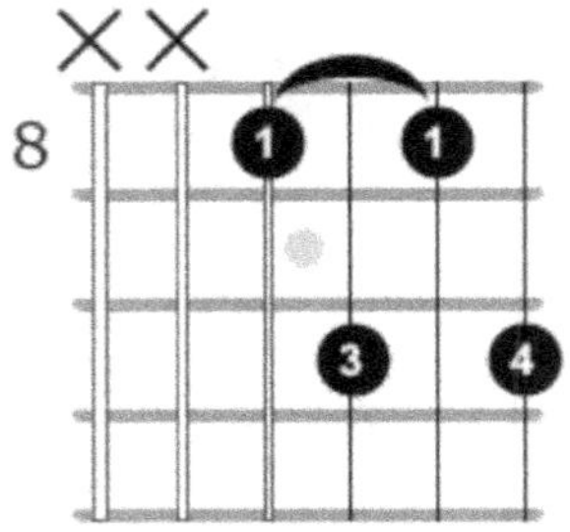

F Major 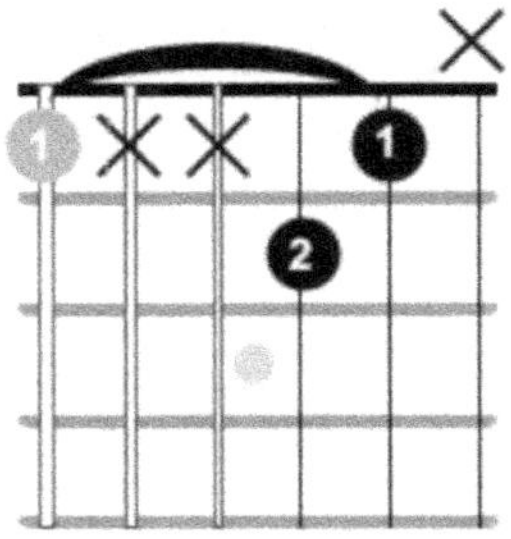 G7/D 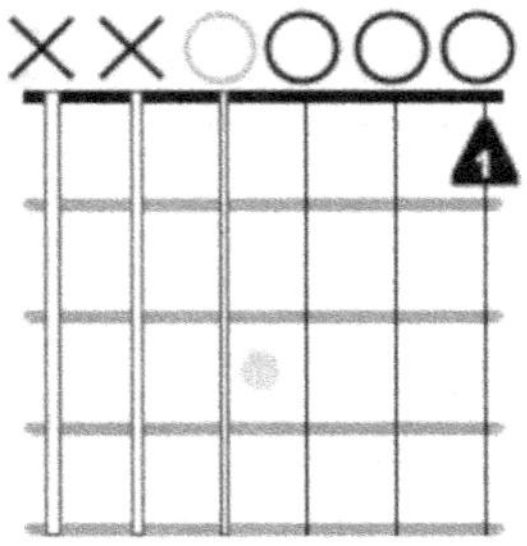 Csus4 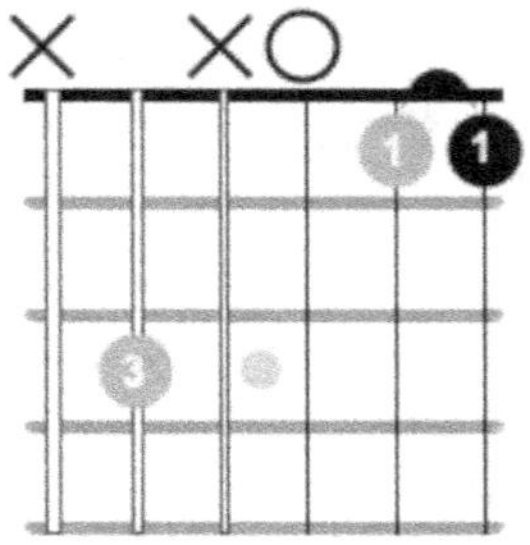 C Major

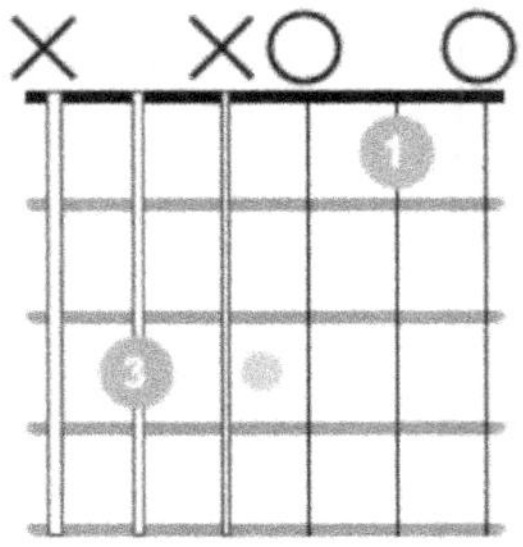

C Major7

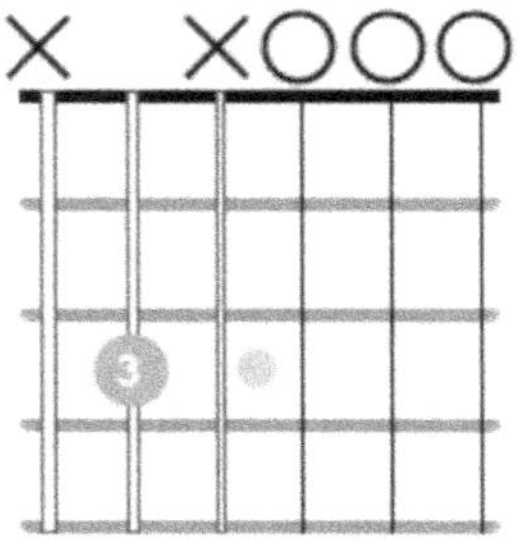

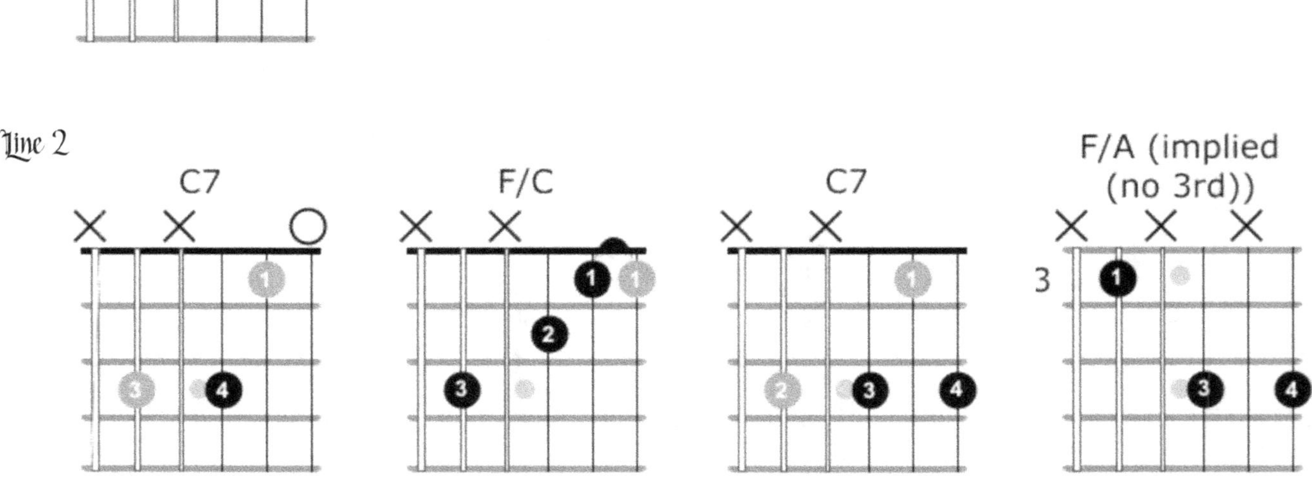

Csus4 - C7	A Major	Dsus4	Dm/C
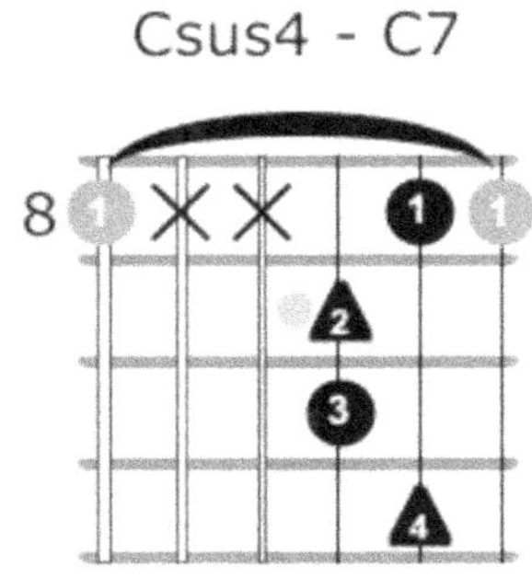	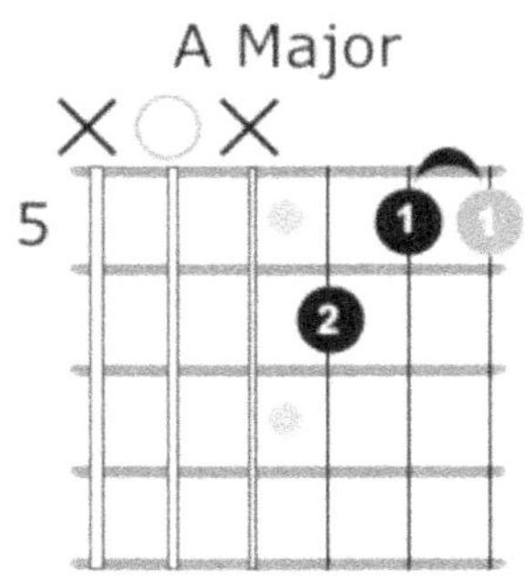	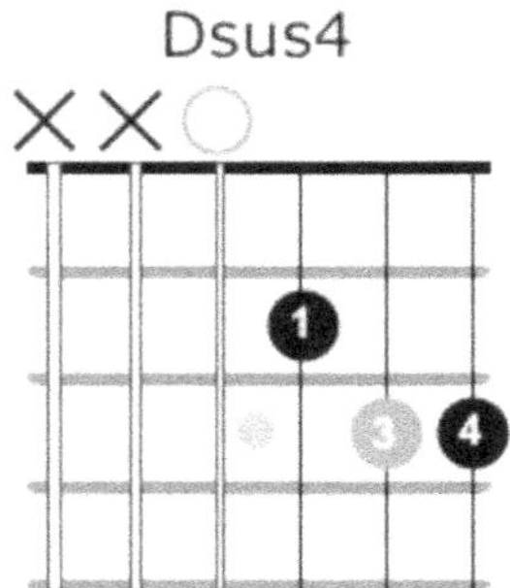	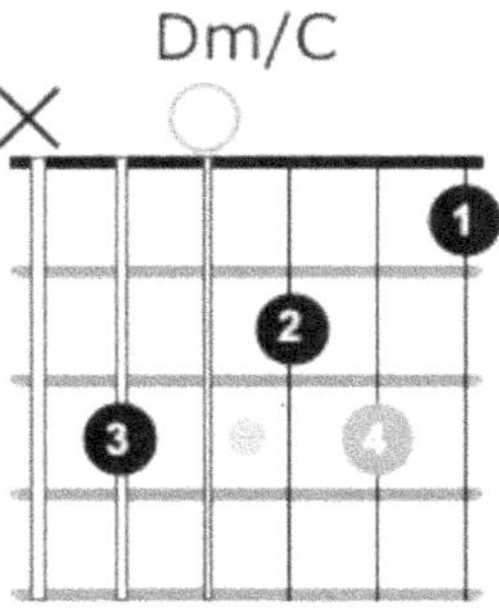

Line 3

G7/B	G7	G7/B	G6
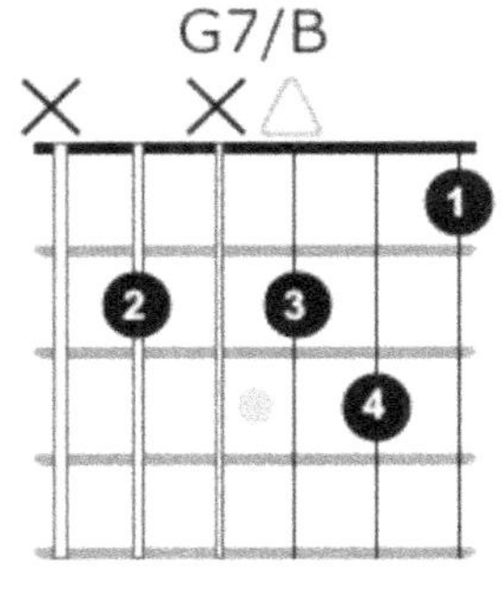	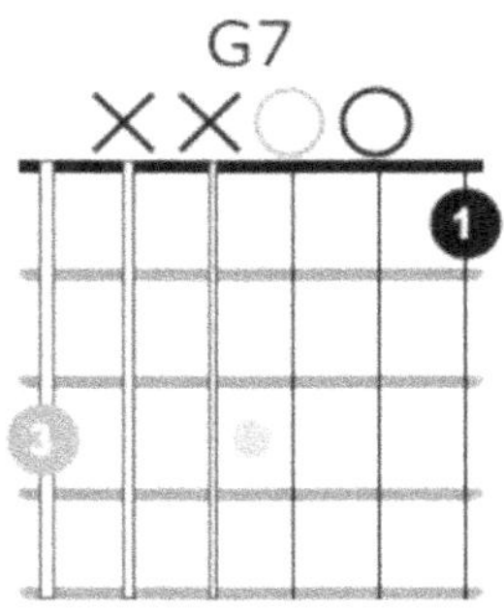	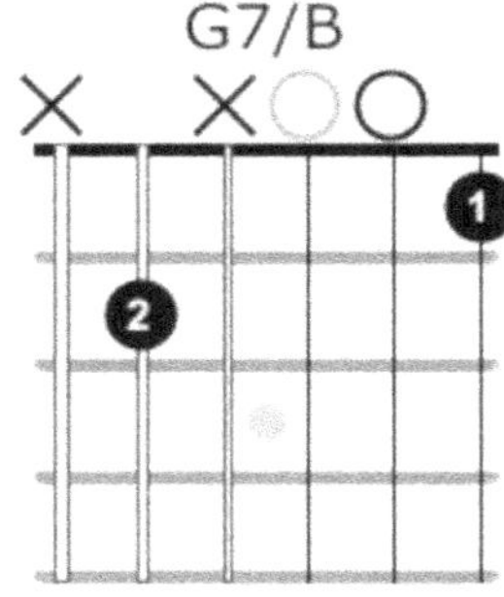	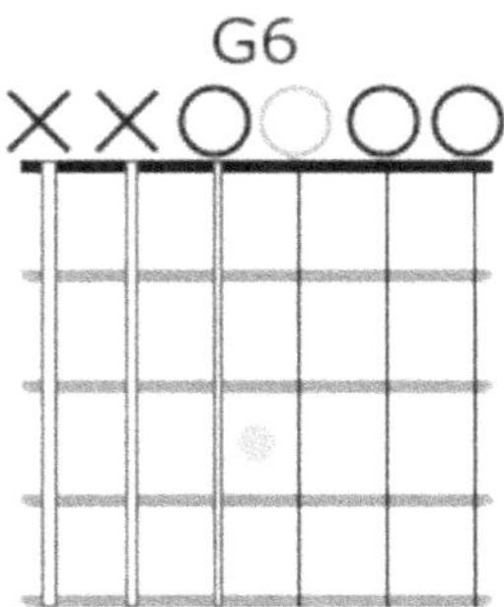

G/F	F/C	F/C	C7
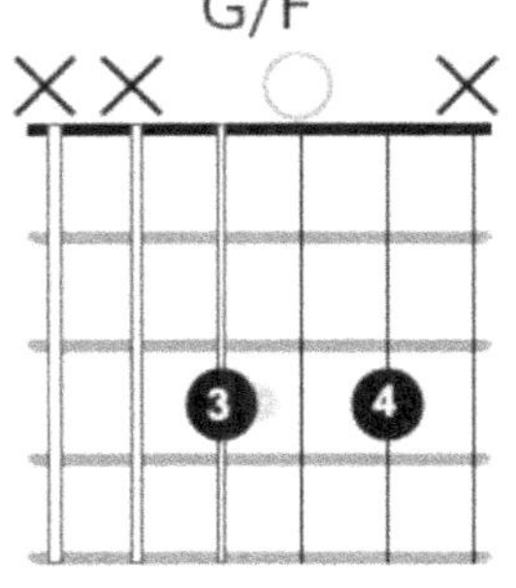	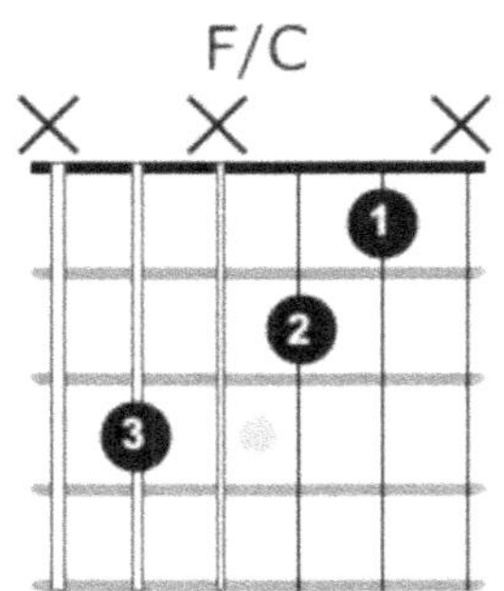	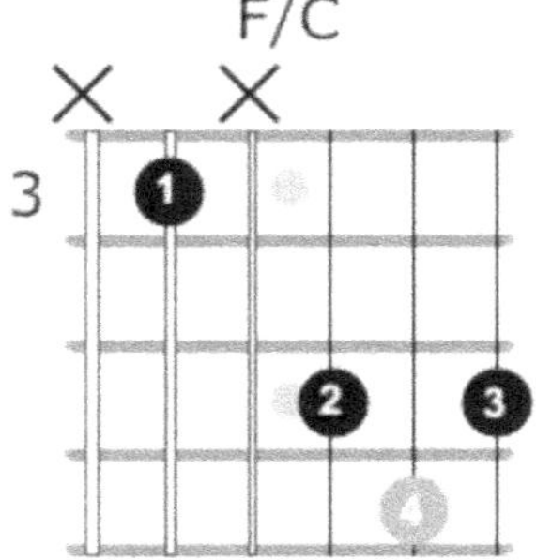	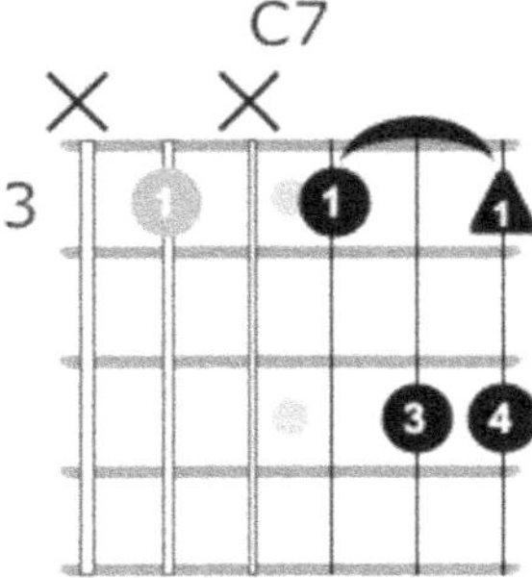

F Major	C7sus4 - C7
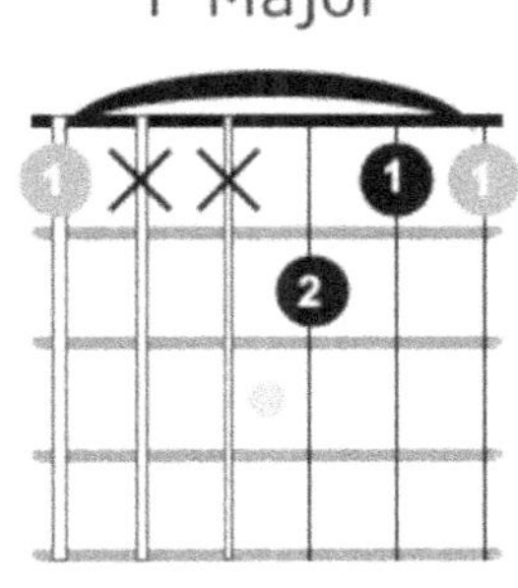	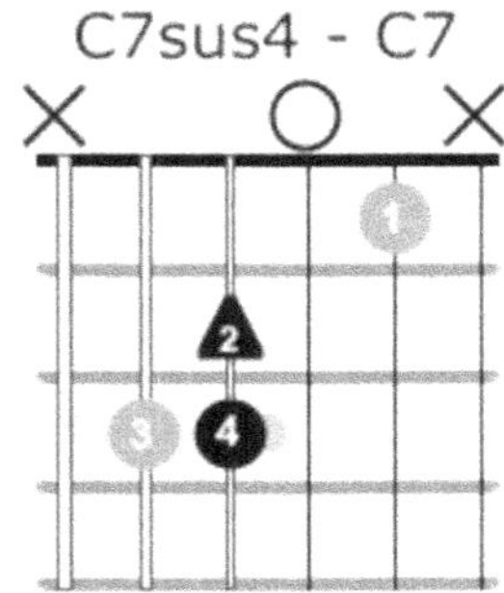

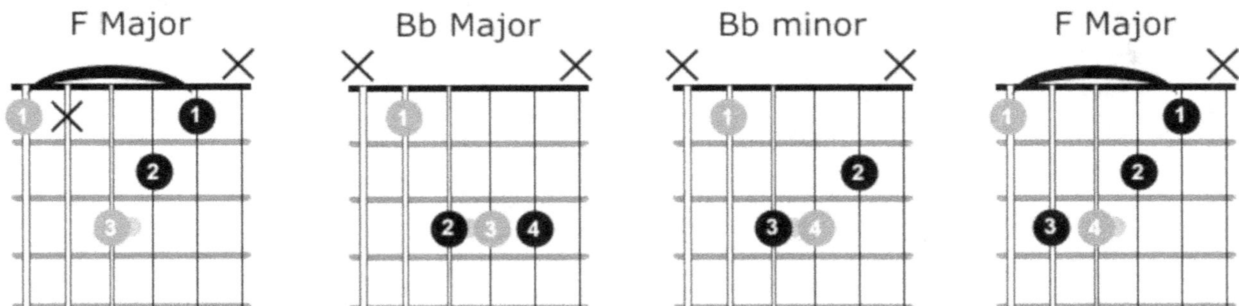

F Major
Bb Major
Bb minor
F Major

O Love That Will Not Let Me Go - Advanced

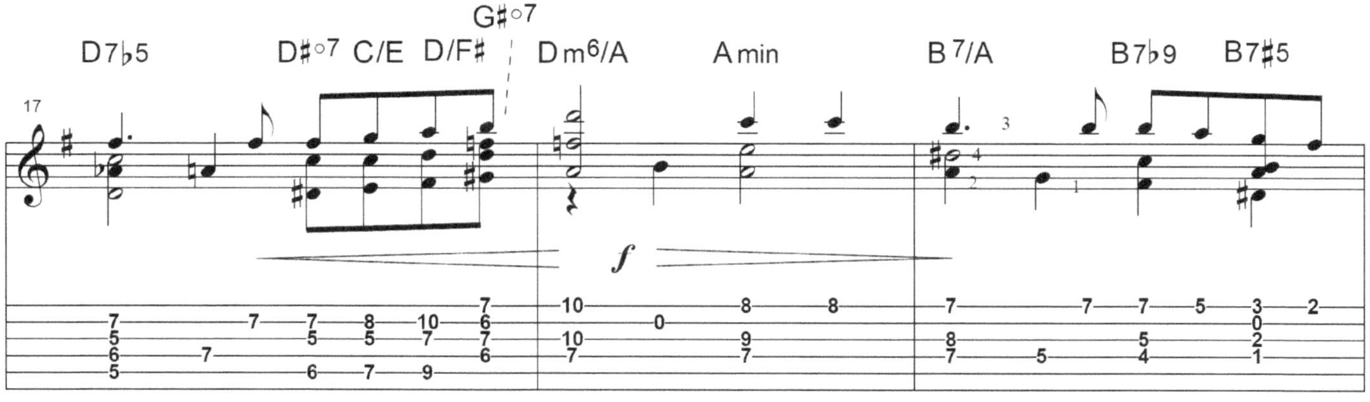

17
D7♭5
D#°7 C/E D/F#
G#°7
Dm6/A
Amin
B7/A
B7♭9
B7#5
f

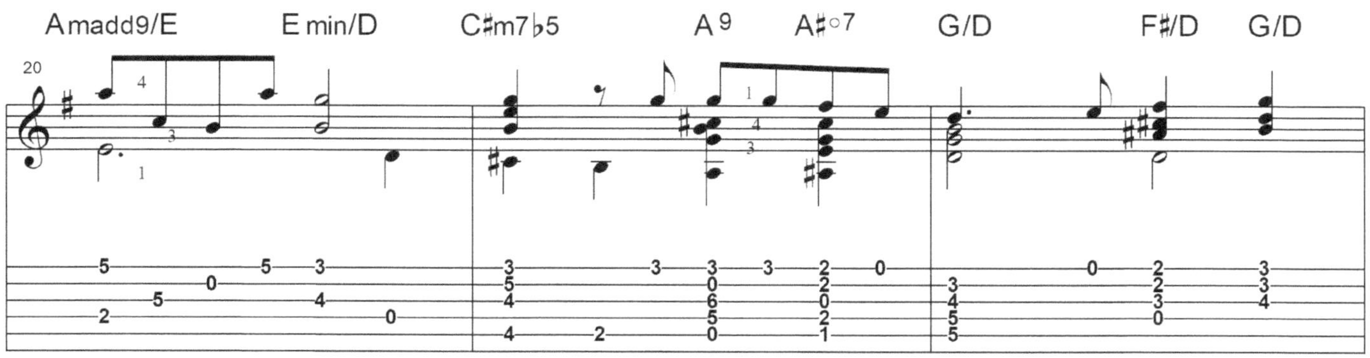

20
Amadd9/E
Emin/D
C#m7♭5
A9
A#°7
G/D
F#/D
G/D

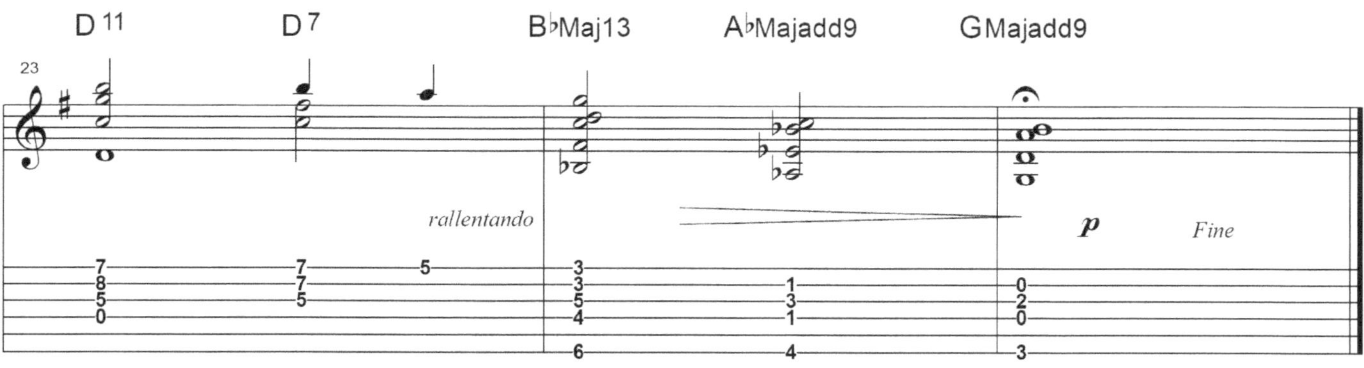

23
D11
D7
B♭Maj13
A♭Majadd9
GMajadd9
rallentando
p
Fine

Chords: O Love That Will Not Let Me Go Advanced

Line 1

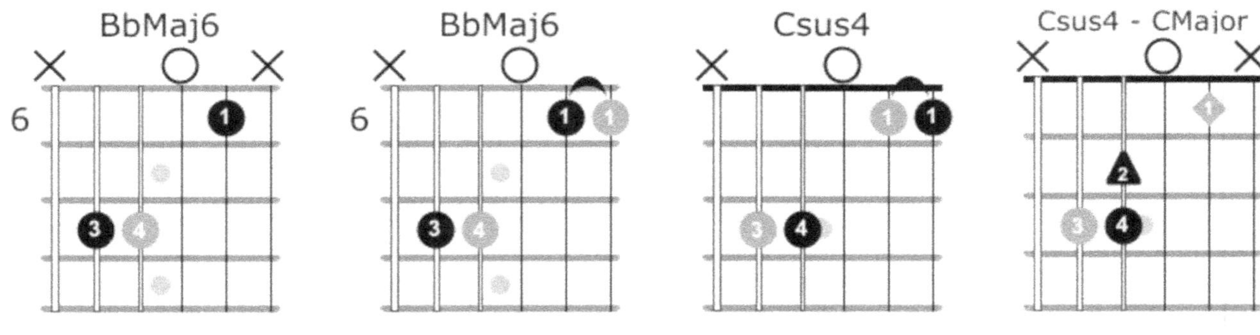

Line 2

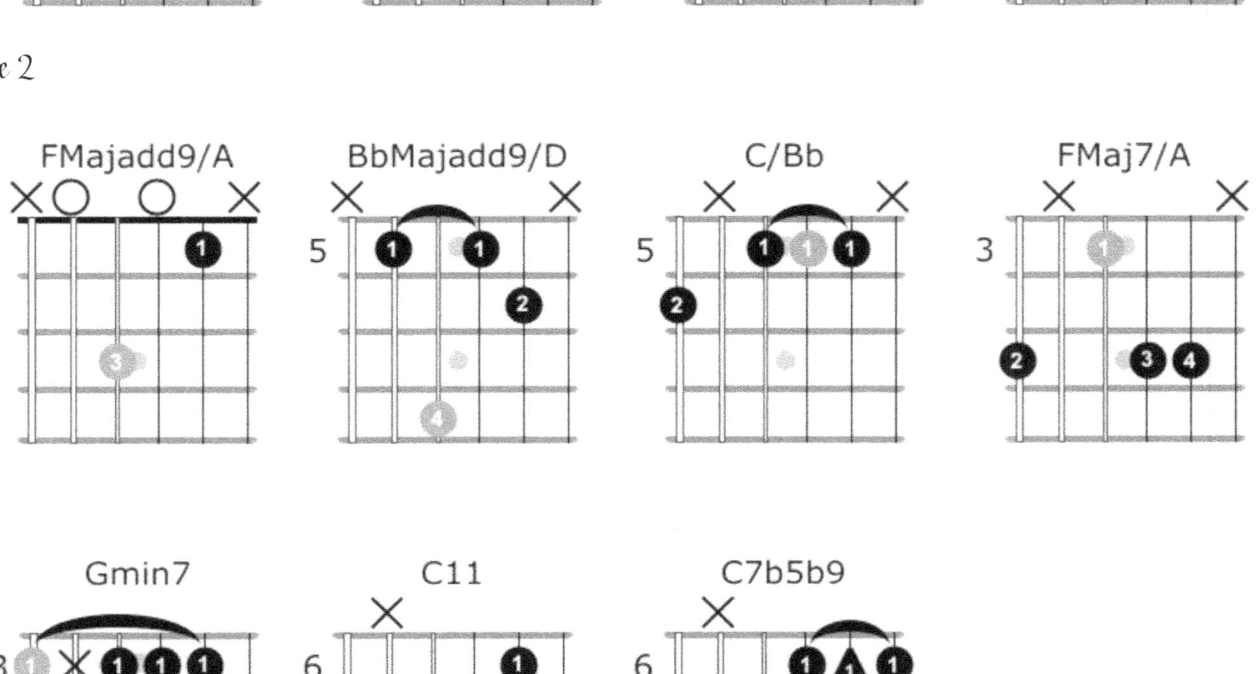

Line 3

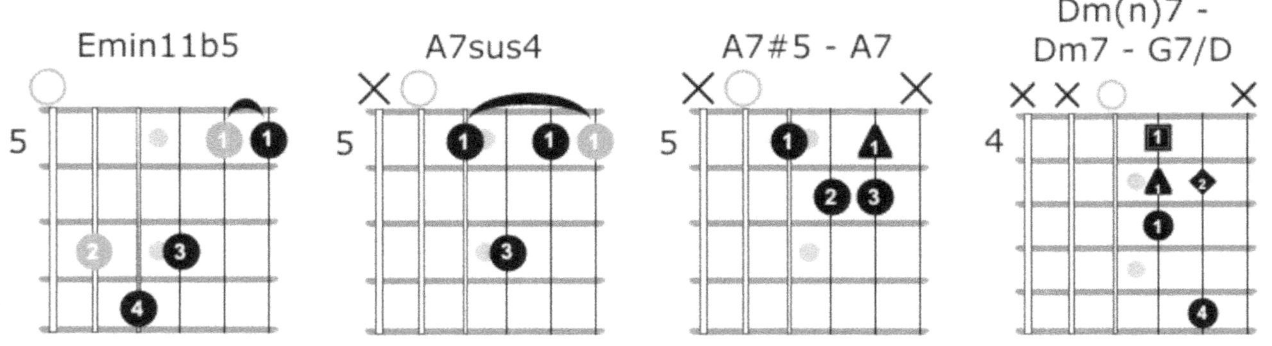

F/G

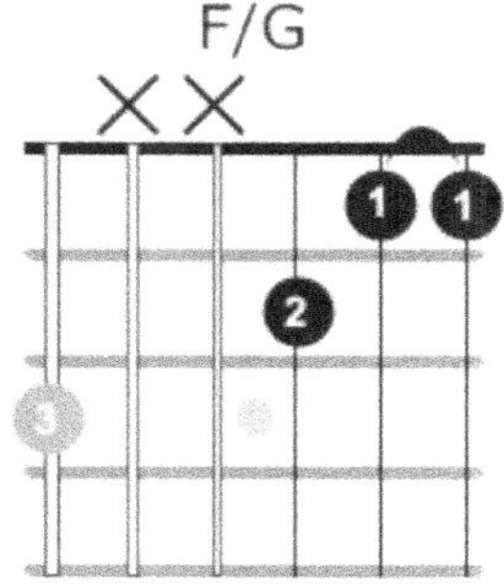

G7

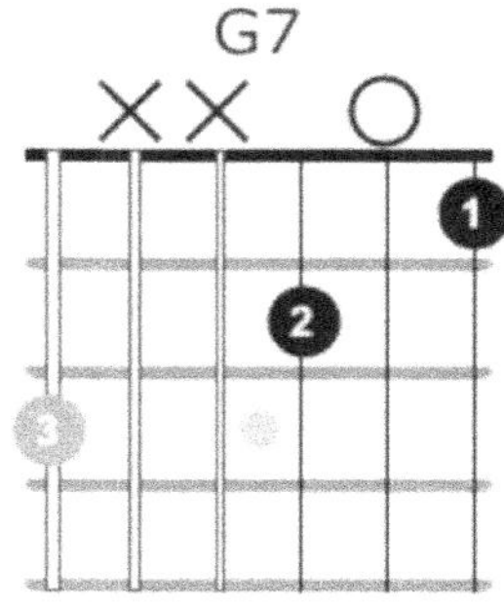

G9#11

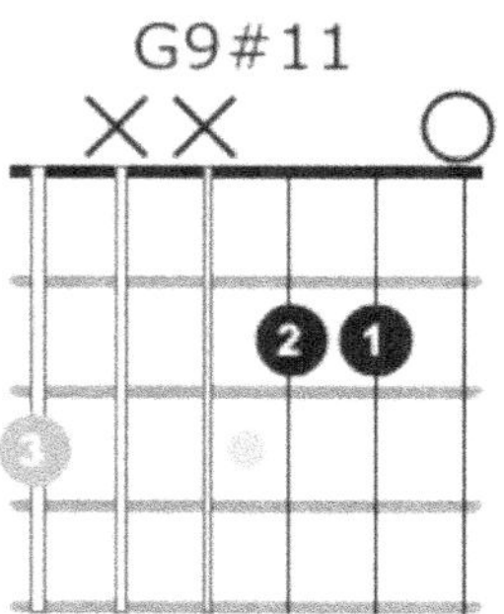

F/C

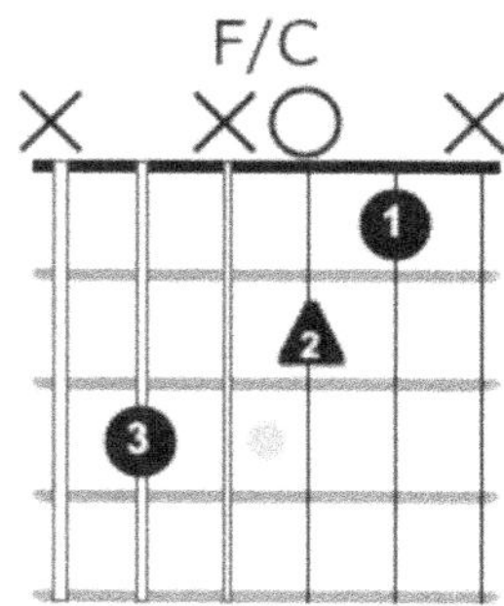

E/C

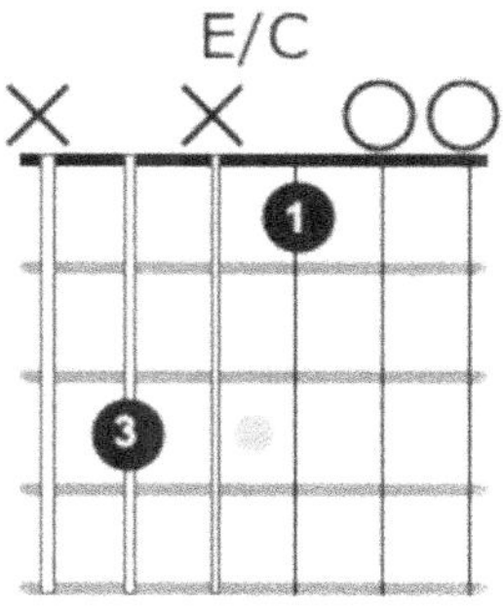

G7/C

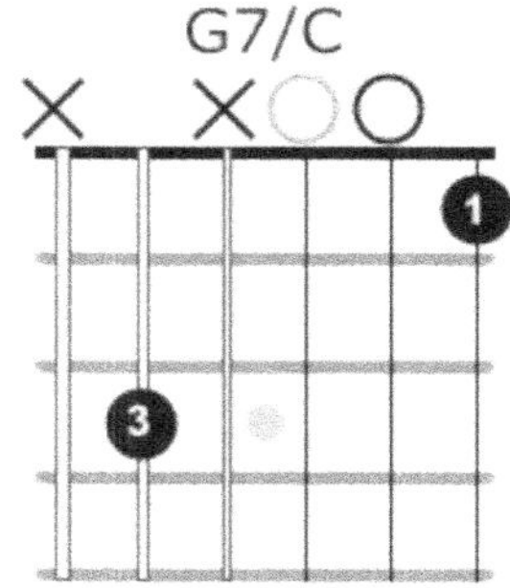

Line 4

C13sus

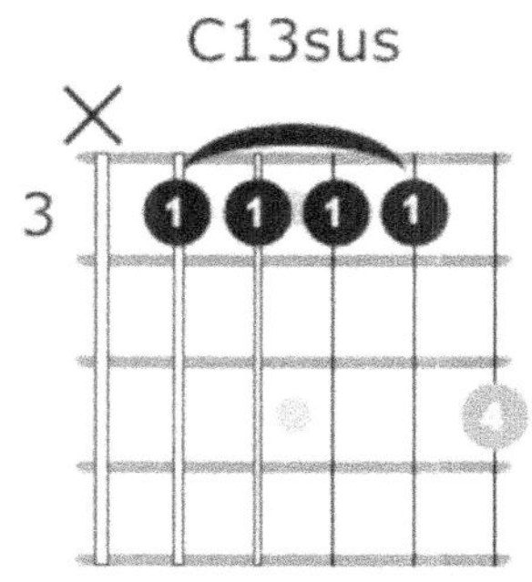

C13b9

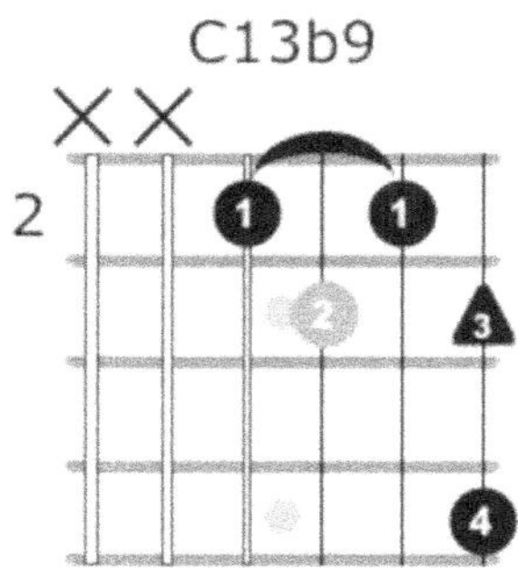

FMajadd9

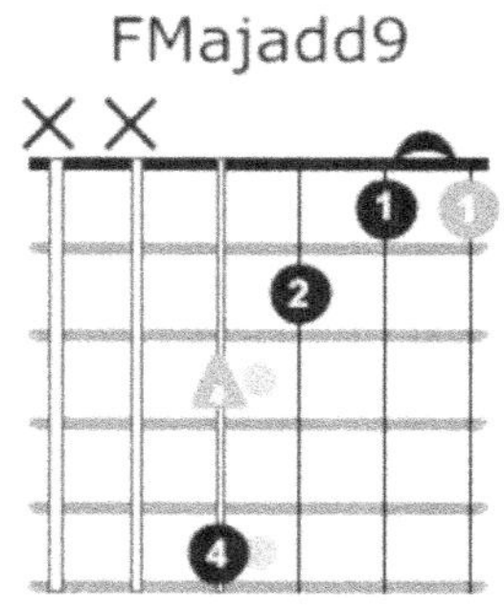

Amin11

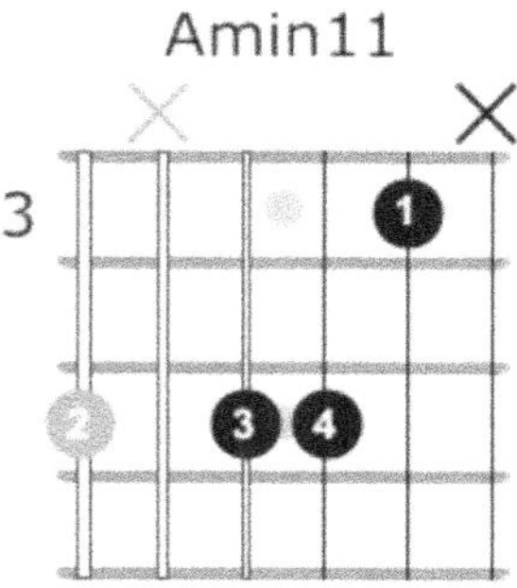

Ab7b5

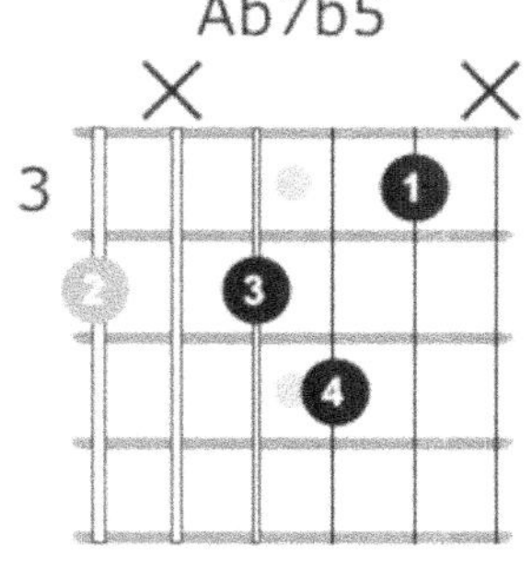

GMaj7

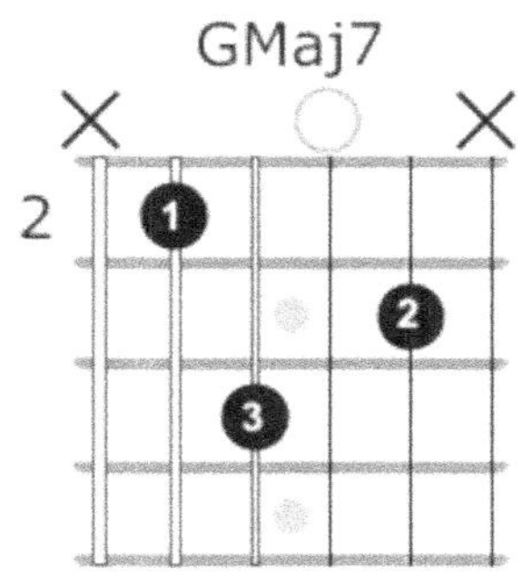

G/B

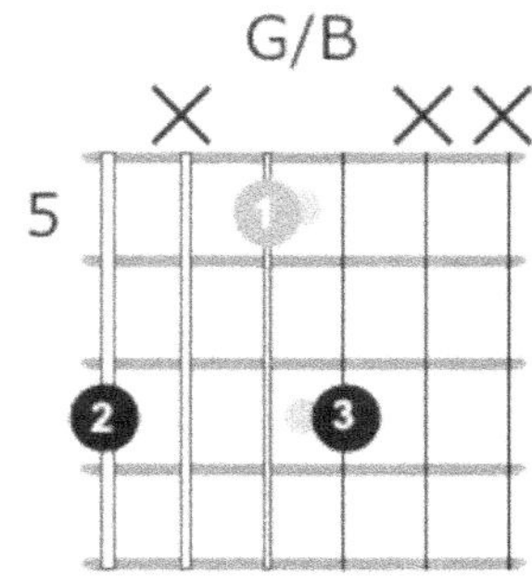

Bbo7

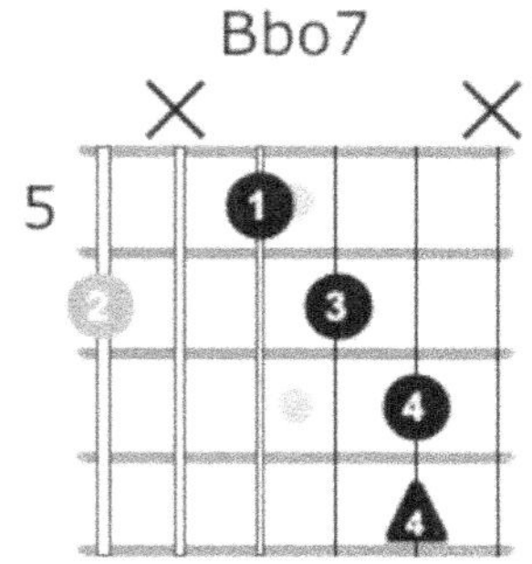

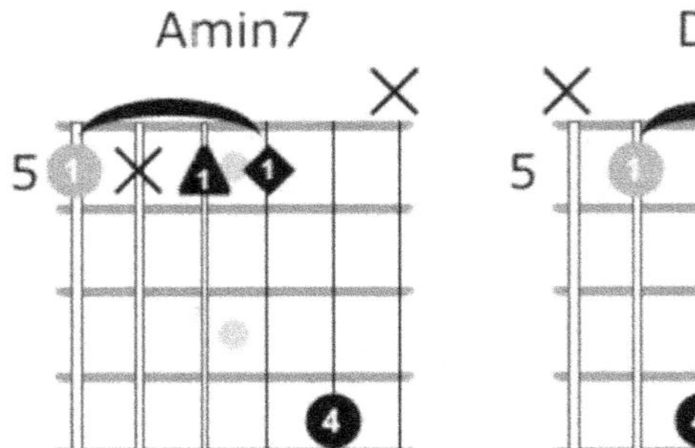

Amin7   D7+

Line 5

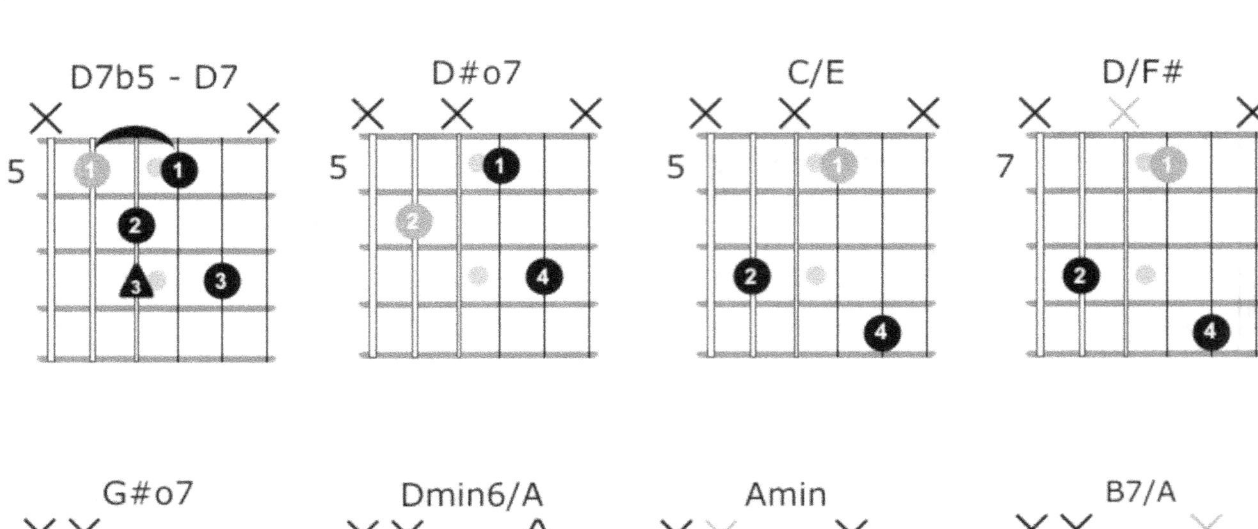

D7b5 - D7   D#o7   C/E   D/F#

G#o7   Dmin6/A   Amin   B7/A

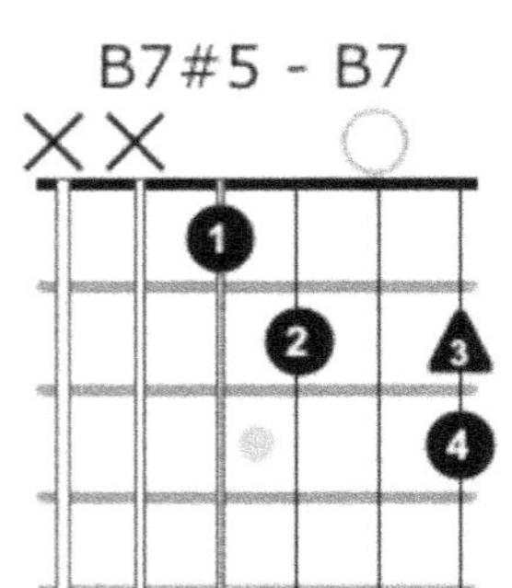

B7#5 - B7

Line 6

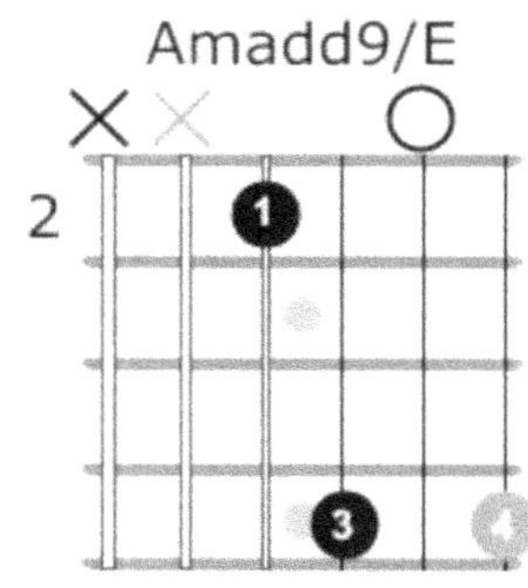

Amadd9/E

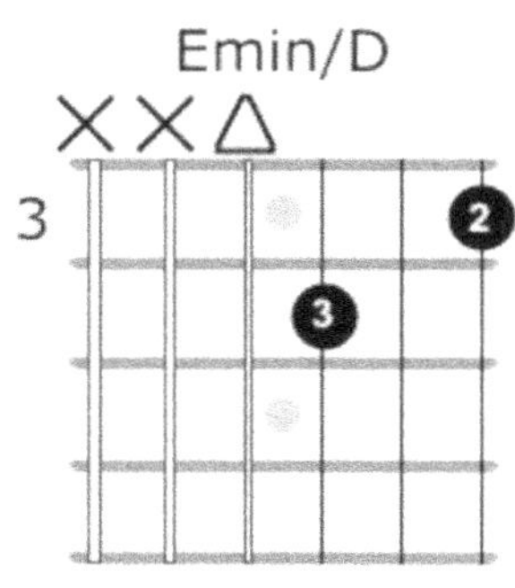

Emin/D

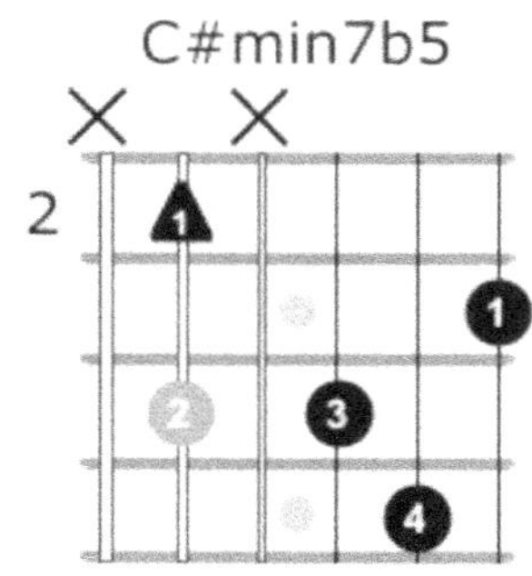

C#min7b5

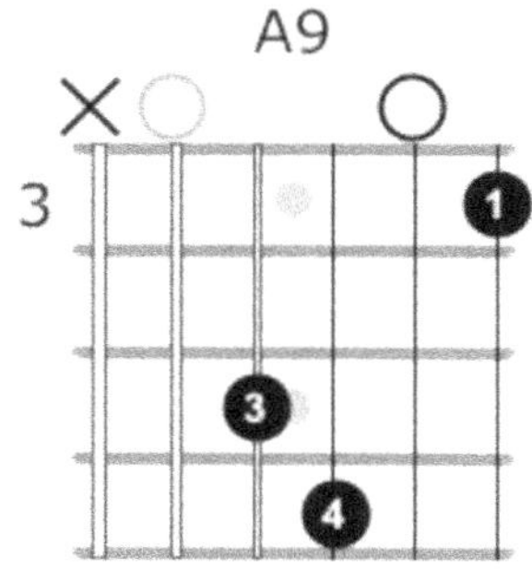

A9

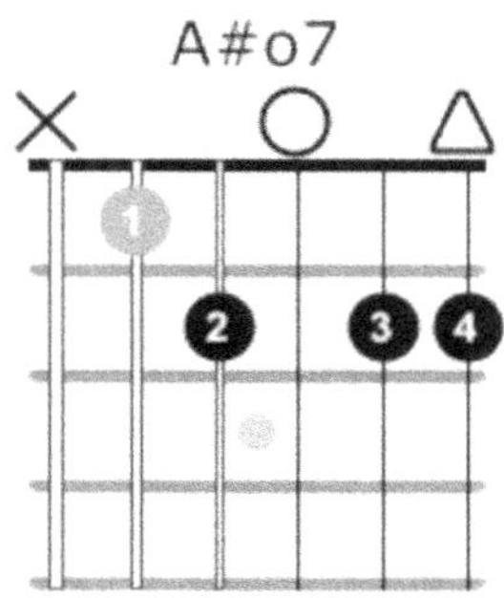

A#o7

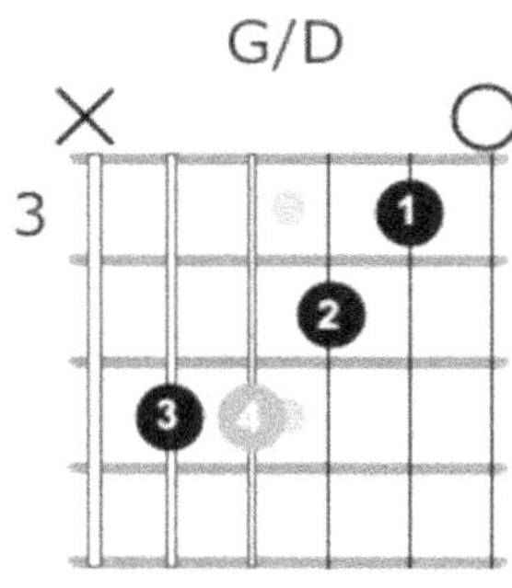

G/D

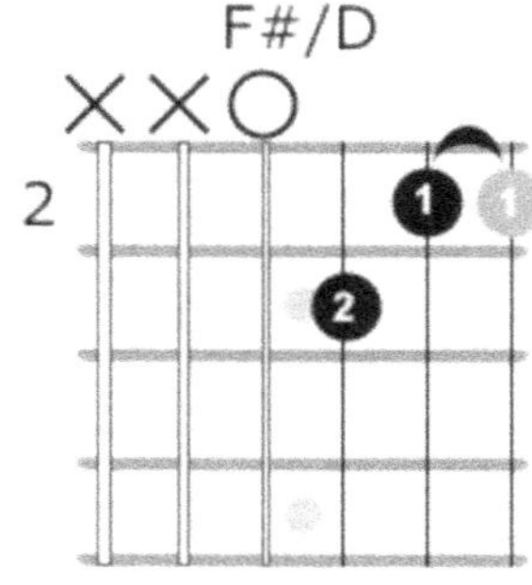

F#/D

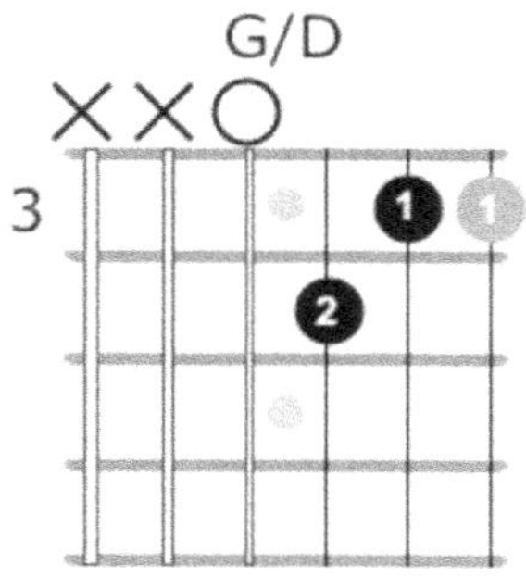

G/D

Line 7

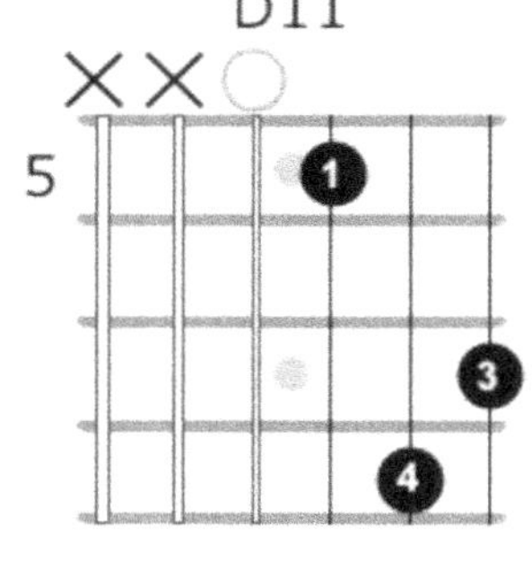

D11

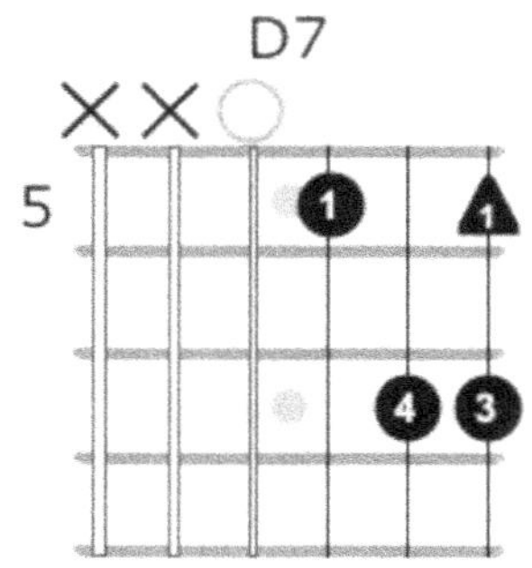

D7

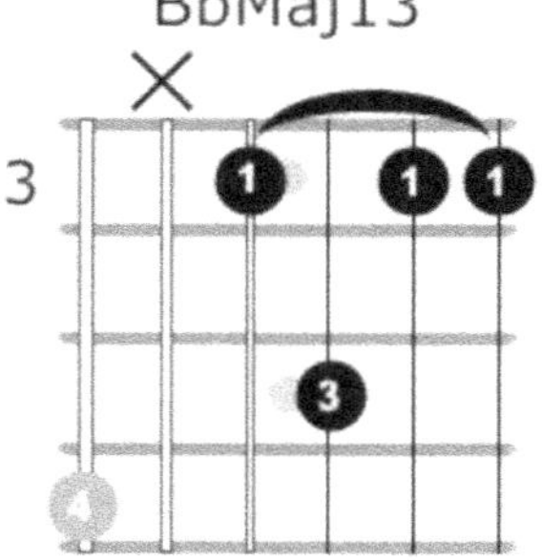

BbMaj13

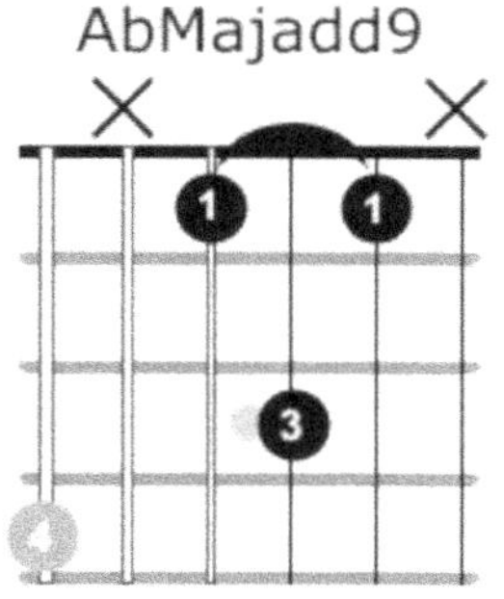

AbMajadd9

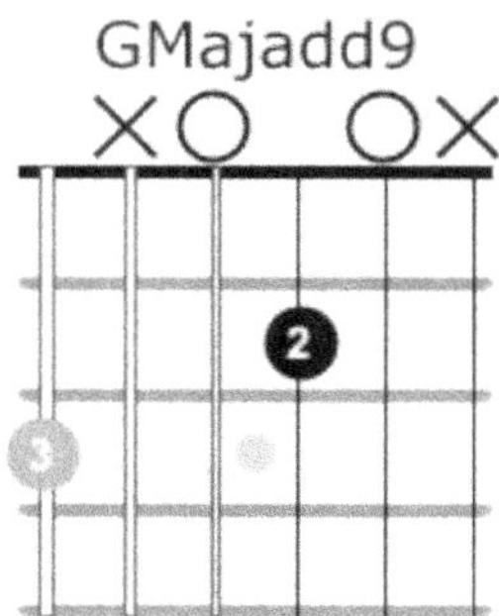

GMajadd9

Hymn 8
The Old Rugged Cross

Resources

Performance of Intermediate version

Audio Talk through of Intermediate version

Performance of Advanced version

Audio Talk through of Advanced version

Use a QR code reader on your cell/mobile phone or tablet to view and listen to the files above. There's a large selection of completely free QR code reader apps available which work on all operating platforms.

To download all resources and other support files, follow the instructions on page 197 of this publication.

Hymn Notes - The Old Rugged Cross

The Old Rugged Cross, is a song that was a firm favourite for several generations of church goers. It was universally known within English speaking Christian circles and beyond.

The song may now not be as popular as it once was but regardless of popularity, it is a lovely song which works really well as a guitar instrumental arrangement.

This is one of only two songs in this book where the music and words were composed by one person. The composer and writer of the lyrics was American evangelist Rev. George Bennard, (1873 – 1958).

The Rev. Bennard was born in Youngstown, Ohio and went on to write a great deal of sacred music over the course of his life.

Rev. George Bennard

Lyrics

Verse 1

On a hill far away, stood an old rugged Cross

The emblem of suff'ring and shame

And I love that old Cross where the dearest and best

For a world of lost sinners was slain

Chorus

So I'll cherish the old rugged Cross

Till my trophies at last I lay down

I will cling to the old rugged Cross

And exchange it some day for a crown

Verse 2

Oh, that old rugged Cross so despised by the world

Has a wondrous attraction for me

For the dear Lamb of God, left His Glory above

To bear it to dark Calvary

Chorus

Verse 3

In the old rugged Cross, stain'd with blood so divine

A wondrous beauty I see

For 'twas on that old cross Jesus suffered and died

To pardon and sanctify me

Chorus

Verse 4

To the old rugged Cross, I will ever be true

Its shame and reproach gladly bear

Then He'll call me some day to my home far away

Where His glory forever I'll share

Chorus

THE OLD RUGGED CROSS - Starter

THE OLD RUGGED CROSS - Starter alternate key

Chords: The Old Rugged Cross

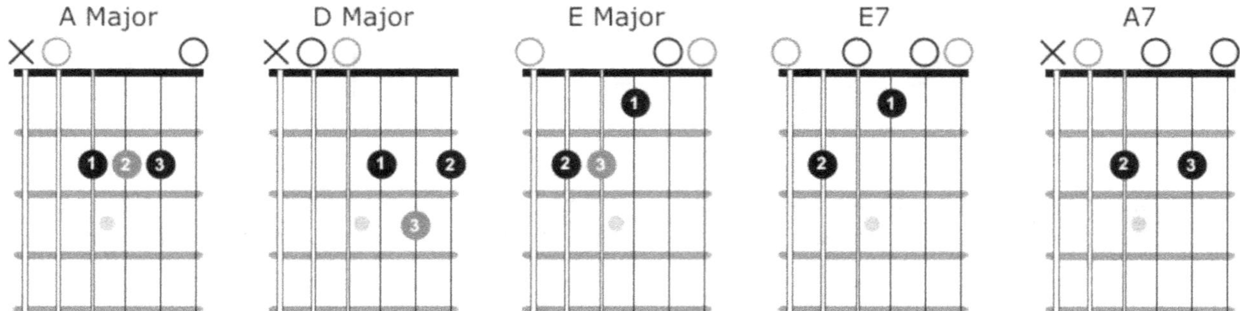

Chords: The Old Rugged Cross Starter Song Alternate Key

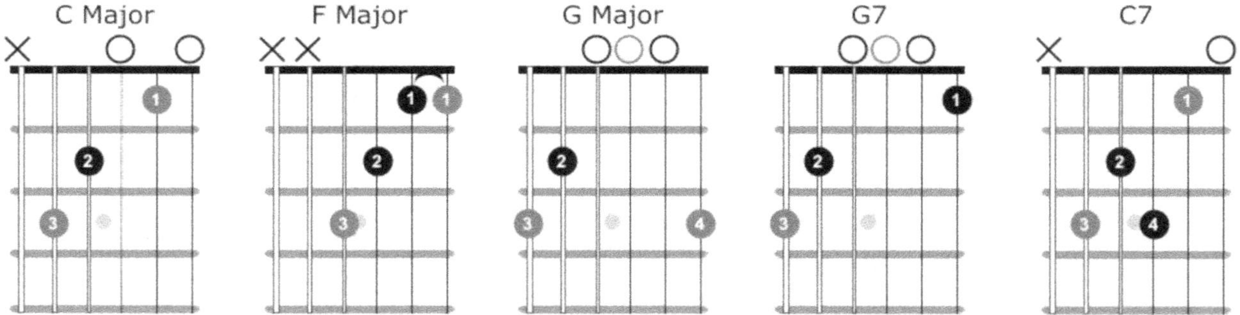

The Old Rugged Cross play along

bpm = 54

Count of 5 then play

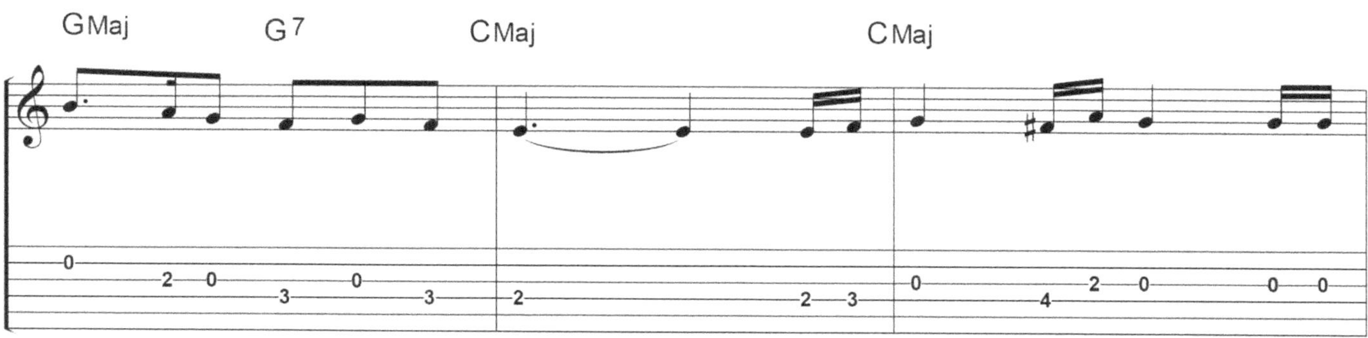

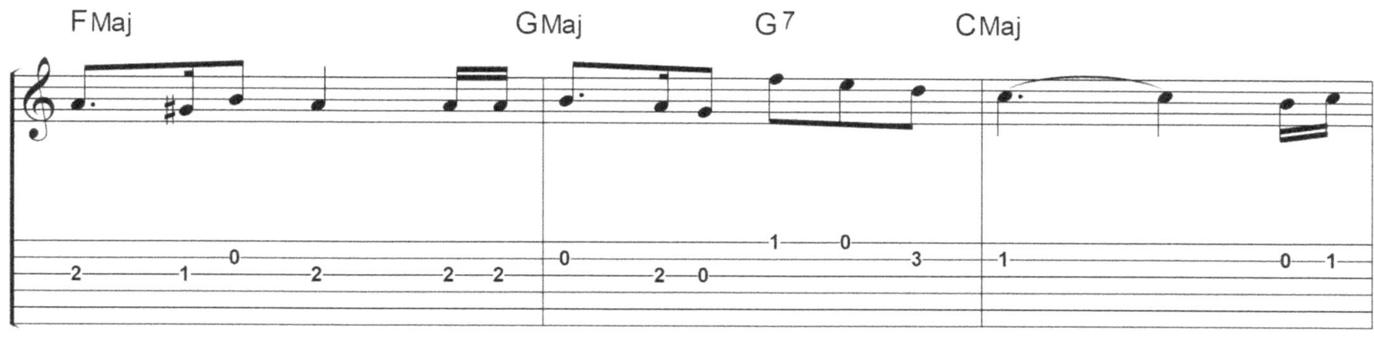

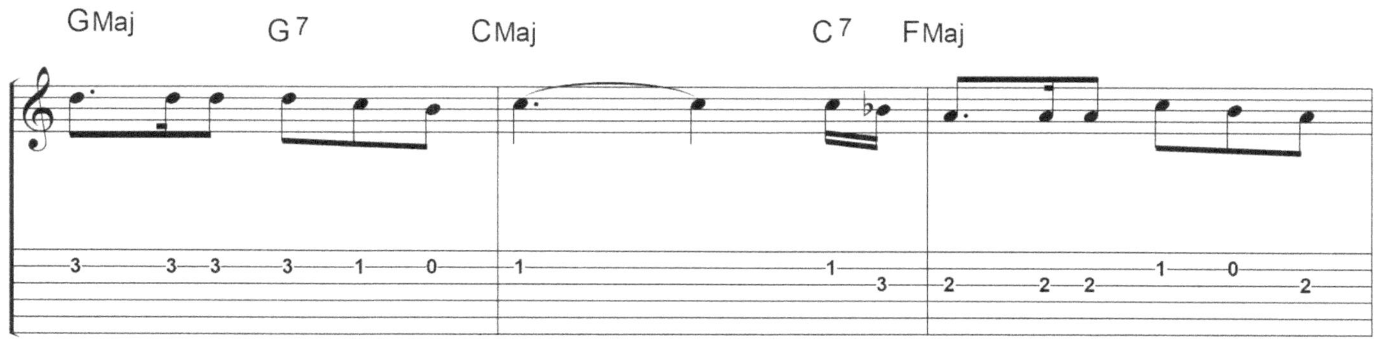

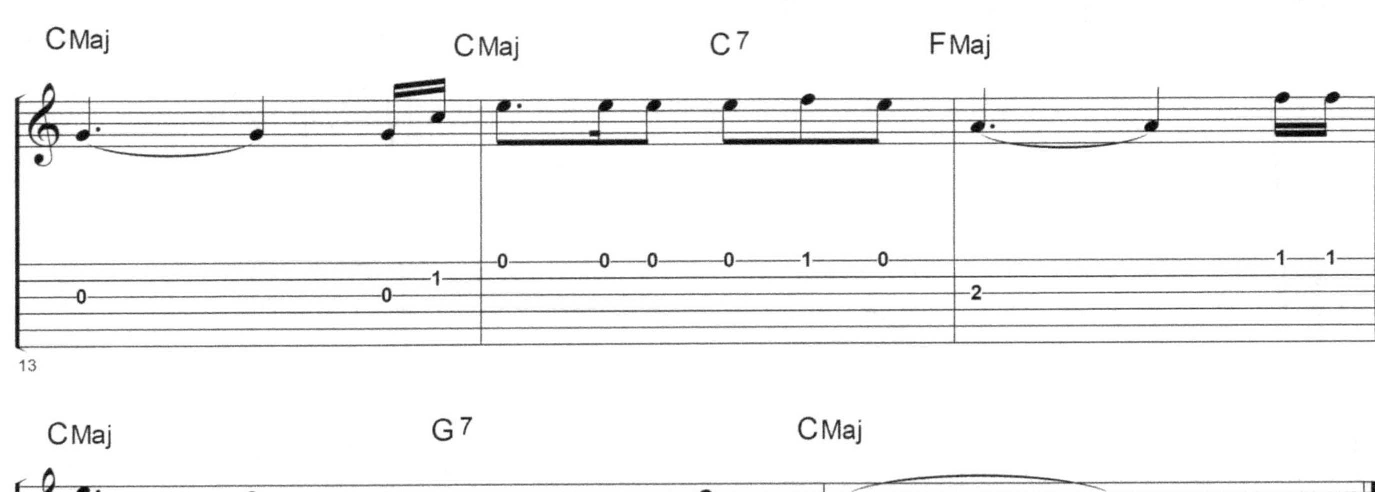

CMaj
CMaj
C7
FMaj
13
CMaj
G7
CMaj
16

THE OLD RUGGED CROSS - Intermediate

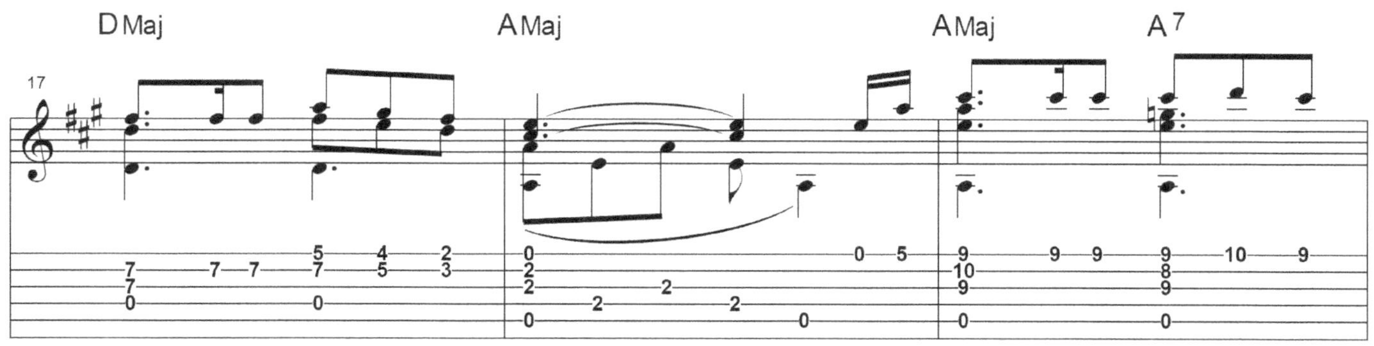

D Maj
A Maj
A Maj
A7
17

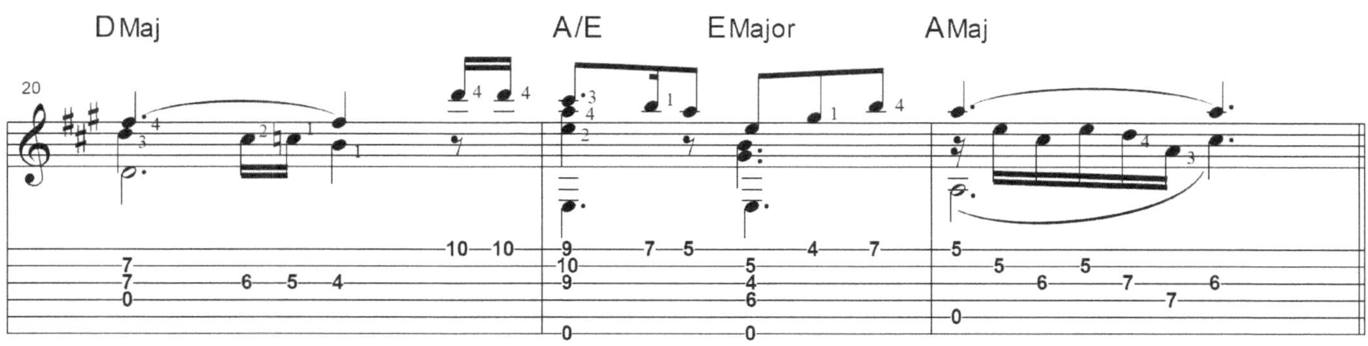

D Maj
A/E
E Major
A Maj
20

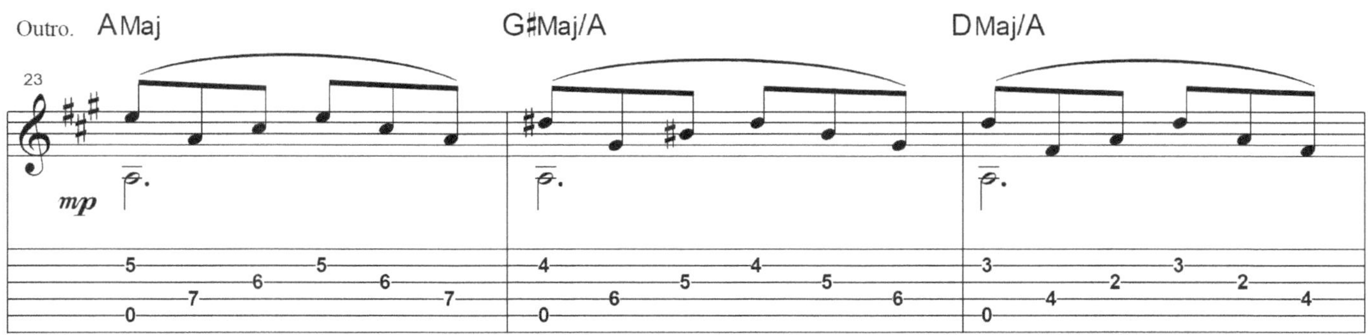

Outro. A Maj
G#Maj/A
D Maj/A
mp
23

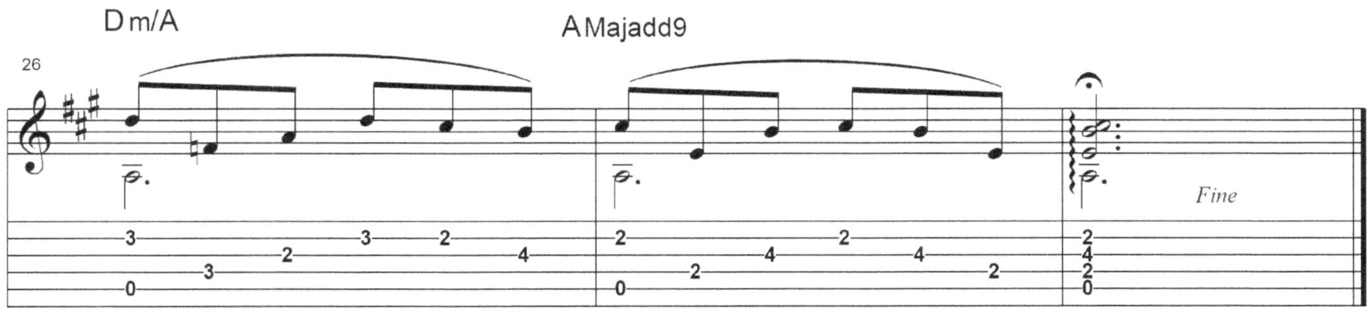

D m/A
A Majadd9
Fine
26

Chords: The Old Rugged Cross Intermediate

Line 1

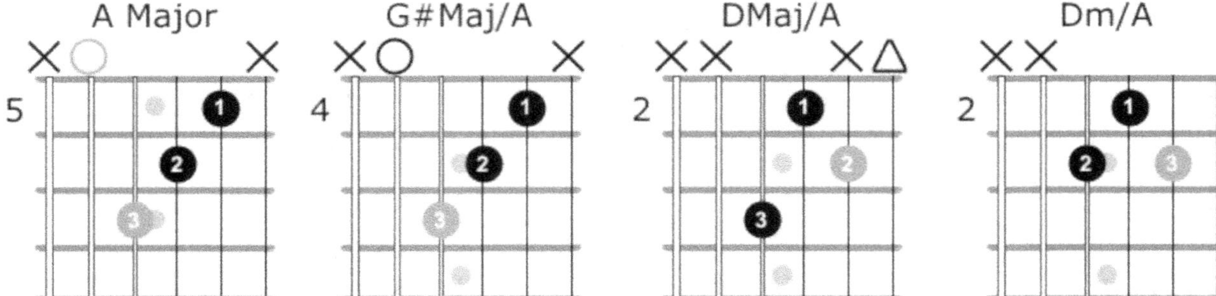

Line 2

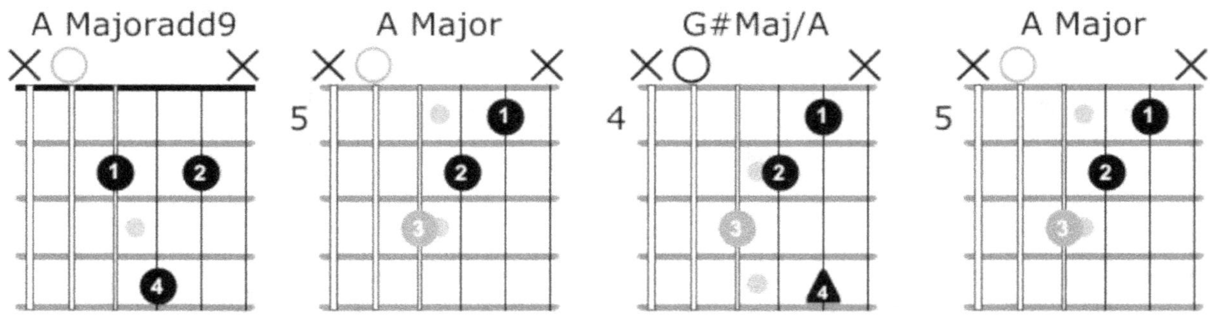

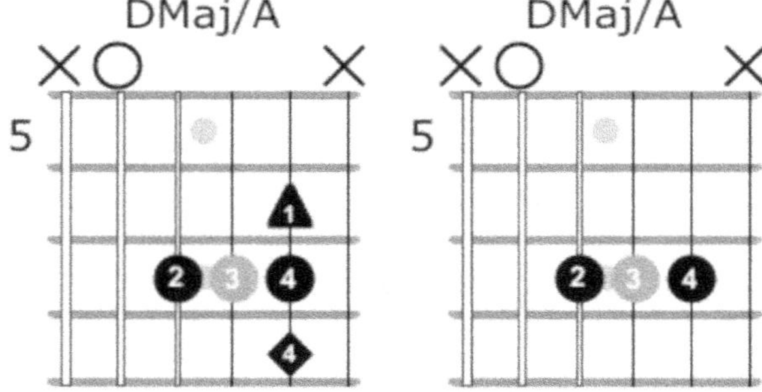

Line 3

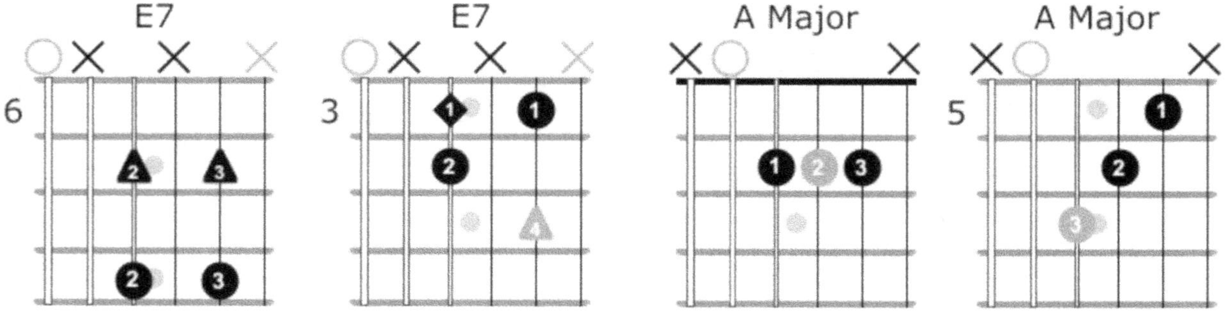

G#Maj/A

A Major

G#Maj/A

A Major

DMaj/A

DMaj/A

Line 4

E7

E7

E7b9

A Major

E7

E7b9

A Major

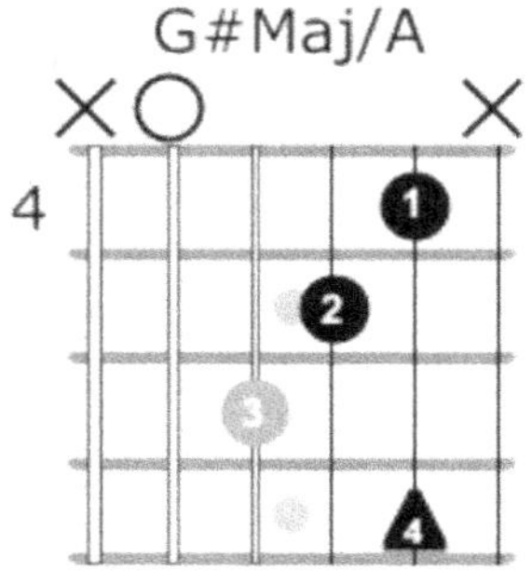

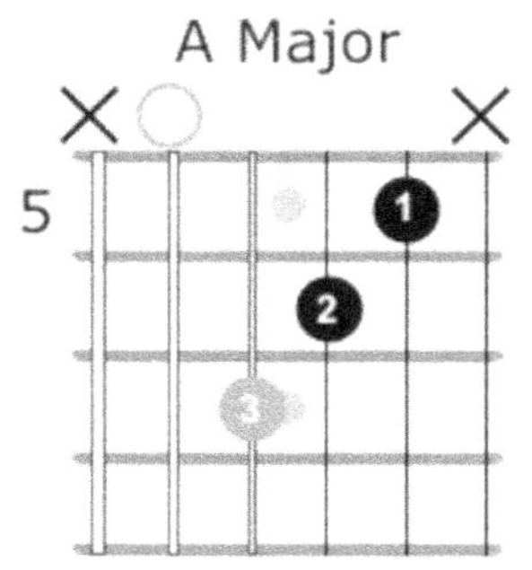

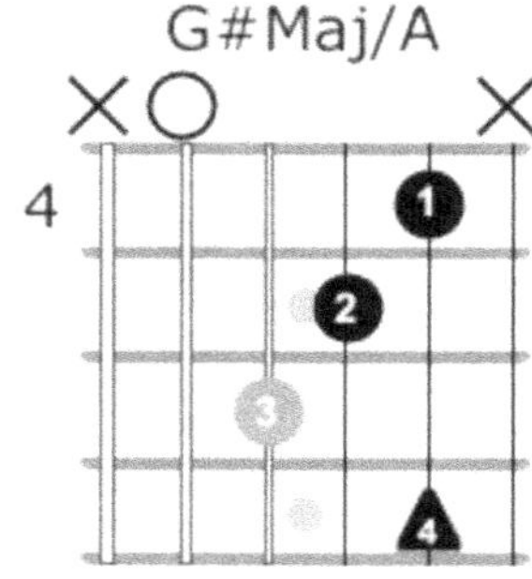

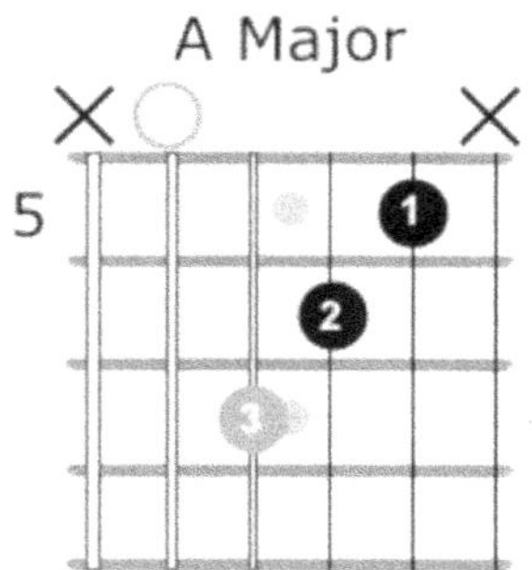

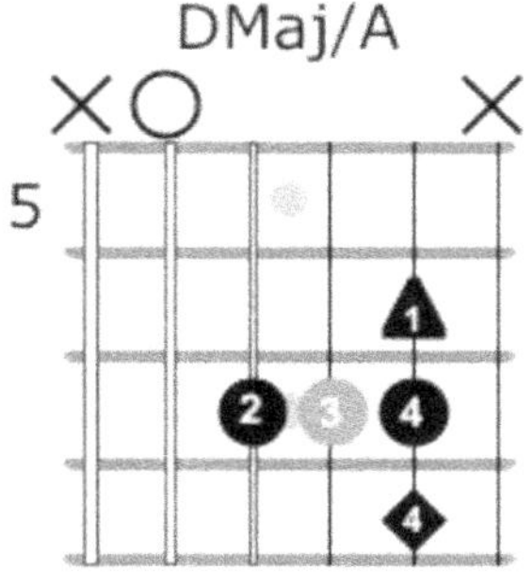

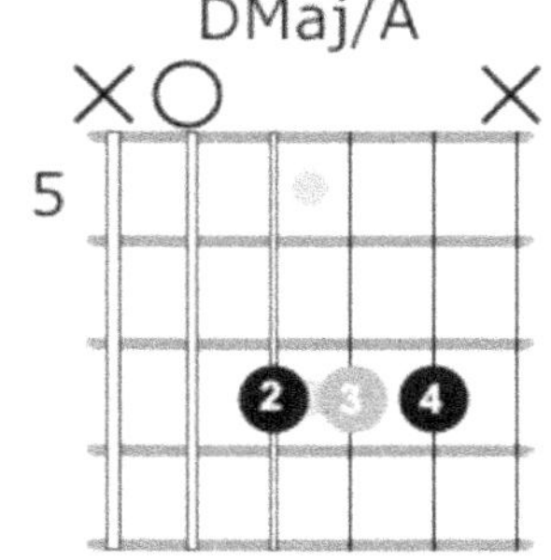

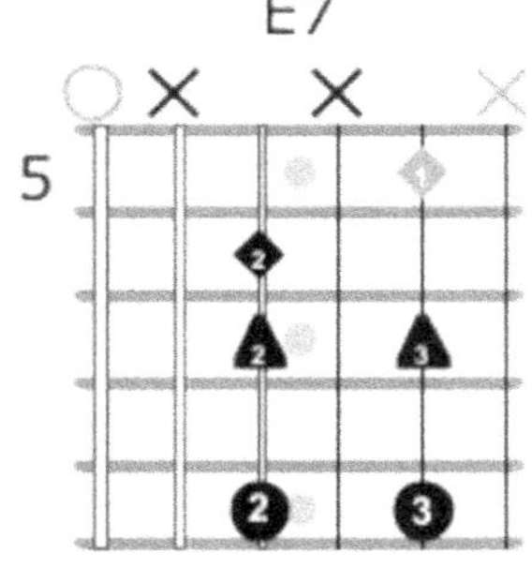

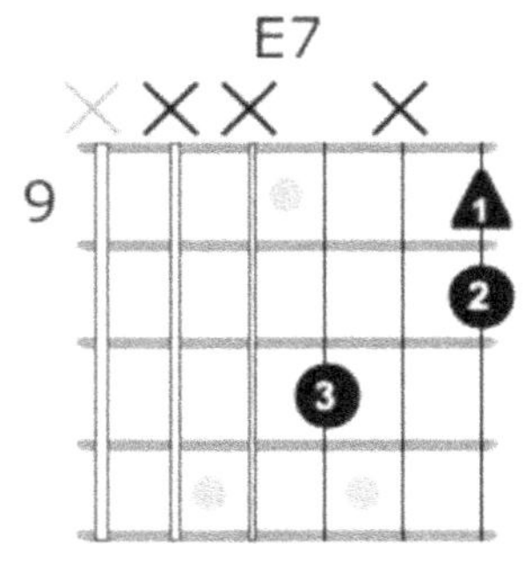

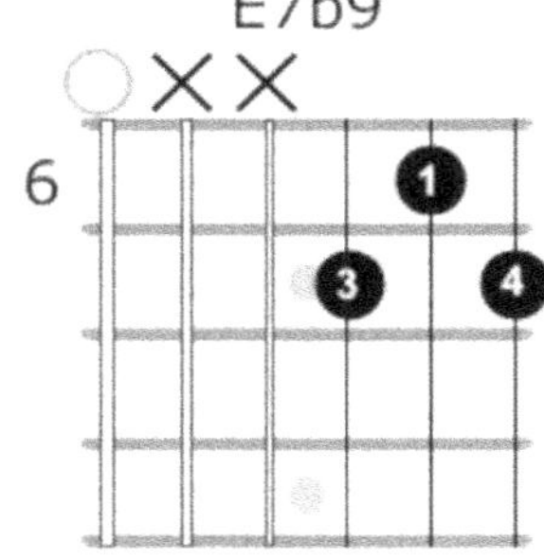

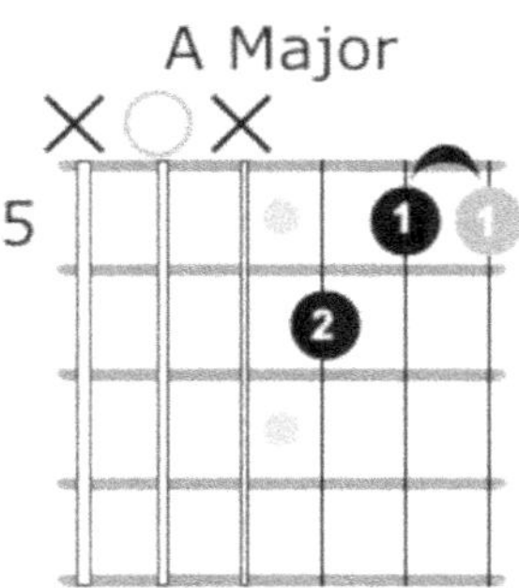

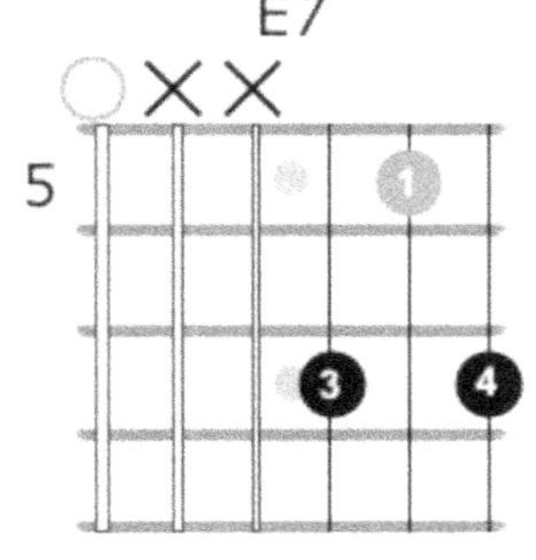

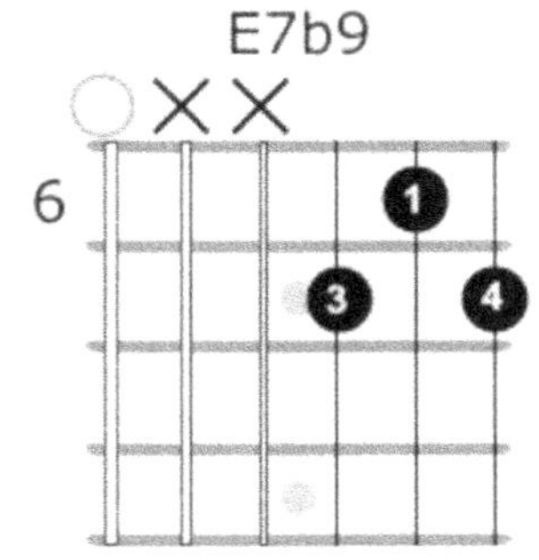

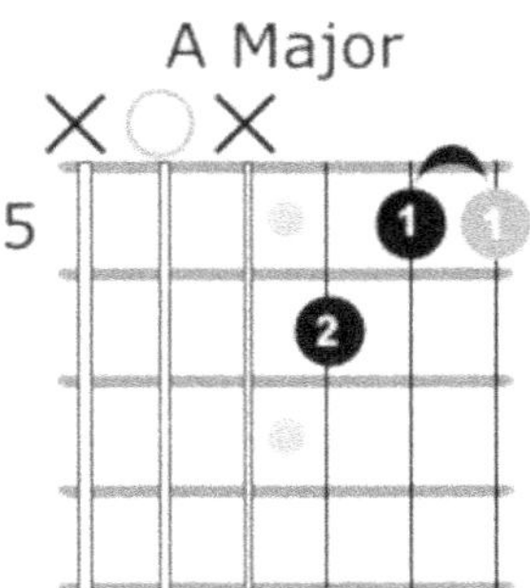

Line 5

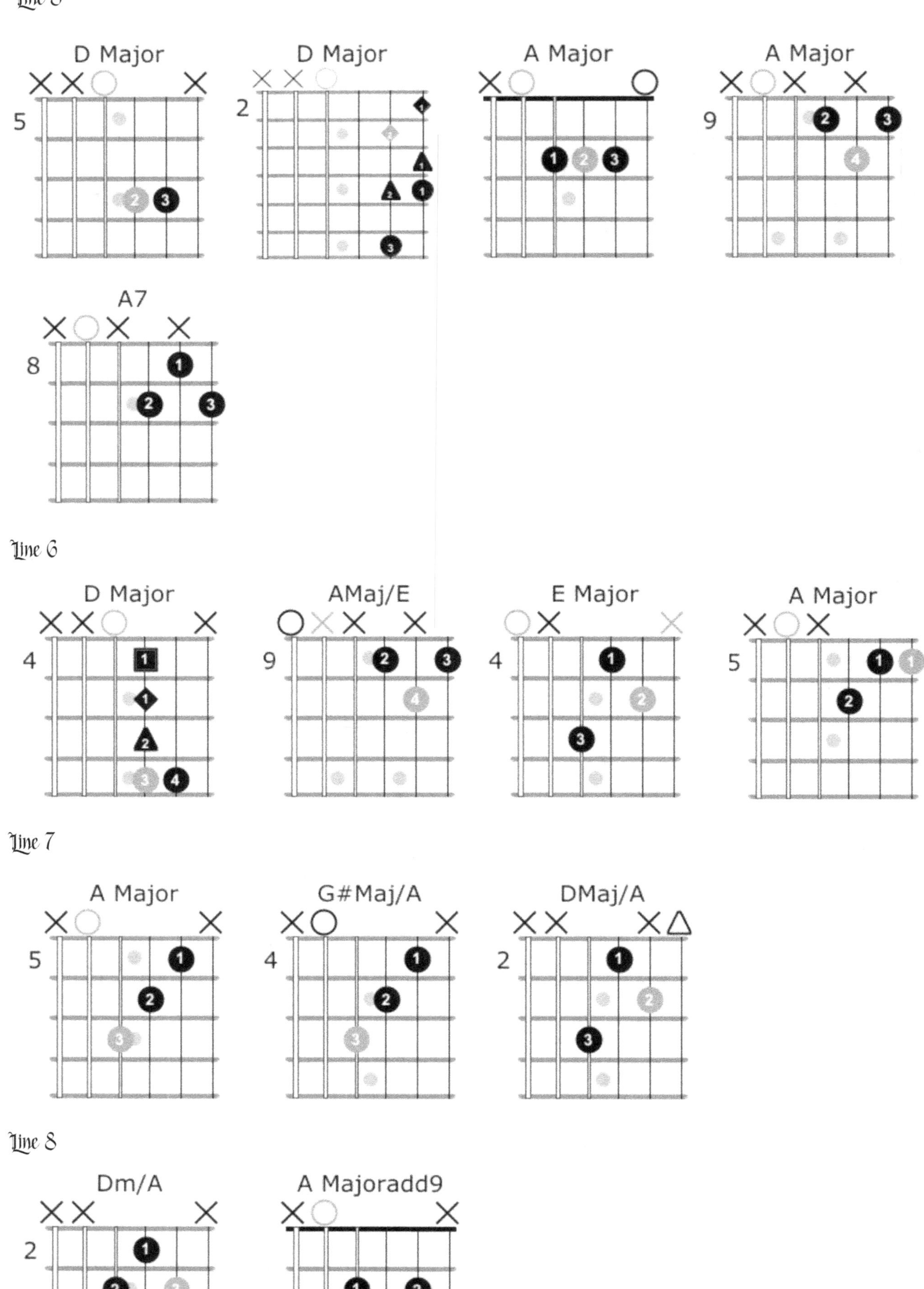

Line 6

Line 7

Line 8

THE OLD RUGGED CROSS - Advanced

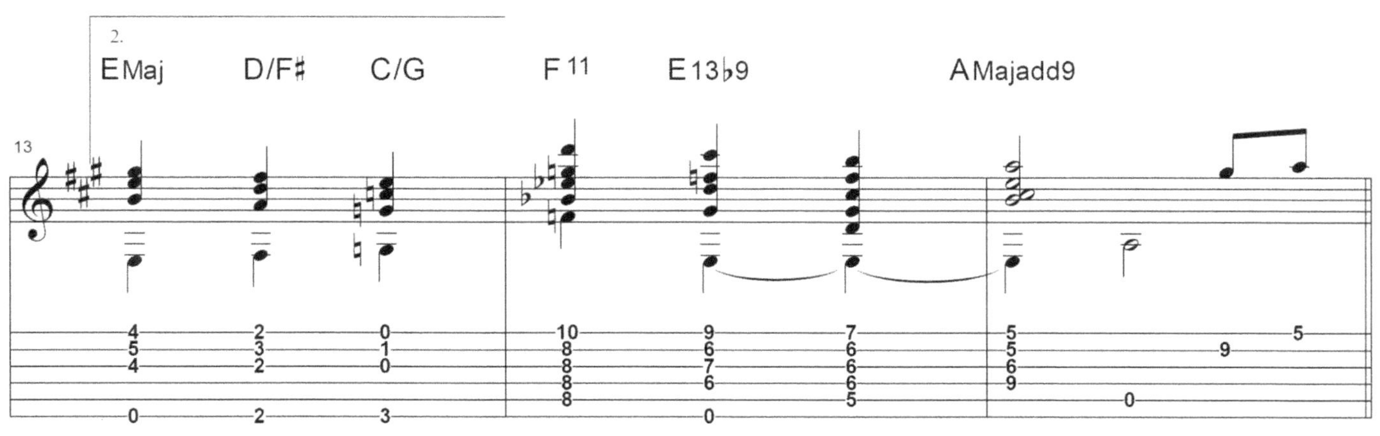
2.
EMaj   D/F#   C/G   F11   E13b9   AMajadd9

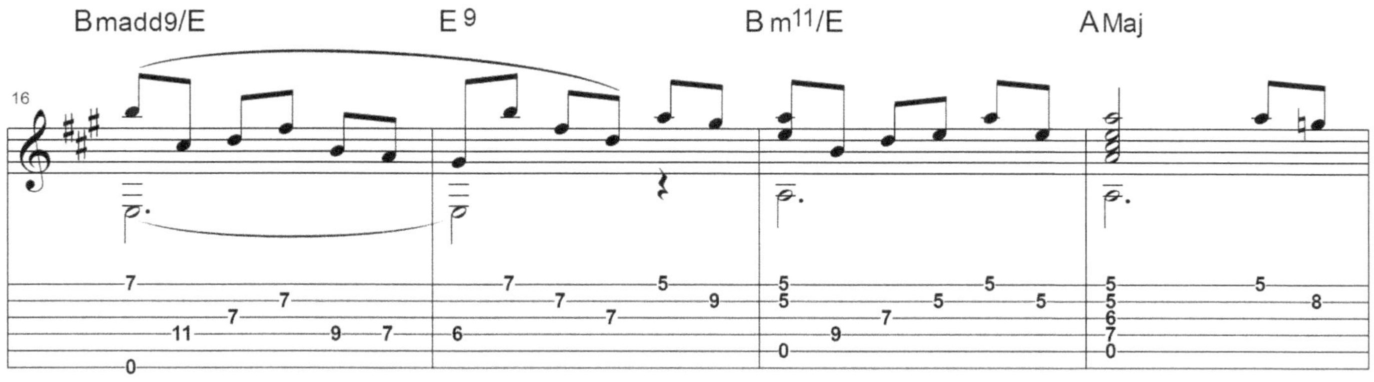
Bmadd9/E   E9   Bm11/E   AMaj

DMaj7   D#o7   A/E

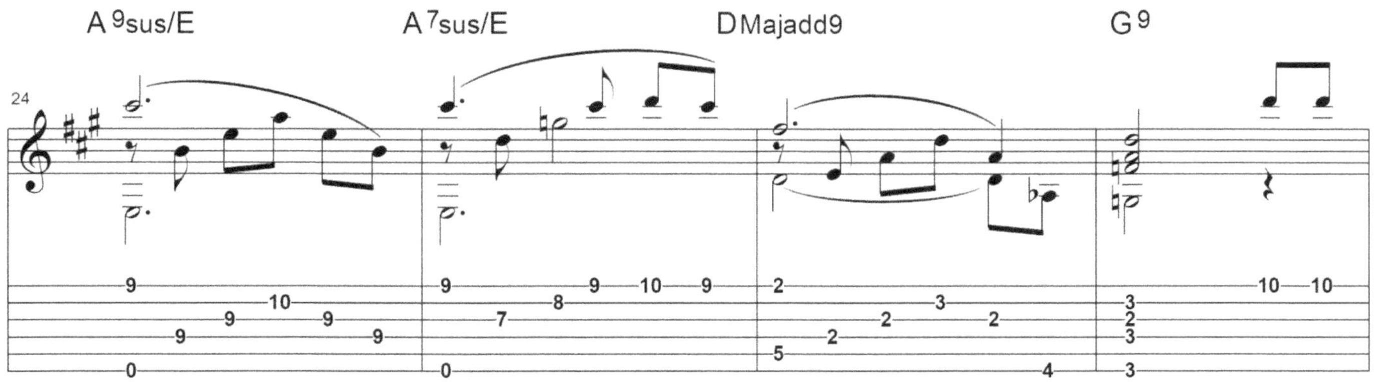
A9sus/E   A7sus/E   DMajadd9   G9

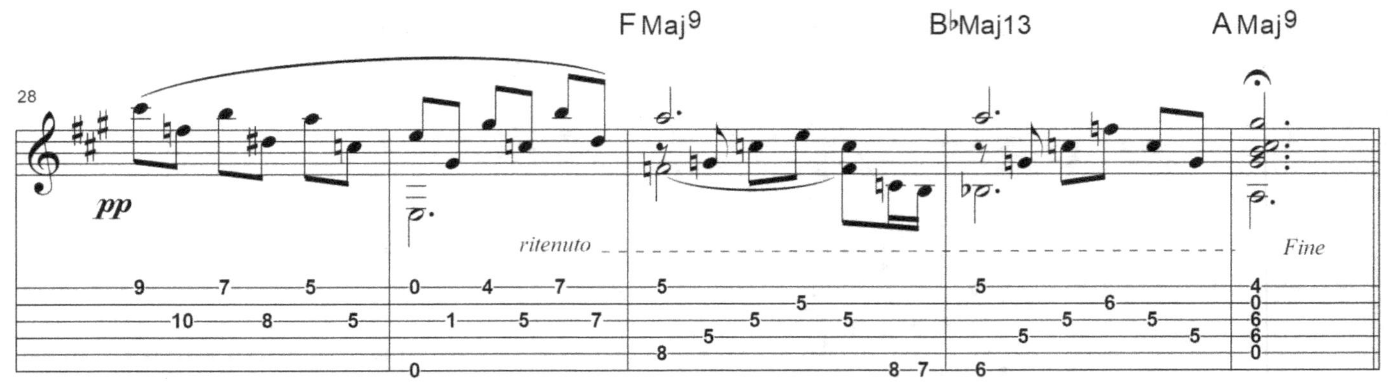

28
pp
F Maj9
B♭ Maj13
A Maj9
ritenuto
Fine

Chords: The Old Rugged Cross Advanced

Note: First two bars are melodic intervals which are not displayed, the chords below begin at bar three.

Line 1

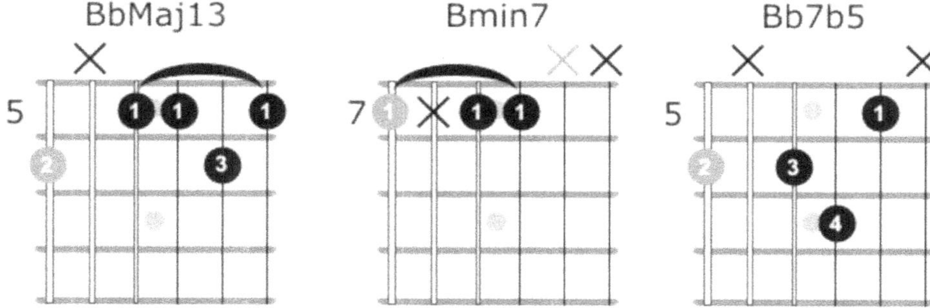

Line 2

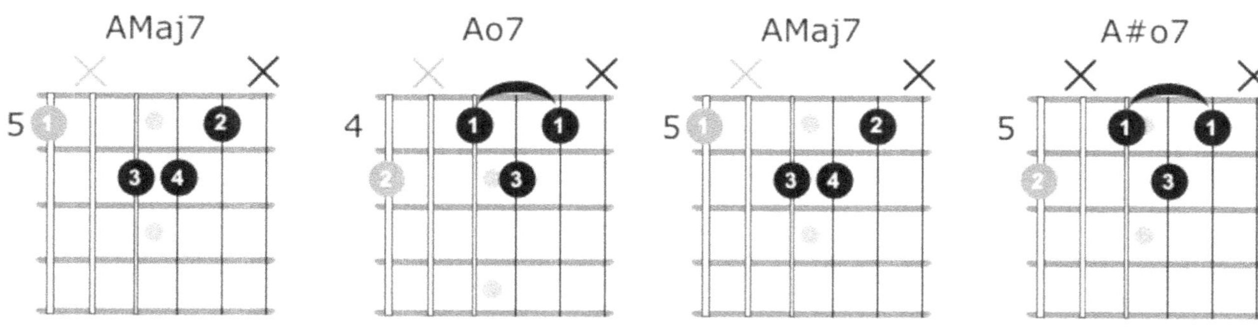

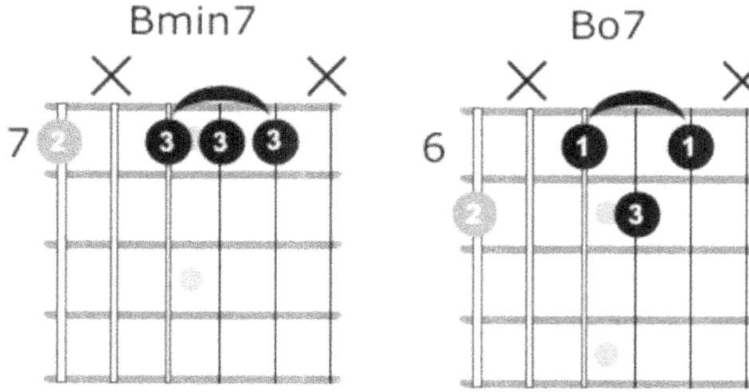

Line 3

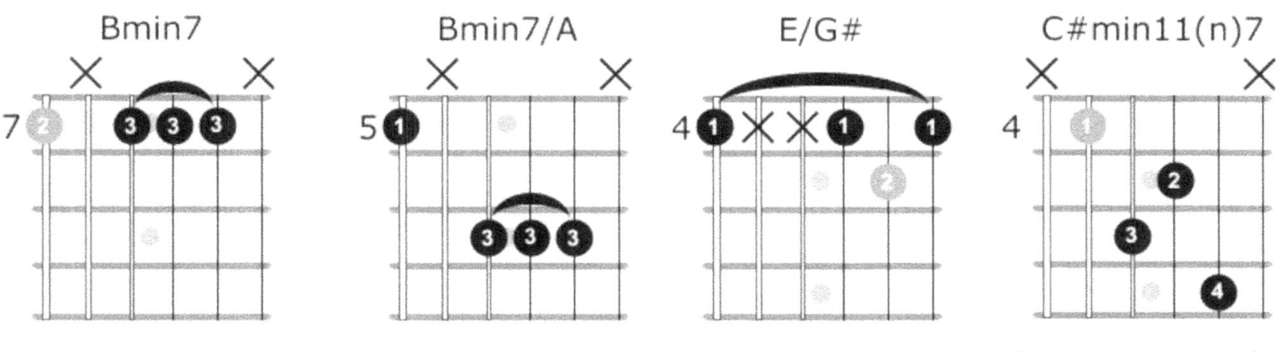

Note: n = natural

G13
Bm7b5/E
E7+
E7b9
3
5
5

Line 4

AMaj7
CMajadd9
FMaj9
Bmin11
5
5
7
5
Bb7
E7
6
6

Line 5

EMajor
D/F#
C/G
F11
4
2
8

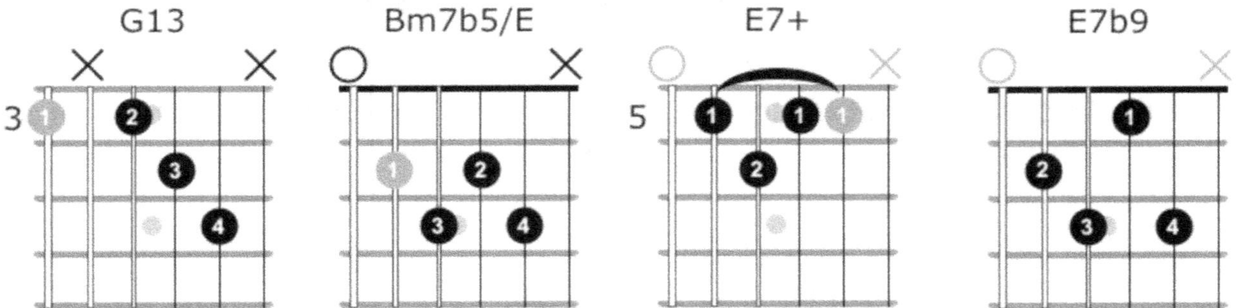

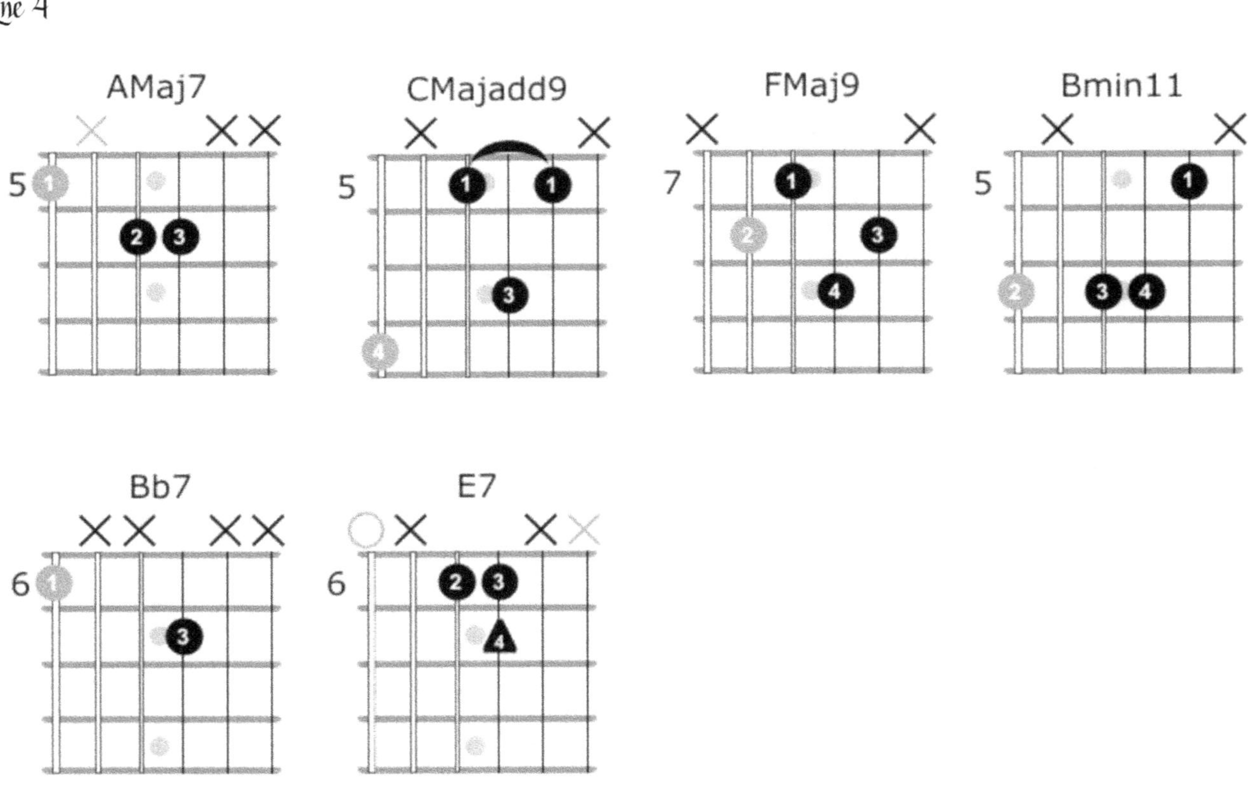

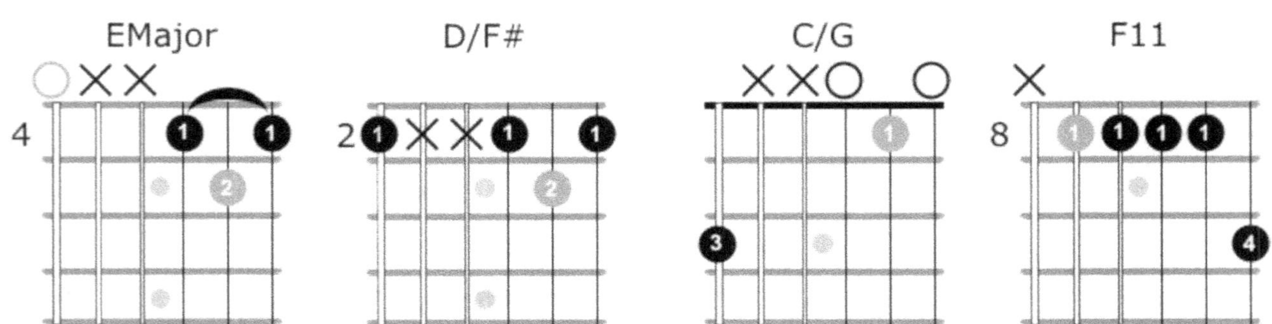

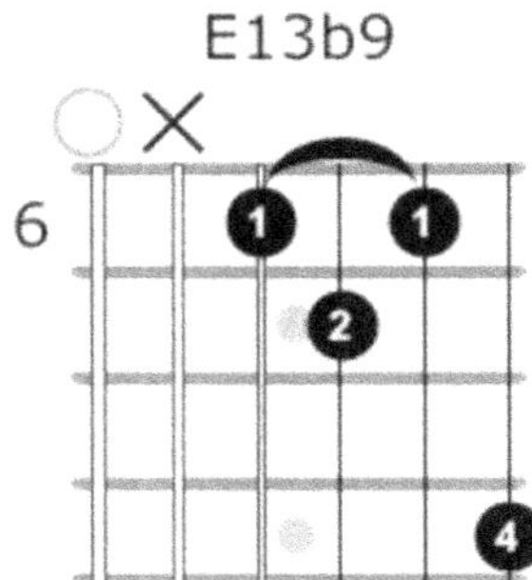

E13b9

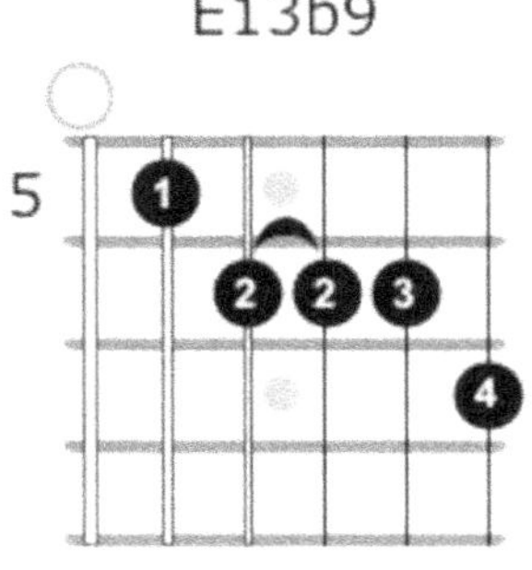

E13b9

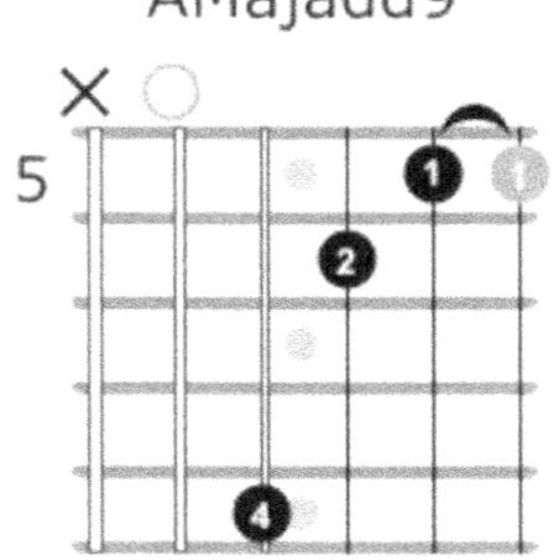

AMajadd9

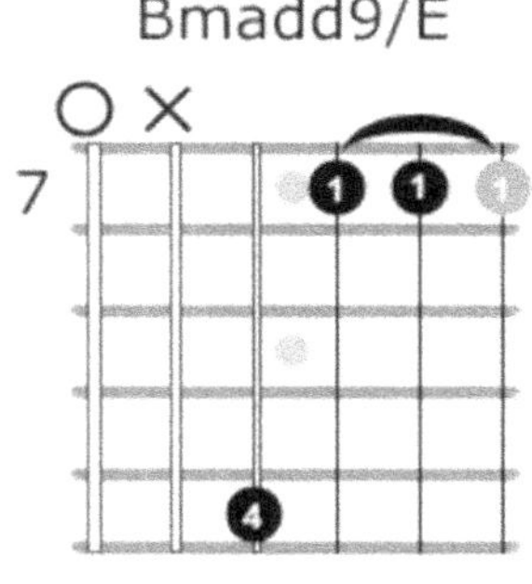

Bmadd9/E

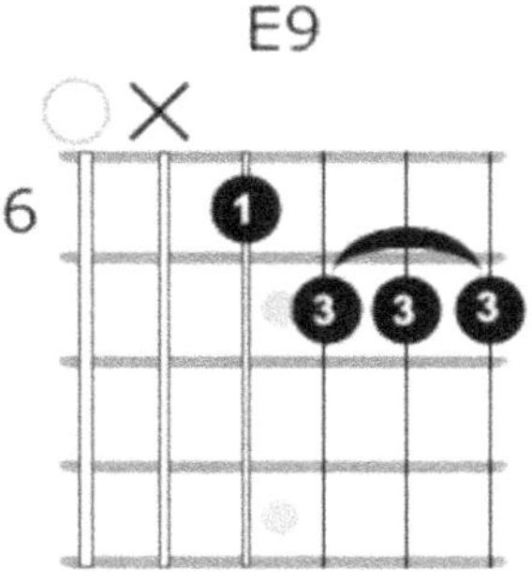

E9

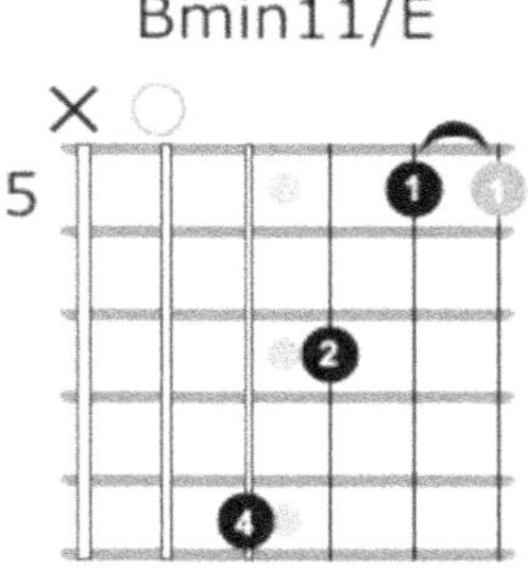

Bmin11/E

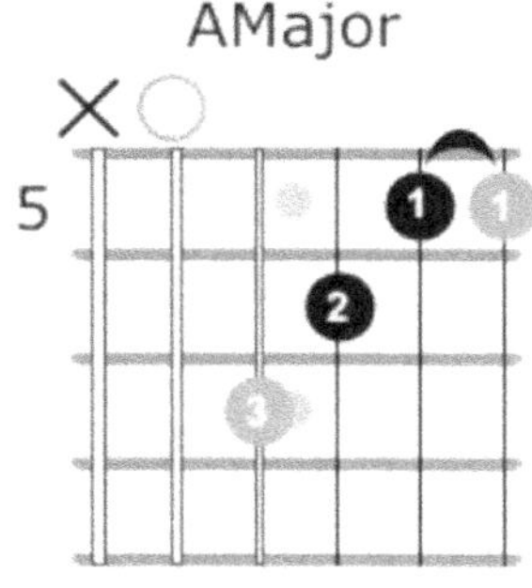

AMajor

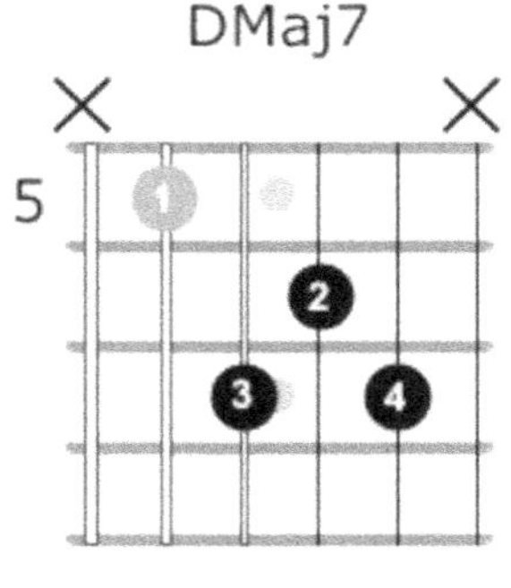

DMaj7

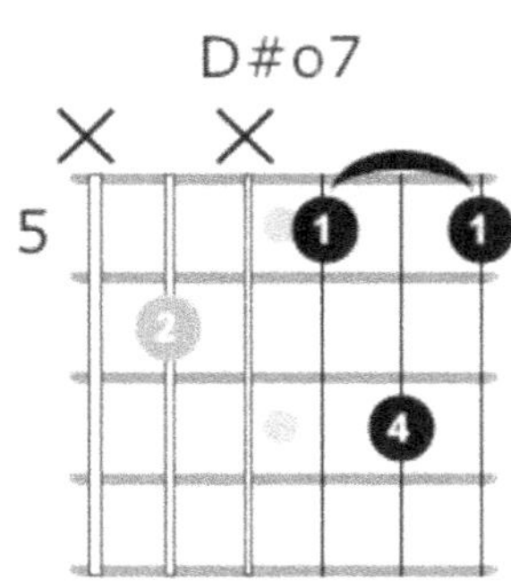

D#o7

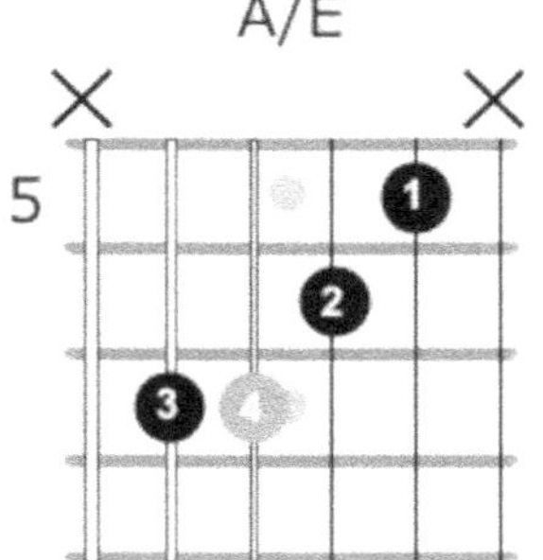

A/E

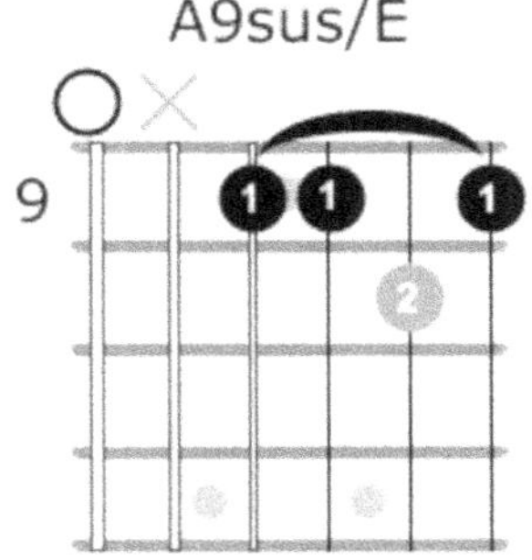

A9sus/E

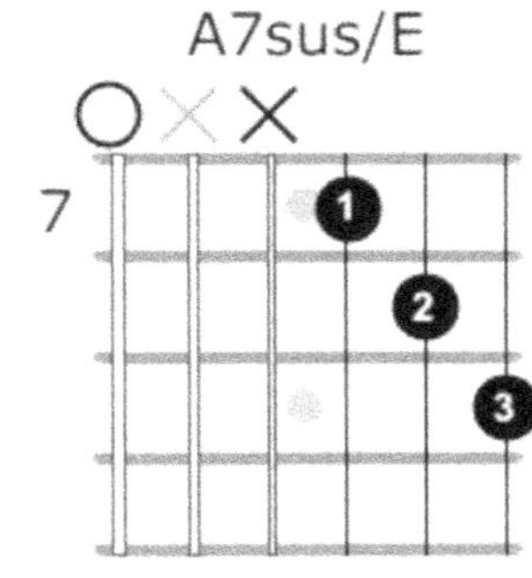

A7sus/E

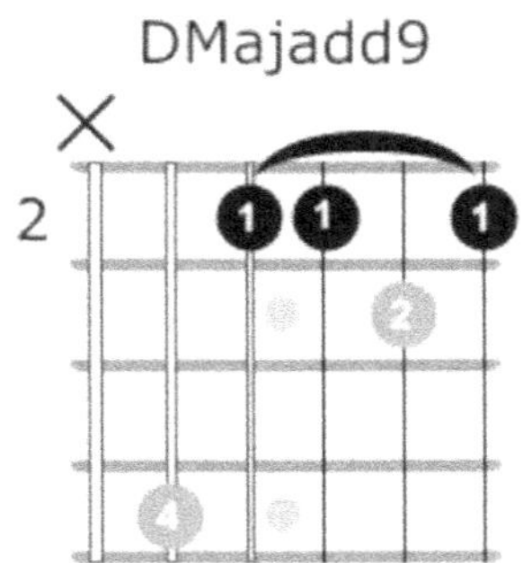

DMajadd9

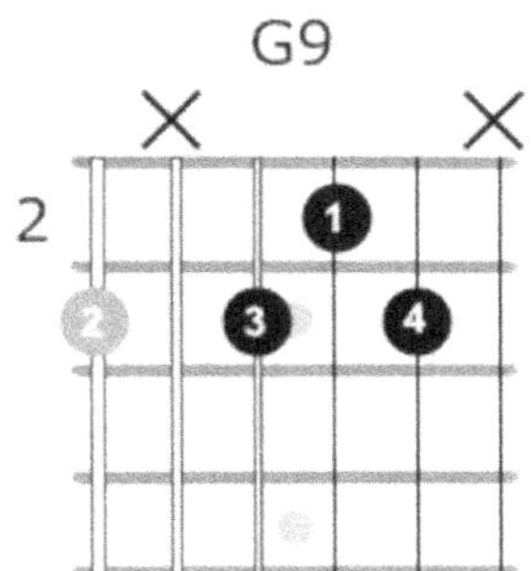

G9

Note: The first two bars of the arrangement are once again played after the G9 chord before these final three chords are played.

Line 9

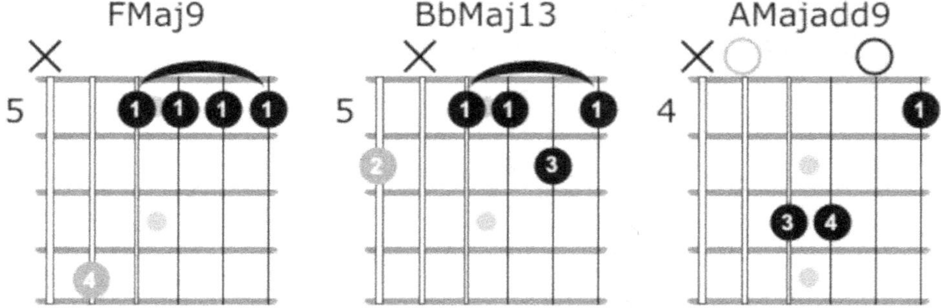

FMaj9
BbMaj13
AMajadd9

Hymn 9
'Tis So Sweet To Trust In Jesus

Resources

Performance of Intermediate version

Audio Talk through of Intermediate version

Performance of Advanced version

Audio Talk through of Advanced version

Use a QR code reader on your cell/mobile phone or tablet to view and listen to the files above. There's a large selection of completely free QR code reader apps available which work on all operating platforms.

To download all resources and other support files, follow the instructions on page 197 of this publication.

Hymn Notes –'Tis So Sweet To Trust In Jesus

Louisa M.R. Stead (1850 – 1917) was born in England. Her burning ambition was to become a missionary for God in China. A thread of tragedy, however, seems to run through many of the lives of the great hymn writers and we find it again in Louisa's life. After moving to America and marrying, she was out with her husband and child near a coastal area when they saw a boy drowning. Her husband jumped in to save the boy but sadly both drowned. From that point, Louisa and her child became destitute. This song was written in response to praying to God to help them. A knock on the door was heard soon after and a hot meal and money had been placed outside the house. Louisa went on to missionary in Africa where she remarried and remained for the rest of her life.

Louisa M.R. Stead   William J. Kirkpatrick

William J. Kirkpatrick (1838 – 1921) was a notable and prodigious musical talent. Born in Ireland, his family emigrated to America when he was very young. A carpenter by trade, William eventually downed his tools after the death of his first wife to work as a musician full time. The composer of the music for the words of this song, William built up an impressive and large catalogue of Christian music throughout his life. He was to become the musical director at Grace Methodist Church in Philadelphia.

Lyrics

Verse 1

'Tis so sweet to trust in Jesus,

Just to take Him at His Word

Just to rest upon His promise,

Just to know, "Thus saith the Lord!"

Chorus

Jesus, Jesus, how I trust Him!

How I've proved Him o'er and o'er

Jesus, Jesus, precious Jesus!

O for grace to trust Him more!

Verse 2

O how sweet to trust in Jesus,

Just to trust His cleansing blood;

Just in simple faith to plunge me

'Neath the healing, cleansing flood!

Chorus

Verse 3

Yes, 'tis sweet to trust in Jesus,

Just from sin and self to cease;

Just from Jesus simply taking

Life and rest, and joy and peace.

Chorus

Verse 4

I'm so glad I learned to trust Thee,

Precious Jesus, Savior, Friend;

And I know that Thou art with me,

Wilt be with me to the end.

Chorus

'Tis So Sweet To Trust In Jesus - Starter

music - William J Kirkpatrick
lyrics - Louisa M. R. Stead

'Tis So Sweet To Trust In Jesus - Starter alternate key

Slowly

music - William J Kirkpatrick
lyrics - Louisa M. R. Stead

Chords: 'Tis So Sweet To Trust In Jesus Starter Song

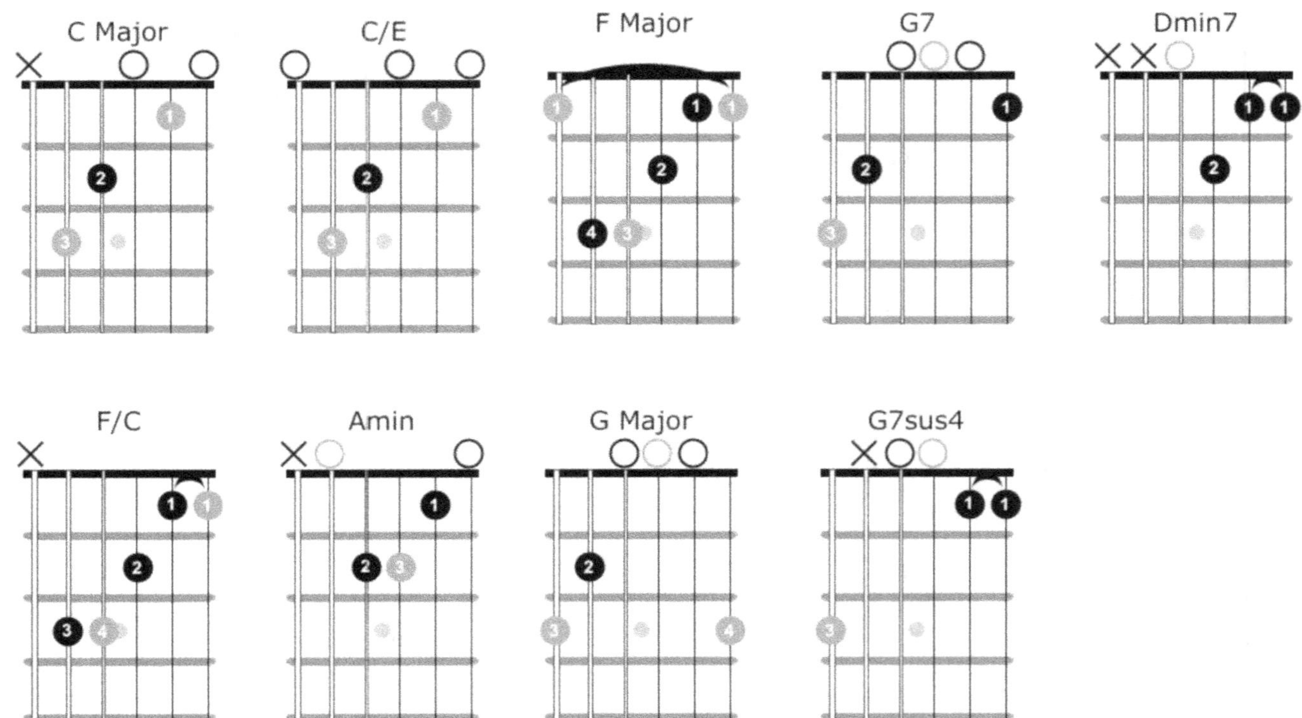

Chords: 'Tis So Sweet To Trust In Jesus Starter Song Alternate Key

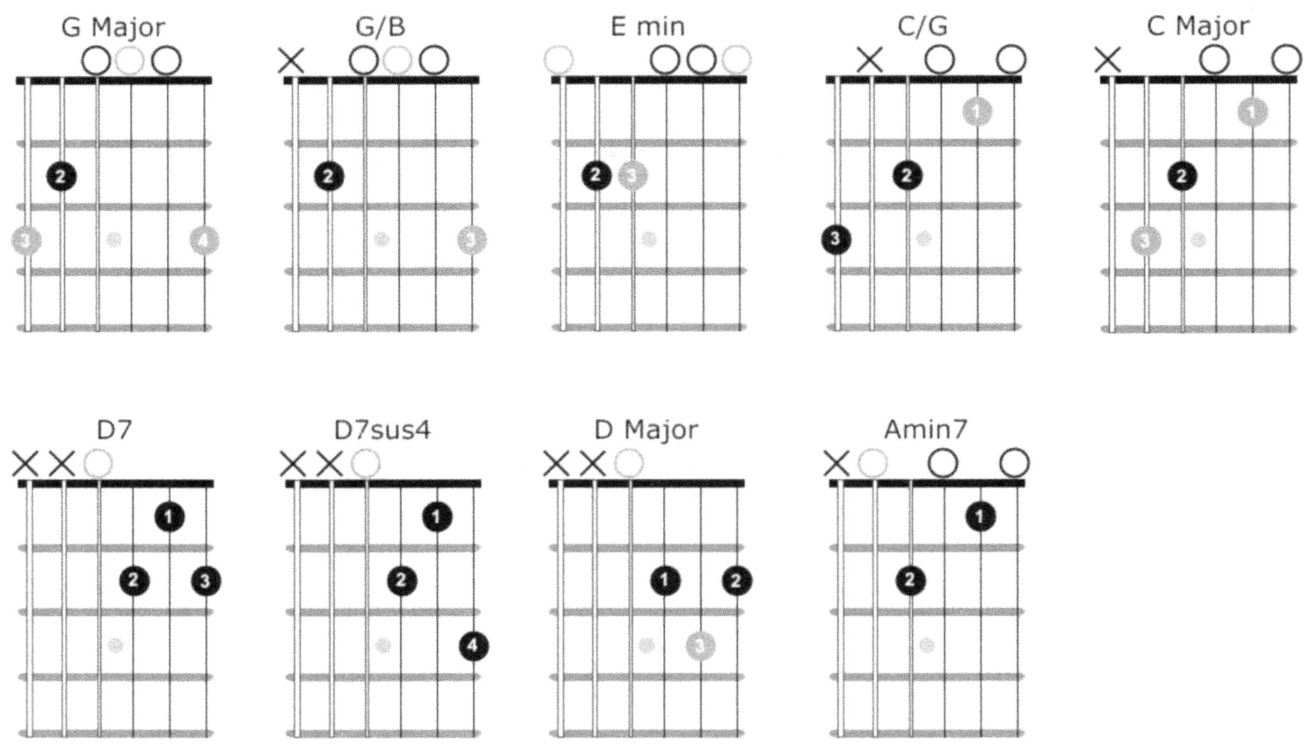

'Tis So Sweet To Trust In Jesus play along

bpm = 80

Abide With Me + Melody
Abide With Me Backing Track

Count of 4 then play

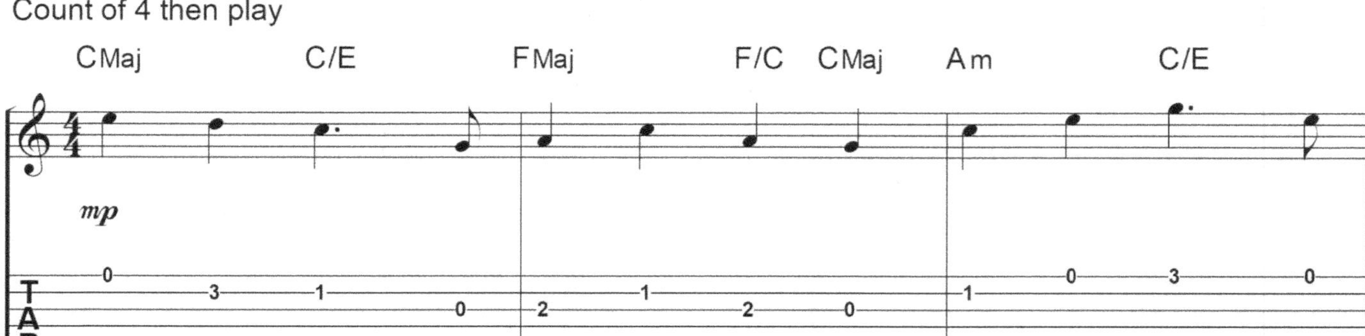

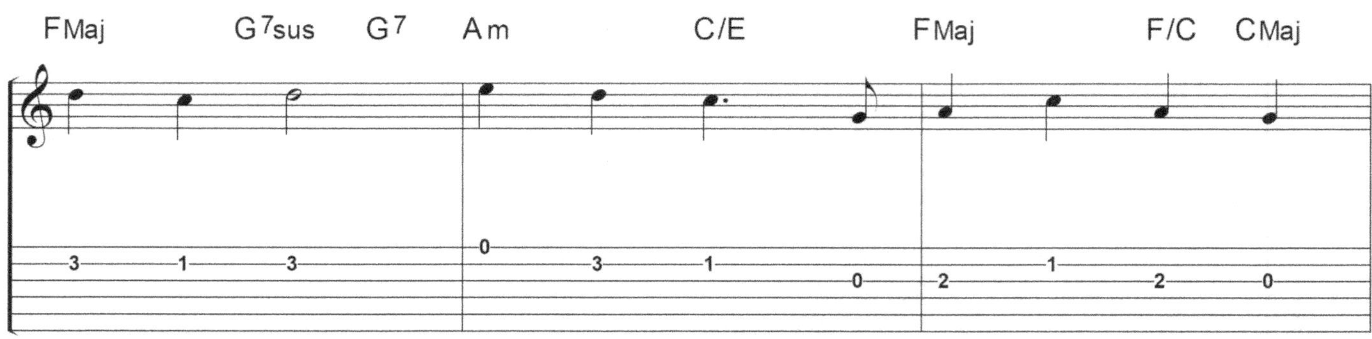

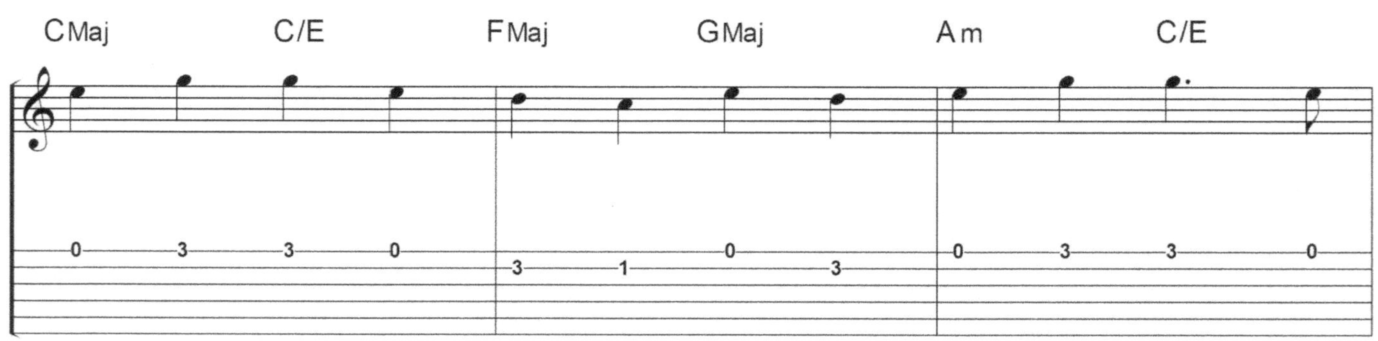

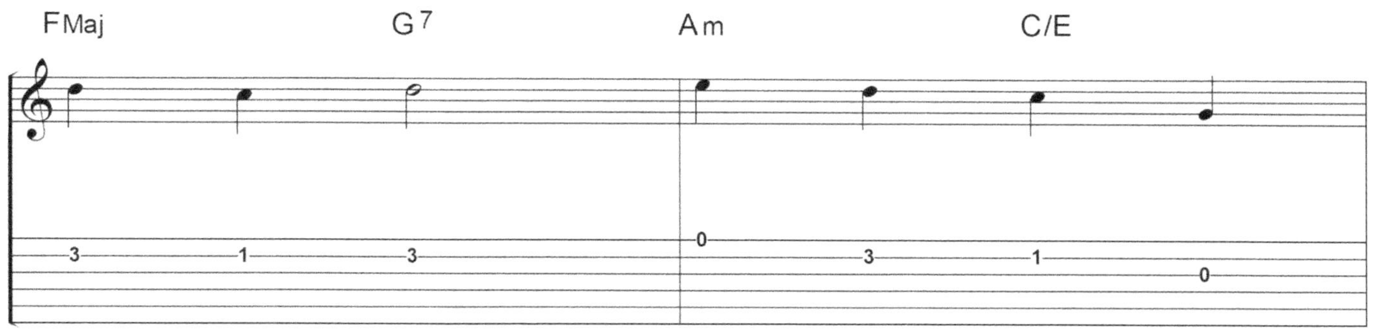

FMaj
G7
Am
C/E

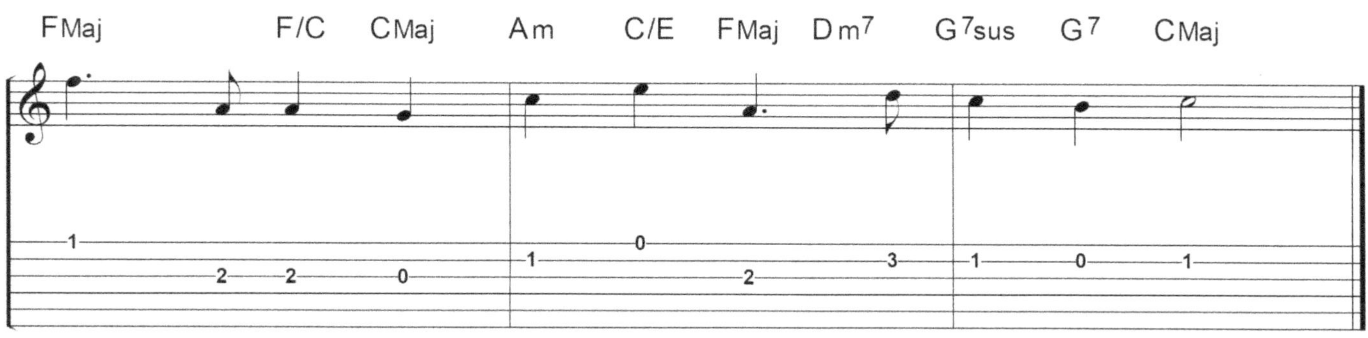

FMaj
F/C
CMaj
Am
C/E
FMaj
Dm7
G7sus
G7
CMaj

'Tis So Sweet To Trust In Jesus - Intermediate

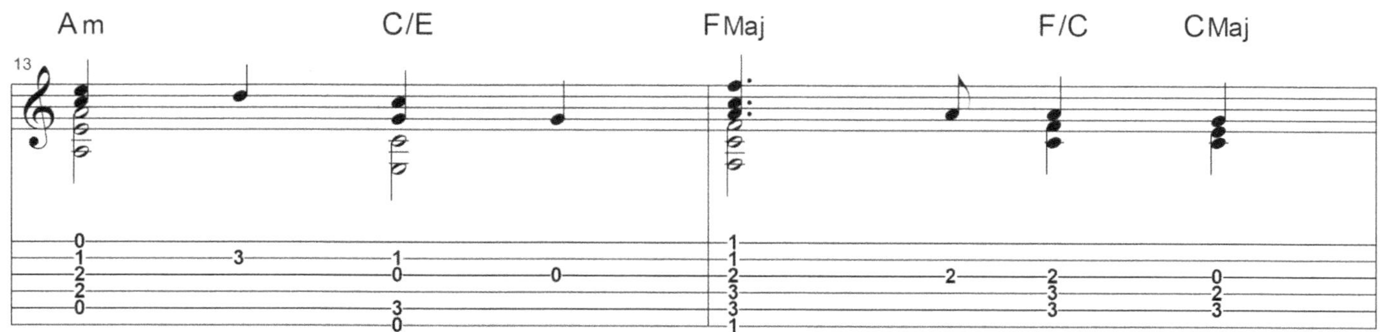

Am
C/E
FMaj
F/C
CMaj
13

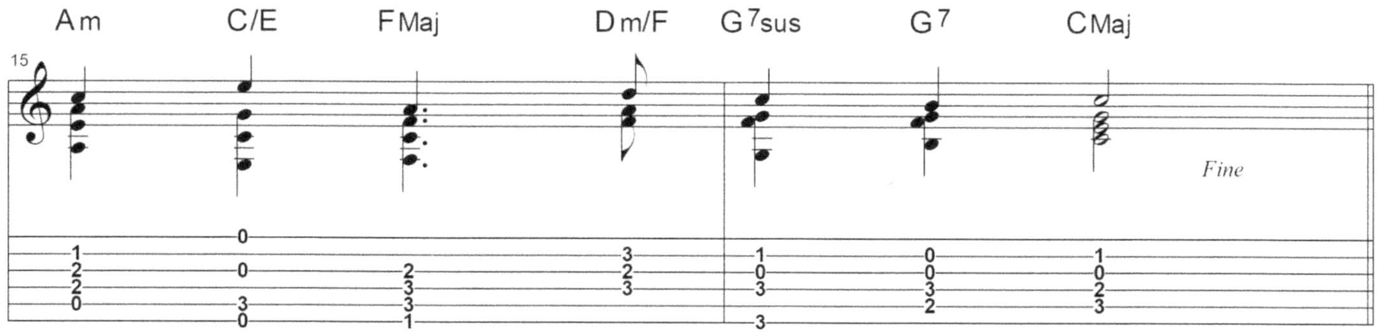

Am
C/E
FMaj
Dm/F
G7sus
G7
CMaj
15
Fine

Chords: 'Tis So Sweet To Trust In Jesus Intermediate

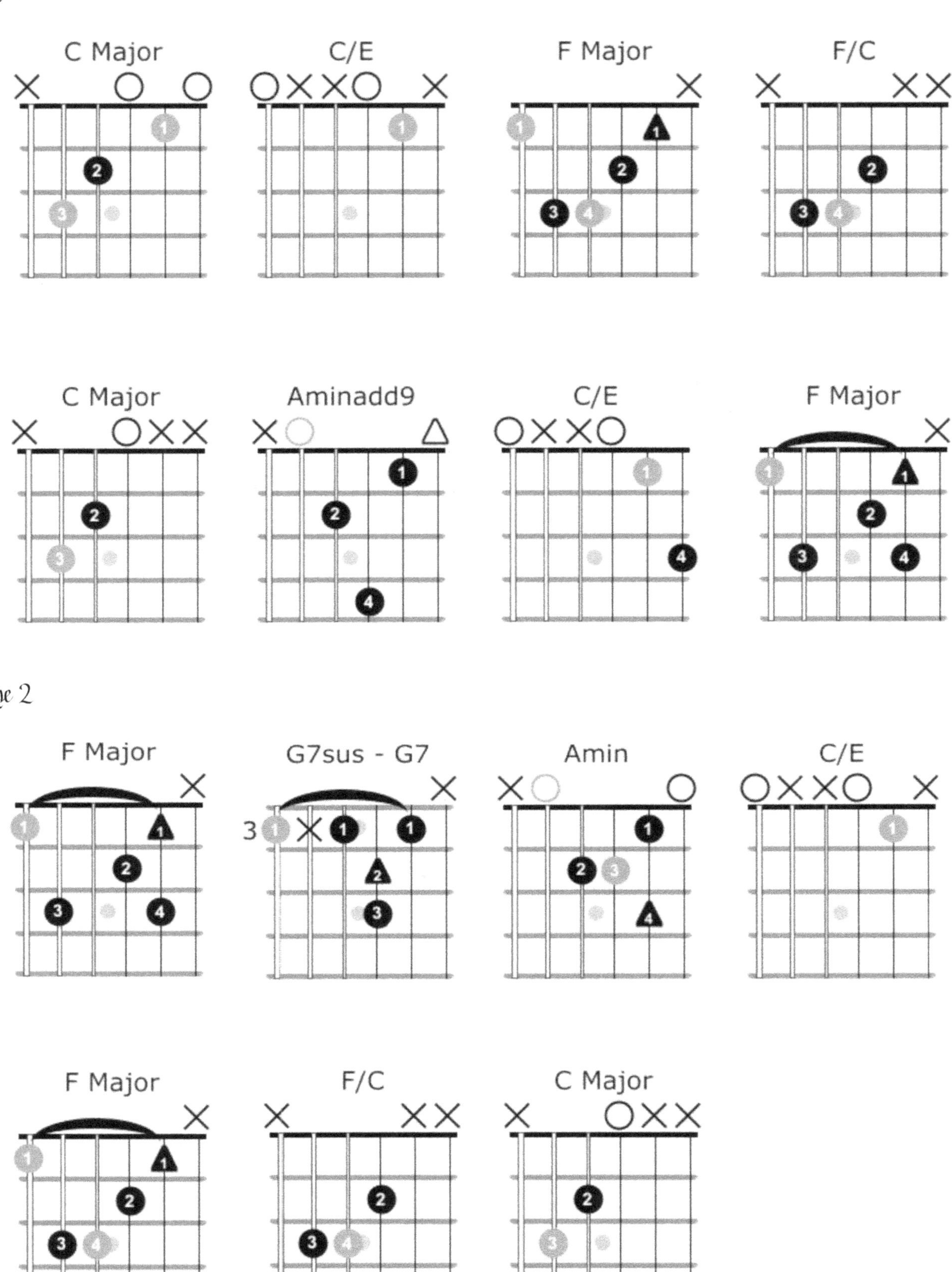

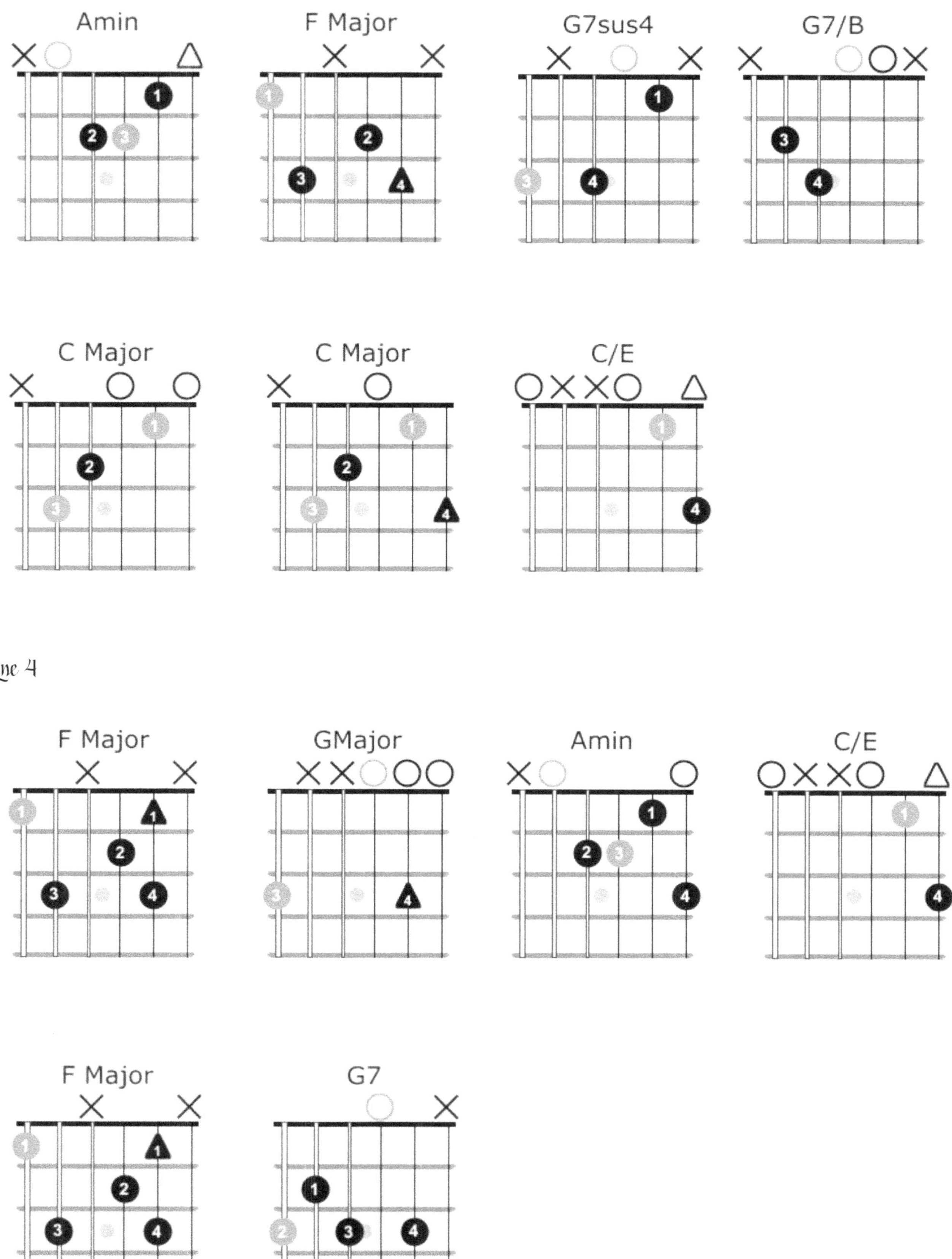

Amin
F Major
G7sus4
G7/B
C Major
C Major
C/E

F Major
GMajor
Amin
C/E
F Major
G7

Line 5

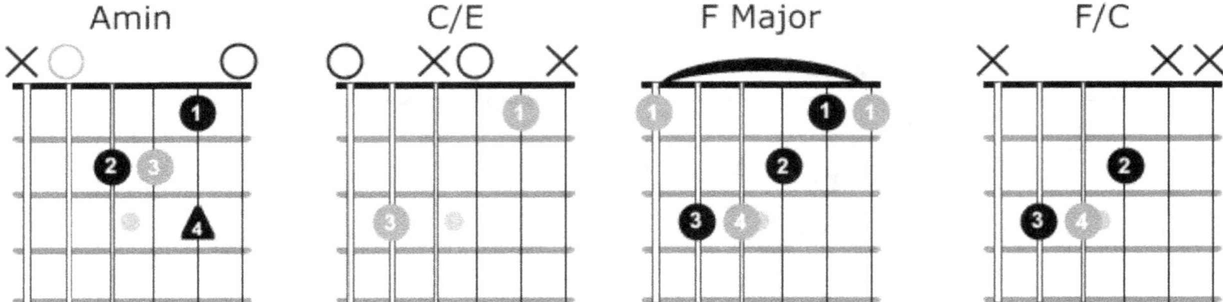
Amin
C/E
F Major
F/C

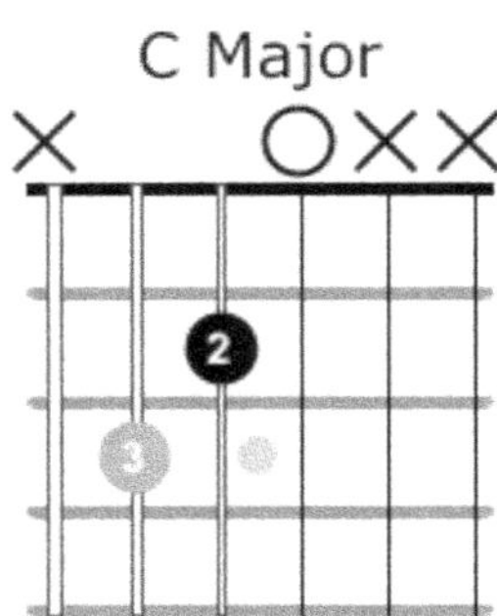
C Major

Line 6

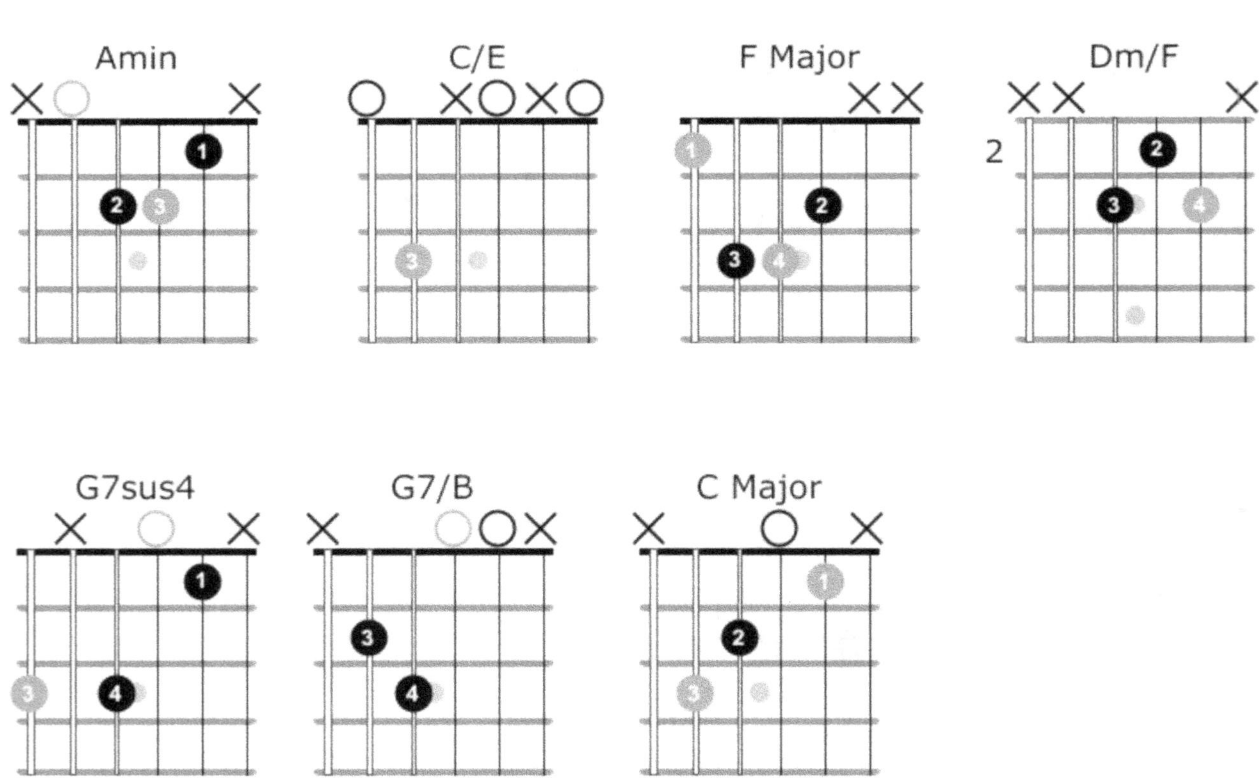
Amin
C/E
F Major
Dm/F
G7sus4
G7/B
C Major

'Tis So Sweet To Trust In Jesus - Advanced

adagio

Arranged by
Ged Brockie

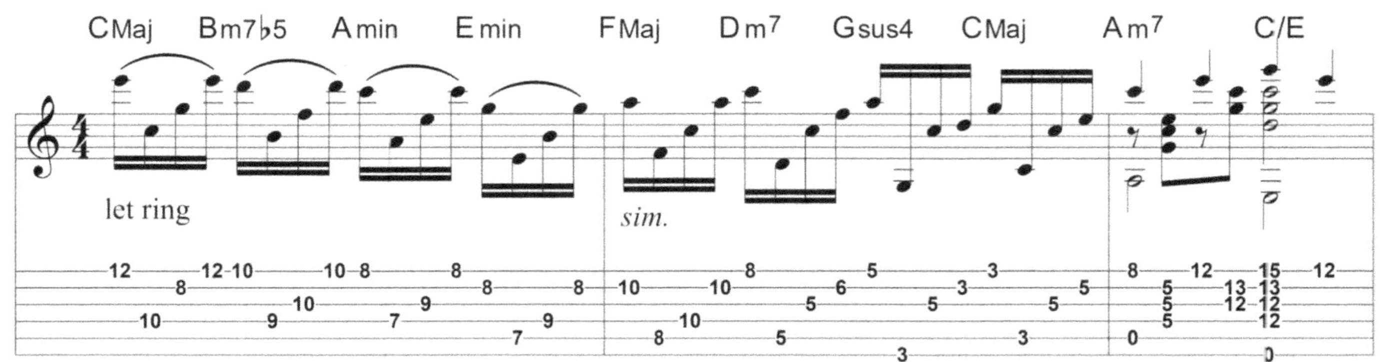

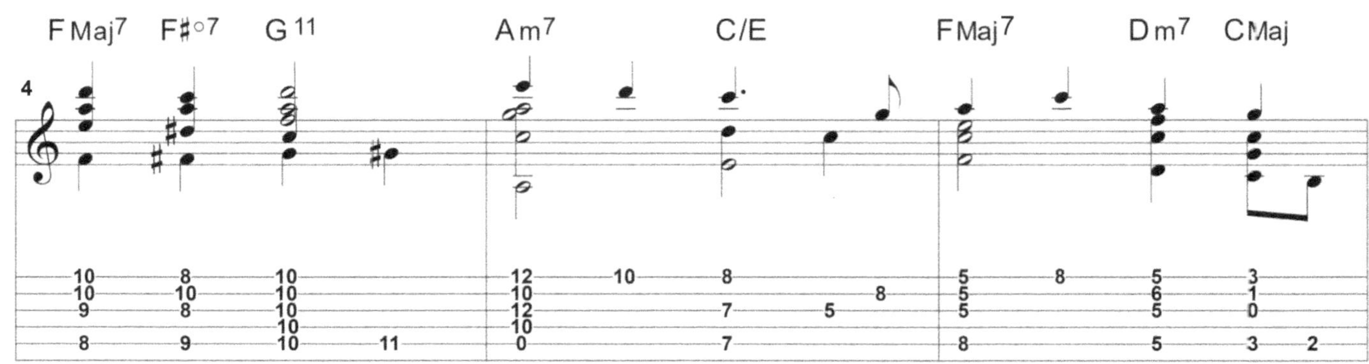

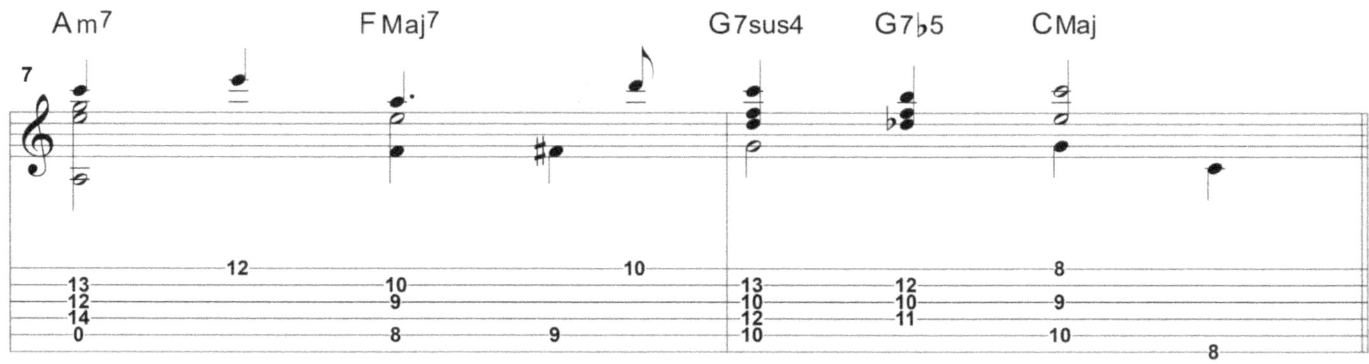

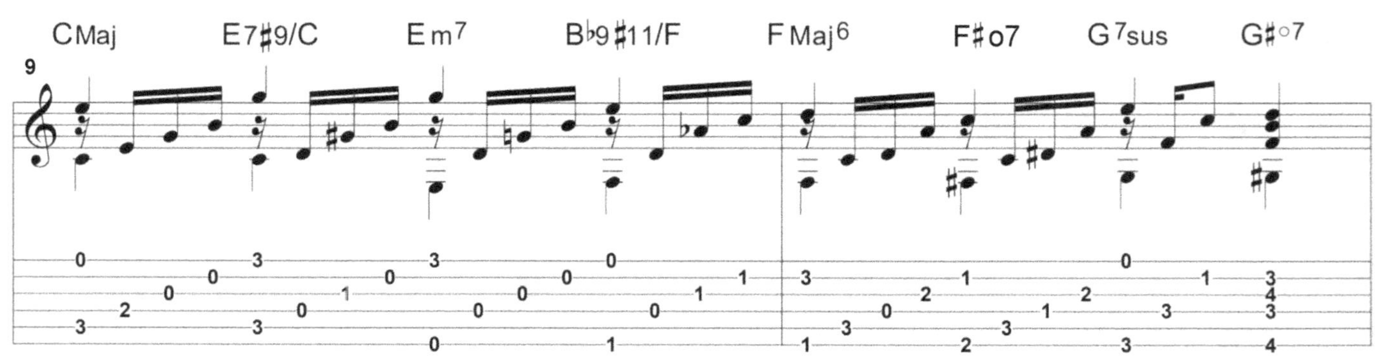

Amadd9   Am7   Em11   FMaj6   G7sus   G#°7
Am   C/E   FMaj9   F/C   CMaj
Dm11   D/F#   G11   G7b9   CMaj7
CMaj   Bm7b5   Amin   Emin   FMaj   Dm7   CMajadd9
let ring
Fine

Chords: 'Tis So Sweet To Trust In Jesus Advanced

Line 1

CMajor

Bm7b5

Amin

Emin

FMajor

Dmin7

Gsus4

CMajor

Amin7

Amin7

C/E

Line 2

FMaj7(13)

F#o7

G11

Amin7

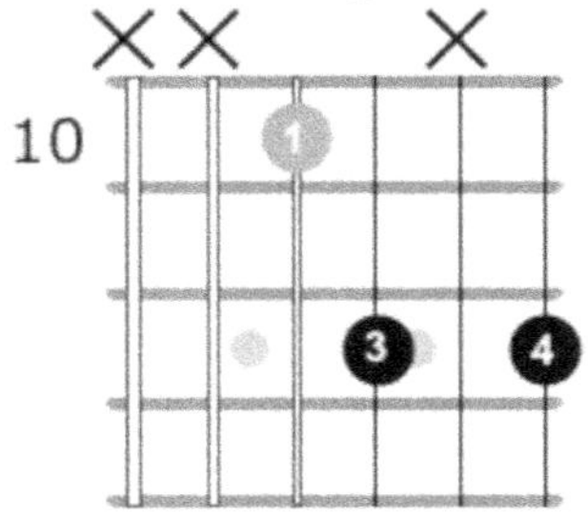

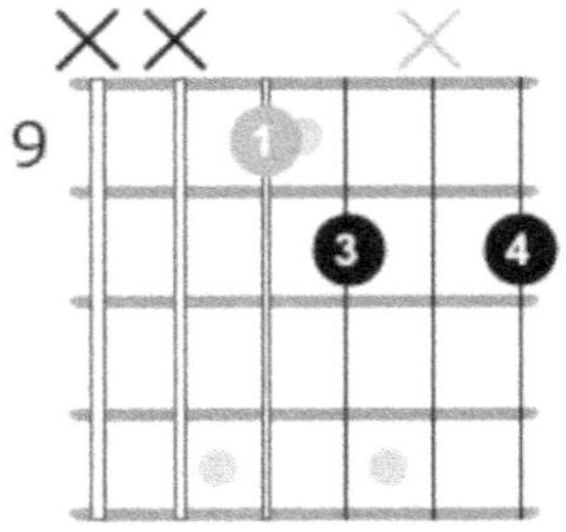

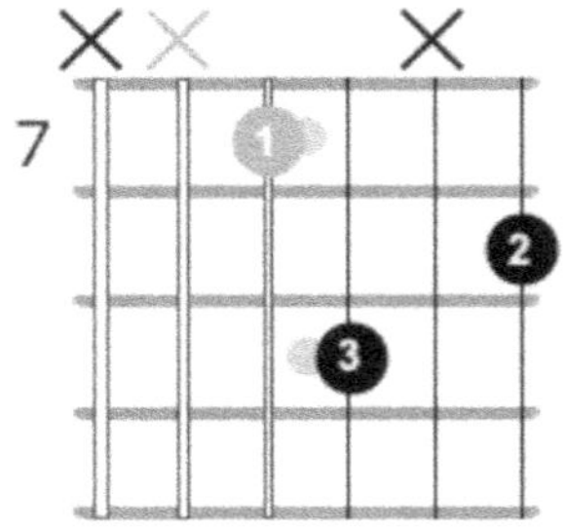

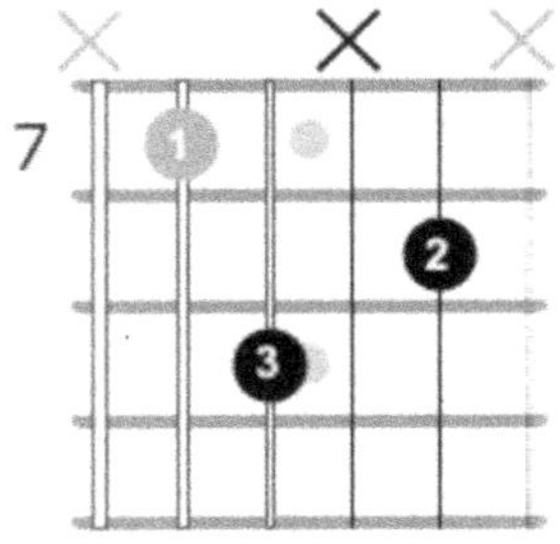

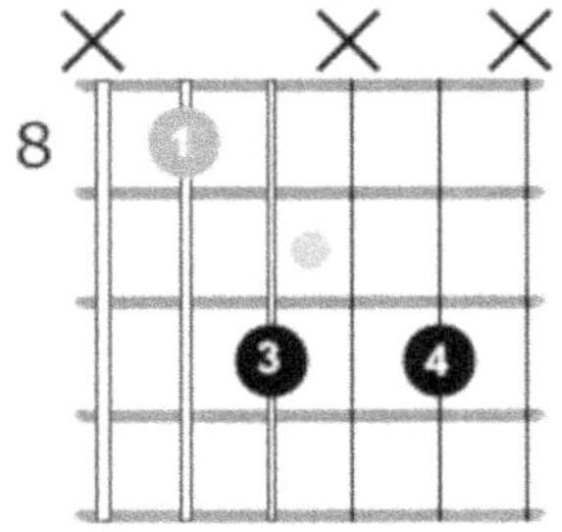

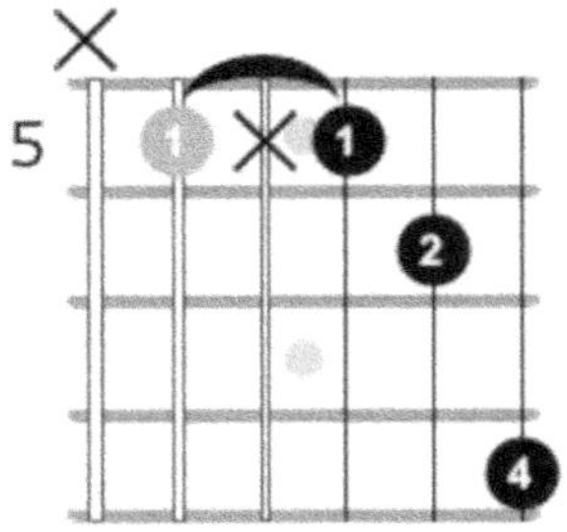

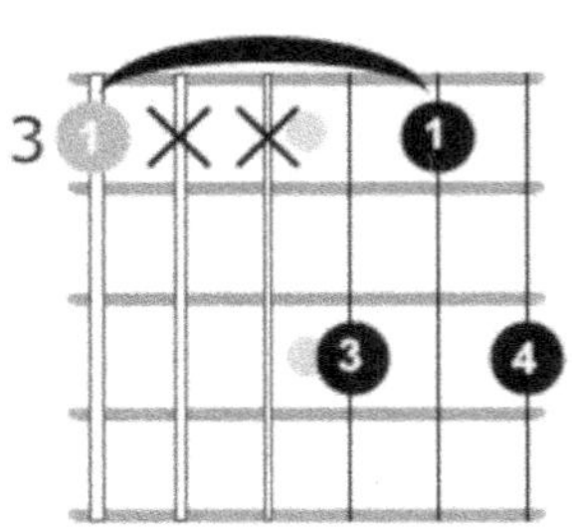

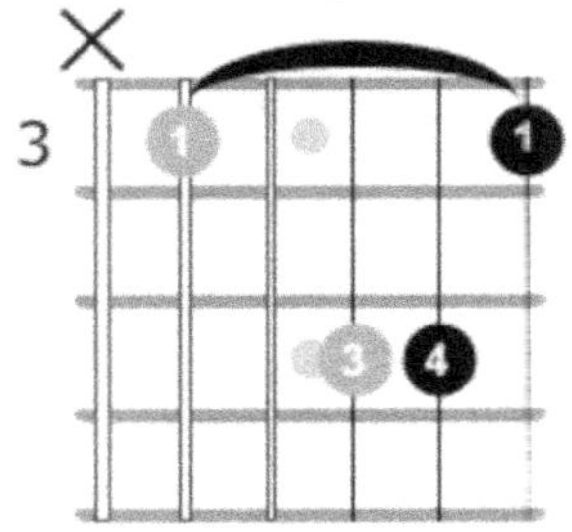

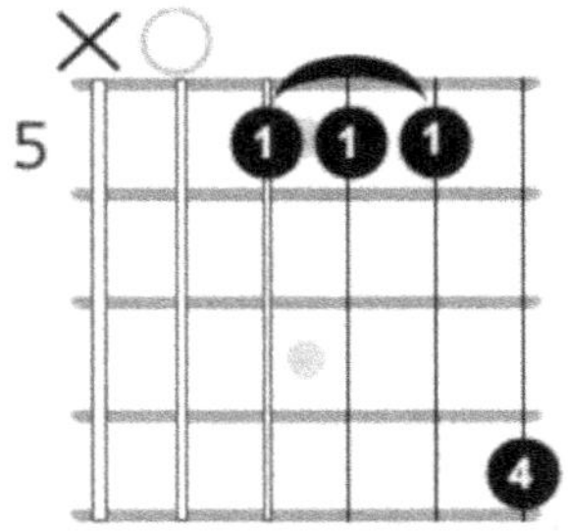

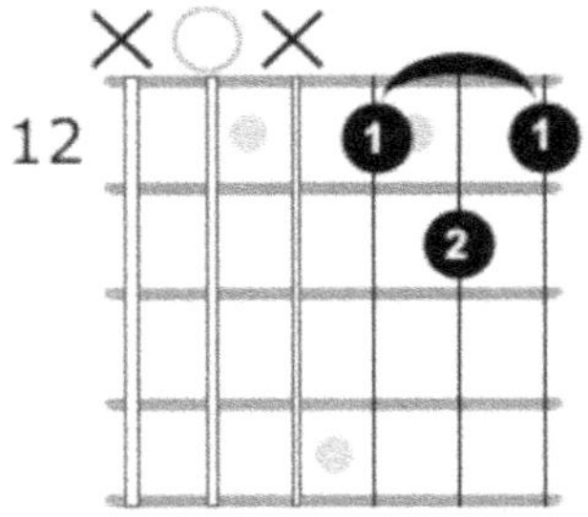

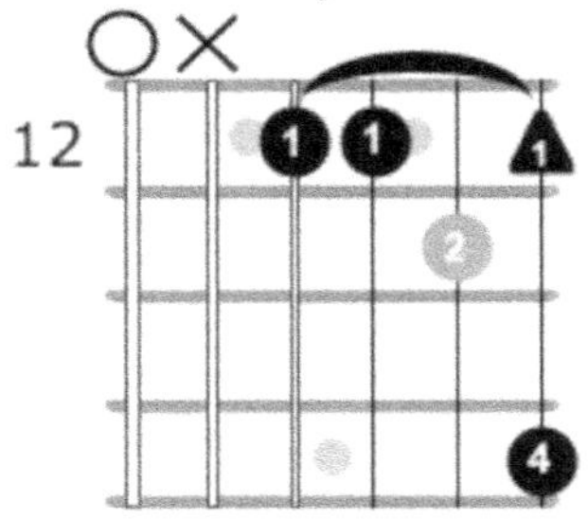

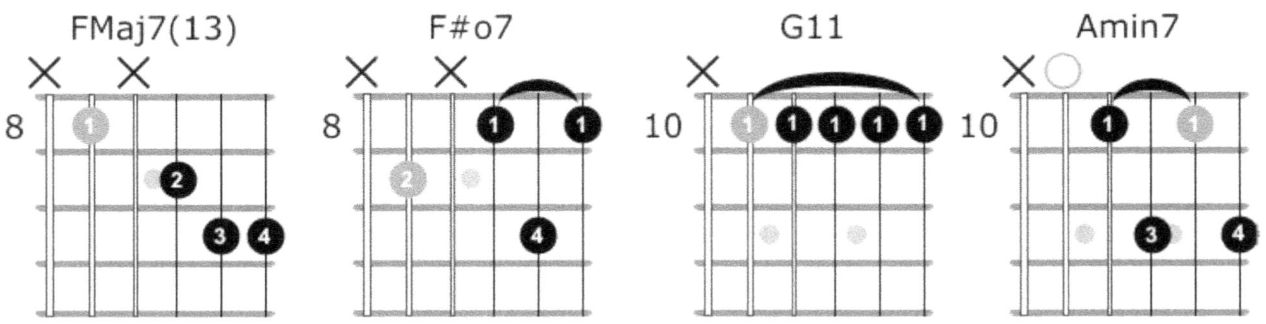

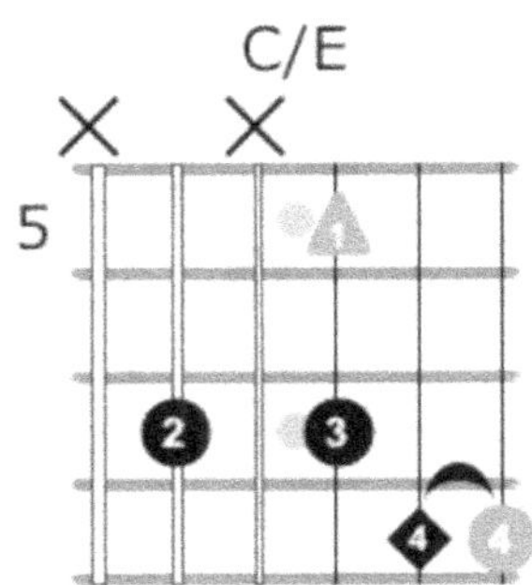

C/E

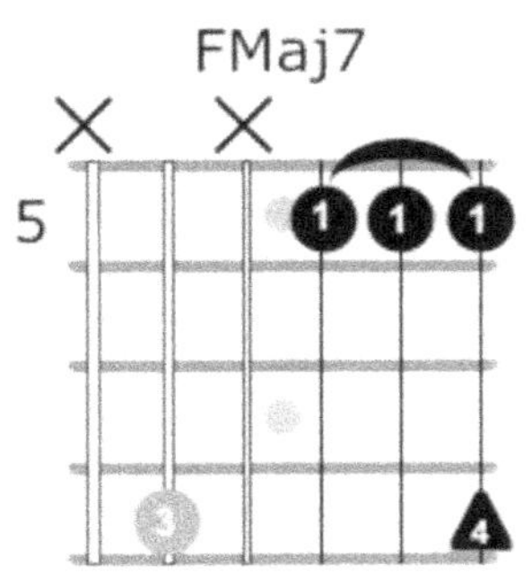

FMaj7

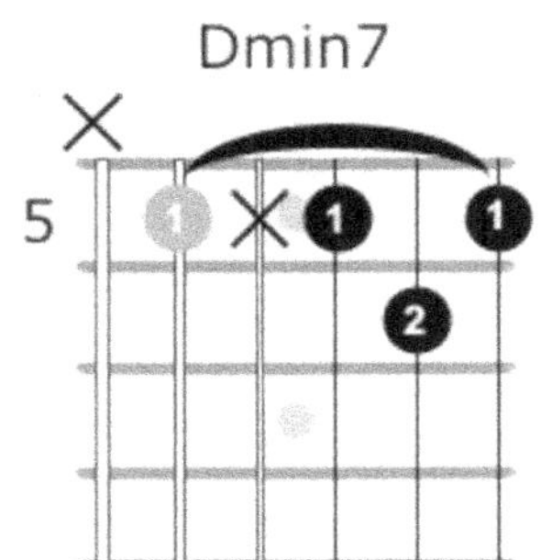

Dmin7

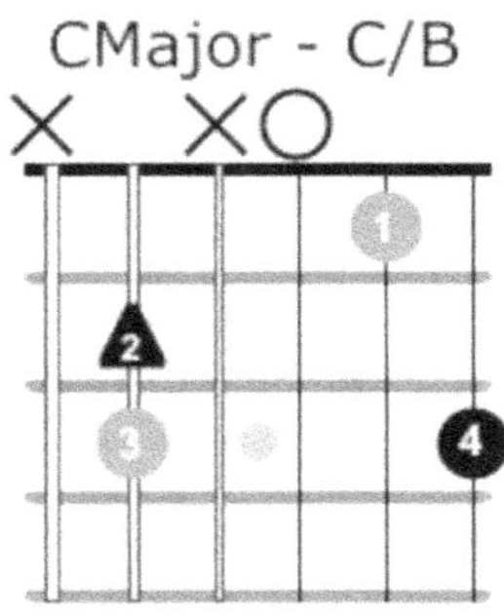

CMajor - C/B

Line 3

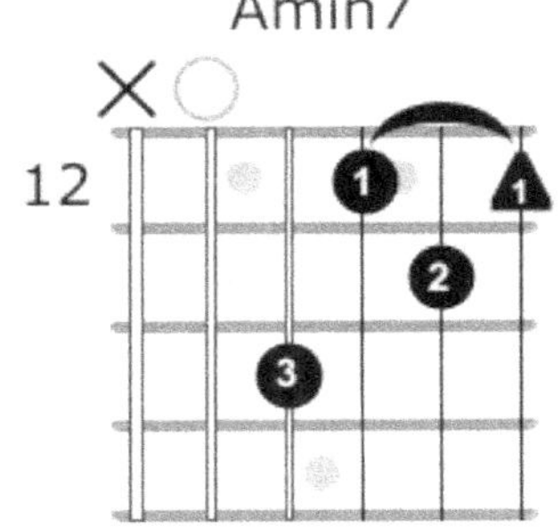

Amin7

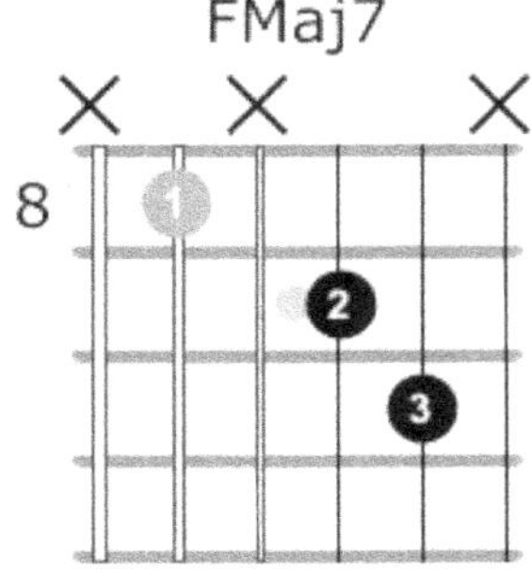

FMaj7

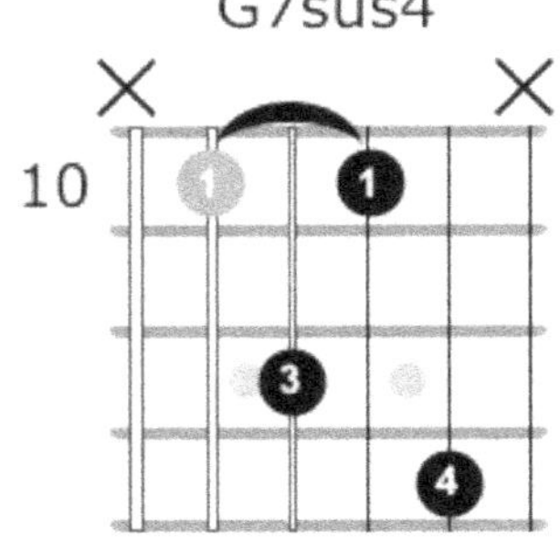

G7sus4

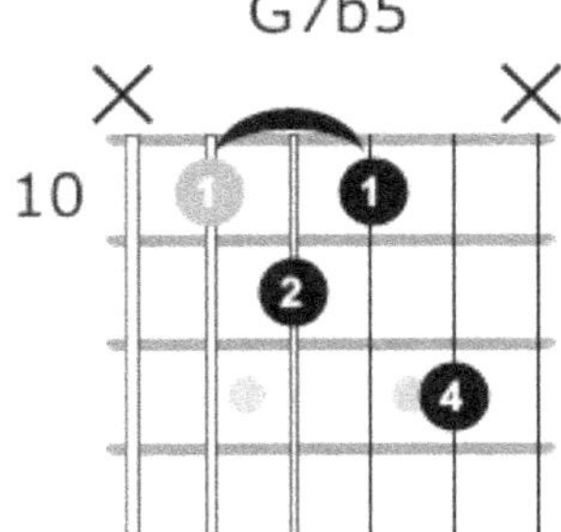

G7b5

CMajor

Line 4

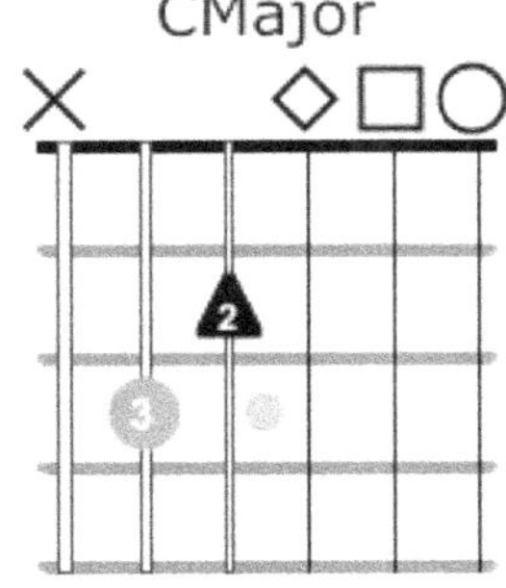

CMajor

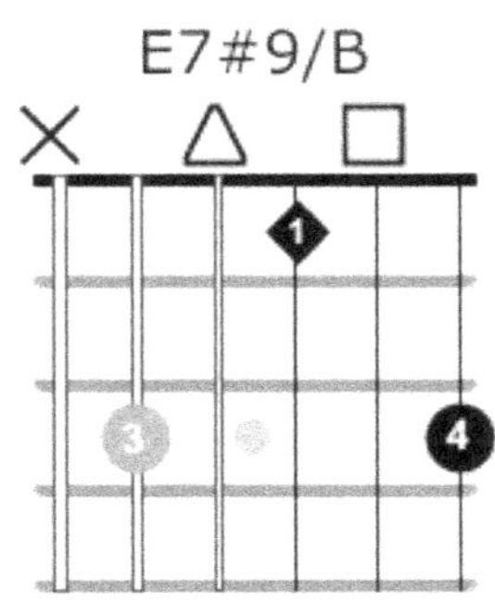

E7#9/B

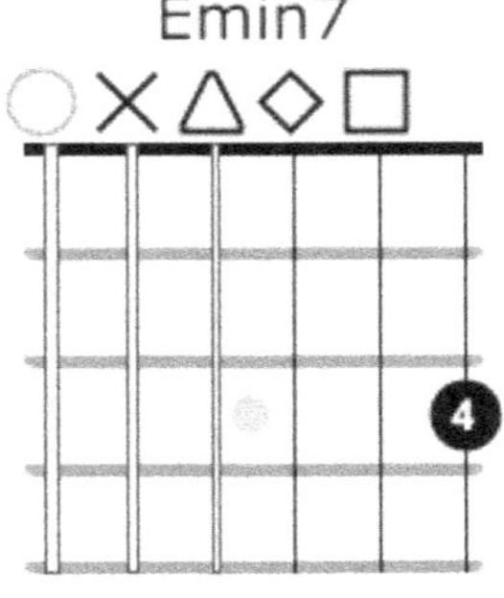

Emin7

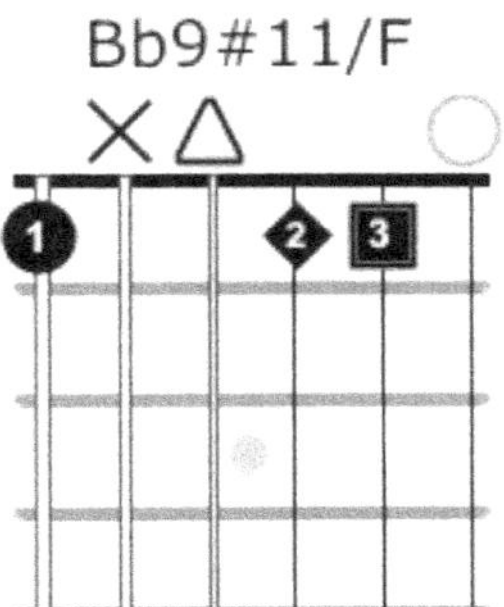

Bb9#11/F

FMaj6	F#o7	G7sus	G#o7
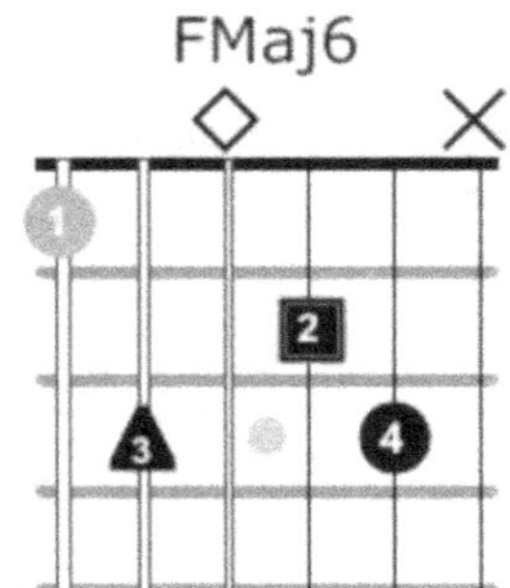	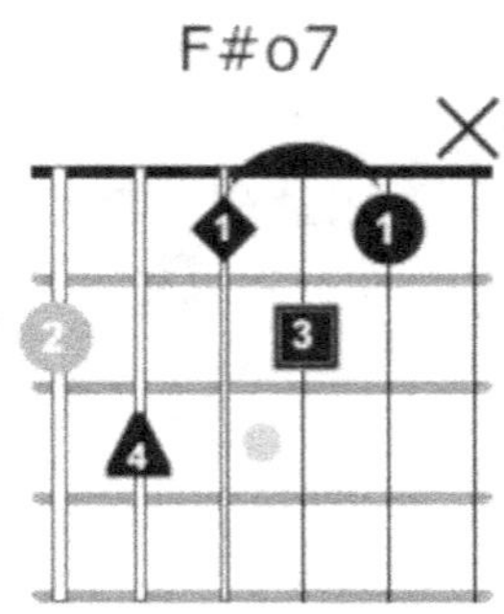	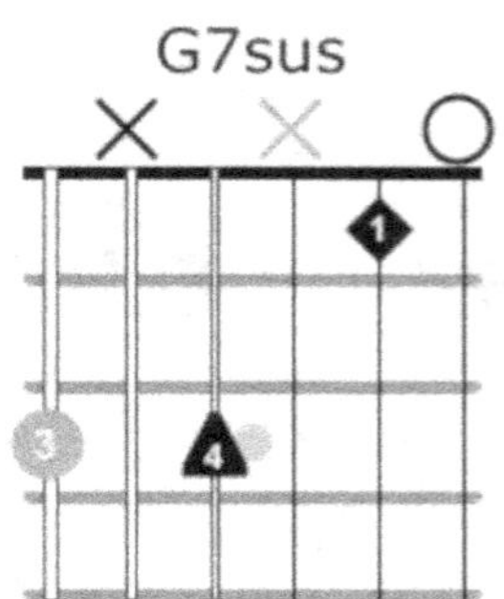	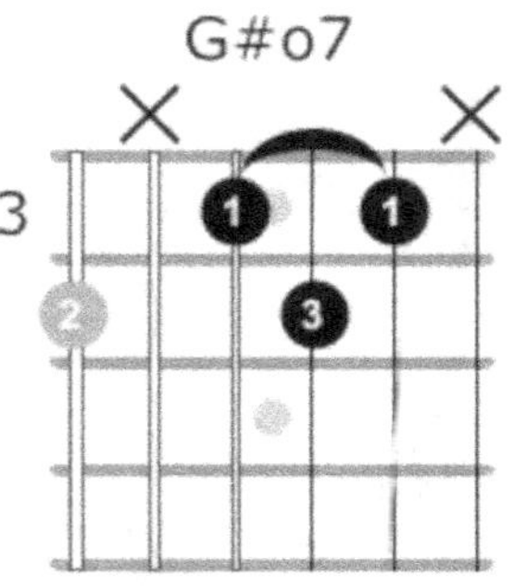

Line 5

Amadd9 - Am7	Emin11	FMaj6	FMaj6
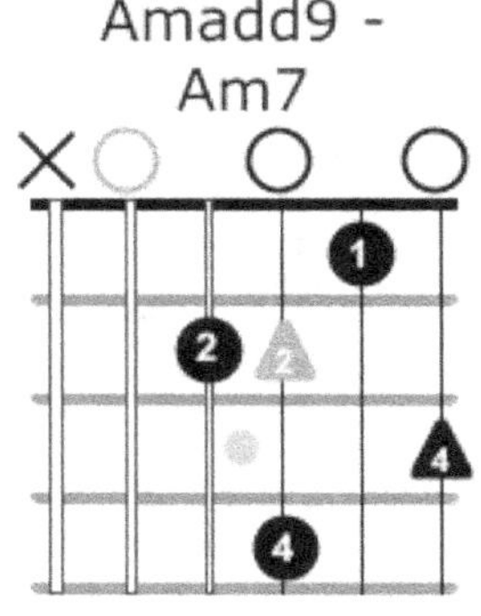	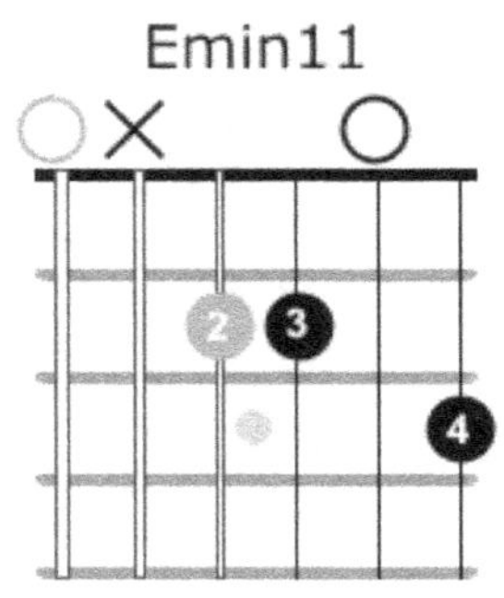	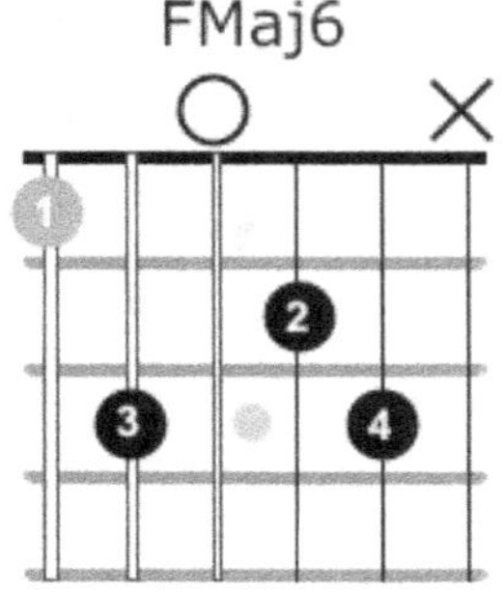	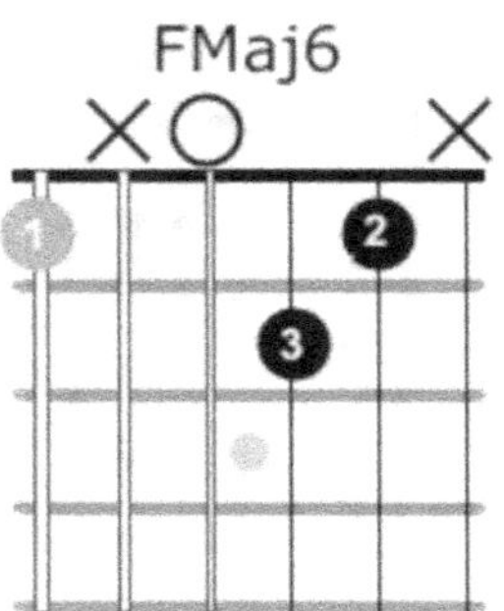

G7sus	G#o7
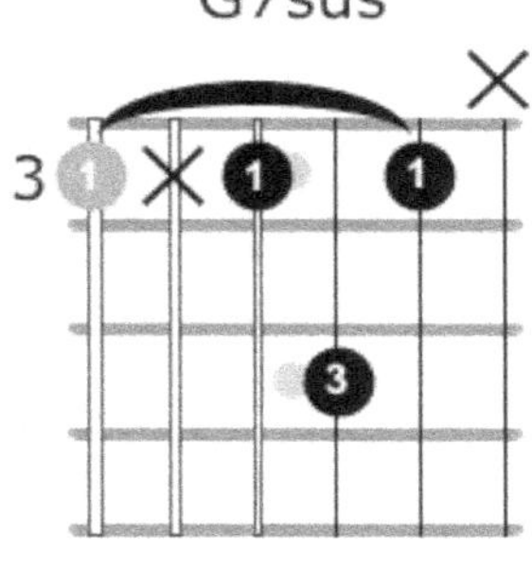	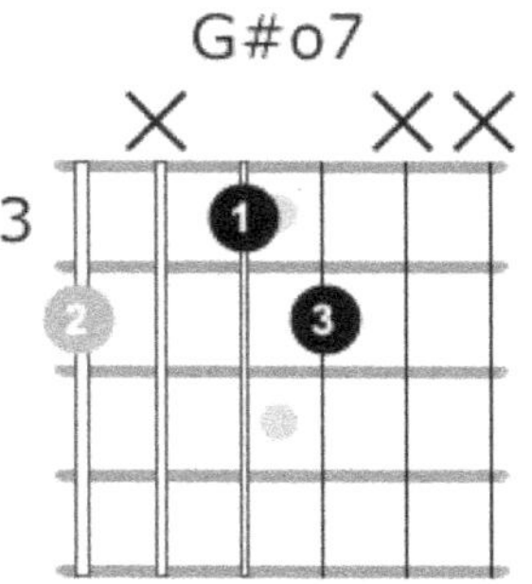

Line 6

Amin7	C/E	FMaj9 (6/9)	F/C
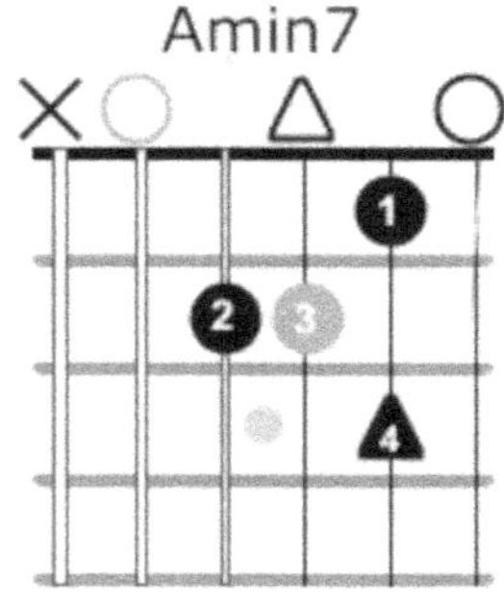	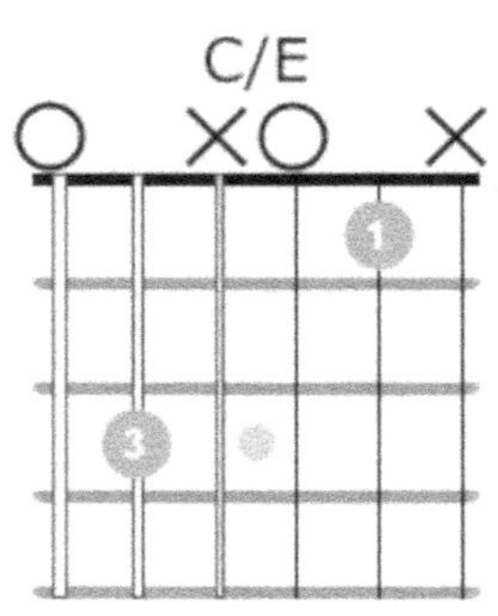	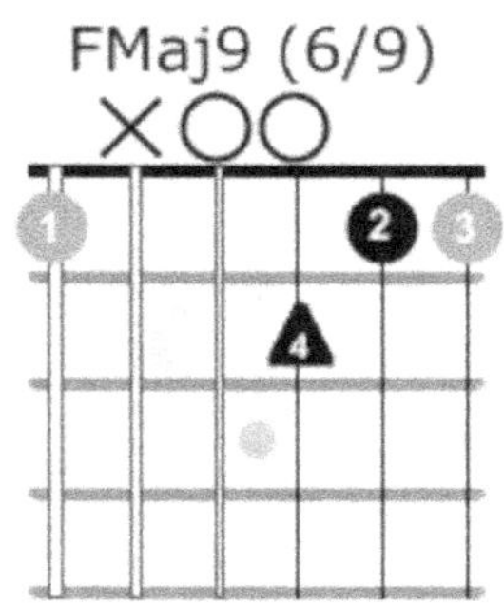	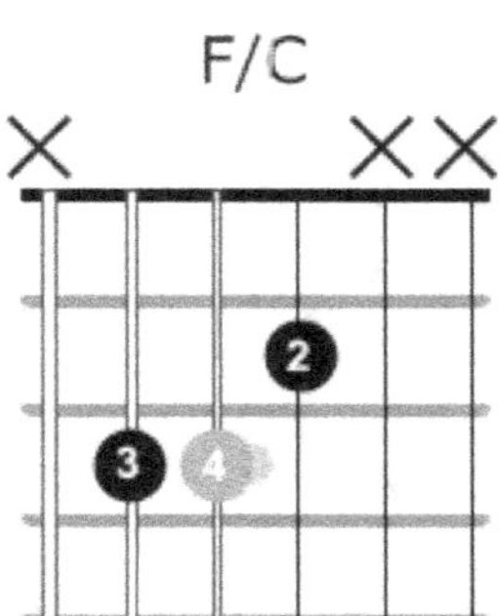

CMajor

Line 7

Dmin11
D/F#
G11 - G7b9
CMajor

Line 8

CMajor
Bm7b5
Amin
Emin
10
9
7
7
FMajor
Dmin7
CMajadd9
8
5
8

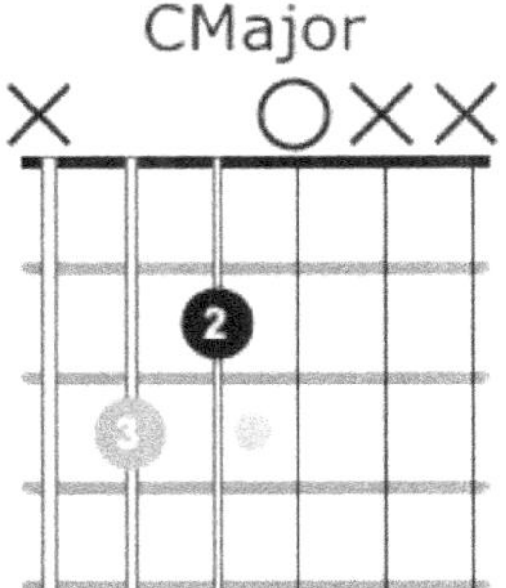

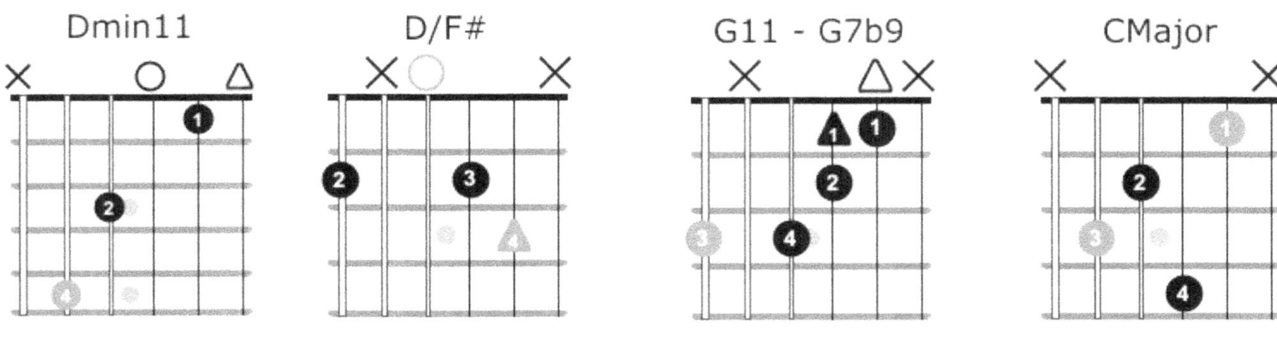

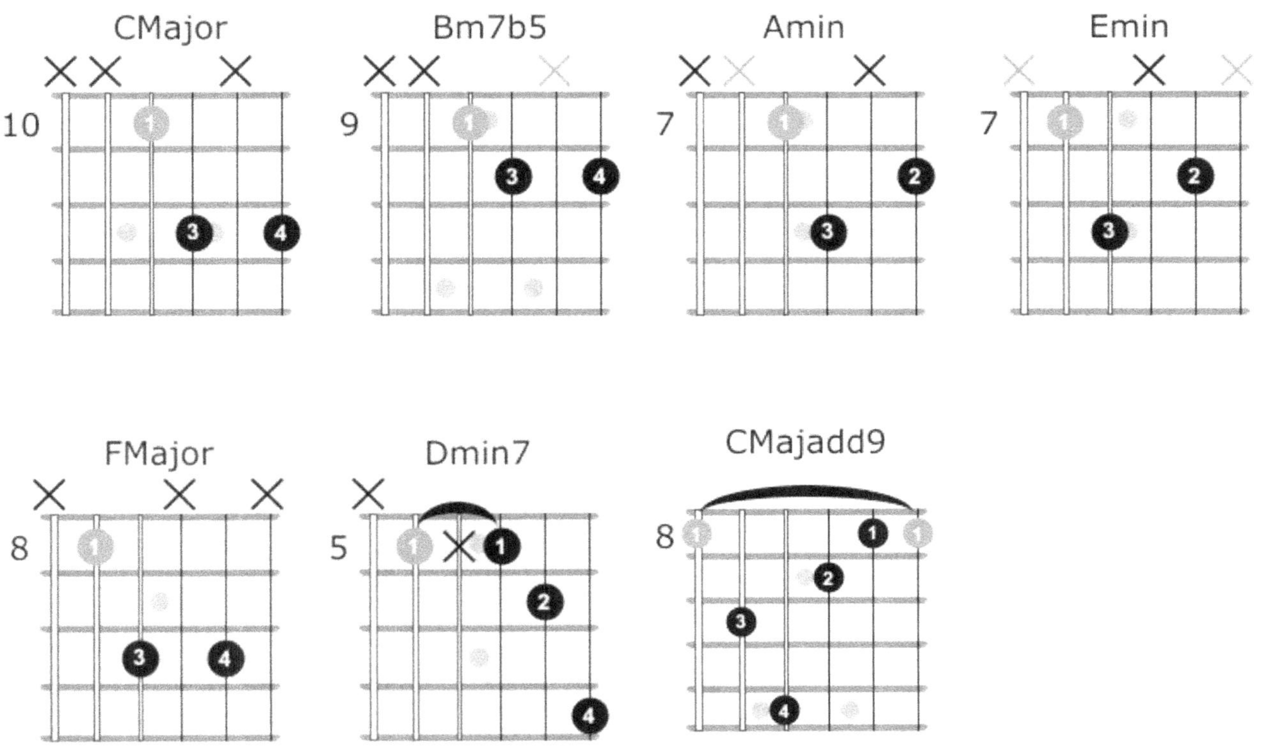

Hymn 10
What A Friend We Have In Jesus

Resources

Performance of Intermediate version

Audio Talk through of Intermediate version

Performance of Advanced version

Audio Talk through of Advanced version

Use a QR code reader on your cell/mobile phone or tablet to view and listen to the files above. There's a large selection of completely free QR code reader apps available which work on all operating platforms.

To download all resources and other support files, follow the instructions on page 197 of this publication.

Hymn Notes – What A Friend We Have In Jesus

Irishman Joseph M. Scriven (1819 – 1886) belonged to a well to do family, however, despite this, calamities seemed to stalk him throughout his life. He wrote the poem "Pray Without Ceasing", which was put to music by Charles Crozat Converse and was re-titled "What A Friend We Have In Jesus".

Joseph was almost married twice, but on both occasions, his then betrothed died. The first lady died of drowning the night before their marriage and the second of illness. He then devoted his life to helping others including assisting people financially. His own death through drowning may have been suicide as he was suffering from depression at the time.

American Charles Crozat Converse (1832 – 1918) was an attorney who also composed songs for the church. Charles was educated in Leipzig where he studied both law and music. He wrote most of his compositions under the pen-names "C. O. Nevers", "Karl Reden", and "E. C. Revons" and even published a guitar method book in eighteen fifty five.

Charles Crozat Converse   Joseph M. Scriven

Lyrics

Verse 1

What a friend we have in Jesus

All our sins and griefs to bear

And what a privilege to carry

Everything to God in prayer

Verse 2

Oh, what peace we often forfeit

Oh, what needless pain we bear

All because we do not carry

Everything to God in prayer

Verse 3

Have we trials and temptations?

Is there trouble anywhere?

We should never be discouraged

Take it to the Lord in prayer

Verse 4

Can we find a friend so faithful

Who will all our sorrows share?

Jesus knows our every weakness

Take it to the Lord in prayer

What A Friend We Have In Jesus - Starter

What A Friend We Have In Jesus - Starter alternate key

Joseph M. Scriven &
Charles Crozat Converse

Steadily

Chords: What A Friend We Have In Jesus Starter Song

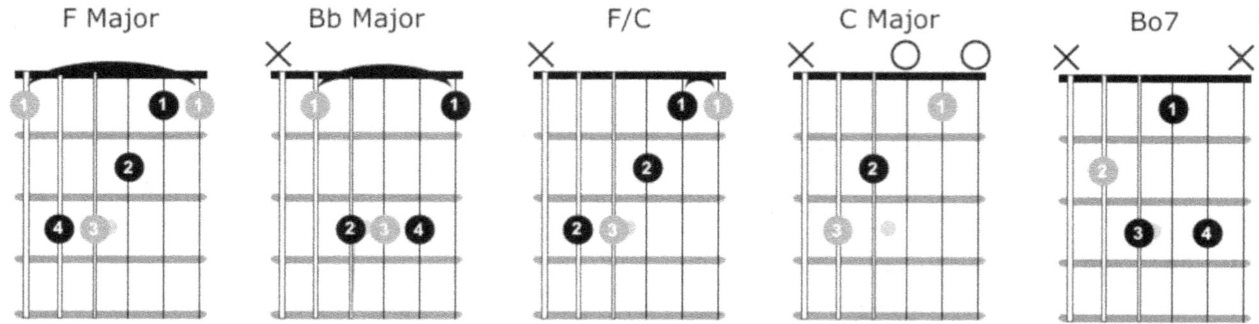

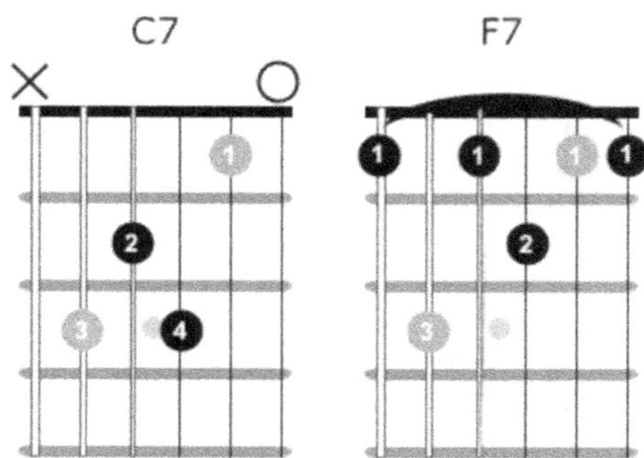

Chords: What A Friend We Have In Jesus Starter Song Alternate Key

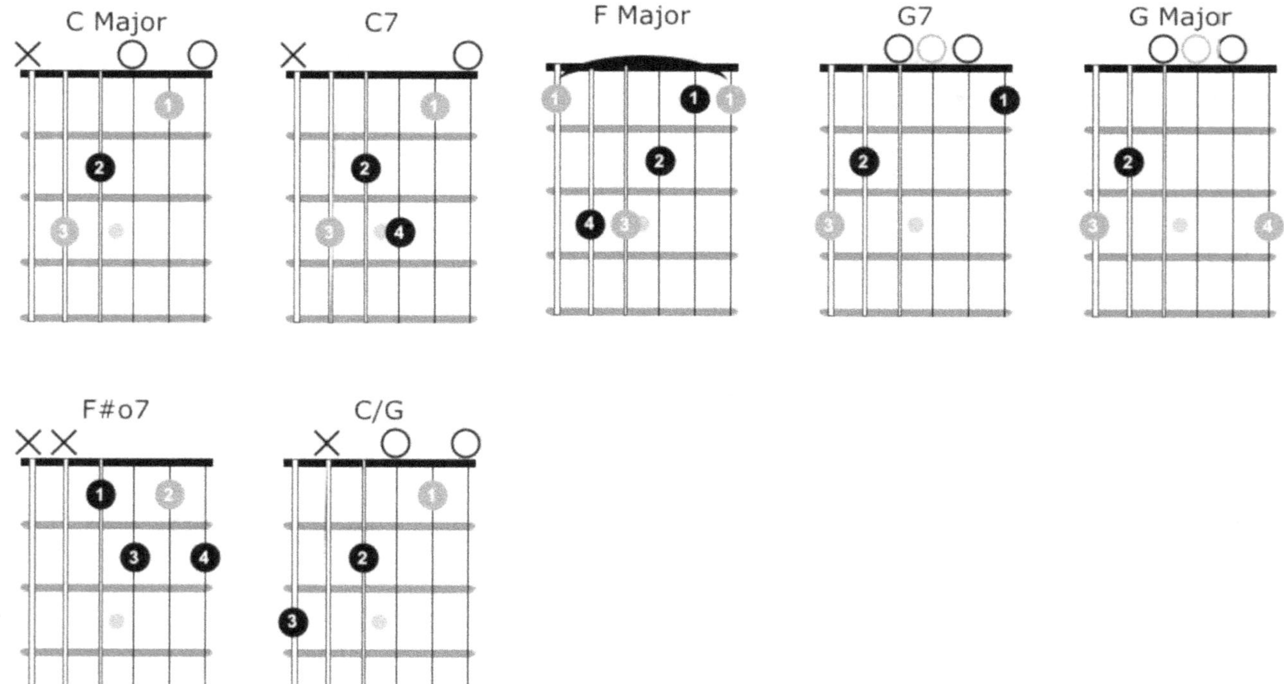

What A Friend We Have In Jesus play along

bpm = 90

Abide With Me + Melody
Abide With Me Backing Track

Count of 4 then play

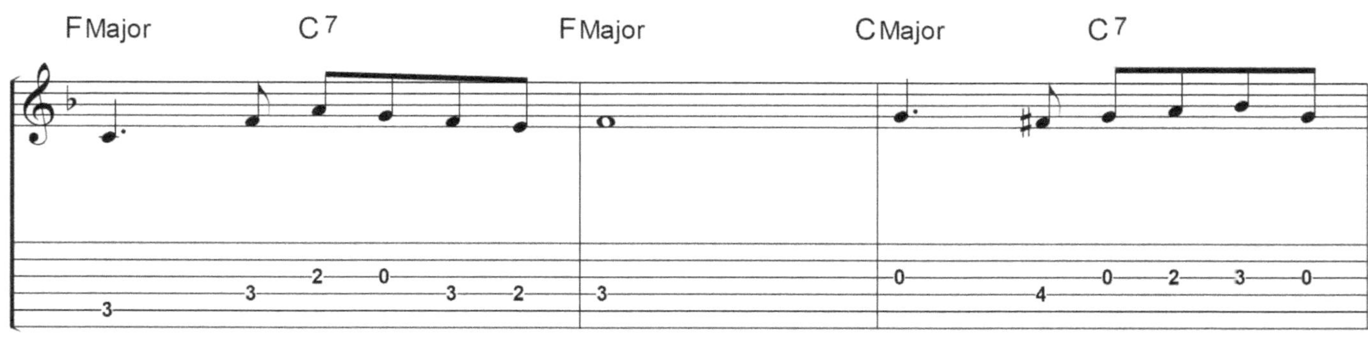

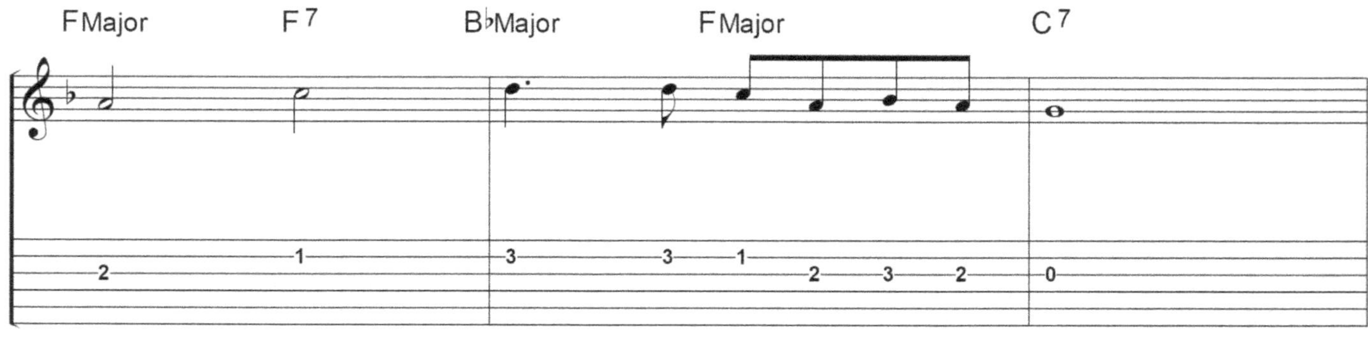

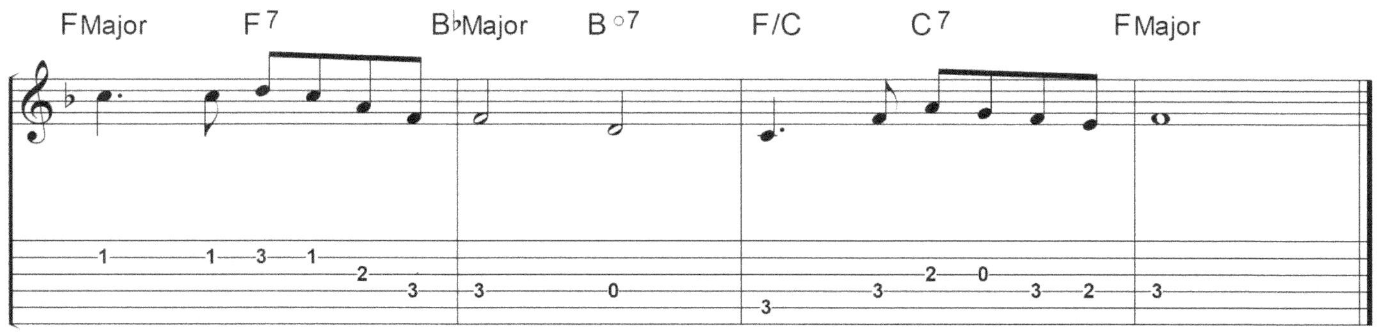

FMajor
F7
B♭Major
B○7
F/C
C7
FMajor

What A Friend We Have In Jesus - Intermediate

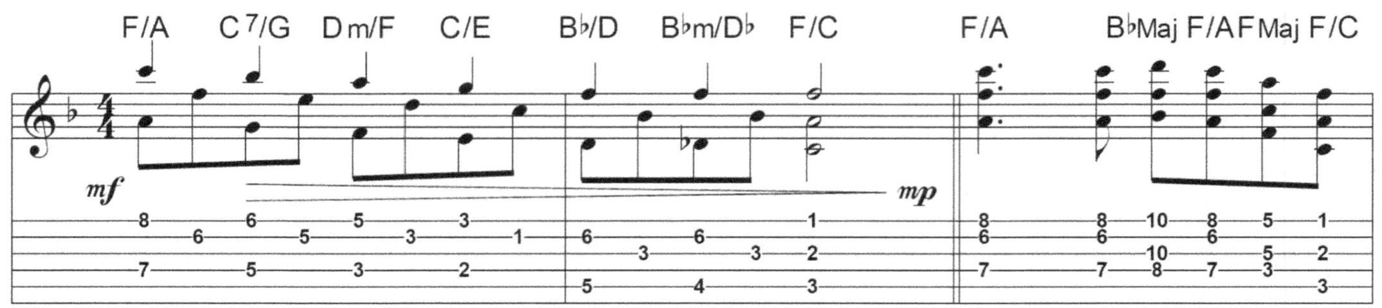

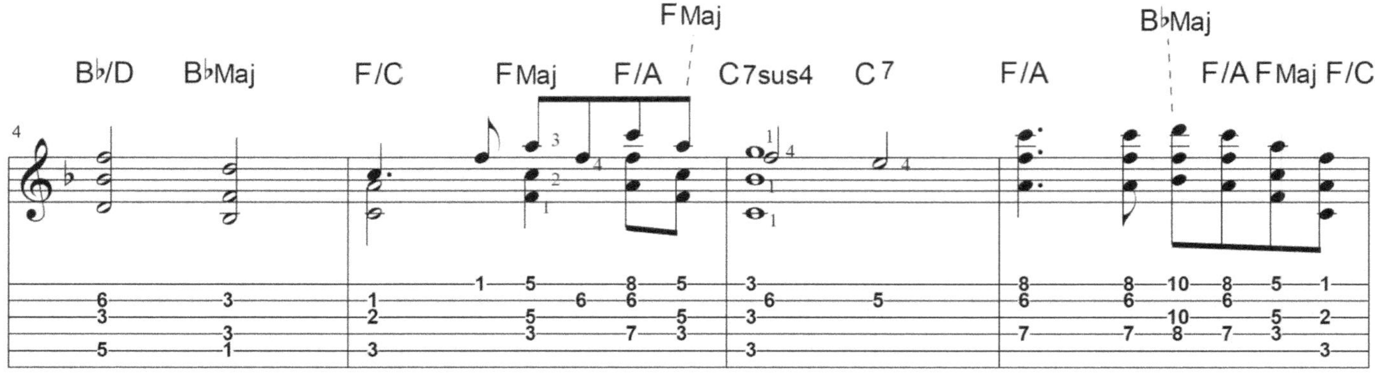

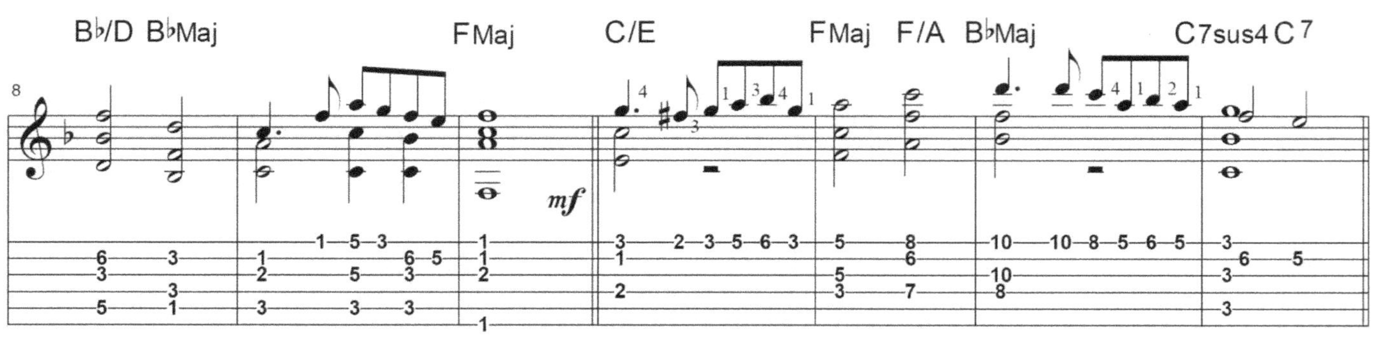

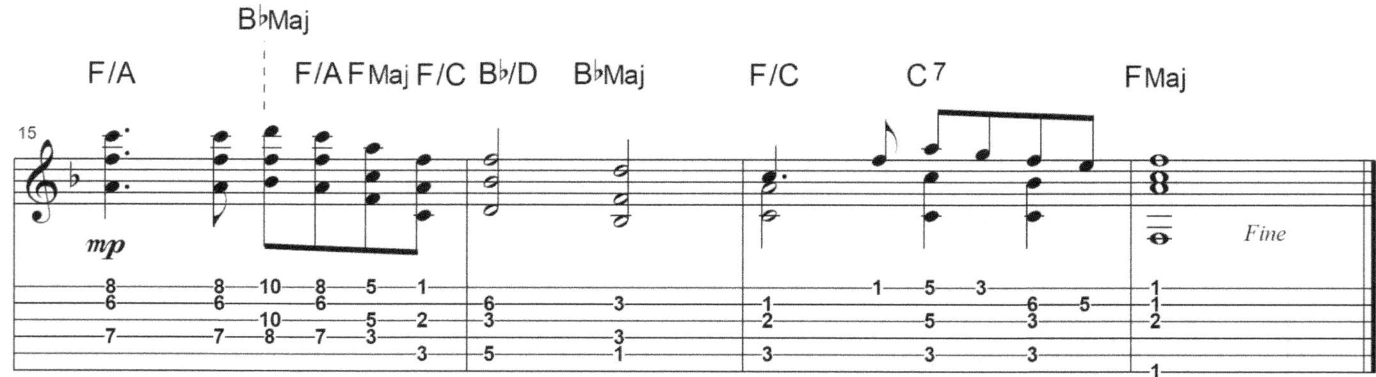

Chords: What A Friend We Have In Jesus Intermediate

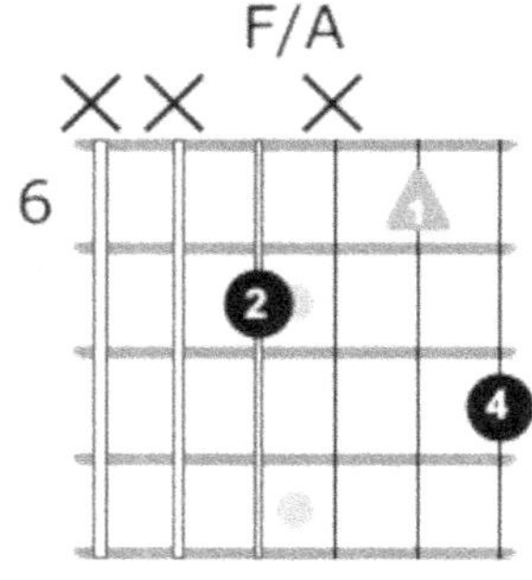

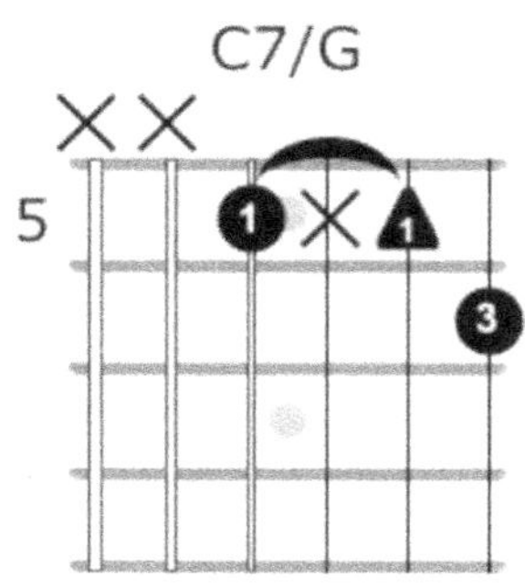

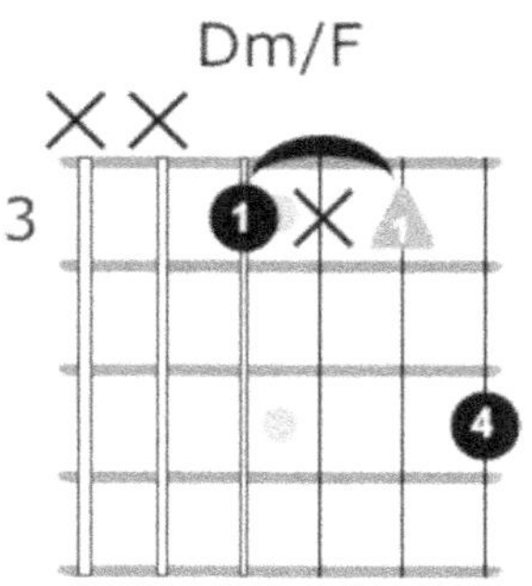

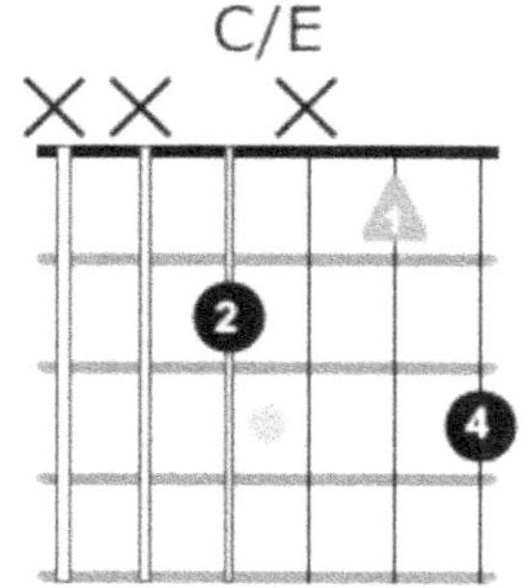

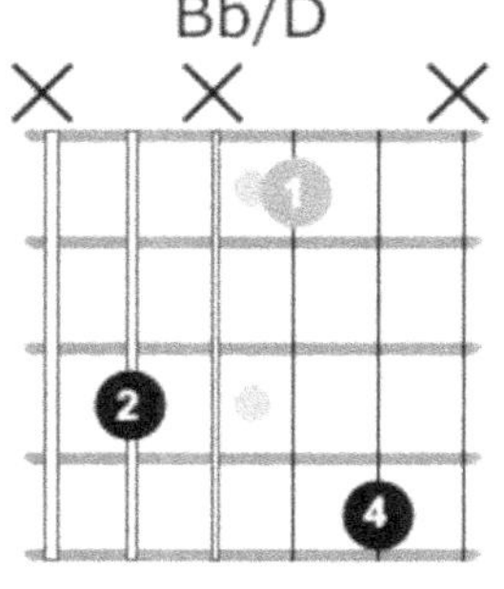

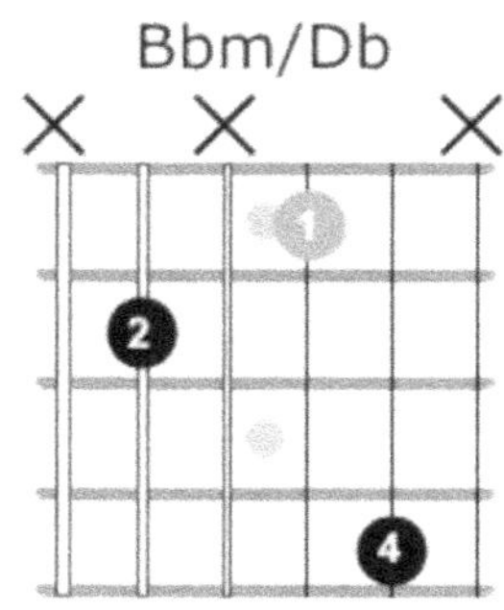

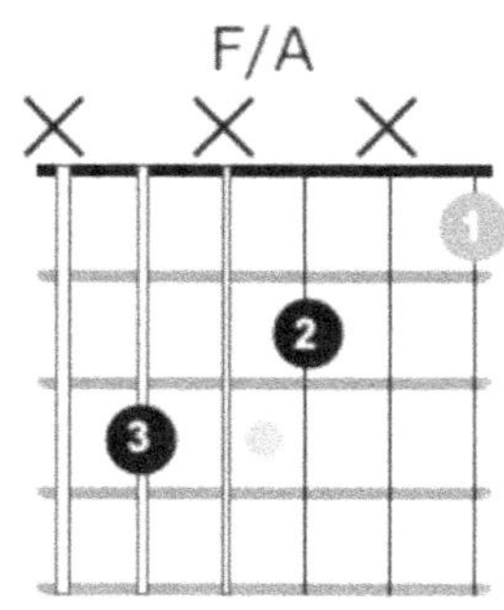

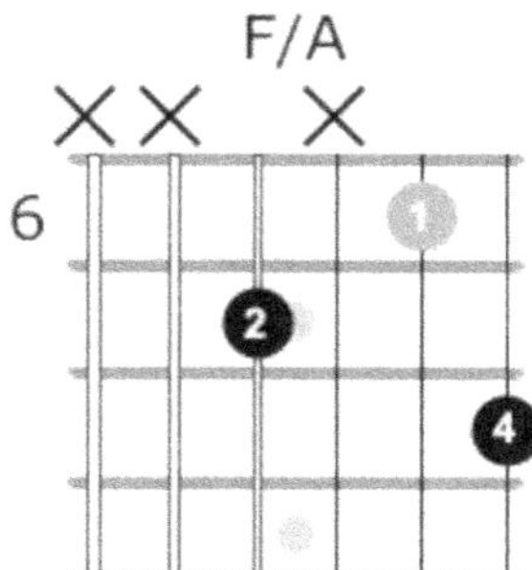

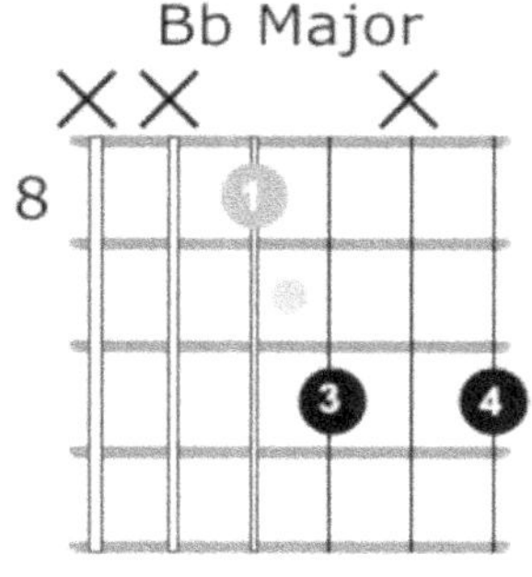

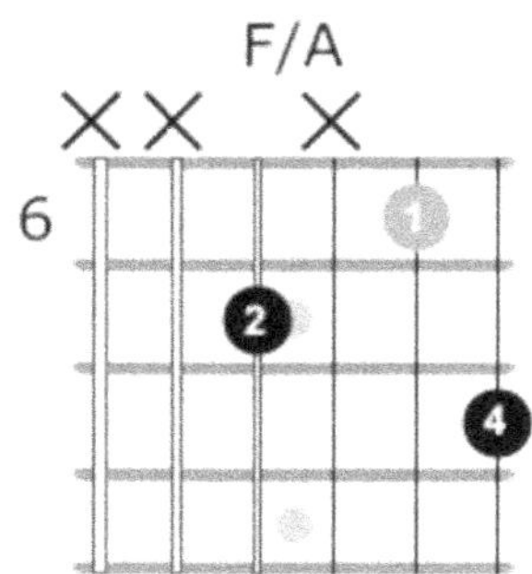

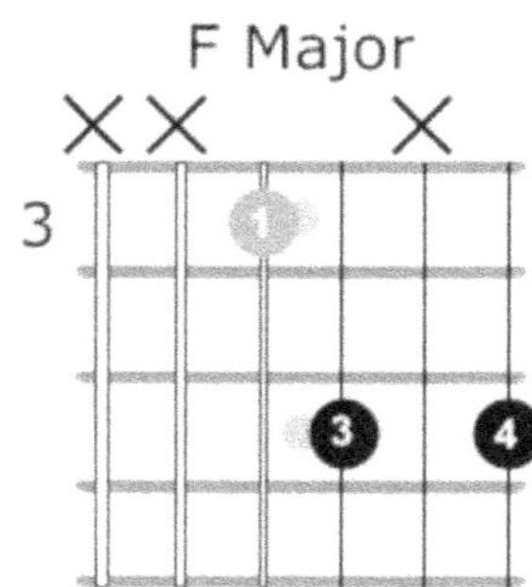

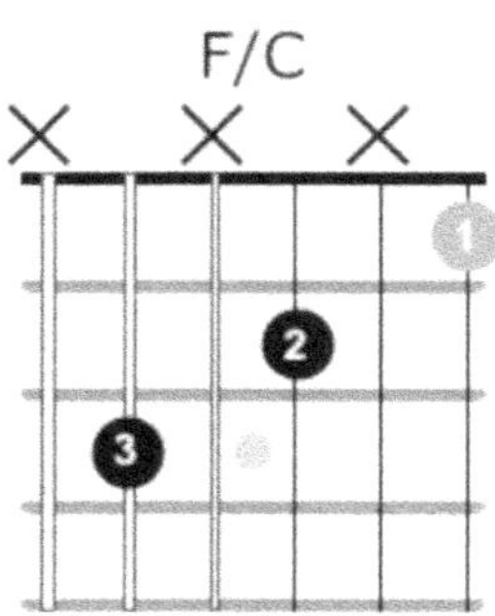

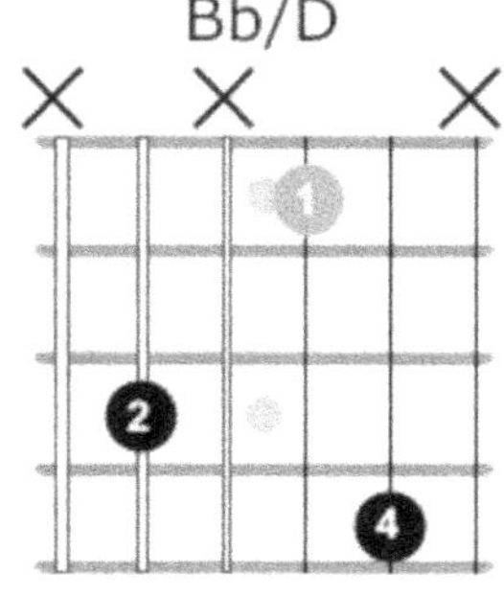

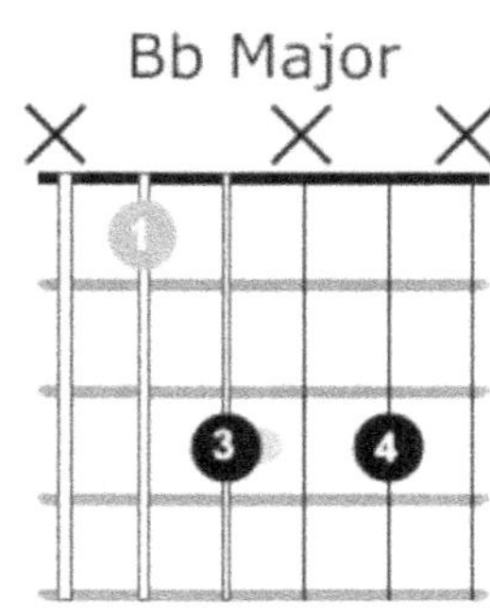

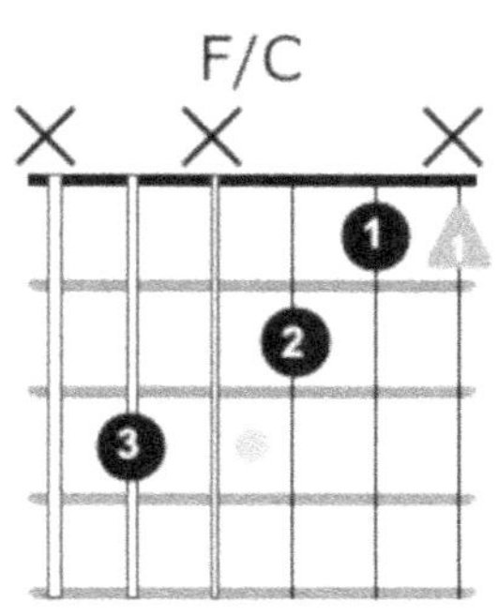

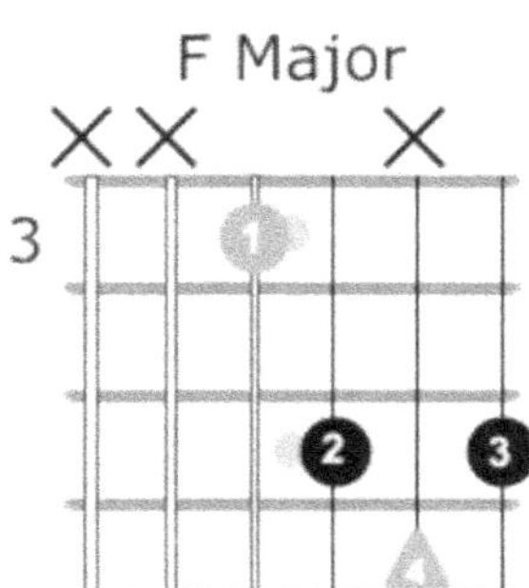

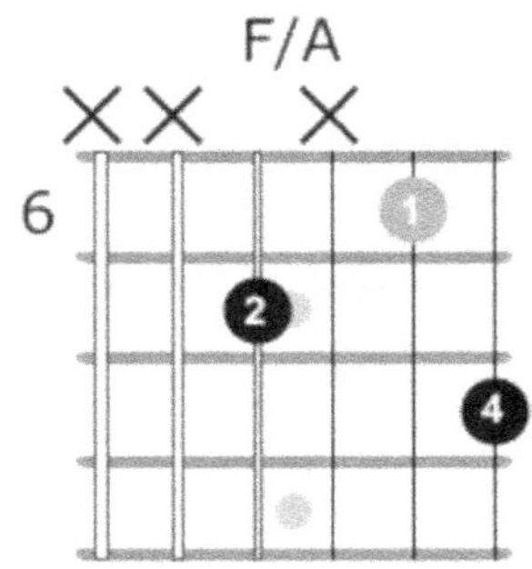

F/A

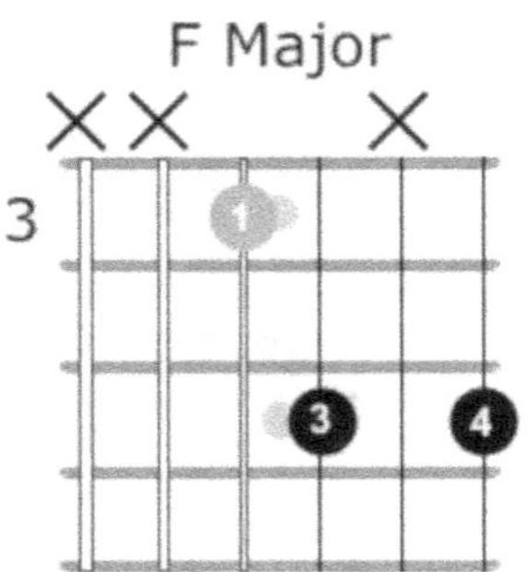

F Major

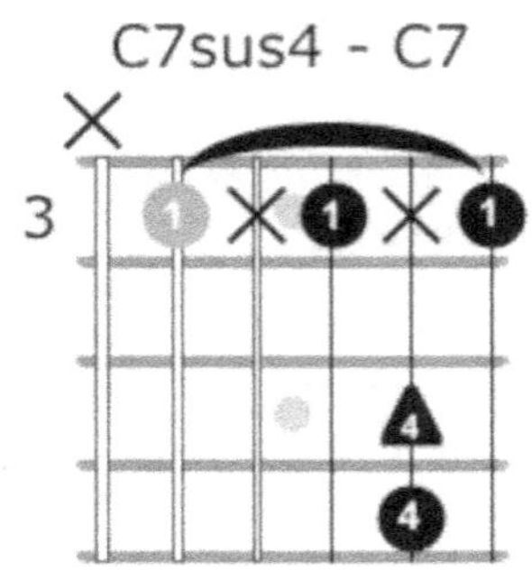

C7sus4 - C7

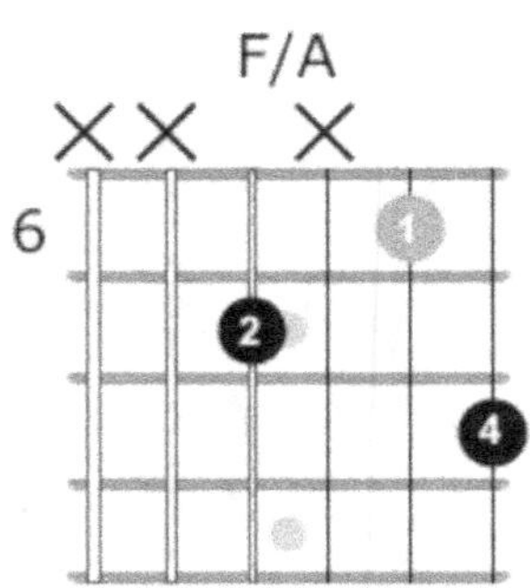

F/A

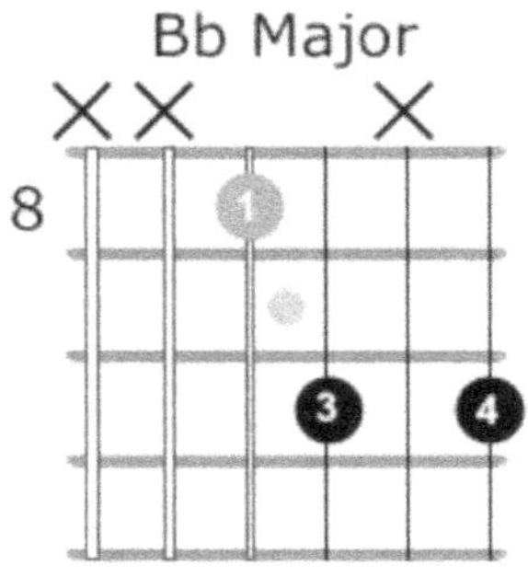

Bb Major

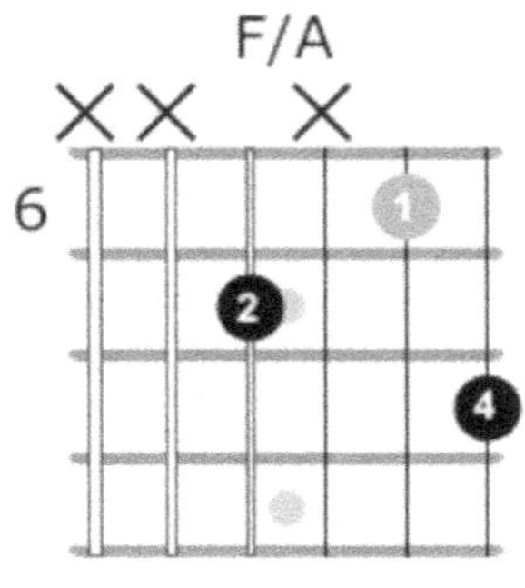

F/A

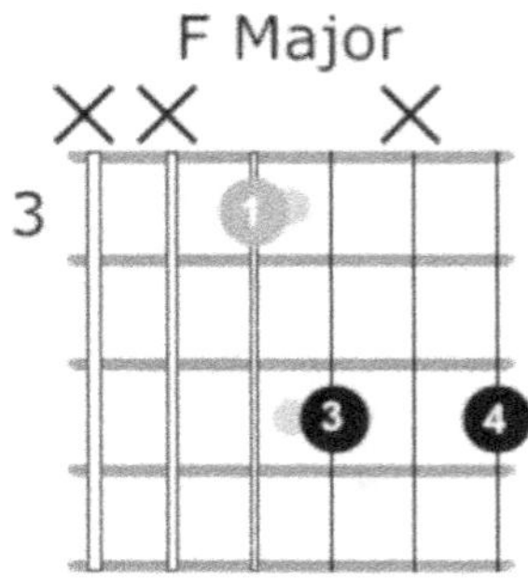

F Major

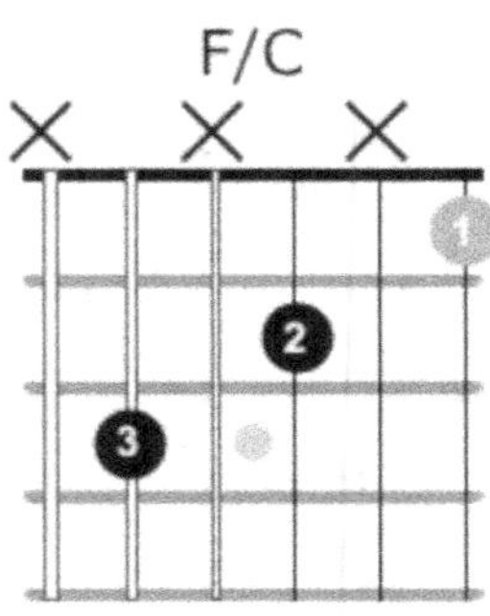

F/C

Line 3

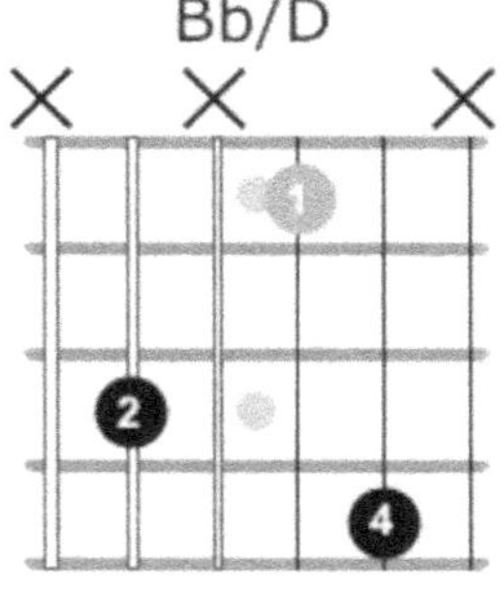

Bb/D

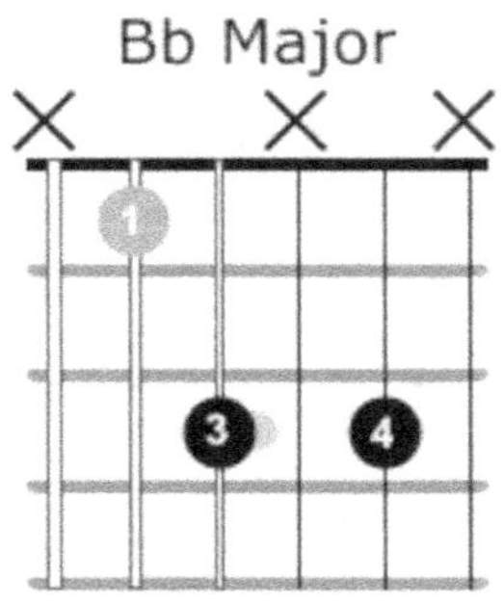

Bb Major

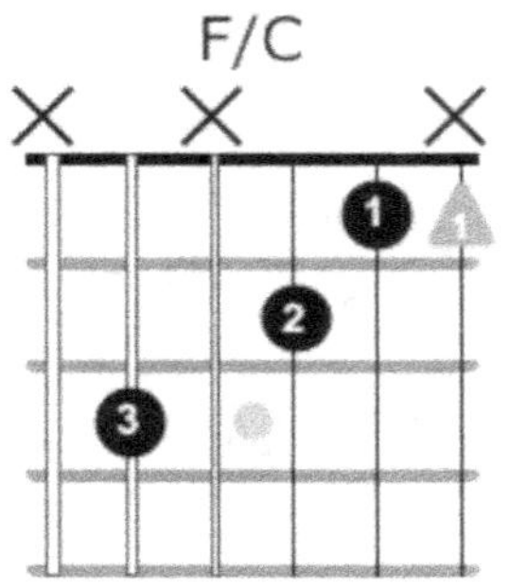

F/C

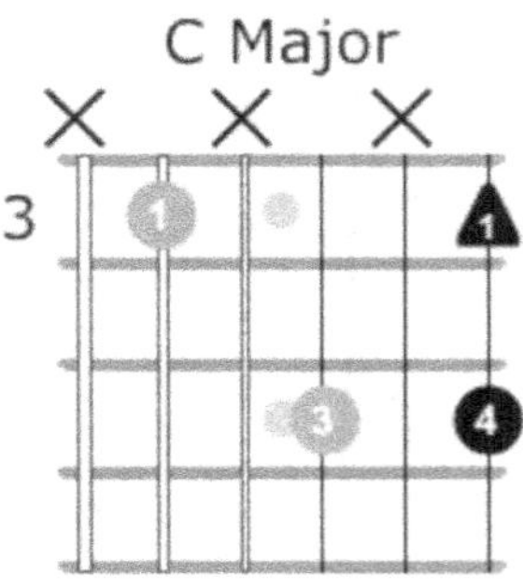

C Major

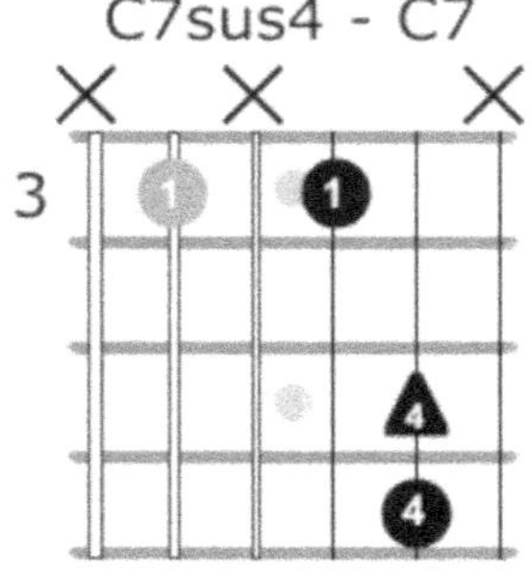

C7sus4 - C7

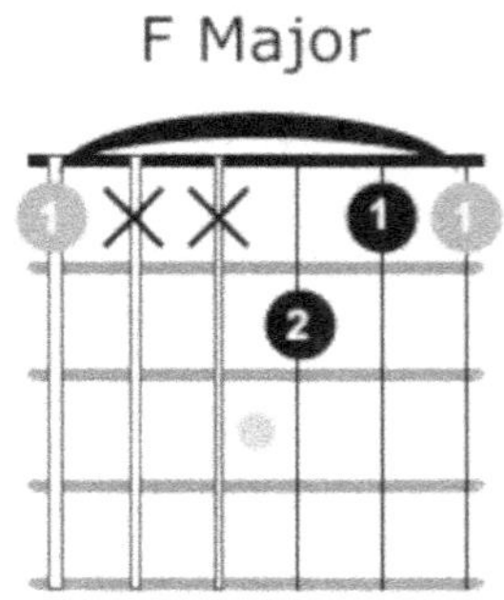

F Major

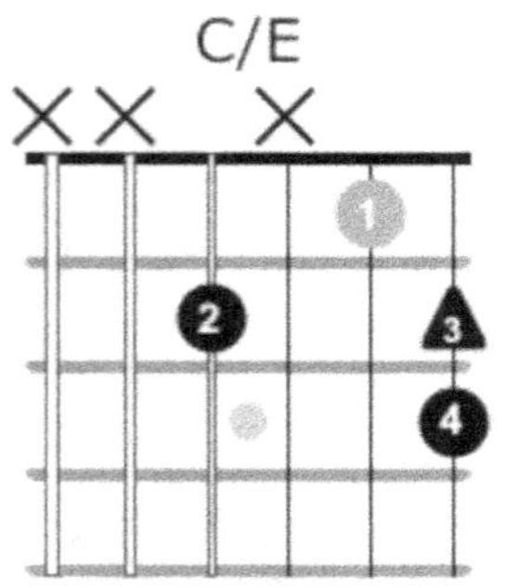

C/E

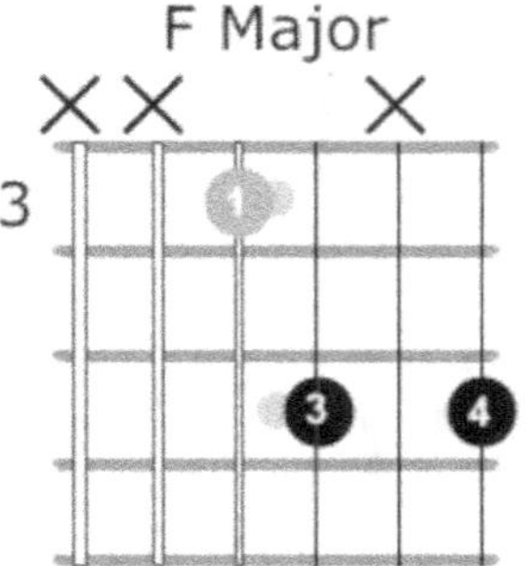

F Major

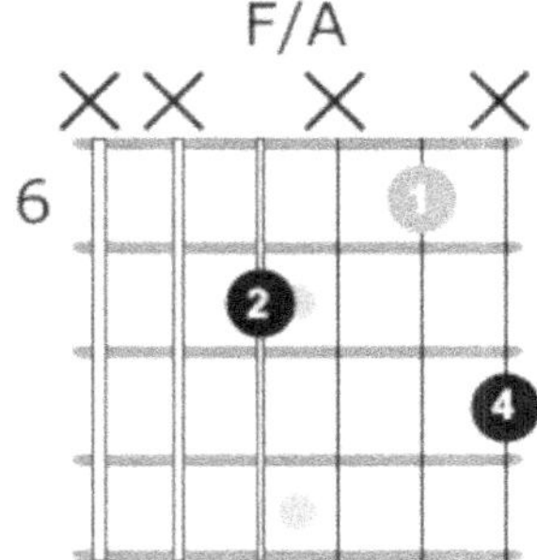

F/A

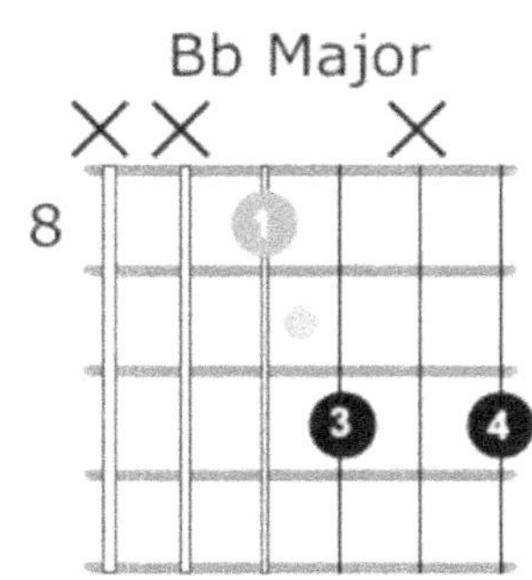

Bb Major

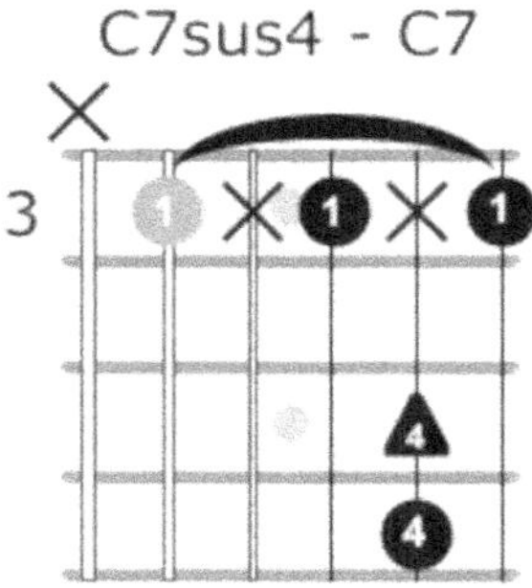

C7sus4 - C7

Line 4

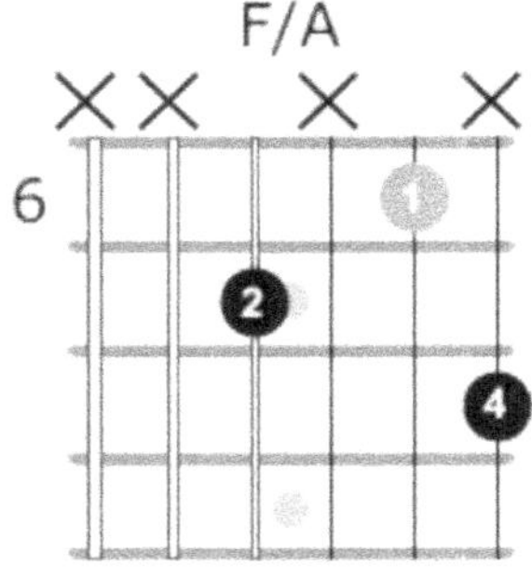

F/A

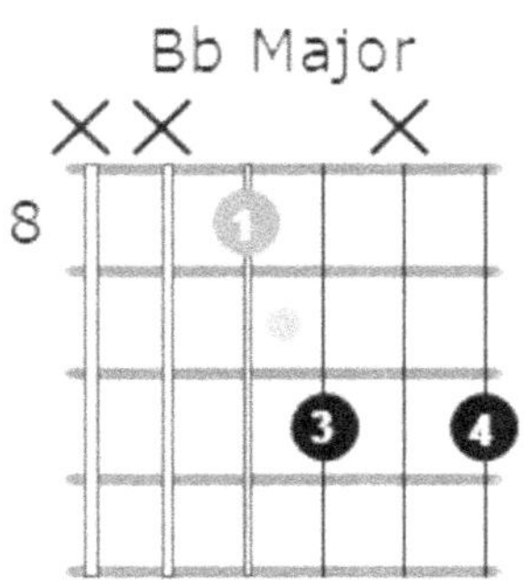

Bb Major

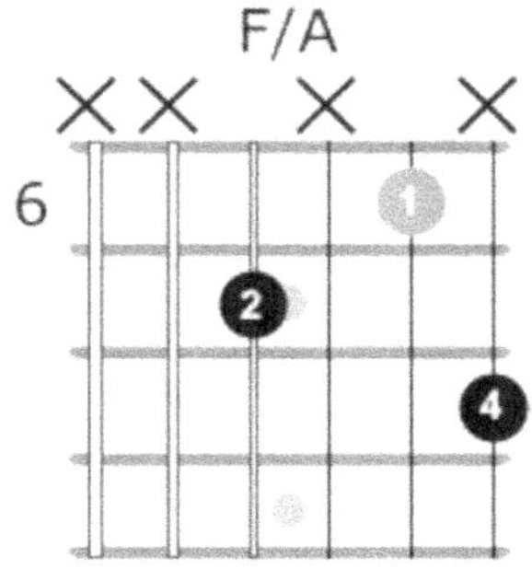

F/A

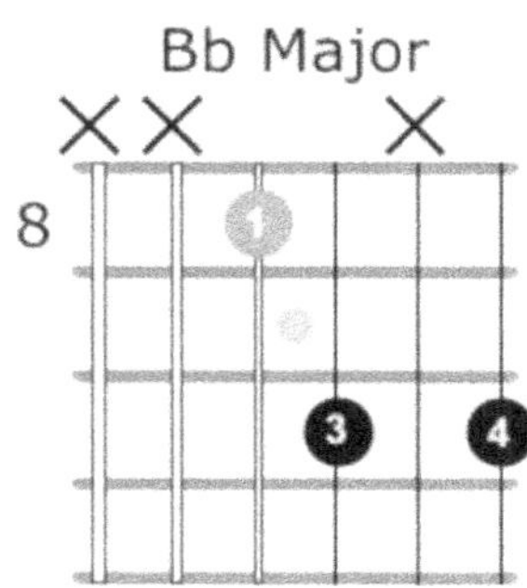

Bb Major

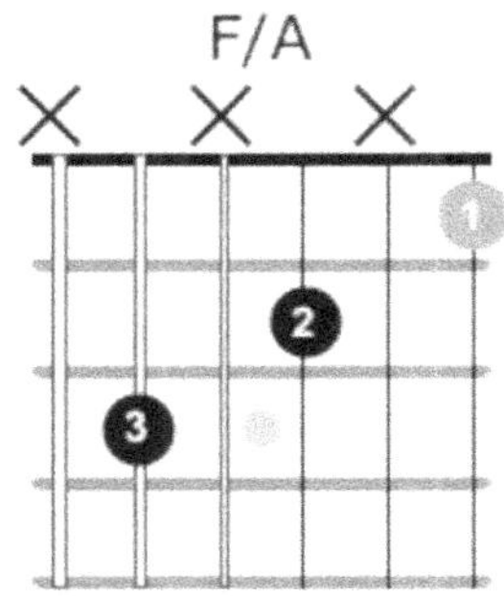

F/A

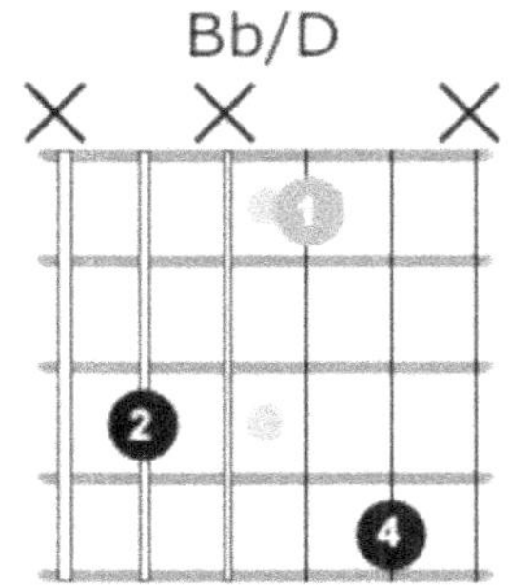

Bb/D

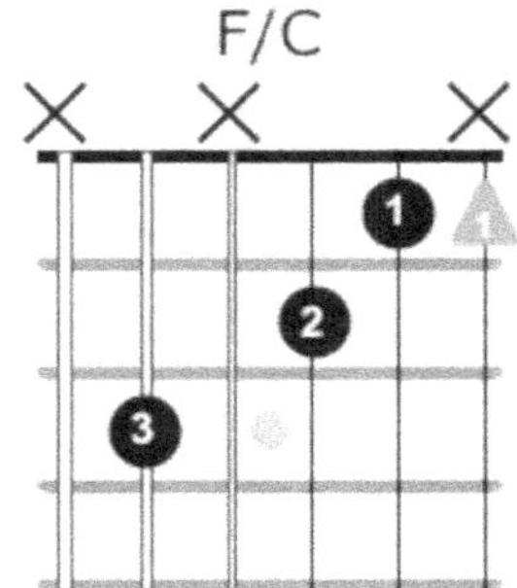

F/C

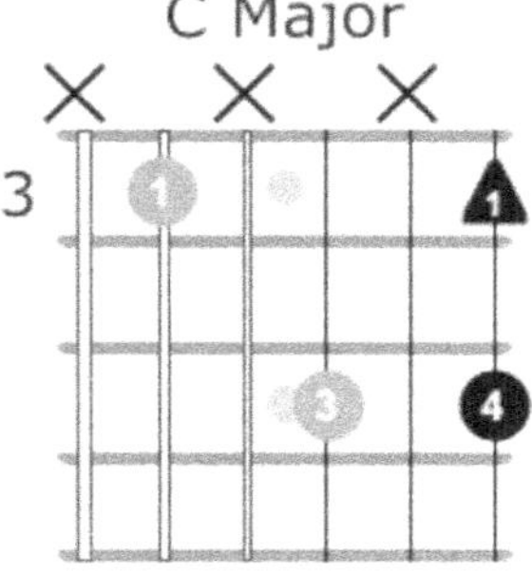

C Major

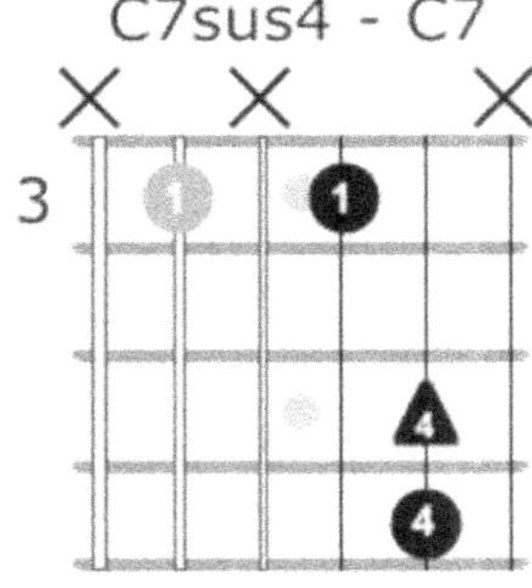

C7sus4 - C7

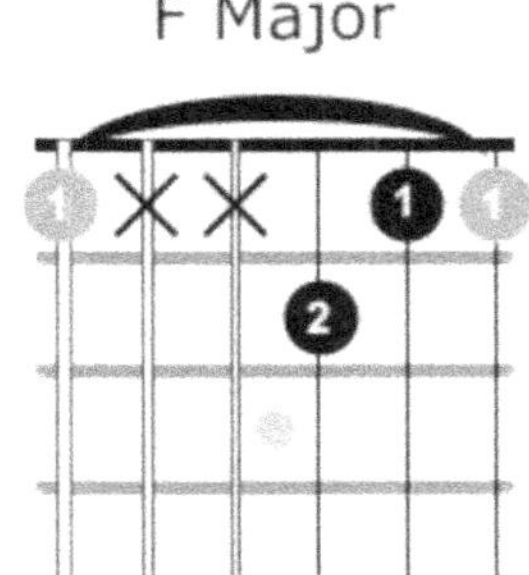

F Major

What A Friend We Have In Jesus - Advanced

G m11
F#o7 G m7
G9+
C7b5b9 C7b9 F Maj7
C m7
B13
mf

Bb Maj7
A m   D7#5b9   G7sus
C7sus

with a swing feel

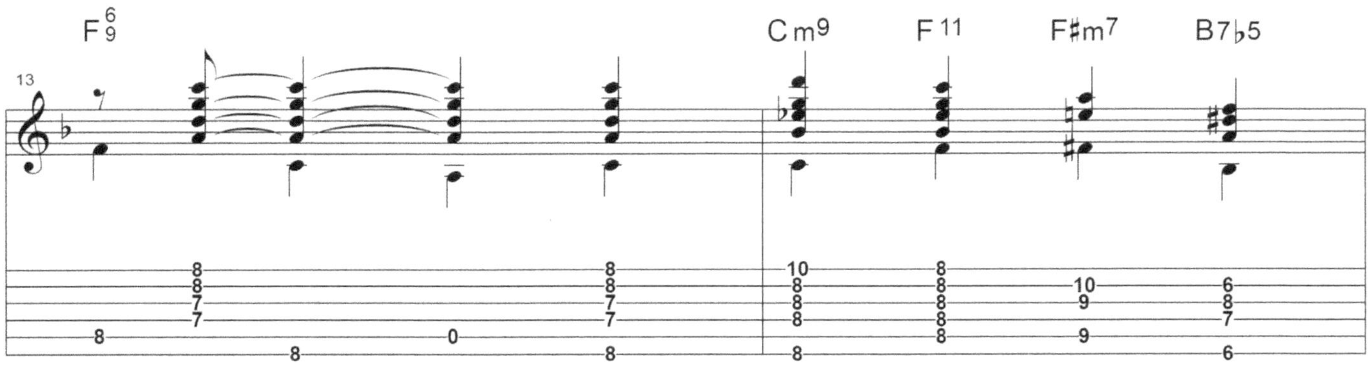

F6/9
C m9   F11   F#m7   B7b5

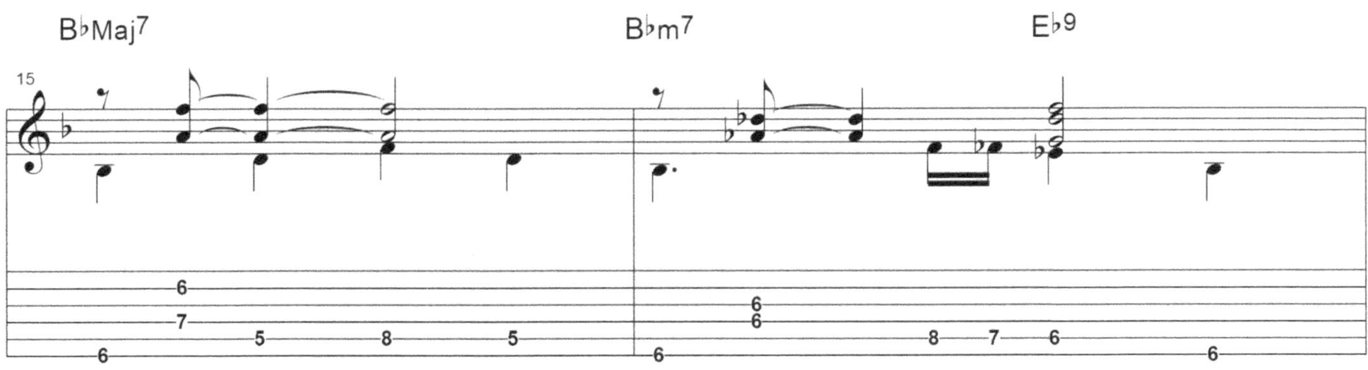

Bb Maj7
Bb m7
Eb9

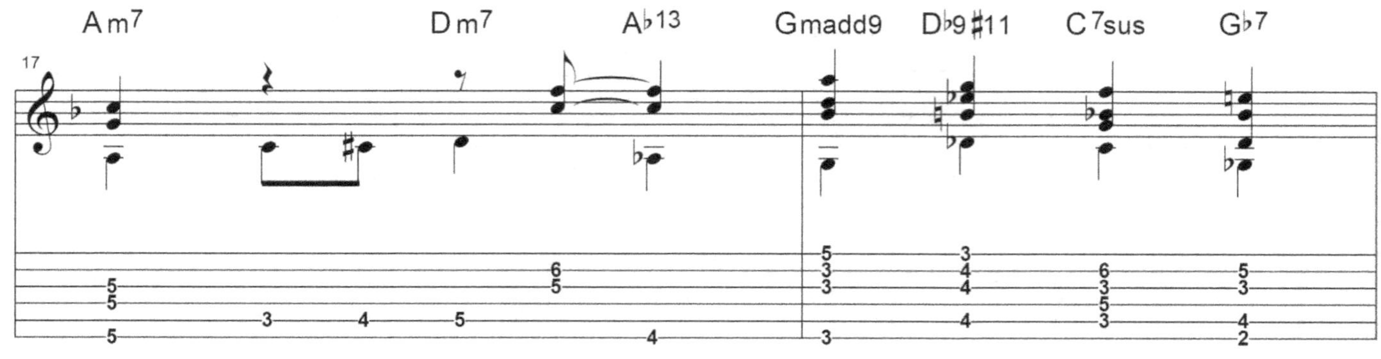

Am7
Dm7
Ab13
Gmadd9
Db9#11
C7sus
Gb7
17

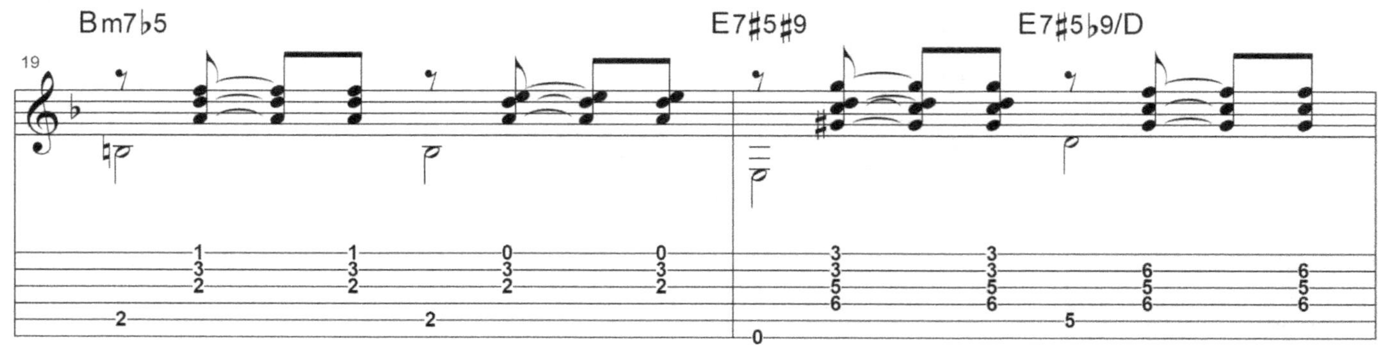

Bm7b5
E7#5#9
E7#5b9/D
19

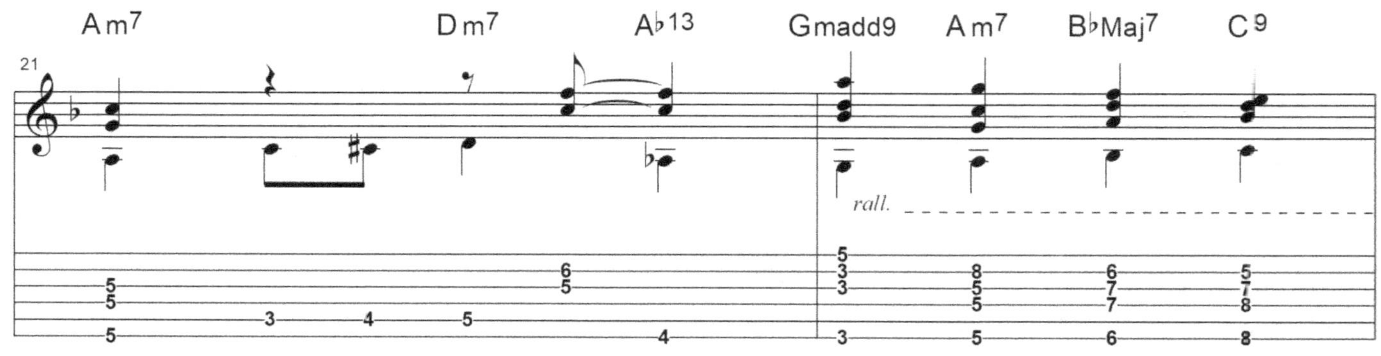

Am7
Dm7
Ab13
Gmadd9
Am7
BbMaj7
C9
21
rall.

DbMaj13
FMaj
23
mp
Fine

Chords: What A Friend We Have In Jesus Advanced

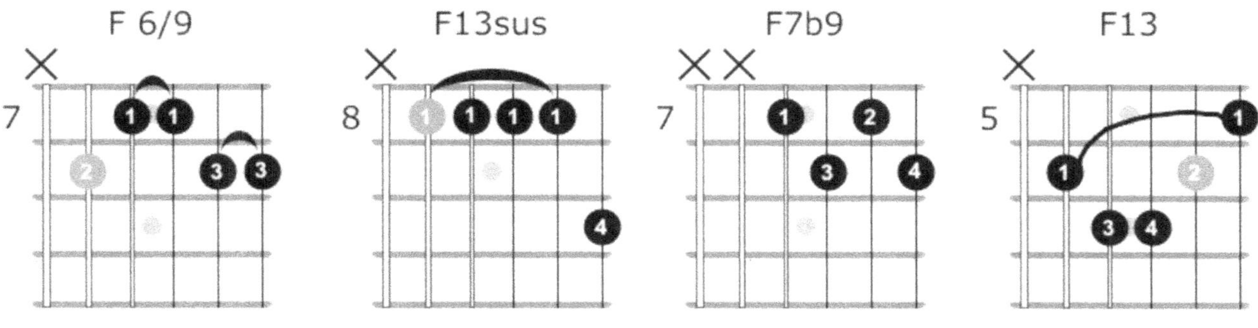

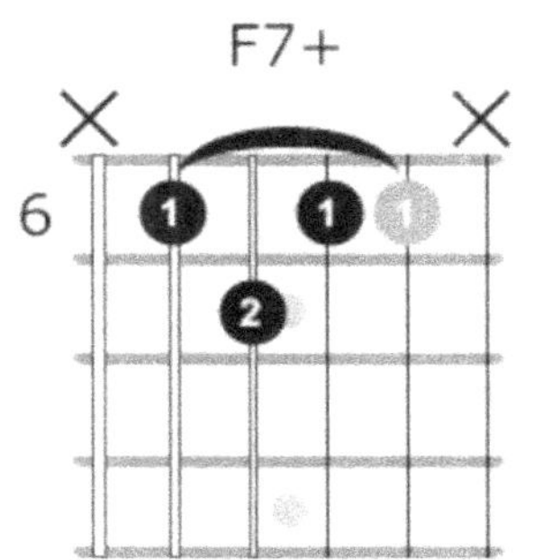

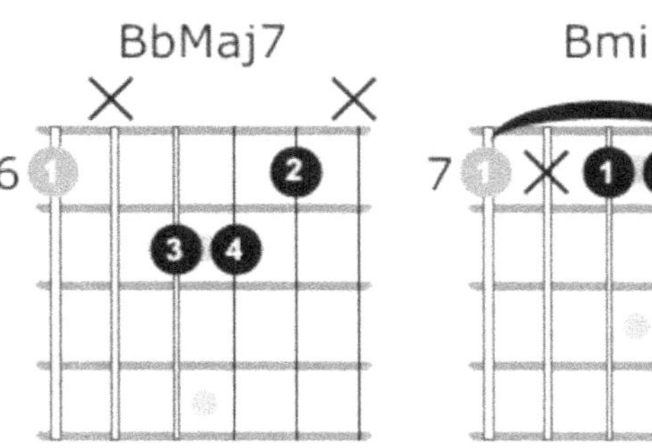

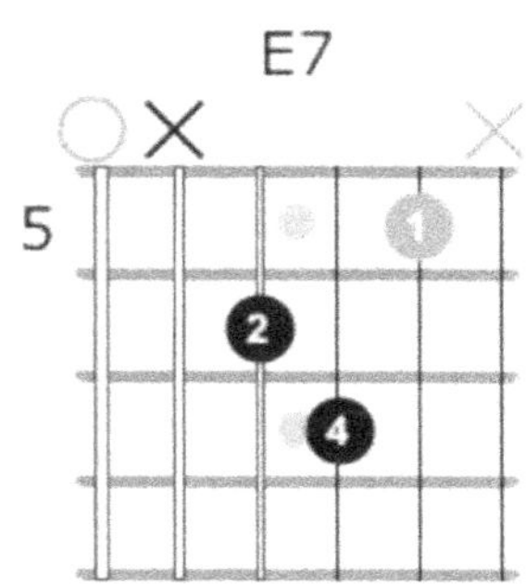

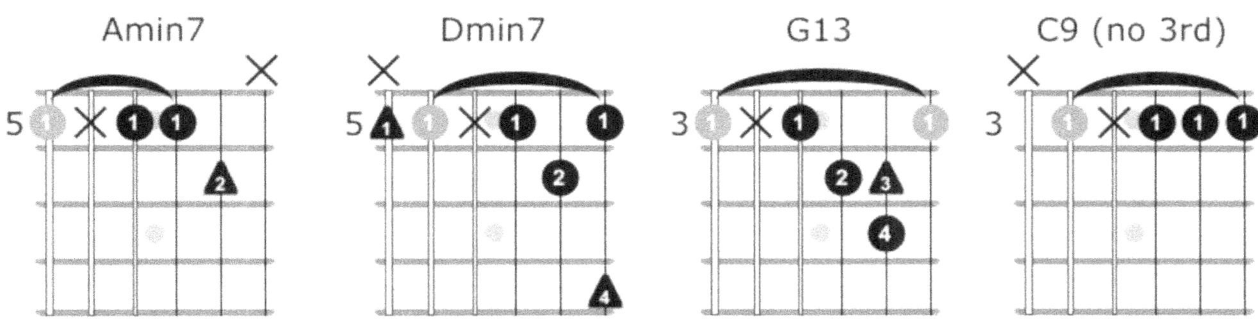

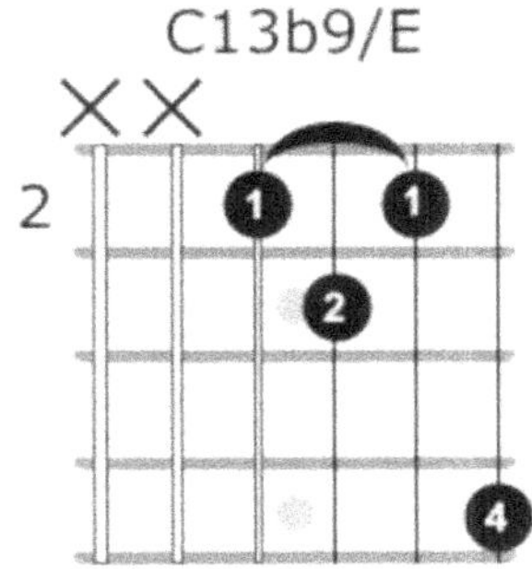

Line 3

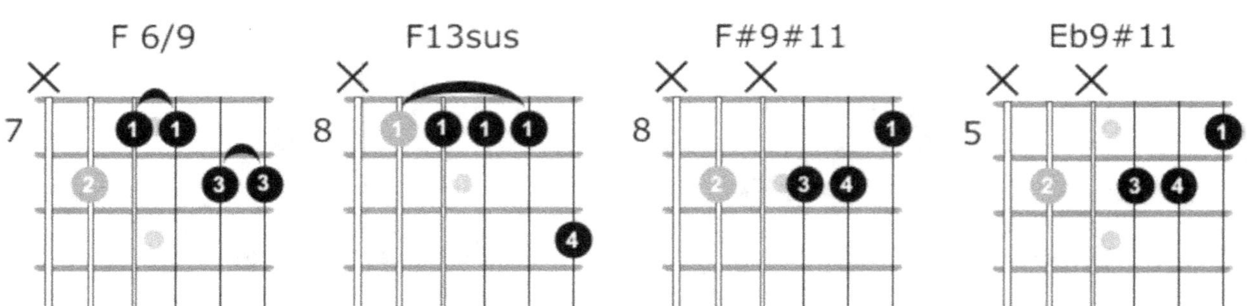
F 6/9
F13sus
F#9#11
Eb9#11

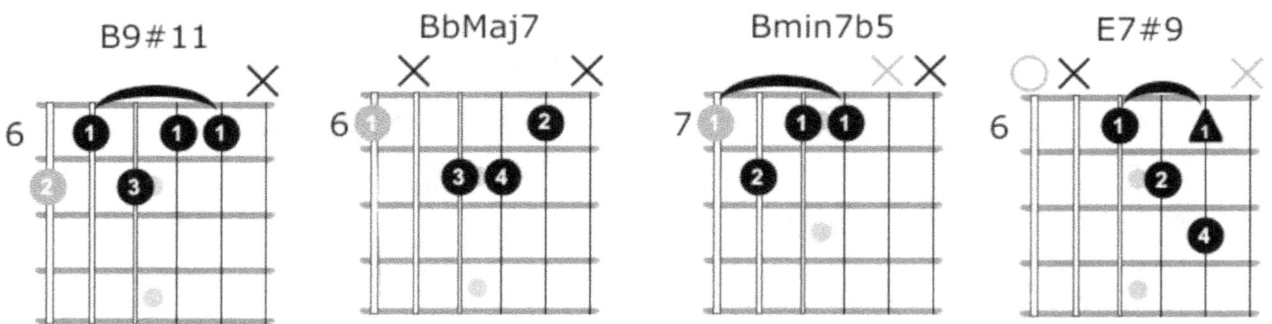
B9#11
BbMaj7
Bmin7b5
E7#9

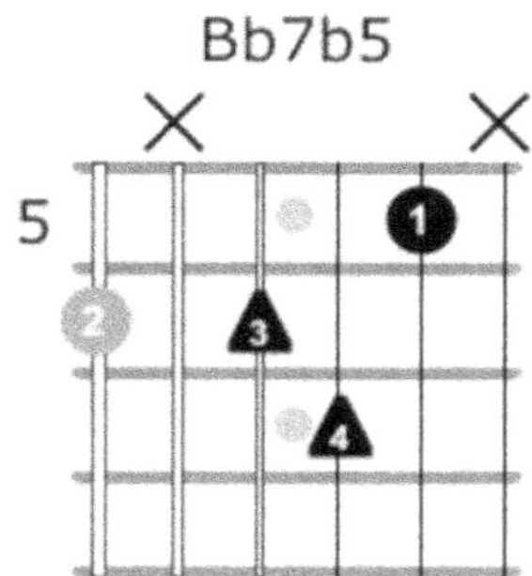
Bb7b5

Line 4

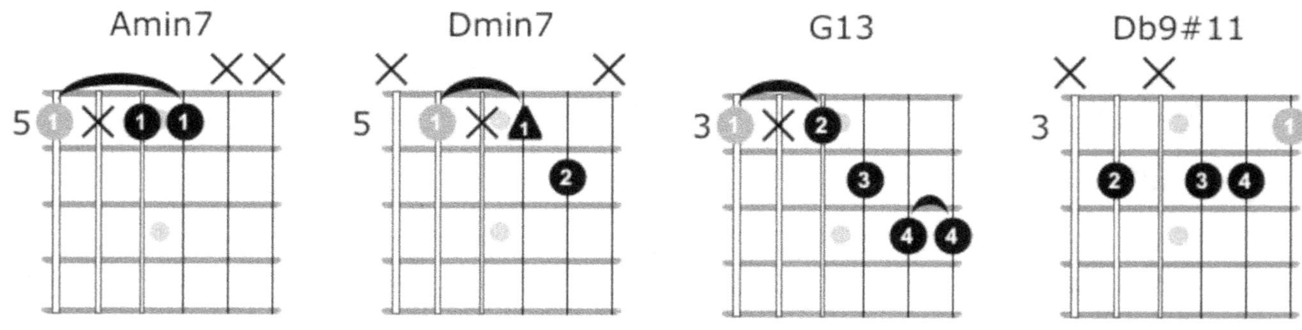
Amin7
Dmin7
G13
Db9#11

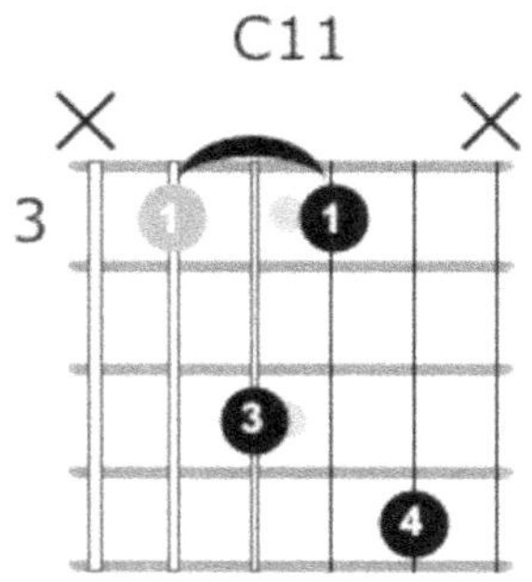

C11

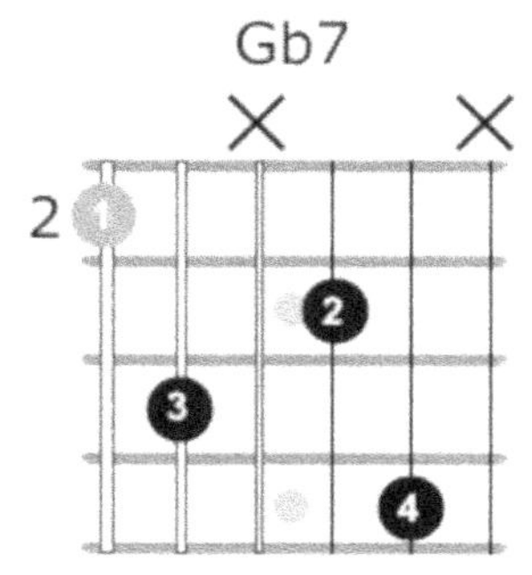

Gb7

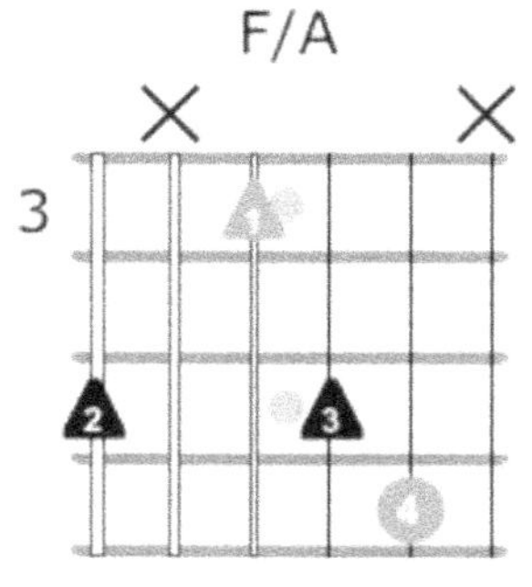

F/A

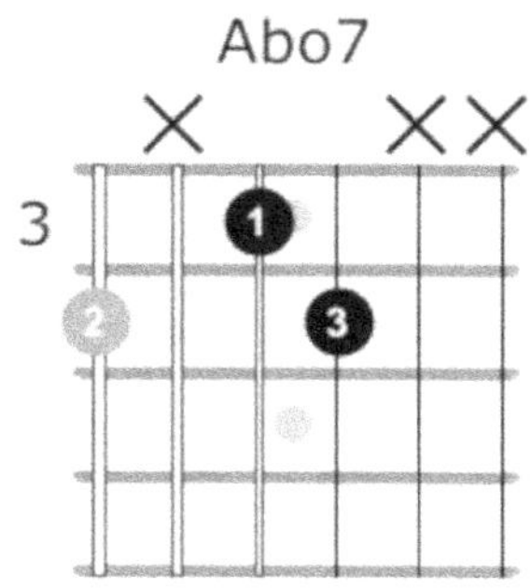

Abo7

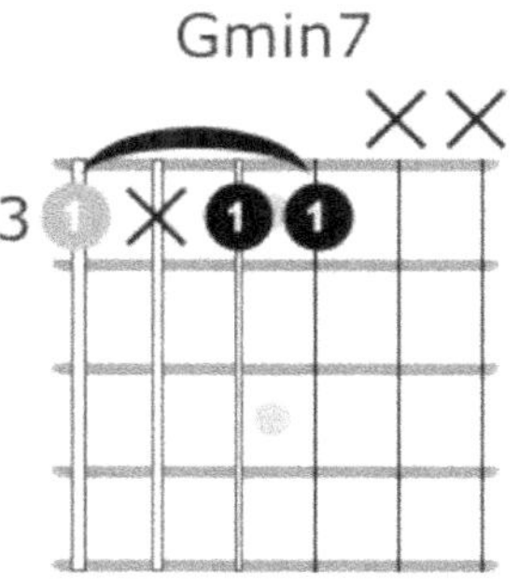

Gmin7

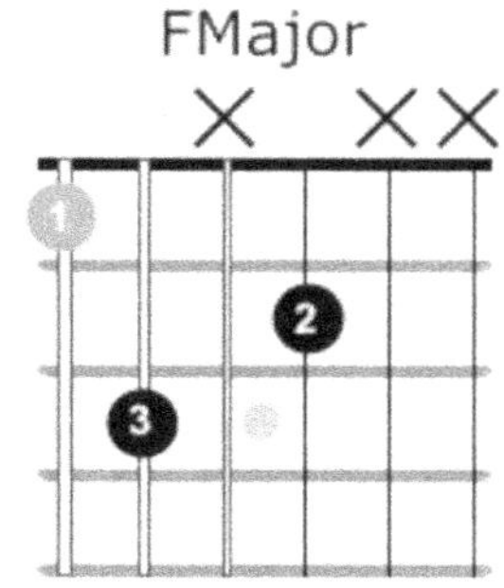

FMajor

Line 5

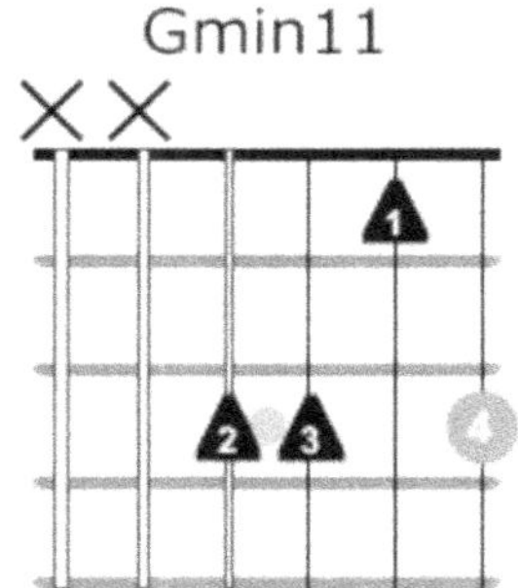

Gmin11

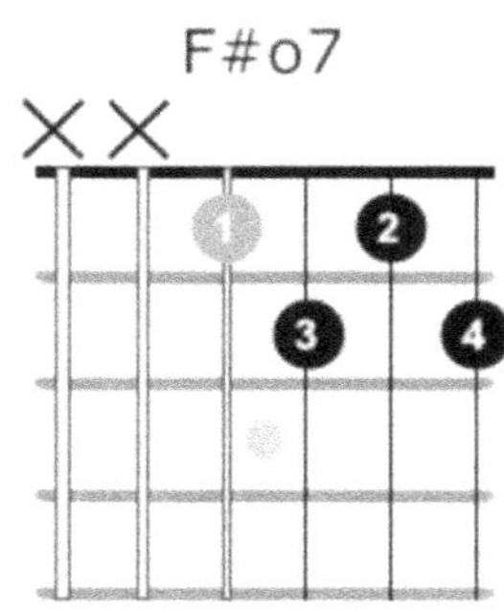

F#o7

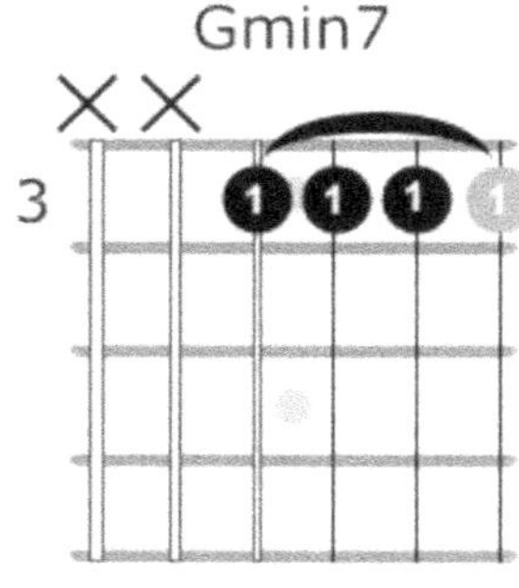

Gmin7

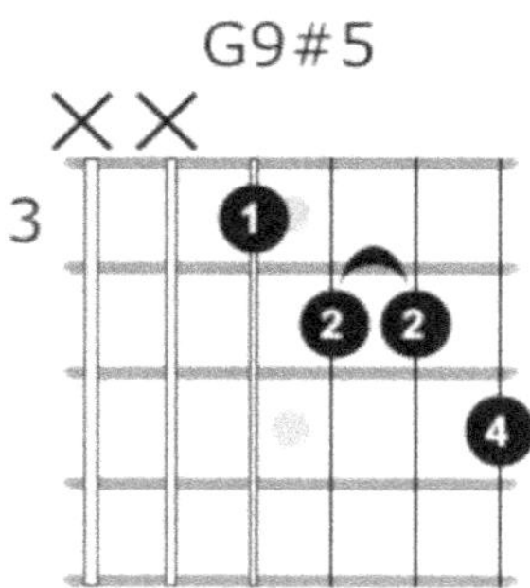

G9#5

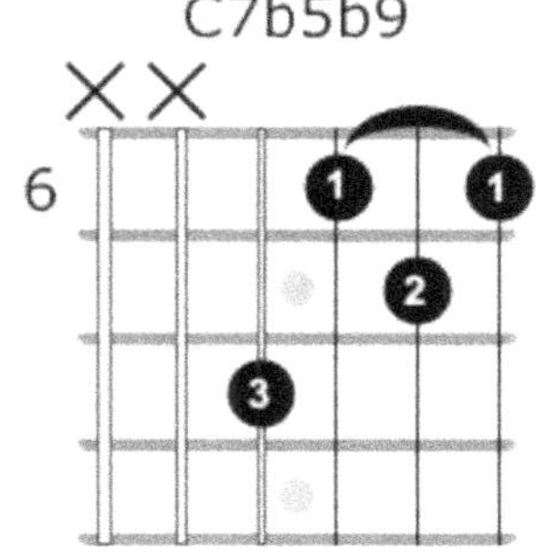

C7b5b9

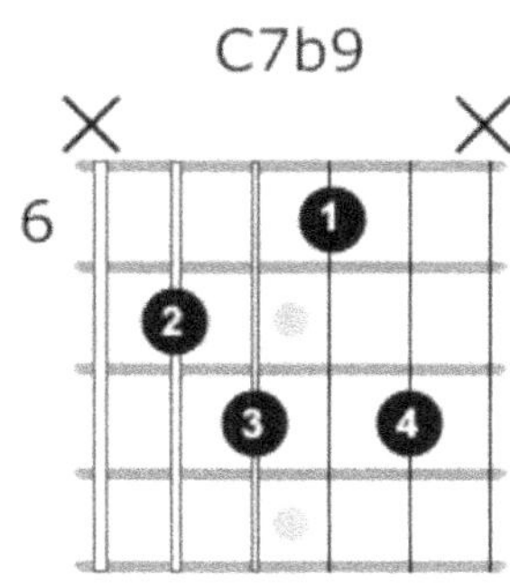

C7b9

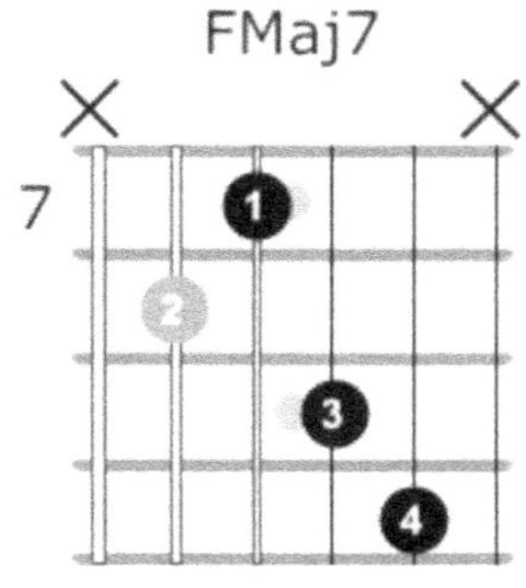

FMaj7

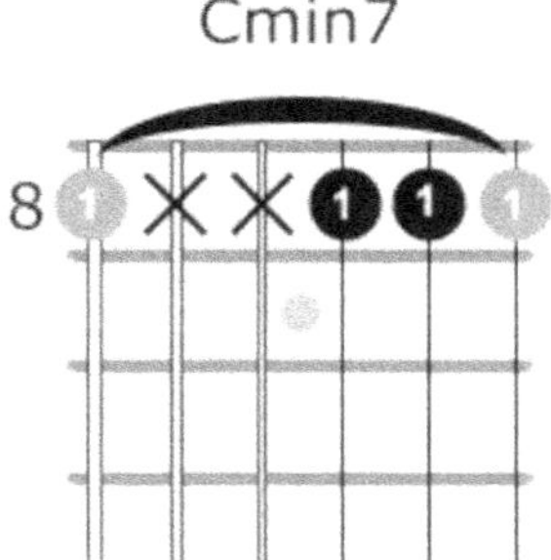

Cmin7

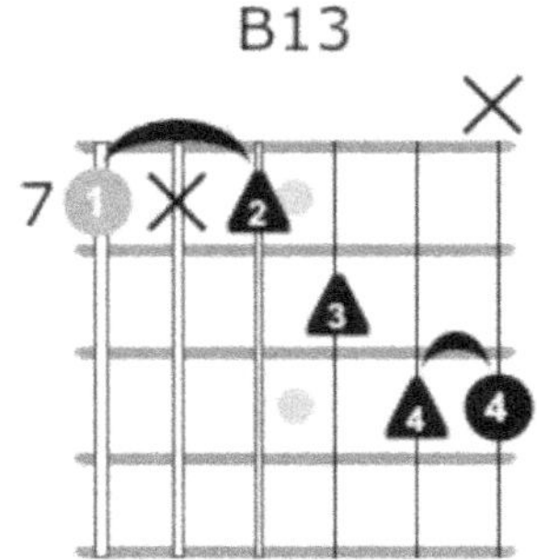

B13

Line 6

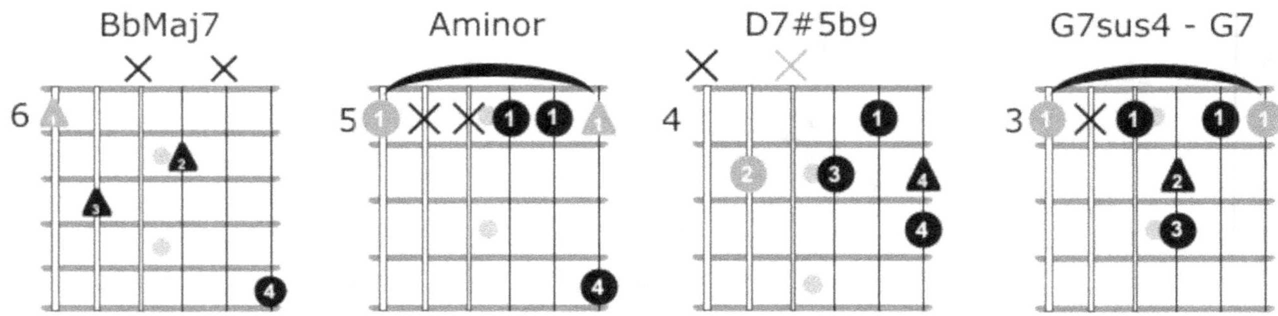

BbMaj7
Aminor
D7#5b9
G7sus4 - G7

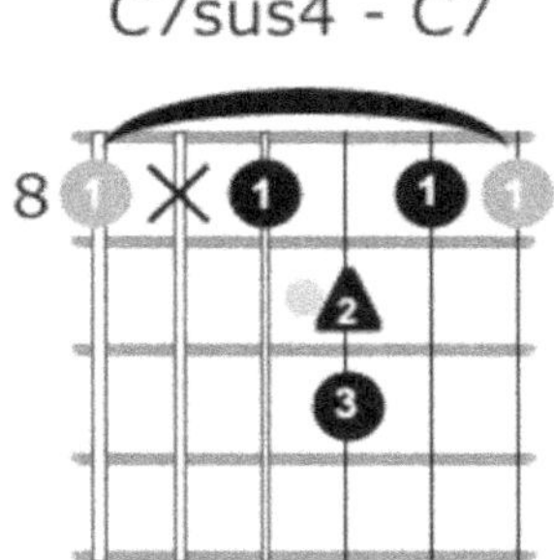

C7sus4 - C7

Line 7

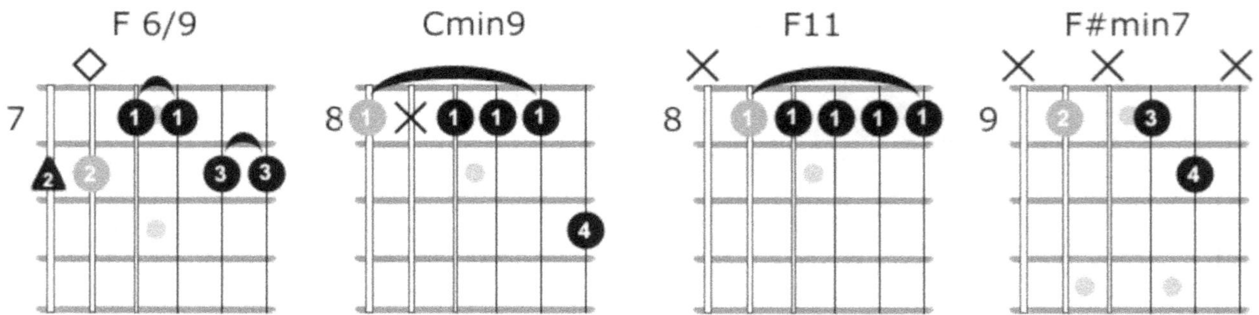

F 6/9
Cmin9
F11
F#min7

B7b5
6

Line 8

BbMaj7
5
Bbmin7
6
Eb9
5

Line 9

Amin7
3
Dmin7
5
Ab13
4
Gminadd9
3
Db9#11
3
C7sus
3
Gb7
2

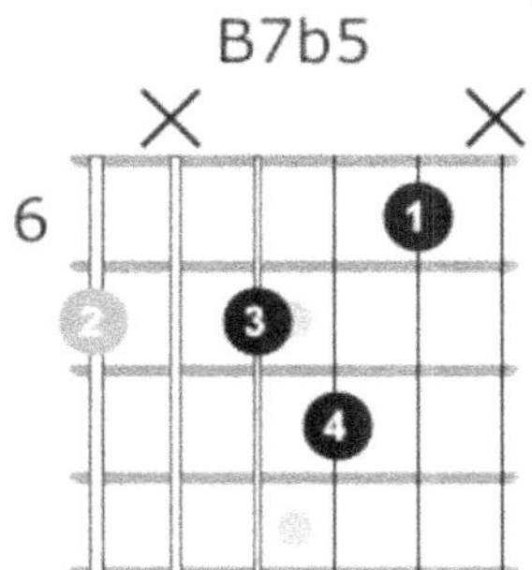

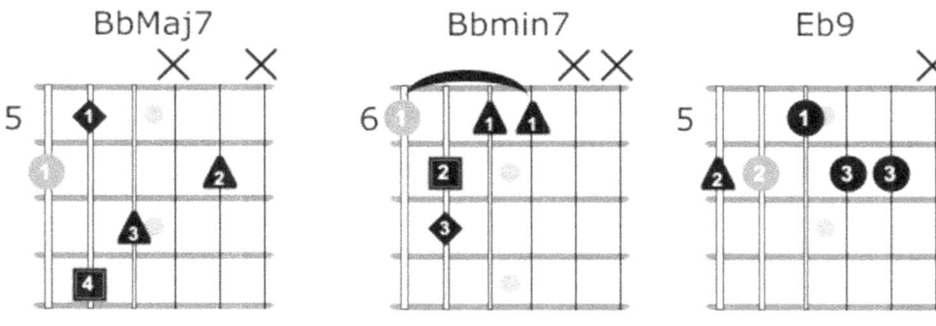

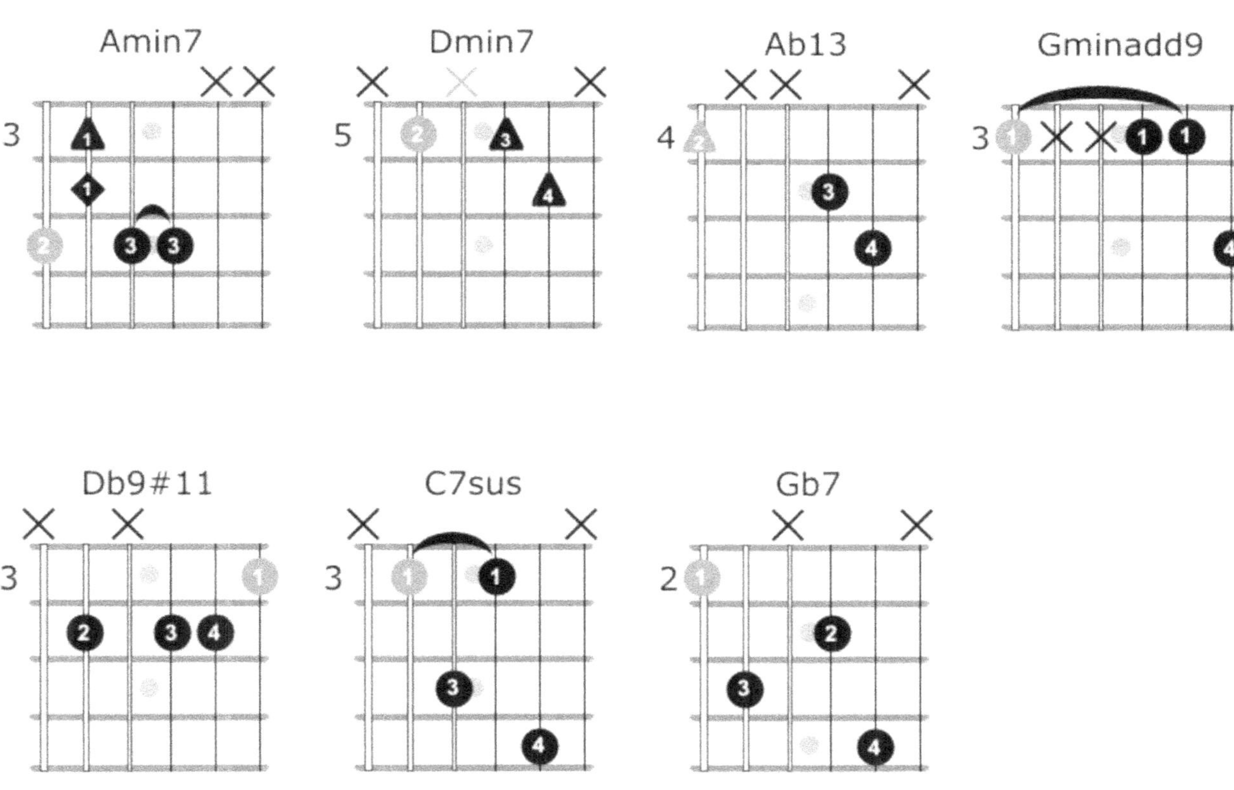

Line 10

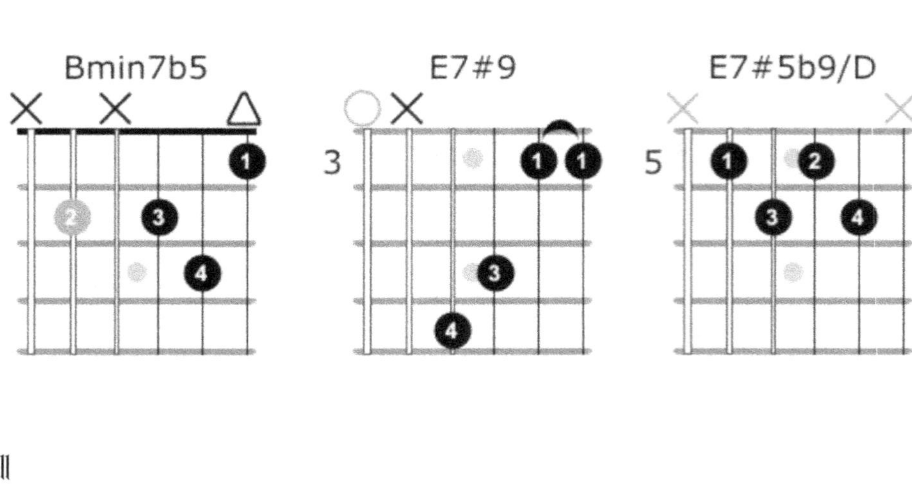

Line 11

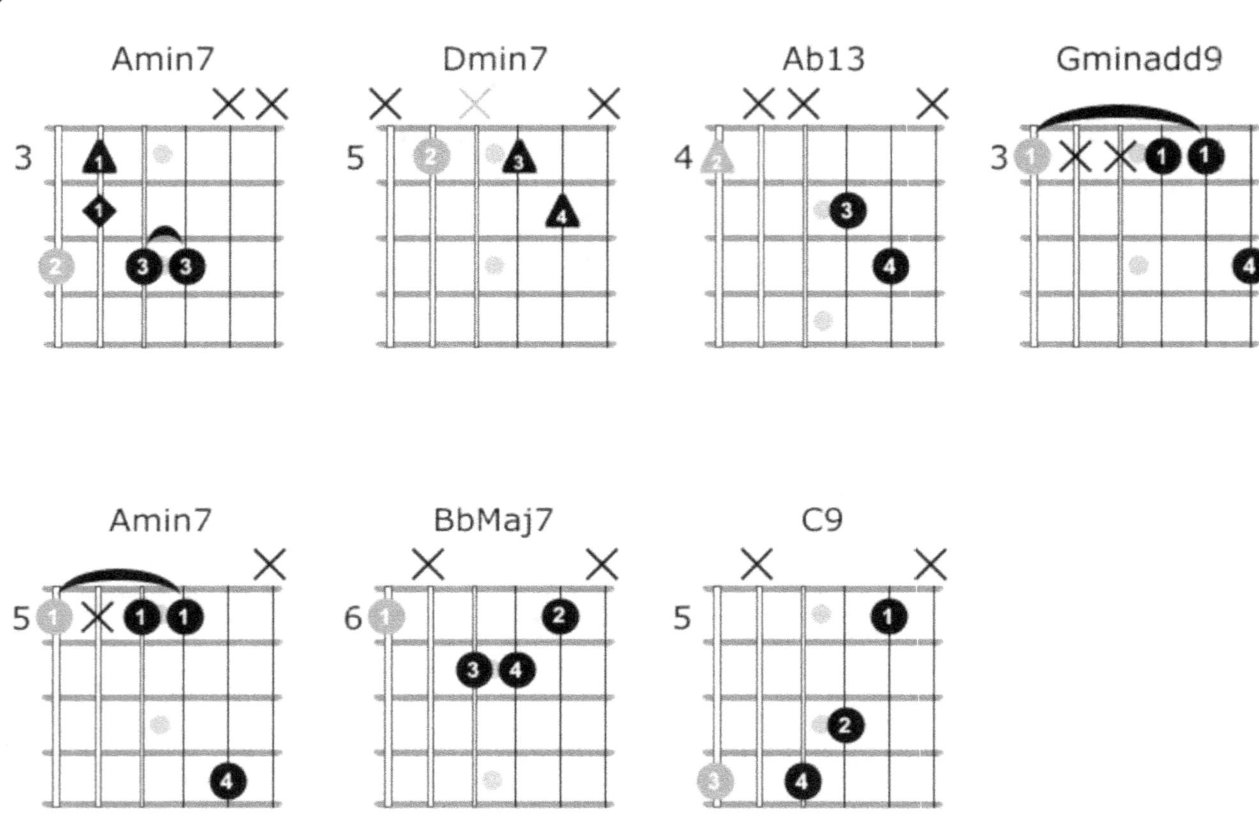

Line 12

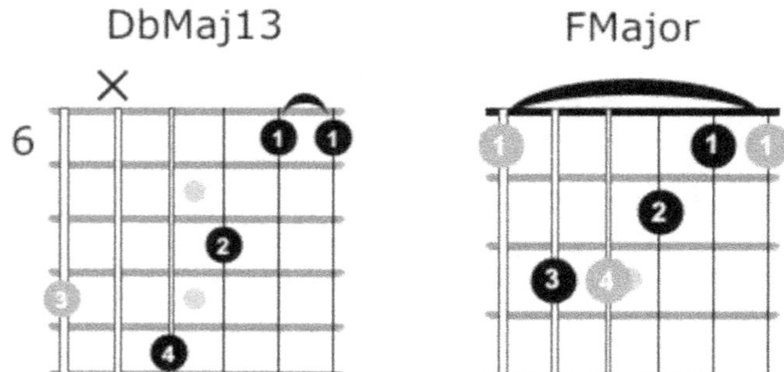

196

GET YOUR DOWNLOAD PACK WHICH SUPPORTS THIS PUBLICATION

1.   Paste this URL in a browser and then follow the download instructions:

https://gmiguitarshop.com/products/songs-of-worship-free-download

2. OR go to https://gmiguitarshop.com

- The search bar is at the top (middle) of the webpage on desktop monitors.

- Type in "Songs Of Worship" and all products relating to this publication will appear. Select the "**free download**…" option.

- **NOTE IT SAYS £10,** but you'll **add the code below** to receive a **100% discount**.

- Once you select from the search, you will be taken to products download page. Tick the "I agree with the terms & conditions" radio box and click the "**ADD TO CART**" button where you will be offered to **VIEW CART** or **CHECK OUT**; this step is up to you. Once you want to finish, view the next step.

- To finalise the transaction, simply click **CHECKOUT**. On this screen you will see the **DISCOUNT CODE** area - add the code (which is shown in bold) below and the price will change to zero. Fill in your details on the page and click **CONTINUE TO PAYMENT**. On reaching the final page, the price will be **ZERO**.

ADD THIS CODE - **SONGSOFPRAISE**

- The download will be sent to you immediately upon finalising all your details.

WHAT IS INCLUDED?

- **Video performances of all intermediate and advanced songs.**

- **20 mp3 files tracks. 10 with melody and 10 backing tracks.**

- **Author narration for all intermediate and advanced arrangements covering musical and technical considerations when learning each piece. Total running time 1 hour 49 minutes.**

Total download size = 832.1MB

THIS IS A LARGE DOWNLOAD, YOU WILL NEED BROADBAND TO DOWNLOAD.

ANY PROBLEMS? CONTACT GMI BY GOING TO THE CONTACT PAGE ON:

www.guitarandmusicinstitute.com

ABOUT GED BROCKIE

Ged Brockie is the creative vision behind GMI - Guitar and Music Institute. A professional musician for over thirty five years, Ged has had the privilege of working with some of the finest musicians from around the world in a variety of musical situations throughout Scotland, the UK and Europe.

Performance: Royal Scottish National Orchestra, the Orchestra Royal Scottish Ballet, Carl Davis, the Scottish Guitar Quartet, concert solo/band work, tours, West End shows on tour, pro/amateur shows, music festivals, TV/radio appearances, session work, educational workshops, music industry appearances, corporate music, cover band work.

Education & Industry Programs: Tutored guitar, composition, writing for film and technology at all levels from high school through F.E. (further education colleges) to higher education (university), created an HND in Jazz guitar for the Scottish Qualifications Authority, commissioned by the SQA for bespoke theory papers as well as sample examples for Higher National qualifications.

Projects: Developed/co-ran the Jazz UK international summer school, pioneered the European arm of the Pacific Northwest Film Scoring Program led by double Emmy winning composer Hummie Mann. Part of a small team that created the Edinburgh Guitar & Music Festival in 2013, worked with Gary Garritan for GPO Jazz software (jazz guitar).

Composition: Compositions include three albums The Last View From Mary's Place (2001), The Mirror's Image (2009) and Signature (2022). Three albums with the Scottish Guitar Quartet (11 titles), two indy feature films, a commission from the Scottish Parliament for music to accompany an HD film about the Scottish Parliament, a fringe show, various adverts for TV and media.

www.gedbrockie.com

SOME OF OUR OTHER GREAT SELLING TITLES

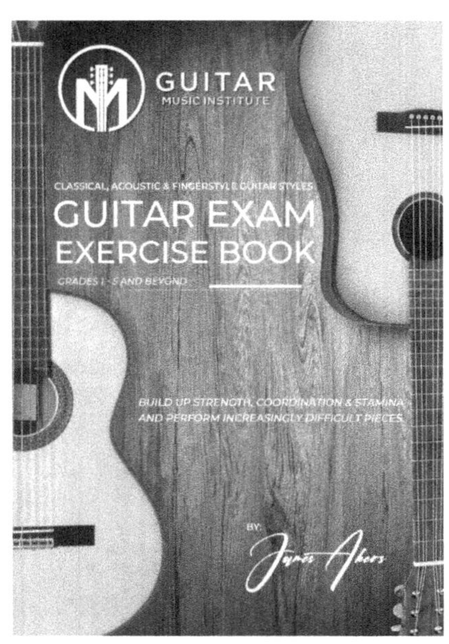

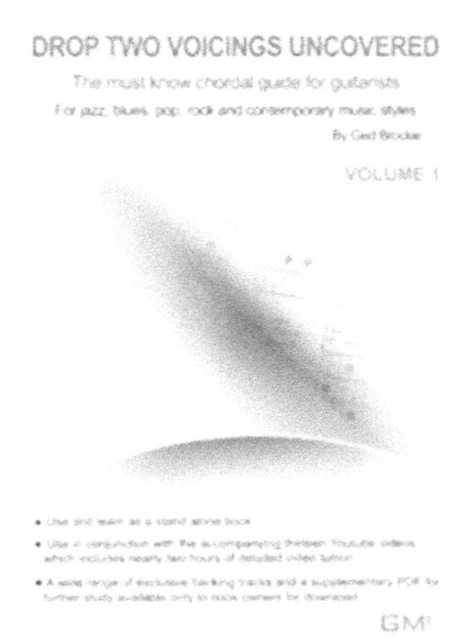

If you enjoyed this publication, then please visit the following websites for more content, lessons, articles, videos, podcasts, free and paid content and more…

We'd also really appreciate a positive review on Amazon if you found this book enjoyable and an addition to your guitar playing experience.

www.guitarandmusicinstitute.com

gmiguitarshop.com

www.gmipremium.com

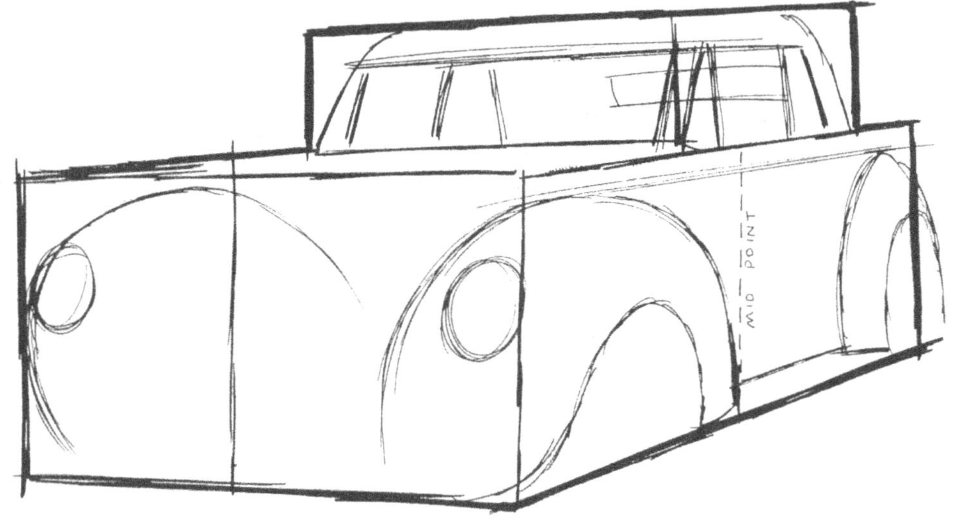

One of the most distinctive cars of the Forties is the **Lincoln Continental** so let's rattle the classic purists by Pro Streetin' one! Copy the two boxes you see here. Start the fenders at the midpoint, the rear fender at the same height. Indicate headlights then carve out that unique roofline.

Rough in the hood, keying off the centerline and just touching the front fender. Block in the blower, blower pulley, carbs, and bug catcher using simple, basic shapes. Indicate a driver too. Loosely oval out the grill areas with angled ellipses cut off by the fender line. Rough in some tires.

Hokay . . . It's time to add more detail to the engine along with some engine noise. Have fun with some body graphics and try to let them follow the body's own styling. Ink all this with your favorite pen adding solid blacks as shown and you're all set to go Pro Street!

HOW TO DRAW MODEL CARS

Next to the real thing, a model car is a great way to study the lines of a body style. You can hold it at **any angle** and have a commanding view of every detail. Wild, tricky, off-beat points of view become fun and easy to do when you've got it, three dimensionally, right in front of you. Be inventive and challenge yourself. Try to pick a view that gets your juices flowin'!

This method can also be helpful in determining what your finished model might look like with the custom modifications you plan to make. Changing and rearranging a design concept is much easier on paper than in plastic. Try to stay loose and let things happen; try to visualize as many variations as you can. Often, a great model is one with a bit of thought behind it, and this is where the thinking begins so let's crank up those pencil points.

Okay . . . Let's fool around with Revell's '41 Willys kit. You rarely see one **customized** so that route might be interesting.

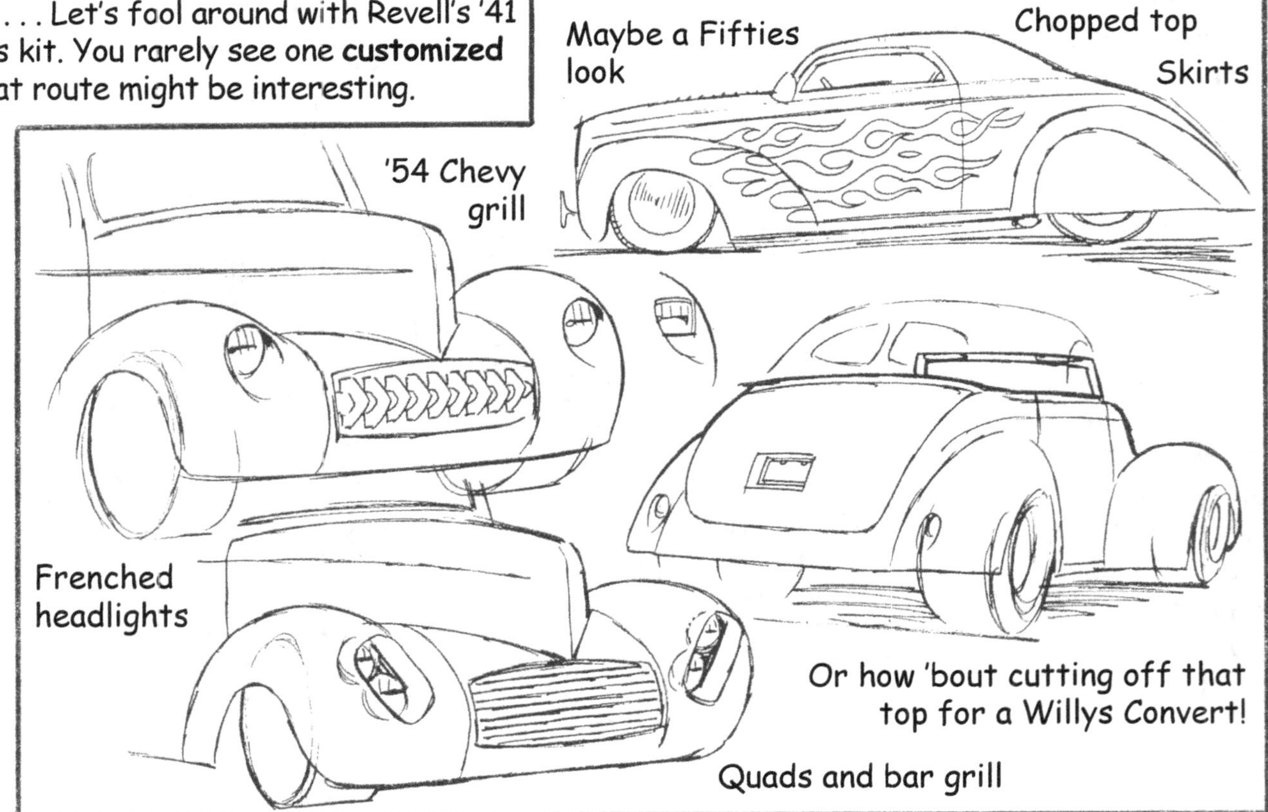

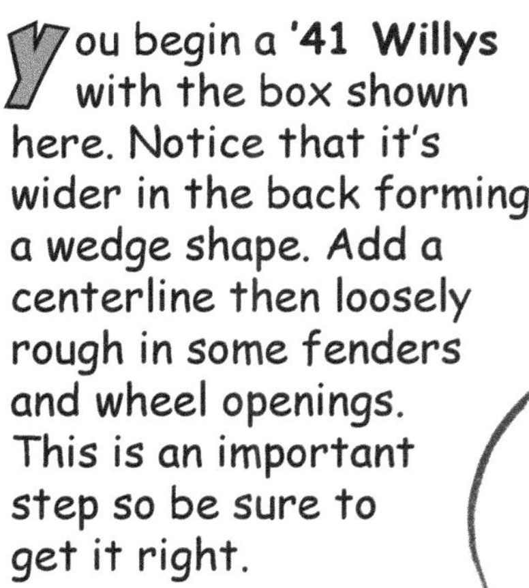

*Y*ou begin a **'41 Willys** with the box shown here. Notice that it's wider in the back forming a wedge shape. Add a centerline then loosely rough in some fenders and wheel openings. This is an important step so be sure to get it right.

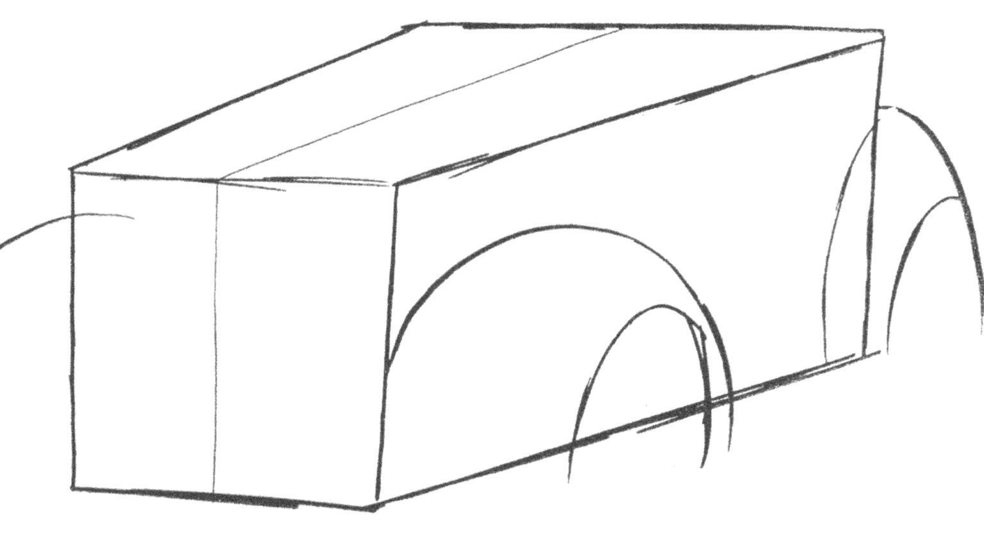

Picking up on that centerline, begin to plot out the curves of the hood; indicating the side body chrome helps flesh out the way the hood flows. The bottom point of the hood is midway in the box. After adding some contour to the trunk area, rough in a windshield.

The grill cavity drops in just below the tip of the hood and runs between the two fender seams. Add some door lines and the body line around the open area. Add big 'n' little tires drawing right through the fenders to get 'em right!

I've decided to go with the canted quad headlights and I've filed the grill cavity edges straight so it now accepts a straight bar grill. Loosely lay in some bucket seats and the basics for a driver. This also might be a good time to cut a hole out of the hood for . . .

. . . The air intake of a blown Chevy rat that I dropped in. Time to go over everything once more, tightening up the detail on the wheels and tires, fender and body lines, and interior. Add side mirrors then rough yourself in as the driver.

Finally, you're ready for some ink; heavy on the outlines, a finer line on the details. Solid blacks give the tires some shape and indicate a super glossy paint job with the help of some white highlights. **Go magic fingers!**

ENGINES

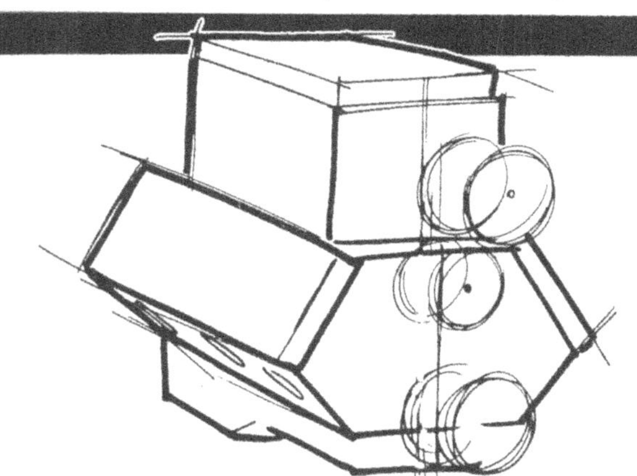

Okay, everybody . . . Let's start with the traditional hot rod engine: a **Ford Flathead V-8** with the works! Study the boxes carefully and block out your engine accordingly. This first step is an important one so make sure you take your time. Notice that the smaller pulley is centered while the blower pulley and the crankshaft pulley are slightly to the right. The exhaust ports are also marked.

Six carbs sit on top of the blower so let's start there. Think of them as soda cans and build from there. Detail the blower a bit and work up the blower belt placement. Water pump pulleys are on the top to the right and the left of the belt. Spark plug holes and wires may be added now along with the fins on the aluminum racin' heads. Rough in the pipes.

Almost there, eh? Check over everything adding more details as you go along. Finish up the carbs like these. Include lots of head bolts, a distributor, and a few brackets as shown. Bring the headers to life then triple chrome 'em! Ink all this in with a ball-point or felt-tip pen and you have a full-race Fifties flattie!

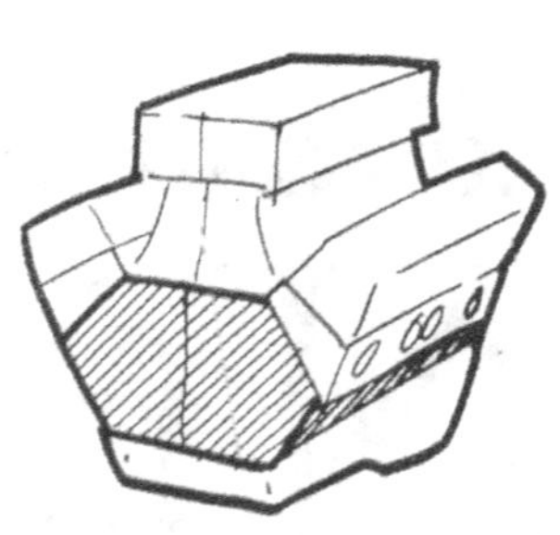

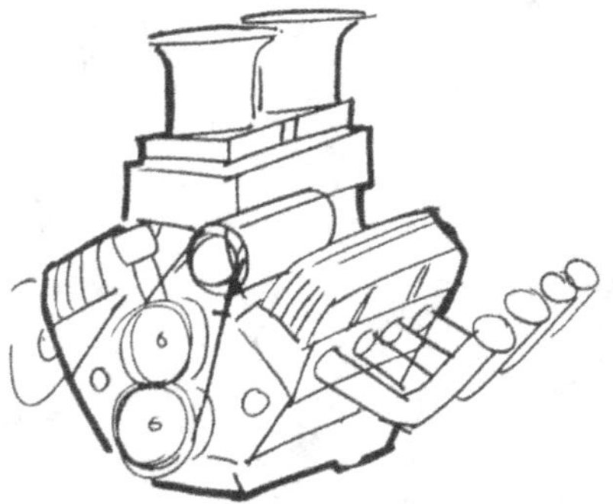

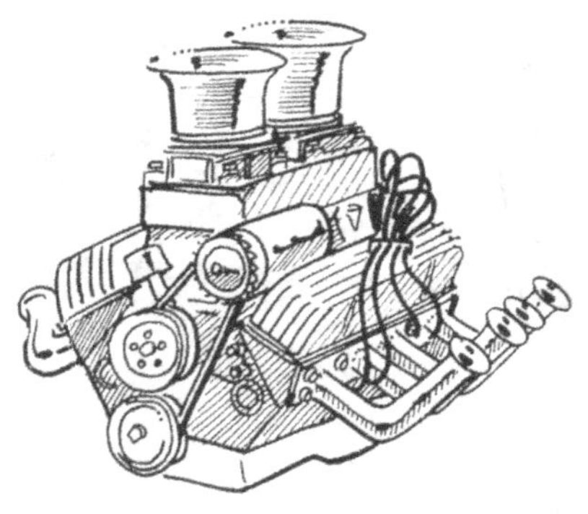

The next engine to make waves was the **Chevy V-8**. Block it in and make sure you get the proportions right. The basic block is shaded and all else bolts on.

Now it gets tricky. Rough in the four-barrel carbs an' stacks. Generator and front pulleys are placed as are headers on both sides.

Presto! The Chevy begins to breathe as you add a few final details. Plug wires, pipes, and a fan belt help make it respectable! Ink it in and it's yours!

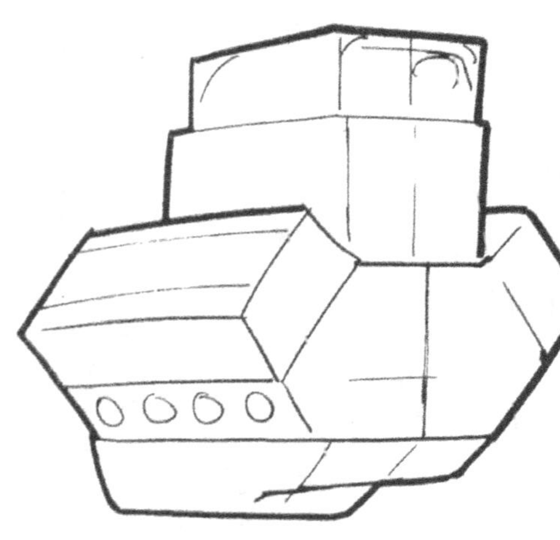

The biggest power plants ever were Mopar products. Lots of rails an' Funny Cars use 'em so let's see what they look like! Keep everything big and husky while you loosely rough in this monster!

Notice the shape of the valve covers and exhaust pipes. **Pencil carefully!**

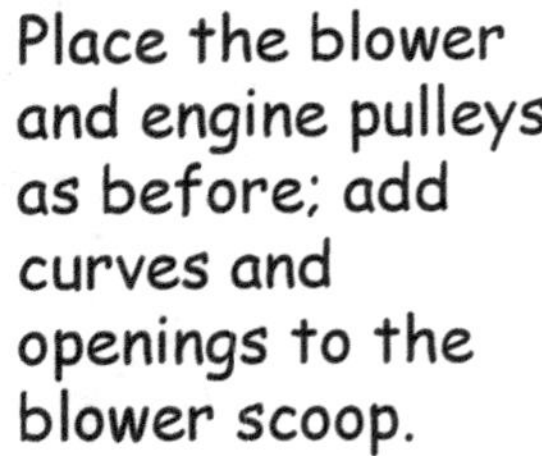

Place the blower and engine pulleys as before; add curves and openings to the blower scoop.

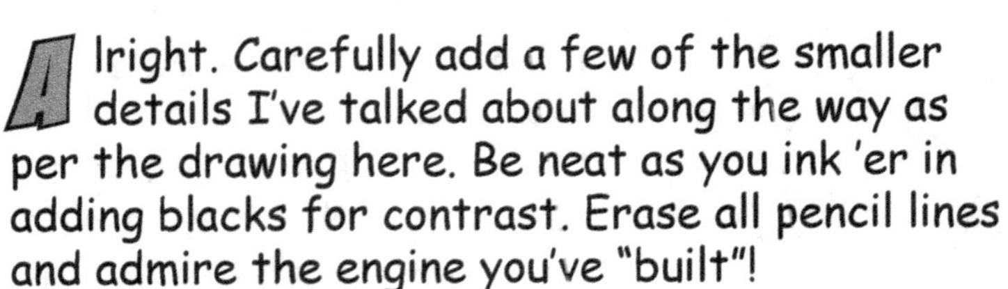

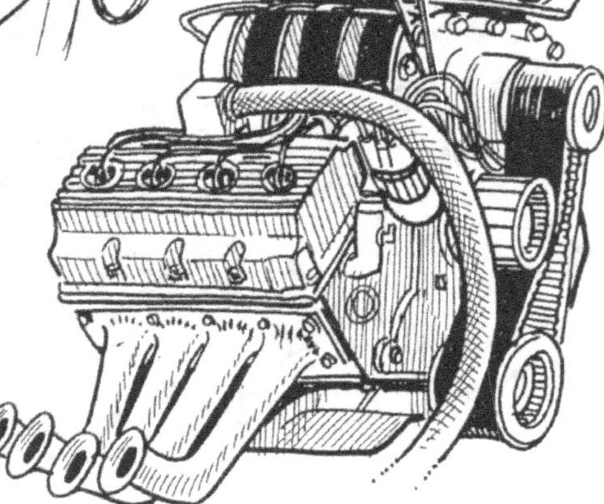

Alright. Carefully add a few of the smaller details I've talked about along the way as per the drawing here. Be neat as you ink 'er in adding blacks for contrast. Erase all pencil lines and admire the engine you've "built"!

FRAMES

Let's take it slow an' easy and do up a frame step by step. Basically, two lengths of boxed steel sit side by side. The frame is joined front and rear with a sporing perch up front.

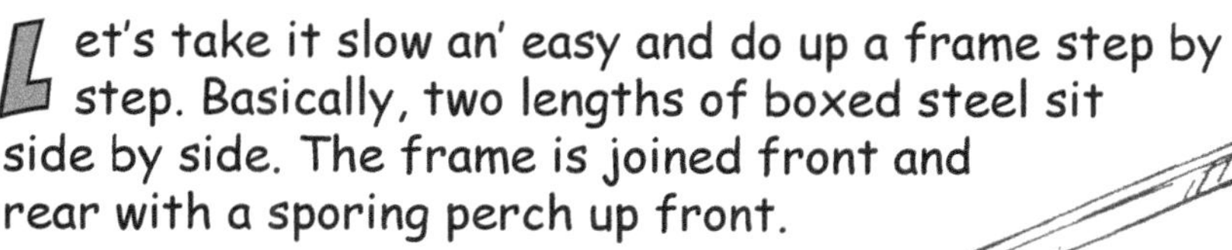

The frame kicks up in the rear to allow for rear suspension.

Rough in the dropped front axle using the centerline to keep things straight. The spring arcs to the center and the shocks bolt up to the brackets.

Add the rear, thinking of it as a ball with a pole shoved through it. Center it up with guide lines, roughing in the coil springs and rear shocks. Draw right through the lines.

Tires are the next step so loosely rough in some thin motorcycle types up front and some big fat slicks out back. Don't worry about the details yet; just concentrate on getting those ellipses lookin' right!

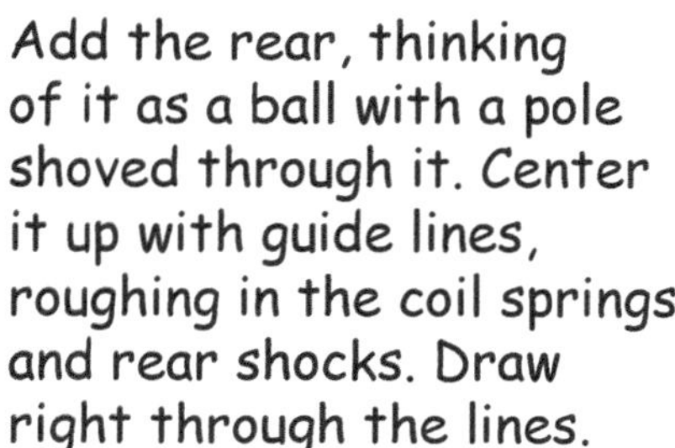

Once again, guide lines help keep all this "even steven." Don't be afraid to use 'em!

*T*he next step oughta' be some kinda' wild engine so pencil in one of your choice or block in the Chevy shown here topping it off with two fours an' chrome stacks.

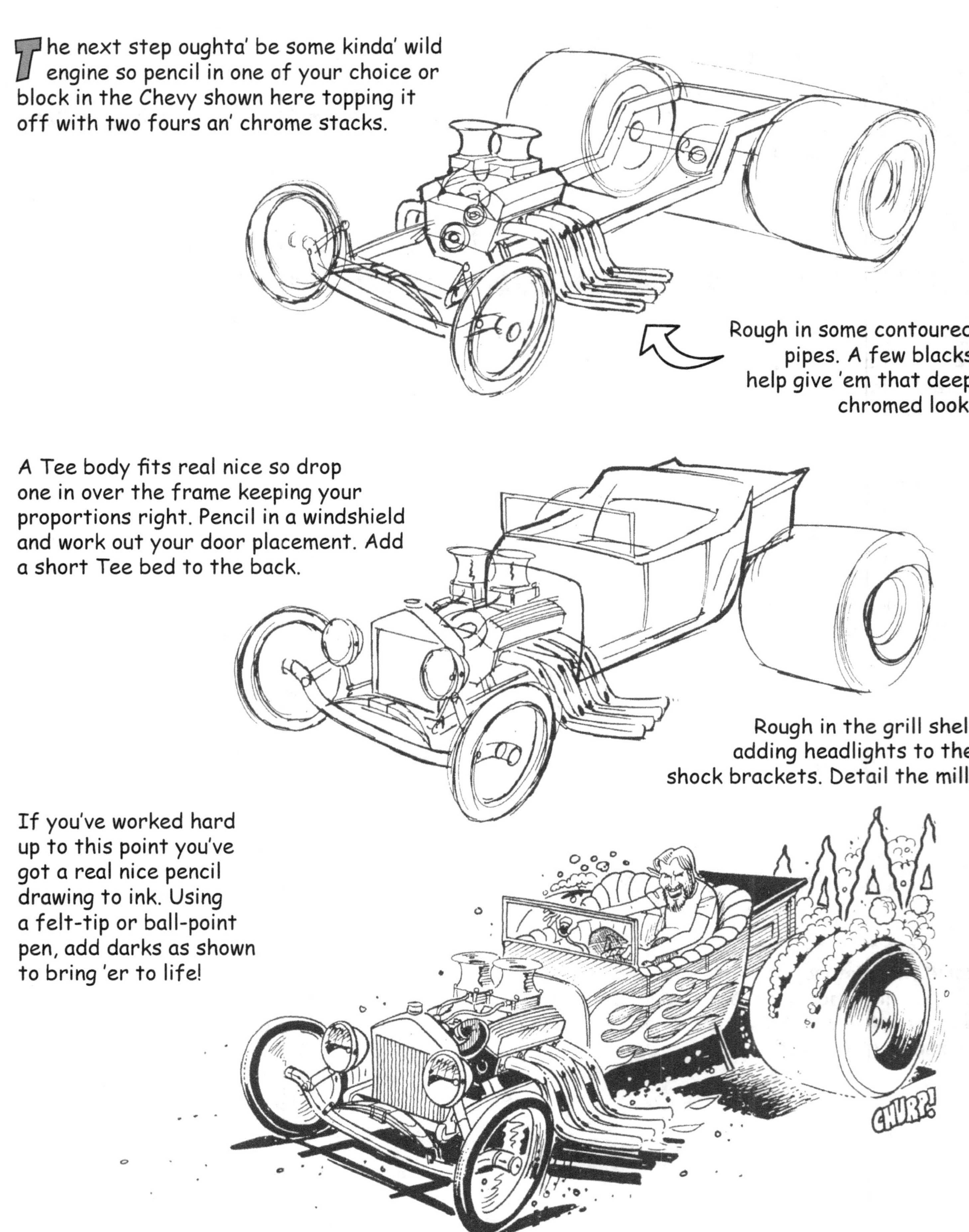

Rough in some contoured pipes. A few blacks help give 'em that deep chromed look.

A Tee body fits real nice so drop one in over the frame keeping your proportions right. Pencil in a windshield and work out your door placement. Add a short Tee bed to the back.

Rough in the grill shell adding headlights to the shock brackets. Detail the mill.

If you've worked hard up to this point you've got a real nice pencil drawing to ink. Using a felt-tip or ball-point pen, add darks as shown to bring 'er to life!